INTIMATE RIVALS

The Council on Foreign Relations (CFR) is an independent, nonpartisan membership organization, think tank, and publisher dedicated to being a resource for its members, government officials, business executives, journalists, educators and students, civic and religious leaders, and other interested citizens in order to help them better understand the world and the foreign policy choices facing the United States and other countries. Founded in 1921, CFR carries out its mission by maintaining a diverse membership, with special programs to promote interest and develop expertise in the next generation of foreign policy leaders; convening meetings at its headquarters in New York and in Washington, DC, and other cities where senior government officials, members of Congress, global leaders, and prominent thinkers come together with CFR members to discuss and debate major international issues; supporting a Studies Program that fosters independent research, enabling CFR scholars to produce articles, reports, and books and hold roundtables that analyze foreign policy issues and make concrete policy recommendations; publishing *Foreign Affairs*, the preeminent journal on international affairs and U.S. foreign policy; sponsoring Independent Task Forces that produce reports with both findings and policy prescriptions on the most important foreign policy topics; and providing up-to-date information and analysis about world events and American foreign policy on its website, www.cfr.org.

The Council on Foreign Relations takes no institutional positions on policy issues and has no affiliation with the U.S. government. All views expressed in its publications and on its website are the sole responsibility of the author or authors.

INTIMATE
RIVALS

*Japanese Domestic Politics
and a Rising China*

Sheila A. Smith

A Council on Foreign Relations Book

Columbia University Press   New York

Columbia University Press
Publishers Since 1893
New York   Chichester, West Sussex
cup.columbia.edu

Library of Congress Cataloging-in-Publication Data
Smith, Sheila A., 1959–
Intimate rivals : Japanese domestic politics and a rising China /
Sheila A. Smith.
pages cm
"A Council on Foreign Relations Book."
Includes bibliographical references and index.
ISBN 978-0-231-16788-8 (cloth : alk. paper)
ISBN 978-0-231-53802-2 (e-book)
1. Japan—Foreign relations—China. 2. China—Foreign relations—Japan.
3. Japan—Politics and government—21st century. I. Title.

DS849.C6S64   2014
327.52051—dc23   2014022523

∞
Columbia University Press books are printed on permanent
and durable acid-free paper.
This book is printed on paper with recycled content.
Printed in the United States of America

c 10 9 8 7 6 5 4 3 2

COVER IMAGE: Prime Minister Koizumi Jun'ichirō pays homage
to the imperial war dead at Yasukuni Shrine, October 17, 2005.
(REUTERS/Eriko Sugita)
COVER DESIGN: *Noah Arlow*

For Ian Hendry Smith

CONTENTS

PREFACE

I began to consider the idea of writing a book on Japan's relations with China in the early 2000s while at the East-West Center in Hawaii. Tensions between Japan and China had erupted over the visits by Prime Minister Koizumi Jun'ichirō to the controversial war memorial, Yasukuni Shrine, and policymakers in Washington were becoming increasingly concerned about the inability of Tokyo and Beijing to put their history behind them. An East-West Center alumnus, Otsuka Takao, president of the Hotel Grand Palace in Kudanshita, offered me the perfect setting for my frequent research trips to Tokyo with my boisterous young son. The hotel was located next to the Yasukuni Shrine, and we often walked among the beautiful gingko trees and towering torii gates in the early hours of the morning when jet-lag made sleep impossible. Aged Shinto priests rustled in their robes from building to building, and I could not help but wonder how this rather anachronistic site had become a focal point in the diplomacy of Asia's two largest nations.

Differences over twentieth-century history were not the only cause of Sino-Japanese tensions. At the beginning of the twenty-first century, new difficulties arose. Trade tensions over the import of shiitake mushrooms and tatami mats began to complicate economic relations. Violence against Japanese at the Asian Cup games in Beijing in 2004 shocked many in Japan. When demonstrators in cities around China protested the revision of Japanese textbooks in March 2005, Japanese businesses also were damaged, further souring public opinion about China. In the corridors of Asian summit meetings, Chinese and Japanese leaders exchanged chilly stares and refused to speak. In 2006, in the midst of this "deep freeze" in diplomatic relations, Prime Minister Koizumi, dressed in full formal wear, paid an official visit to the Yasukuni Shrine on August 15, the day of the Japanese commemoration of the end of the war. A few weeks later, he resigned after five years as Japan's prime minister.

For a while, Koizumi was blamed for the downturn in Tokyo's relations with Beijing, and his successors seemed to make progress in changing the tenor of the relationship. Other factors continued to plague diplomatic ties, however. Public attitudes toward China were hardening. China's economy grew, and the economic interdependence that had anchored Japan's relationship with China created unforeseen frictions. The new UN Convention on the Law of the Sea raised questions about maritime claims, and the East China Sea became more and more populated with survey ships and new, more modern, naval vessels. Even regarding the deeply sensitive issue of historical memory, the Koizumi era was not the first entanglement of China policy with Japanese domestic politics and popular sentiment, and it would not be the last. In Japan, this intimate contact with a changing China was unnerving to many and called into question the premises of Japan's postwar identity.

The Sino-Japanese relationship seemed impervious to the efforts of political leaders and government bureaucrats to find common ground. In the fall of 2006, Koizumi's successor, Abe Shinzō, traveled to Beijing to begin a process of reconciliation and to craft a new, "mutually beneficial" relationship for China and Japan. Two years later, after a reciprocal visit by the popular Chinese premier, Wen Jiabao, to Japan, President Hu Jintao met in Tokyo with Prime Minister Fukuda Yasuo. The May 2008 Hu-Fukuda summit laid out an ambitious agenda of cooperation, including joint energy development in the East China Sea and a food safety agreement. But the diplomatic accomplishment was short-lived. The East China Sea agreement was never implemented, and the food-poisoning case involving imported frozen Chinese dumplings took another two years to resolve. To make matters worse, a relatively small incident in September 2010 involving a Chinese fishing trawler and two Japan Coast Guard vessels blossomed into the biggest postwar crisis in Sino-Japanese relations and opened a rift between Beijing and Tokyo that continues today. Equally important, the flare-up of tensions over the sovereignty of the Senkaku Islands (known as the Diaoyu Islands in China) provoked a domestic debate over Japan's ability to manage a rising China.

The last forty years of Japanese-Chinese diplomatic relations have rested on a simple premise: economic interdependence would be the path to postwar reconciliation between the peoples of both countries. At first glance, this reliance on close economic ties seemed to be a successful strategy for overcoming political strains, and it ensured an opportunity for greater prosperity for Japanese and Chinese alike. Moreover, there was plenty of evidence of good feelings between the people of Japan and China. The Japanese response to the Sichuan earthquake and the Chinese willingness to allow that aid to be delivered spoke to the progress achieved by Fukuda and Hu in their Tokyo meeting just days before. Several years later, Beijing returned the kindness by delivering aid to Japanese in Tohoku after the Great East Japan Earthquake. Japanese investment in China continued to grow, and Chinese goods, services, and now investment flowed into the Japanese economy, signaling a new era of mutual prosperity. In 2009, a new reformist political party with a desire for even closer relations with China and a commitment to historical reconciliation came into power in Tokyo.

Yet for all this evidence of a desire for better diplomatic relations, new irritants fostered greater frustration, and Sino-Japanese relations worsened. In 2010 and again in 2012, the rapid escalation of contention over a small group of uninhabited islands, long managed quietly by both governments, revealed this deepening distrust. For years, groups of Japanese and Chinese activists in small fishing boats braved the choppy and dangerous waters of the East China Sea to place their country's flags on the Senkaku Islands. Their governments, meanwhile, worked to keep their claims from disturbing the broader goal of Sino-Japanese cooperation. At the end of the first decade of the twenty-first century, however, it was the governments of China and Japan that sought to assert and defend their sovereignty with maritime forces and, by early 2013, with their militaries.

Long before talk of a "rising" China became popular, I sensed trepidation among many in the Japanese government about this relationship. Those familiar with China saw difficult times ahead for the Chinese people and argued for patience with a changing China. Others were less knowledgeable about China but increasingly concerned about Japan's ability to adjust to its rapidly changing neighbor. The task of adjusting, however, belonged not only to diplomats, political leaders, and experts. Rather, the broad influences associated with a changing China were felt across Japanese society, making this moment of geostrategic change a complex challenge for many in Japan. While diplomats continue to grapple with finding a way to resolve the island tensions, the domestic politics surrounding many of the challenges in Japan's relations with China have changed over the decade. A new balance of interests have emerged, which neither determine greater conflict nor impede greater cooperation with Beijing. Yet more and more, Japanese are calling for an improvement in their own government's ability to contend with the diverse ways that China's growth in regional economic and security affairs has altered Japan's interests. This book takes a closer look at Japan's effort to adjust to China's emergence.

Nonetheless, I realize that this is more than simply a research project of interest to Japanese or scholars of Japan. The relationship between Japan and China seems to point toward larger questions about our era in world politics. Despite much debate about the phenomenon of China's rise, far less is understood about how and why other societies are responding. Today I recognize just how difficult it will be for policymakers to manage the anxiety in our societies about a world that is interdependent and, at the same time, unpredictable. In Asia, too, this anxiety about the future is magnified by the daily complexities associated with China's rise, and the worry about the capacity of other societies to adjust is palpable. In the context of this geostrategic shift, policymakers in Japan and China will need to work harder to find common ground, as will policymakers in the United States. Japan and China will need to accommodate the changing balance of interests in the relationship between their societies. Across the Pacific, our ability to build relationships and find solutions to shared problems across rapidly and not so rapidly transforming societies also will be tested.

ACKNOWLEDGMENTS

My ability to complete this project has been immensely strengthened by the support of many. I must acknowledge with gratitude the incredible scholars who shaped my approach to the study of Asia at Columbia University: James William Morley, Carol Gluck, and Gerald Curtis tutored me in modern Japan; and Jack Snyder and Robert Jervis taught me to bring rich history and regional expertise to the study of international relations. In 2006, I was awarded an Abe Fellowship by the Social Science Research Council, with funding from the Japan Foundation Center for Global Partnership, allowing me to make two extended research visits to Tokyo. There I was affiliated with Keio University's Center for Contemporary Chinese Studies in the East Asia Research Institute as a guest of the renowned China scholar Kokubun Ryōsei. Keio was a wonderful place to visit, a beautiful campus with dynamic and engaging scholars of Northeast Asia.

During this complex project, my colleagues at the Council on Foreign Relations (CFR) provided generous support and intellectual stimulation. I would like to thank Richard N. Haass, president; James M. Lindsay, director of studies; and Elizabeth C. Economy, director of Asian studies, for their support and encouragement. My research associates have made it all possible. Early on, Sophia Yang kept the Japan Program running with great aplomb and professionalism while I continued my research in Japan. Charles McClean worked tirelessly through the final stages of the writing, contributing research assistance and a keen editorial eye as the pages turned into chapters and the chapters turned into a manuscript. He also was unfailingly steady in his support as I juggled a complicated schedule to find writing time. In Tokyo, Tsuneoka Chieko accompanied me to interviews with the Japanese advocates and interests whose stories are such an integral part of this book. Quite literally, this book could not have been written without Chieko's persistence and precision. Finally, I thank the talented group of interns at the Japan Program who kept me up to date on the next emerging crisis: Murai Hideki, Minoura Haruna, Iioka Keiko, Naiki Miyuki, Jennifer Ijichi, Ashley Sutton, Katayama Go, Shimada Yuko, Joelle Metcalfe, Yoshihisa Yuki, and Jingtian Gong.

I owe a different sort of debt to the Kuruba family. From my early study of the Japanese language to my research today on politics and foreign policy, I have had a willing group of respondents to my never-ending questions. The late Kuruba Kenji would talk with me into the night about Meiji and Showa Japan and his own experience as a young naval officer in the final days of the war. Kuruba Hiroko, too, shared her insights into wartime and early postwar Japan; taught me how to read the Kōjien as well as operate an electronic dictionary; and, today, at the age of eighty-eight, teaches my son o-hajiki and go and still makes the best harumaki. I am deeply grateful that Keiko, Michiko, and Izumi; their husbands; their children; and now their children's children, continue to invite me to call the Kuruba family my own.

But beyond this special window onto generational change, I, like so many Japan scholars before me, have rarely found a door closed in Japan. As you will see from this book, my research led me to some interesting sites and introduced me to many people in Japan who had little contact with American academics and their research ambitions. Yet with only a few exceptions, my requests for interviews and follow-up information were tolerated and even welcomed. Despite the sensitivity of my questions, I was offered information and insights. Many who have come to know me over the years continue to try to correct my misapprehensions about their country and to challenge my conclusions. Many in the Japanese government have taken time to discuss their work with me, and I have gained invaluable insights from their perspectives; and many of Japan's senior political leaders and bureaucrats directly responsible for managing the increasingly difficult relationship with Beijing have given generously of their time. I was privileged to interview four of Japan's prime ministers for this book: Nakasone Yasuhiro, Fukuda Yasuo, Abe Shinzō, and Noda Yoshihiko. I also discussed Japan's relations with China with four of Japan's foreign ministers over the past decade: Kōmura Masahiko, Nakasone Hirofumi, Okada Katsuya, and Maehara Seiji. Fukuda Yasuo and Sengoku Yoshito, cabinet secretaries to Prime Ministers Koizumi Jun'ichirō and Kan Naoto, respectively, also granted me multiple interviews. I have done my best to acknowledge in the notes those whom I could acknowledge, but many others asked that their conversations remain off the record.

Little did I know that my research would become the stuff of headlines around the globe and crises at the highest levels of governments, including my own. Asia policymakers in the United States also deserve my gratitude for their insights into and thoughtful feedback on my work. Academics and experts are allowed the luxury of thinking out loud without direct reference to what may happen next, but those in government must communicate intentions across the intricate and fragile pathways of diplomacy, all amid contentious domestic politics. As I witnessed in the most recent episode of tensions between Tokyo and Beijing, U.S. policymakers have a direct role in the response to diplomatic crises and maritime confrontation between Beijing and Tokyo. I therefore now have a more immediate appreciation of just how much the success or failure of individual policymakers can shape outcomes.

I also benefited greatly from the generosity of scholars and friends in Japan and the United States. Let me thank first the members of my CFR study group, who provided early advice and encouragement: Richard C. Bush, Victor Cha, Elizabeth Economy, Carl Green, L. William Heinrich, Fred Hiatt, Mike M. Mochizuki, Stanley Roth, Richard J. Samuels, and Adam Segal. In addition, I thank Akiba Takeo, Jeffrey Bader, Kurt Campbell, Ralph Cossa, Carolyn Fleisher, Michael J. Green, Susan Griffin, Charles Grubb, David Janes, Funabashi Yōichi, Ishiba Shigeru, Ishii Masafumi, Chris Johnstone, Katō Yōichi, Kobayashi Yōtaro, Michael McDevitt, Nagashima Akihisa, Sasae Kenichiro, Michael Schiffer, J. Thomas Schieffer, Seguchi Kiyoyuki,

Allan Song, Takahara Akio, Takamizawa Nobushige, the late William J. Tyler, Umemoto Kazuyoshi, and so many others for their insights and support. My father, Ralph Edward Smith, read every word in every draft and assiduously provided editorial feedback. As a retired naval officer who served most of his career in the Pacific, he continues to have an avid interest in the geopolitics of Asia. His dedication to this book may have been born of a different motive, but I could not have asked for a more thoughtful critic.

Projects of this sort cannot be completed without the support of family and friends. Let me thank first my parents, Ralph and Barbara Smith. I must thank Margaret Rulon-Miller and Louisa Rubinfien, who have been my dearest companions since college, and continue to give me courage in all that I do. Finally, a special note of gratitude is due my son, Ian. As a young boy, he was always happy to don his backpack and head for Tokyo, Beijing, Okinawa, and even Washington, D.C., to help Mom with her research. I am even more delighted that my teenager still smiles and says, "Sure, Mom, let's go!" when I ask if he's up for another trip to Asia. It is in the hope that he continues to find the world an inviting and exciting place that I dedicate this book to him.

ABBREVIATIONS

ADIZ	Air Defense Identification Zone
APEC	Asia-Pacific Economic Cooperation
AQSIQ	General Administration of Quality Supervision, Inspection, and Quarantine
ASDF	Air Self-Defense Force
ASEAN	Association of Southeast Asian Nations
ASIF	Association for the Safety of Imported Food
ASW	Anti-Submarine Warfare
BSE	Bovine Spongiform Encephalopathy
CCP	Chinese Communist Party
CIE	Civil Intelligence and Education Section
CLCS	UN Commission on the Limits of the Continental Shelf
CNOOC	China National Offshore Oil Corporation
DPJ	Democratic Party of Japan
EEZ	Exclusive Economic Zone
FAO	Food and Agriculture Organization of the United Nations
FDI	Foreign Direct Investment
GHQ	General Headquarters
GSDF	Ground Self-Defense Force
HACCP	Hazard Analysis and Critical Control Point
ICJ	International Court of Justice
ISR	Intelligence, Surveillance, and Reconnaissance

ITLOS	International Tribunal for the Law of the Sea
JAPIT	Japan Association for the Promotion of International Trade
JAS	Japan Agricultural Standard
JCCU	Japan's Consumer Cooperatives Union
JCG	Japan Coast Guard
JCIEA	Japan-China Importers and Exporters Association
JCPTA	Japan-China Trade Promotion Association
JSP	Japan Socialist Party
LDP	Liberal Democratic Party
MAFF	Ministry of Agriculture, Forestry, and Fisheries
METI	Ministry of Economy, Trade, and Industry
MEXT	Ministry of Education, Culture, Sports, Science, and Technology
MFN	Most-Favored Nation
MHLW	Ministry of Health, Labor, and Welfare
MLAT	Mutual Legal Assistance Treaty
MLIT	Ministry of Land, Infrastructure, Transport, and Tourism
MOD	Ministry of Defense
MOU	Memorandum of Understanding
MPS	Ministry of Public Security
MSA	Maritime Safety Agency
MSDF	Maritime Self-Defense Force
NATO	North Atlantic Treaty Organization
NPA	National Police Agency
NPO	Non-Profit Organization
NSC	National Security Council
ODA	Official Development Assistance
PRC	People's Republic of China
ROC	Republic of China (Taiwan)
ROE	Rules of Engagement
ROK	Republic of Korea
SDF	Self-Defense Force
TMG	Tokyo Metropolitan Government
UNCLOS	United Nations Convention on the Law of the Sea
USSR	Union of Soviet Socialist Republics
WHO	World Health Organization
WTO	World Trade Organization

INTIMATE RIVALS

1

CONTENDING WITH CHINA

In the final days of campaigning for the Japanese Upper House election in July 2013, Prime Minister Abe Shinzō visited Japan's southernmost islands of Okinawa Prefecture. His conservative party was in trouble there because of a long-standing political dispute over a U.S. military airfield. Yet Abe did not go to champion the U.S.-Japan alliance; instead he went to the outlying islands of Ishigaki and Miyako, the first visit there by a Japanese prime minister in forty-eight years.[1] In these last hours of a definitive election, Abe chose to praise the Japan Coast Guard and Air Self-Defense Forces for defending their nation against China.

Tensions between Japan and China had been brewing for years, but the territorial dispute over isolated islands in the East China Sea prompted particularly strong emotions in Japan. Indeed, when he returned to the prime minister's office in December 2012, Abe inherited an escalating crisis that seemed headed for a possible armed clash over the disputed Senkaku Islands.[2] Chinese and Japanese leaders had set aside this territorial dispute during the final phase of negotiations for the 1978 Treaty of Peace and Friendship and had worked together ever since to keep this issue off their diplomatic agenda. But a Chinese fishing trawler captain changed that in September 2010 when he deliberately rammed two Japan Coast Guard ships near the islands, prompting his arrest by the Japanese government. The Chinese and Japanese governments were at loggerheads for weeks afterward, with Beijing raising diplomatic pressure on Tokyo until it released the captain.

The domestic repercussions in Japan continued, however. A little more than a year later, Ishihara Shintarō, the erratic governor of Tokyo, announced that he would purchase these islands from their owner because the national government was incapable of defending their sovereignty against China.[3] The Noda Yoshihiko cabinet moved to complete the national government's purchase of the Senkakus in an effort to prevent Governor Ishihara from further inflaming the dispute with Beijing.[4] But it was too late. Beijing no longer was interested in returning to a quiet management of their differences. The Chinese reaction to Noda's purchase of the islands was swift and severe. Demonstrations erupted throughout the country, with widespread damage to Japanese companies, and the Chinese government introduced its own ships to the islands' waters to assert its sovereign control.

The diplomatic crises with Beijing over the islands stirred those in Japan who had long thought that their postwar security choices had left their country vulnerable. Japanese politicians vied with one another in their calls for defending Japanese sovereignty over the islands. After the purchase of the islands, Abe campaigned for the presidency of the Liberal Democratic Party (LDP), advocating that government officials be stationed on the islands to assert Japan's "effective control" (*jikkō shihai*) in the face of the Chinese sovereignty challenge. By the time Abe's conservatives won a landslide victory in the Lower House on December 16, 2012, Senkaku nationalism was no longer a marginal cause in Japanese politics; the defense of Japanese sovereignty over the islands was now the rallying cry of Japan's ruling party.

The escalating tensions between Japan and China quickly raised regional concerns when their two militaries were added to the mix. In December 2012, a small Chinese surveillance aircraft entered Japanese airspace over the disputed Senkakus, initially undetected by air defense radar. Japanese fighter jets scrambled, leading the new LDP government to review its rules of engagement (ROEs) for air defenses. Subsequently, Chinese fighter jets were added to the mix of surveillance flights near the islands, and new competition for airspace was added to the maritime tensions. A month later, as 2013 began, a

Chinese naval vessel locked its fire-control radar on a Japanese Maritime Self-Defense Force frigate. After the Japanese government made this incident public, the Chinese government began investigating the incident, and while the Ministry of Defense denied that it had even taken place, it did acknowledge that these kinds of military interactions were dangerous and could lead to war.[5] The following fall, however, a new Chinese announcement provoked concerns about rising military tensions yet again. China stated that it was imposing an air defense identification zone (ADIZ) across the East China Sea, and the Ministry of Defense called on all aircraft crossing this area to report their intentions to Beijing in advance. Included in the ADIZ were the disputed islands.[6]

This escalating territorial dispute drew global attention to the deepening rift between Tokyo and Beijing. No longer able to negotiate their differences, the leaders of China and Japan turned to others around the world for support. At the United Nations General Assembly in September 2012, Japanese and Chinese leaders vented their frustration—and argued for their interpretation of the dispute. Prime Minister Noda articulated his country's respect for the Charter of the United Nations, which calls on nations to "settle disputes in a peaceful manner based on international law."[7] In contrast, China's foreign minister, Yang Jiechi, concluded his speech asserting Chinese sovereignty over the Diaoyus by contending that Japan's national purchase of the islands was an "outright denial of the outcomes of the victory of the world anti-fascist war and poses a grave challenge to the postwar international order."[8] According to Yang, Japan "stole" these islands from China. Uninhabited, rocky islands far from the shores of either country thus became the emblem of contest over national identity and global influence. By the end of 2013, Chinese ambassadors in London and Washington, D.C., were writing op-eds condemning Japan as a "revisionist" power with deep "militarist" values. Japan's ambassadors also took up their pens in an effort to dispute Chinese claims.[9]

Tokyo and Beijing, too, sought to shape Washington's reaction to their dispute. Tokyo turned to its alliance partner to help deter and dissuade further coercive action by Beijing, and Beijing cautioned Washington to remain neutral. As the confrontation in the East China Sea escalated dangerously, the Obama administration strongly urged both Japan and China to remain calm and to pursue a peaceful resolution of their differences. In October 2010, after Japan and China had their first round of confrontation over the Chinese fishing trawler incident, Secretary of State Hillary Rodham Clinton reasserted the U.S. position that the Senkaku Islands were covered by article 5 of the bilateral U.S.-Japan security treaty.[10] Then when the tensions escalated dramatically in September 2012, Secretary of Defense Leon Panetta traveled to Asia to reiterate the U.S. defense commitment but also to urge restraint by both governments.[11] Even Congress weighed in with a joint resolution on the U.S. interests in the dispute.[12] Fear of miscalculation—and an inadvertent clash between Asia's two largest powers—pushed Washington to urge calm and restraint while also bolstering Japan's southern air defenses to enhance deterrence. In December 2013, Vice President Joe Biden traveled to Northeast Asia to try to dampen China's ADIZ ambitions and to reassert the U.S. position that it would not change its own military operations in response.[13] But Tokyo remained skeptical of Washington's support in its contest with Beijing.

SINO-JAPANESE TENSIONS

Territorial nationalism is a potent force in domestic politics, and the Japan-China clash over the disputed Senkaku Islands ushered in a particularly dangerous moment in their relationship. Japan's tensions in its relationship with China did not begin with the island dispute, however, as their difficulties in resolving policy differences had first become evident a decade earlier. Although not all aspects of the complex Sino-Japanese relationship have been contentious, political leaders in Japan have found compromise more and more difficult as popular enthusiasm for China has faltered. Chinese leaders, too, have seemed unable to fulfill agreements or to reach a compromise.

Many factors have contributed to the tensions between Tokyo and Beijing. For more than a decade, the rise in China's economic influence, coupled with the expansion of its military power, signaled a potentially significant transition of geopolitical power. The anticipation of a much stronger China, possibly hostile to Japan, increasingly fed Japanese perceptions of their relationship with Beijing. China's neighbors in Asia, particularly U.S. allies, face many challenges in confronting this rising power. Greater proximity, economic dependency, and a new emerging *regional* balance of power create competing choices. Japan's difficulties with China suggest the need for a better analysis of these competing influences, and Tokyo's experience offers a critical case study of the adjustments required of a status quo power.

Another important factor is the continued differences over the legacy of the past and the terms of Japan's postwar settlement. The San Francisco Peace Treaty, signed in 1951 and restoring Japanese sovereignty in the wake of the United States' seven-year occupation, did not include Japan's two "rising" neighbors, the Republic of Korea (ROK) and the People's Republic of China (PRC). In 1950, although the Korean War divided the peninsula, a full-fledged government had yet to be formed in the ROK. In addition, the United States recognized the Kuomintang (Guomindang) government of Chiang Kai-shek, and when Beijing fell to the Chinese Communist Party (CCP) in 1949, the United States and its soon-to-be Cold War ally in Tokyo refused to recognize the newly formed mainland government.[14] It took decades for Japan to conclude separate peace treaties with its neighbors. The Japan-ROK Treaty on Basic Relations was not concluded until 1965, and the Japan-PRC Treaty of Peace and Friendship was not negotiated until after President Richard Nixon's historic trip to China in 1978. Territorial disputes and other issues related to the postwar settlement were subject to contemporary revisionist politics in all three Northeast Asian nations, and unresolved differences over history and compensation became lightning rods for nationalist sentiment.

The emergence of China as a regional and global power only exacerbated the dissatisfaction with the terms of the postwar peace between Japan and its neighbors. Then in 2012, intensifying difficulties with Seoul and Beijing over island disputes reinforced the idea that Tokyo's strategic position in Northeast Asia was deteriorating. In 2014, Japan's territorial disputes over islands with three of its Northeast Asian neighbors—Russia, South Korea, and China—still remained unresolved. The changing Northeast Asian balance of power was gradually creating unease over Tokyo's defenses.

Finally, tensions over the island dispute gave new urgency to Japan's debate over military reform, and soon after taking office, the Abe cabinet announced that it would review the previous government's national defense plan. For more than a decade, Japan's military budget had not grown, and adjustments to the changing balance of forces in the region had been put off. Equally important, the United States and Japan had not undertaken a strategic review of their alliance since 1997 and still were focused on implementing a post–Cold War realignment of forces. Much had changed in the region since then. Long an advocate of reinterpreting Japan's constitution to lift some of the constraints on Japan's military, Abe appointed an advisory committee to review the legal basis for expanding Japan's right to the use of force in cooperation with other nations, including the United States, and he proposed an increase in Japan's defense spending. In New York in September 2013, Abe confirmed to an American audience that Japan would not be the "weak link in the regional and global security framework where the U.S. plays a leading role," yet he had his eyes on China:

> We have an immediate neighbor whose military expenditure is at least twice as large as Japan's and second only to the U.S. defense budget. The country has increased its military expenditures, hardly transparent, by more than 10 percent annually for more than 20 years since 1989. And then my government has increased its defense budget only by zero point eight per cent. So call me, if you want, a right-wing militarist.[15]

Abe's reference to Chinese criticism of his agenda reflected Beijing's insistence that he was the problem.

While Abe's views on Japan's defense and its postwar history have never been in doubt, the acrimony between Tokyo and Beijing has become more and more personal. Beijing has not always been critical of Abe, however. As the newly elected prime minister in the fall of 2006, he was openly welcomed in Seoul and Beijing as the statesman who would repair strained relations and open the way for a "mutually beneficial" relationship. Nonetheless, when he returned to power in 2012, the Japan-China relationship had already deteriorated considerably. Abe did not create these tensions, though, and in fact, he called for high-level talks again with the new Xi Jinping leadership in Beijing. But his diplomatic success in his first term in office did not translate into success in his second term.

A Decade of Diplomatic Strain

Signs of a changing bilateral relationship already were evident at the turn of the century.[16] Over the next decade, repeated frictions between Tokyo and Beijing on a variety of policy problems reflected the growing popular concern over China's influence, and the diplomatic relationship swung from confrontation to reconciliation and back again.[17]

With each problem, the Japanese government seemed increasingly unable to resolve its differences with Beijing. Prime Minister Koizumi Jun'ichirō (2001–2006) presided over roughly half the decade of strain between Tokyo and Japan, and for a time, Beijing attributed many of these difficulties to him. Moreover, Koizumi's insistence on visiting the controversial Yasukuni Shrine was seen as the primary cause of China's criticism of Japan. When Koizumi stepped down, diplomats in Beijing and Tokyo unveiled a sophisticated diplomatic blueprint of high-level summitry designed to thaw the chill of the Koizumi years,[18] and it was Abe who led the Japanese effort to repair relations. The culmination in May 2008 was Hu Jintao's visit to Japan, the first in a decade by a Chinese president. Prime Minister Fukuda Yasuo, son of the prime minister who had welcomed Deng Xiaoping on his first visit to Tokyo in 1978, welcomed Hu and proudly announced their new vision for "mutually beneficial relations based on common strategic interests."[19]

But this high-level diplomacy did not end the difficulties in the Japan-China relationship. New issues drew public criticism. Even after the Hu-Fukuda summit in 2008, the two governments continued to struggle to manage Japanese fears over poisoned frozen dumplings imported from China. Consumers boycotted Chinese goods, and the criminal investigation of the incident resulted in tense recriminations from both governments. In 2010, a Chinese fishing trawler in waters near the disputed Senkaku/Diaoyu Islands created the worst diplomatic standoff between Tokyo and Beijing since normalization. Popular animosity in both countries ratcheted upward as their political leaders feuded openly. After the two-week confrontation ended and tempers cooled, diplomats began yet again to return to the diplomacy of reconciliation, but with little progress. Again in 2012 the two countries were at odds over their island dispute. In mid-August, Chinese activists landed on the Senkakus; the Noda cabinet followed through on its purchase of the islands from their owner; and widespread anti-Japanese demonstrations followed in China. Compared with the fishing trawler incident, tensions between Beijing and Tokyo escalated dangerously as popular antagonisms soared, and even the two militaries became engaged. The carefully orchestrated diplomatic effort to steady the Japan-China relationship had failed.

At home, the Japanese were struggling to find a new approach to governance, and this affected their diplomacy with China as well. Japan was handicapped by its leaders' inability to stay in office long enough to develop a rapport with their Chinese counterparts. Japan's protracted political transition, which began in the early 1990s with the breakup of the conservative LDP, left the Japanese people feeling less confident in their own government. With the notable exception of Koizumi's five-year tenure, Japan's prime ministers changed virtually every year. Then in 2009, Japanese voters chose a new party to rule Japan. The arrival of the Democratic Party of Japan (DPJ)—a new, untested political party—did not restore public confidence in government but shook it even further, especially in its handling of foreign affairs. Japan's relations with Washington were strained over the basing of U.S. military forces in Okinawa, and despite the DPJ's commitment to closer ties with Seoul and Beijing, Japan's regional relationships also suffered. Not all the blame can be placed on the DPJ, though, as their leaders were confronted with two unprecedented political crises with Beijing over the islands. Nonetheless, successive DPJ prime ministers had to contend with harsh criticism at home from their conservative opposition as well as the public.

Both Japanese liberals and conservatives found it increasingly difficult to find partners among the new generation of Chinese leaders. The LDP had been in office for decades, and the earlier generation of its leaders had developed close ties with the leaders of the Chinese Communist Party. As a new force in Japanese politics, the DPJ did not have this legacy and had to work at building relationships with China's leaders. Once the DPJ became the ruling party, Ozawa Ichirō, the party's secretary-general, took 143 new DPJ Diet members to visit with the Chinese leadership, a move that the Japanese media (and members of conservative party) suggested was evidence of his "pro-China" position.[20] Even though Ozawa had cultivated ties with leading Chinese Communist Party members over many years, the DPJ was unable to translate those personal connections into political capital when the 2010 crisis over the Chinese trawler erupted. Despite repeated efforts to communicate with top party leaders, including sending Hosono Gōshi, one of Ozawa's protégés, to Beijing, the DPJ government found that China had little interest in compromise as tensions escalated.[21] Even those in the LDP with well-maintained ties to China's leadership found it difficult to find channels of communication in Beijing.

The Japanese public, too, was increasingly skeptical of the Chinese government. While personal ties between Japanese and Chinese leaders have weakened, Japanese public opinion of China has gradually soured. By 2013, according to a poll conducted by Genron NPO and the *China Daily*, 90.1 percent of Japanese said they had a negative attitude toward China,[22] even though more and more Japanese have had firsthand experience of China. China was the number-one destination for Japanese tourists; in fact, Japanese account for the greatest number of foreign visitors to China. As of 2013, more than 3.5 million Japanese had visited China each year, with the number climbing 70 percent from 2000 to 2010.[23] In addition, more than 125,000 Japanese live in China.[24] Similarly, more than 1 million Chinese citizens have visited Japan, and after visa restrictions were lifted in 2011, more are expected each year.[25] China was the number-two country of origin, behind South Korea, for visitors to Japan. Many Chinese students study in Japan, and more and more Chinese are finding Japan an attractive destination for second homes. Needless to say, Chinese products, firms, and capital affect Japan's domestic economy in new ways, although this economic interdependence has not forestalled the perception in Japan that the Chinese government was becoming uncooperative with or even hostile to Japan.

REACHING A RESOLUTION—OR NOT

Diplomacy alone has been insufficient to bridge the growing number of differences between Tokyo and Beijing. The failure to solve problems has led to growing frustration among the Japanese public. While China cannot be held accountable for all the difficulties in the relationship, adjusting to its growing influence is a new challenge for both governments. For Tokyo, however, many of the old ways of managing its relationship with Beijing no longer are effective. All countries in Asia, in fact, must adjust to the changing nature and origin of China's economic and military influence. For countries like Japan, which live in interdependent economies and in geographic proximity to a transforming China, the task is persuading their own citizens that their governments are well equipped to guide that adjustment. To date, successive governments in Japan have found adjustment problematic, with a wide array of domestic interests and advocates demanding greater protection from Chinese influence. Not all the issues, however, have involved Chinese behavior directed at Japan; nonetheless, China's pursuit of its expanding interests is affecting Japanese interests in new ways.

The Japanese experience also demonstrates the public's heightened sensitivity to the perception of greater Chinese influence on their society. The repeated tit-for-tat escalation in tensions between Japan and China suggests a tendency toward confrontation between the two governments. But as this book demonstrates, this was not driven by a strategic decision to confront China. On the contrary, accommodation rather than confrontation seems to have been the diplomatic choice.

Japan's leaders have not been able to implement this choice, however, for mainly domestic reasons. Policy differences across a range of issues reveal the complex assortment of Japanese who see their choices affected by Chinese behavior. The domestic factors supporting—and opposing—collaboration with Beijing will shape the resolution of these problems. Crafting a set of shared diplomatic goals with Beijing thus is only one part of Japan's effort. A much less appreciated—but equally important—requirement is managing the Japanese interests that will ultimately be affected by China's policy decisions. While many in Japan anticipated the rise of Chinese influence on global and regional relationships, very few predicted how much that influence would shape Japan's domestic politics. More often than not, this homegrown criticism has been directed just as much at the Japanese government as at Beijing.

Four Cases of Contention, 2001–2014

The domestic interests forming Japan's relationship with China are many, and their ability to determine the Japanese government's decision making on China varies as well across policy issues. Four such cases offer insights into the domestic interests that influenced Japanese policymaking on China over the past decade: Prime Minister Koizumi's visits to the Yasukuni Shrine, the effort to negotiate shared use of the East China Sea, the *gyōza* (dumpling) food-poisoning incident, and the *Senkaku shokku* (Senkaku shock), which began with a Chinese fishing captain's provocation of the Japan Coast Guard in 2010 and ultimately produced a standoff two years later between Japanese and Chinese patrols claiming sovereignty over the disputed Senkaku/Diaoyu Islands.

Two of these cases revolve around old issues, issues that evoke powerful popular sentiments and threaten Japan's national identity. The first is the Japanese state's effort to memorialize its war dead. The controversial Yasukuni Shrine has been the focus of conservative efforts to pay tribute to those who died in the name of the emperor in World War II, a war of aggression and imperial ambition in China as well as against the United States in the Pacific. Prime Minister Koizumi's commitment to visit Yasukuni on the date of Japan's surrender, August 15, led to a deep spiral downward in the Japan-China relationship. It also reopened public debate over the status of the shrine and the leaders designated as class-A war criminals. Seven years later, Prime Minister Abe reopened this debate over the shrine's significance, revealing the gap between domestic Japanese views and the international understanding of Yasukuni's meaning. Even Washington was concerned that Abe was deliberately raising tensions in the region.

A second bone of contention, as yet unresolved, is the effort to navigate differences in the maritime boundaries in the East China

Sea. These differences date from the early 1970s and were part of the normalization talks between Tokyo and Beijing that led to the 1978 Treaty of Peace and Friendship. Japan's maritime interest in the East China Sea includes access to resources, such as fisheries, seabed minerals, and energy resources, as well as the broader debate over how to delineate Japanese and Chinese territorial and exclusive economic zone (EEZ) boundaries according to international law. The UN Convention on the Law of the Sea (UNCLOS) presented a new effort to define the maritime economic rights of coastal states and to resolve conflicts over contested areas. China challenged not only Japan's long-standing territorial claims to the Senkaku Islands but also its interpretation of its maritime boundaries and claims. Efforts to negotiate a shared approach to joint research on seabed energy resources went nowhere, and the upswing in China's maritime activities in and around Japan's waters became a cause for protest and contention. Both the issue of Japan's war memory and its maritime rights in the East China Sea rose to the top of the bilateral agenda and became the sources of a dispute that was much more public than ever before.

The two remaining disputes reveal more potent public sensitivities that have taken center stage in Japan-China diplomacy. One is Japan's dependence on food imports from China. Imports of agricultural products, such as vegetables and rice, were on the rise. Cheaper and more easily available than Japanese vegetables, these imports had broad appeal to Japanese consumers. Moreover, Japan's food-processing industry had moved offshore to Chinese locales where cheap labor and proximity to agricultural products resulted in less expensive goods back home. On January 30, 2008, imported poisoned dumplings prompted a widespread investigation into China's role in supplying Japan's food. The *gyōza*-poisoning case, however, revealed the limits of Japanese oversight in Chinese factories and the lack of effective domestic procedures for ensuring consumer safety in Japan.

The last case is as old as the postwar relationship. The differences between Beijing and Tokyo over the sovereignty of the Senkaku/Diaoyu Islands were clear during normalization talks in the late 1970s, but today this territorial dispute has flared up in Japan as a potent emblem of national identity. The growing civic activism has brought fishermen and activists alike across the East China Sea to attempt landing on the uninhabited islands. In September 2010, however, the provocative behavior of a Chinese fishing-boat captain instigated a sharp escalation in bilateral tensions. Nationalistic efforts to assert Japan's control over the islands—for years the domain of small activist groups and local politicians—went mainstream after Governor Ishihara announced a campaign to raise money to purchase the islands and the LDP, in opposition at the time, argued to inhabit them. The national government's long-standing effort to keep the islands off the bilateral agenda with Beijing was no longer workable at home. National purchase became the only way of forestalling conservative calls for a more assertive defense of Japan's sovereignty over the islands. In addition, this issue became fodder for domestic political gain as frustration with the national government's leadership gave upcoming politicians a tactical advantage.

Domestic Interests and Japan's China Policy

In each case, Japan's policy differs and thus reflects the variety of interests associated with that policy's outcome. Cumulatively, however, these cases offer some insight into whether there is a broader nationalist or anti-China advocacy developing in Japanese politics. In other words, is there evidence of serious—and mounting—advocacy for resisting Chinese power? Have preferences in Japan shifted sufficiently to persuade the government that compromise in negotiation with Beijing ought to be abandoned? What issues can the Japanese government compromise on, and which will elicit a domestic backlash? Is there evidence of a consensus in Japan on the impact of China's rise, and if so, what does that consensus mean for Japanese behavior?

None of these cases represents deliberate behavior by China that is intended to cause Japan harm, nor does Japan's policymaking reflect a similar intention. Rather, in large part these cases are contentious because they resist a clear-cut resolution, and the negotiation of conflicting interests demands compromise. These are the issues over which we would expect interest groups to forge alliances and/or over which broad-based anti-China sentiment might find a foothold. These are the very issues in which domestic pressures on the government to either stand up to China or resist compromise should be most conspicuous. Therefore, these cases allow insight into the potential for new coalitions to emerge in Japan, coalitions with preferences that would impinge specifically on the Japanese government's ability to negotiate with China.

All four of these cases pertain to issues that resonate in the debate over Japan's postwar identity. The Yasukuni Shrine has long been seen as a contentious issue between Japan's conservative nationalists who seek to restore honor to the Japanese state and postwar liberals who argue for the protections of popular sovereignty in Japan's postwar constitution. Chinese officials often present a slightly different narrative, framing their criticism as aimed at Japan's "militaristic" or "right wing" leaders rather than against the Japanese people. In both narratives, the question really is about whether Japan today is—or ought to be—different from prewar Japan. Issues such as Japan's differences with China over the maritime boundary in the East China Sea and the territorial dispute over the Senkakus have obvious implications for Japan's security policy and its commitment to resolve differences through diplomacy and multilateral dispute resolution mechanisms rather than by military force. Even the food safety issue is embedded in a domestic debate over self-reliance and the extent to which Japan should commit to a liberal trading order and open its market to foreign goods. Rallying around the call for a new approach to Japan's public policy choices in any of these cases would not necessarily be equivalent to resisting China (or adopting an anti-China policy stance). Yet as China's rise continues, Japan's success or failure at negotiating its interests with Beijing will affect the tolerance in Japan of the vulnerabilities that have attended its postwar foreign policy commitments supporting self-restraint on the use of military force and a liberalized global market economy.

Finally, if China's rise is producing greater nationalistic sentiment in Japan, then the question is whether that sentiment will be translated into political activism. And if so, by whom? If China's influence is producing more support for a nationalistic agenda, then the evidence should emerge from these cases of contention. Domestic interests converge around each policy area, but do these repeated frictions with China offer an opportunity to advocate and mobilize around the cause of greater Japanese nationalism? If so, then those interests active in one case should be creating networks of cooperation with interests across issue areas. In addition, do these advocates seeking to influence the debate over Japan's national choices and preferences find common cause with others who also want their government to take a firmer stance toward China? Japan's strategic effort to oppose or join with China will need advocates to lead it and will need domestic support if it is to be executed successfully. The domestic interests on which Tokyo's strategic choices vis-à-vis China are based will be an important determinant of diplomatic success. Differentiating those seeking a role in making Japan's strategic choices from those seeking Japanese government protection of their own interests is the first step in understanding the impact of domestic politics on Japan's choices. A second task is considering the balance of advocacy in Japan on policies related to China to determine whether perceptions of China may be sufficient to prompt a significant realignment of Japan's postwar politics.

The disputes over territory and over sharing the East China Sea are issues for which agreement seems remote. Despite the seeming trend toward confrontation, however, Tokyo and Beijing have found ample room for compromise. A less appreciated aspect of Japan-China relations is the relationship between China policy and the pressures at home for policy reform in Japan. Over the past decade or more, there has been a considerable rethinking of some Japanese policies in order to better adapt to the new China.

Japan's dissatisfaction with relying on a strategy of political reconciliation with China based solely on economic cooperation had already become evident by the late 1990s. The end of the Cold War changed the geostrategic context in which Beijing and Japan had been operating since signing the Treaty of Peace and Friendship of 1978. But Japan's domestic politics also were in flux, and the political transition away from the LDP's single-party dominance created new questions about Japan's foreign policy goals, especially with regard to its relationship with China and the United States and about the ability of Japan's government to create and sustain a new diplomatic strategy toward Beijing.

This elite consensus was accompanied by a deterioration of Japanese public opinion regarding China. Popular sensitivities to what seemed to be a greater vulnerability to Chinese decision making has complicated Japanese policymaking. Here, contentious incidents rather than long-standing cooperation have encouraged the debate about China's rise and what it means for Japan's own governance. Each case that I examine in this book offers insights into the way that Chinese influences on Japanese society are perceived and into the relations among the various domestic actors and agents shaping Japan's domestic policymaking on China.

Taken together, these cases also offer some suggestions for the future. The ability of both governments to manage each other's vulnerabilities will determine the trajectory of Japan-China relations. By their very nature, these issues suggest competing rather than complementary interests, and left unresolved, they carry the potential for aggravating popular anxiety in Japan and creating support for confrontation with China. To be successful, Japanese leaders must persuade their public that cooperation with China will reduce Japan's vulnerabilities rather than exacerbate them.

2

DIPLOMACY AND DOMESTIC INTERESTS

From normalization until the turn of the twenty-first century, Japan's relations with China were guided more by the legacy of the past and the need for postwar reconciliation than by the logic of geopolitics. Japan's identity as an Asian power had been formed over a long and complex history of cultural and economic interactions with China.[1] In the nineteenth century, when the contest for global resources reached Asia, Japan was determined to open its society to compete with the West. But Japan's modernization led to its own imperial ambitions, and at the beginning of the twentieth century, it went to war with China. Japan's desire to compete with the European powers had altered both nations, and in many ways, its rise as a great power came at China's expense.

Japan's attempt to dominate Asia ultimately failed, with a catastrophic loss of life. After World War II and Japan's occupation by the United States and its allies, Japan and China did not resume diplomatic ties for more than two decades. Economic ties were to be the path to reconciliation, with Japan fostering China's economic development. By the beginning of the twenty-first century, however, China's remarkable economic transformation began to change the relationship, with its success ushering in a new era of Asian relations in which both China and Japan exerted considerable regional and global influence.

Japan's views of this new China are linked to its envisioned position in the region and the world. Anticipation that China will one day overtake Japan in both wealth and military power has created uncertainty about not only their relationship but also Japan's own global standing and security. Will a rising China overshadow Japan? Will China's increasing material power and influence translate into a more assertive attitude toward Japan, and how will China's greater influence affect the long-standing Japanese alliance with the United States?[2] Like many other Asian countries, Japan is grappling with a fundamental change in the Asia Pacific, one that touches both its economic prospects and its security. For Tokyo, this is not a theoretical problem;[3] it already is beginning to shape its policy choices. Tensions with Beijing have steadily multiplied, and negotiations have become more difficult. Japan's experience with the new China provides a window on the unique characteristics of that bilateral relationship and also reveals common concerns about the trajectory of Asian international relations. How Japan responds to China's growing economic and military influence will shape the region for years to come.

In many ways, Japan's policy debate mirrors the U.S. debate. China experts in America have cautioned the United States to be aware of how U.S. policy affects Beijing's calculations,[4] and likewise, China has scrutinized the United States and its goals.[5] The various interpretations of Beijing's ambitions continue, with suggestions for U.S. policymakers ranging from encouraging China to become a "responsible stakeholder" to urging Washington to avoid the lure of the "G-2 mirage" and to "buck China."[6] For those who worry about the inevitability of China's future dominance, the mechanics of past transitions in major power relations provide a cautionary tale. Rivalries abound, and wars seem inevitable; Germany's rise in the early 1900s and its assertion of its interests in Europe are often used to suggest a parallel with contemporary Asian politics. The Japanese, too, have begun to adopt this reference to modern European history. At the World Economic Forum at Davos, Switzerland, in January 2014, even Prime Minister Abe, in describing the dynamic between Japan and China, succumbed to this temptation when he compared contemporary tensions in East Asia with those in 1914 and the competition of the European powers before World War I.[7]

However the trajectory of Chinese power unfolds, regional perceptions of Beijing's influence merit careful attention, as they also affect how Asian countries—particularly U.S. allies—see the United States. Conflict with China means that many of these countries, including Japan, have pursued even closer ties with Washington. For others, though, this may be too risky. While U.S. policy experts continue to explore avenues for directing Chinese behavior, Japanese experts see China as less susceptible to their influence and more focused on Washington. Sensitivity to the United States' acknowledgment of Chinese power, such as its effort to define a "new major power relationship," colors Japanese assessments of the impact of China's rise on their own country's interests.[8] For many Asian countries, the region's international relations are not driven solely *by* China; they also are largely determined by perceptions of, and worries about, how the United States and its allies might respond *to* China.

No power in Asia has felt the changing influence of China as keenly as Japan. China's economic growth has provided opportunity for Japanese investment and trade; it has stimulated a reorganization of Japanese networks of production; and Chinese consumer demand will drive Japanese product development in the years to come. Because China and Japan depend on each other for their own national economic success, despite political tensions, this economic interdependence has remained largely unchanged. But other factors shape the relationship as well. Geography brings Japan close to China's military modernization.[9] Japan is offshore the continent of Asia, its maritime boundary stretching from the tip of the Korean Peninsula to the southwestern Japanese islands. From Japan, it is only a thirty-minute flight to Taiwan to the south and a one- to two-hour flight to most cities on the Chinese coast by commercial jet, albeit less by military aircraft. On the sea, Japanese fishing boats and other civilian ships share the East China Sea with Taiwanese, Chinese, and Korean counterparts. Protecting that coastline poses a considerable challenge for the Japan Coast Guard and other maritime agencies,[10] and as Chinese maritime interests have widened, the East China Sea and the straits between the Japanese islands have become a natural route of egress for civilian and military vessels seeking the open ocean.

Diplomacy has not yet proved to be a reliable instrument for solving Japan's tensions with China. After the first diplomatic "chill" that developed during the latter years of the Koizumi Jun'ichirō cabinet, leaders in Beijing and Tokyo sought to redefine their bilateral relationship to accommodate the new balance of interests in the relationship. Yet even this high-level summitry could not stem the repeated frustrations. Just two years after the Fukuda-Hu summit, the island dispute quickly derailed the governments' effort to create "mutually beneficial relations based on common strategic interests."

China's economic growth alone, however, cannot explain this diplomatic impasse between Tokyo and Beijing. Its future remains unpredictable, and its effort to raise the standard of living for all its citizens remains incomplete. Indeed, despite all the country's economic accomplishments, most Chinese today have a quality of life far inferior to that of most Japanese. China's per capita GDP remains around one-tenth of Japan's, and environmental degradation threatens the health and safety of its citizens.[11] Income disparity remains a serious social problem, and the slowing rate of growth in China will make the Chinese people's expectations of improving the quality of their lives even more difficult to achieve.[12] This will likely keep the attention of the country's leaders firmly focused on their domestic challenges and will complicate Beijing's international ambitions. Nonetheless, even though China's rise as a global power is not yet complete, the potential of a more powerful Beijing antagonistic to Japanese interests infuses foreign policy thinking in Tokyo today.

JAPAN AND CHINA: A NEW DYNAMIC

China's ascension in 2010 to the number-two spot in the world economy was widely interpreted as a sign of Japan's eclipse (figure 2.1).[13] Foreign direct investment was bypassing Tokyo and Osaka and heading to China's burgeoning urban centers. Trade between China and the rest of the world was booming, and by 2005, China had become Japan's largest trading partner, with China trade comprising 20 percent of Japan's total trade.[14] Moreover, besides transforming the Japanese economy, the Chinese economy was outperforming it on the global stage.[15]

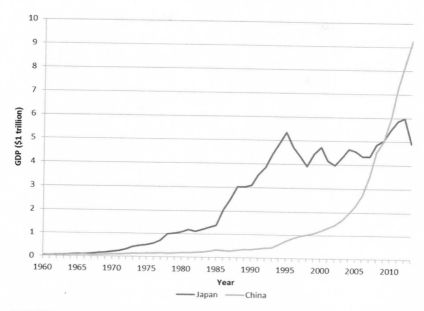

FIGURE 2.1 Japan's and China's GDP. Data is in current U.S. dollars. (Data Catalog, World Bank, last updated April 16, 2013, http://datacatalog.worldbank.org/)

China's interests in the Asia Pacific now were challenging the economic ties that, for decades, had been the foundation for Japan's regional leadership. Ever since its own economic rise in the 1960s, Japan has been the ascendant power in Asia, providing much needed trade and investment to a region largely composed of developing economies. Japanese companies built infrastructure and facilitated technology transfers to the newly emerging economies in Southeast Asia, and Japan's "developmental state" became the model of Asian forms of state capitalism.[16] By the 1980s, Japan led a "flying geese" formation of Asian economies.[17] It had also become a major advocate for regional institution building, played an important role in the formation of the Asia-Pacific Economic Community and later the ASEAN Regional Forum, and sought to play a similarly dominant role in Asia Pacific political institutions.

Japan began to fade from regional affairs by the late 1990s just as China began to become a more integral diplomatic player in Asia. Since then, it has been Beijing rather than Tokyo that has influenced regional dynamics. Asian responses to China's rise reveal that most Asian states are no longer looking to Tokyo, but focusing their attention on whether the United States can counter Beijing's influence.[18] Japan is no longer seen as the dominant influence in the region. In Southeast Asia, "soft" balancing through diplomatic and economic means and a reliance on ASEAN-based regional institutions have been the predominant recourse of the smaller states on China's periphery.[19] Domestically, virtually every Asian country has found that more and more national economic choices have had some bearing on its relations with China. Indeed, the impulse of all Asian powers, large and small, has been to hedge their bets.

Japan has been no exception. Since the beginning of the postwar era, Tokyo's alliance with the United States and its diplomacy with the People's Republic of China (PRC) have been at odds. Although the Cold War dampened the tension, when the two Asian nations normalized relations in 1978, the balancing act between Japan's historic ties to the Asian mainland and its postwar alliance with the United States was made manageable by China's turn toward creating a market economy. Beijing's economic success and its emergence as a global economic force, however, raised new pressures on Japanese diplomacy. Richard Samuels argues that Japan sought a "dual hedge," seeking economic benefit from Beijing while relying on the United States to provide security assurance.[20] In Japan, Samuels found evidence that foreign policy experts are not, however, unanimous in their support for this "dual-hedging" strategy in the face of China's rise. Mike Mochizuki sees greater continuity in the Japanese debate and argues that China's increasing economic power exaggerates what has long been part of Tokyo's foreign policy goals: an effort to find greater autonomy of choice in its relationship with China while still maintaining its alliance with Washington.[21] Both Samuels and Mochizuki, however, point out the tension in Japan's alliance relationship with Washington and the effort to develop closer relations with Beijing, a tension that has brought greater contest over the past decade as the shift in regional and global power in the direction of China has become more conspicuous.

Yet hedging as a strategic response can become difficult to sustain when domestic interests are competing for policy attention.

These interests are often driven by factors independent of the strategic logic that focuses on the systemic consequences of China's rise. Instead, domestic interests perceive of and react to their own experience of Chinese power, and as a result, they become active advocates for government attention. In other words, the domestic impact of China's power also guides Japan's response. Failure to explore the domestic politics that lead the adjustment to a new source of global power overlooks the pressures on governments trying to adjust to geopolitical change. Carefully calibrated strategies can be easily derailed by popular emotions and political opportunity. Much of the policy debate on how to manage a changing China has not taken into account the domestic pressures that confront government policymakers.

Japan's strategic response to China's economic rise has yet to be clearly articulated and has not reflected a unity of purpose between Japan's government and private actors. For example, Japanese business leaders have rarely wavered in their support for greater economic interdependence, and indeed, Japanese investment in China has continued to grow even as Japanese government officials have become more wary of diplomatic compromise with China. Even though diplomats and political leaders continue to advocate the "win-win" opportunities of cooperation with China, they are stumbling from controversy to controversy, proving that the interests of Tokyo and Beijing are not often in sync. Increasingly punctuated by crises and, most recently, by the clash of maritime agencies over the territorial disputes in the East China Sea, the relationship between Japan and China seems to resist past diplomatic formulas for sustained cooperation. Despite their shared economic interests, neither government seems to have a viable strategy for coping with their political differences.

Japan has been unable to hedge in its strategy toward China largely because of domestic interests. In the past, there was a coalition of support for a conciliatory policy toward China. Cooperation with Beijing was the objective, based on the premise that closer relations between the two countries was in Japan's best interests. To be sure, the basic lines of contention over China policy were identifiable in postwar politics. Japan's progressives and conservatives have disagreed over the need for apologizing for its wartime conquest of China; Japan's politicians and business leaders have taken different approaches to managing their bilateral relations; and the Japanese public has seemed torn between the desire to reconcile over the past and to craft a new relationship for the future.[22]

But the domestic debate over China policy has been far from static. As the Chinese economy grew and the relationship with Japan became more interdependent, domestic support in Japan for a diplomatic accommodation of China's internal transformation began to shift. China's economic and military choices raised awareness of the possibility for a more contentious China in the future, and despite Beijing's efforts to articulate its strategy of a "peaceful rise," Tokyo's relations with China seemed increasingly and consistently fraught.

Beyond Japan's political and bureaucratic elites, the constellation of interests with a stake in Japan's policy toward China also grew. Japan's business elites continued to be strong supporters of a close relationship with China, but at times they seemed overshadowed by more virulent voices with a distinctly anti-China tone. The business community still claims a central role in the China policy debate, but it plays a less visible role than in the past. Popular opinion of China, too, began to cool. Japan's own economic difficulties undoubtedly played a role, but the tensions with China over history and trade made for less public support for compromise with Beijing. Focused on the Chinese government's criticism of Japan, popular skepticism over Chinese intentions rose as policy differences emerged, creating a much more precarious domestic climate in which to argue the merits of cooperation with China.

Diplomatic frustrations with China coincided with the 1990s effort to reform Japanese politics. Advocates of reform, such as the LDP politician Ozawa Ichirō, sought a more competitive party system, with alternating parties in power offering new policy choices. Japanese voters then would exercise their choice for building a "new Japan" through the electoral process.[23] Preoccupied with this new era of political reform, Japan's bureaucracies had to contend with the growth in Chinese influence while politicians paid scant attention to the need for a coherent strategy vis-à-vis China. As a multitude of parties and personalities contended for political power, Japan's conservatives looked for coalition partners in the most unlikely of places. The LDP even joined forces with its postwar nemesis, the Japan Socialist Party (JSP), and the JSP's leader, Murayama Tomiichi, became the prime minister of Japan in 1994. Prime Minister Murayama reached a compromise with Japan's conservatives on an issue of deep ideological contention—a clear and heartfelt apology for Japan's twentieth-century history—and this seemed to bring an end to their postwar ideological feud. But even this was not to last.

Political power in Japan became more diffuse, and only one leader, Koizumi, managed to sustain his hold on power long enough to reconsider Japan's evolving strategic position. Koizumi tried to persuade Beijing of the two countries' mutual interests but was unsuccessful in moving forward their debate over the past. With his repeated visits to the Yasukuni Shrine, Koizumi enraged Chinese leaders and ended his tenure in office with a "freeze" in diplomatic relations. In 2009, the LDP lost power to the Democratic Party of Japan (DPJ), ushering in a new but ultimately frustrated effort to negotiate a new "mutually beneficial" relationship with China. Uncertainty was becoming the norm in Tokyo's political relations with Beijing, and Japan's politicians could not build a partnership with China's new emerging leaders. For more than forty years, Japan's diplomacy toward China had been driven by the hope for reconciliation, but in Japan, there was a greater focus on a more reciprocal—and less apologetic—premise for Japan-China relations.

FROM RECONCILIATION TO RECIPROCITY

Japan's objectives in its relationship with China have evolved since the conclusion of the 1978 peace treaty. Perhaps most important initially was the end of the Cold War dynamics that had determined the strategic context of normalization. China's dependence on Japanese economic assistance dwindled as its own economy took off, and postwar reconciliation proved illusory as political sensitivities over historical memory intensified nationalistic impulses in both societies.

As many scholars of the Sino-Japanese relationship have noted, the bilateral relationship seemed resistant to stability. Diplomacy between Tokyo and Beijing was never completely smooth, and yet the two governments extensively enlarged their policy cooperation to include a complex array of interests. As Ming Wan points out in his seminal study of Sino-Japan relations, "Sino-Japanese relations peaked in 1978, with subsequent cooperative periods never matching the heights of collaboration reached those years,"[24] and over time, the "emerging rivalry" between the two was unmistakable.[25] Explanations for the rocky diplomatic relationship vary. Ming Wan finds structural causes, as does Tanaka Akihiko, who situates Japan's foreign policy within a changing Asia. For Tanaka, who has written extensively on Japan's relations with China, it is the end of the Cold War and the blossoming of Asian regionalism that best frame the Japanese experience with China.[26]

Other Japan experts on China look more closely at who managed the bilateral relationship and to what end. For some, the shift from a relationship defined by the terms of reconciliation to one that could withstand the pressures of the new strategic context after the Cold War provides an important frame for considering the changing patterns in Sino-Japanese relations. Kokubun Ryōsei analyzed the management of Sino-Japanese relations in Iwanami shoten's new six-volume series on Japan's diplomacy (*Nihon no gaikō*).[27] He breaks Japan's relationship with China into three phases, roughly twenty years apart, each with a distinct pattern of relationship management. The first, 1952 to 1972, covers the period before normalization when Tokyo recognized the Republic of China (ROC) in Taibei; the second, 1972 to 1992, spans the era when Beijing saw Tokyo as a valuable economic partner after its decision to open its economy; and finally, the recent period from 1992 to the present includes both the rise of Chinese global economic influence and the domestic shift in Japan from a single-party-dominant government to a protracted period of political transition. For Kokubun, it is this coincidence of the emergence of Chinese global influence and domestic political change in Japan that created the contentious and unpredictable nature of the Sino-Japanese relationship today.

Another perspective relies more on the intertwined history of the national identity struggles of China and Japan. In her historical overview of the Sino-Japanese relationship, Mori Kazuko finds a complex reflection of both nations' idea of "postwar" in their efforts to build a "special relationship" defined by China's effort to modernize and Japan's struggle with its past. More recently, Japanese writing on contemporary China has sought to explain to a Japanese audience the sources of "anti-Japan" sentiment in China. In addition, many Japanese scholars take a more issue-oriented approach to examining the Sino-Japanese relationship.[28] Regardless of their approach, however, virtually all agree that by the end of the twentieth century, Japan's relationship with China had reached a critical turning point.

A new strategic consensus began to emerge as Japan's interests were challenged by China. Over time, four aspects of Japanese policy proved to need rethinking. The first was the end of the Cold War and its impact on Japan's assessment of its diplomatic role in Asia. From the Cold War's definition of an East-West divide to the more culturally driven sense of difference between the advanced economies of the West and the developing economies of Asia, Japan developed a strategy for mediating between China and the liberal democracies of the United States and Europe. Second, Tokyo's early reliance on mutual economic interests as the primary determinant of Japan-China relations could not be sustained as China's economy grew and Japan's stalled. Japan's own economic growth prospects became more closely tied to Chinese economic performance, and new factors, including Chinese economic policymaking, began to affect bilateral economic ties. The third factor was the awareness of the limits of reconciliation diplomacy for guiding Japan's relations with China. High-level state visits and Japan's effort to state its remorse for its war effort in China had only limited success in ending China's criticism of Japan's past military behavior. Finally, the Taiwan Straits crisis in 1996 alerted many Japanese policymakers to China's potential use of military force in Northeast Asia, raising yet another concern for Tokyo's military planners.

Bridging Diplomatic Divides

Until normalization in the 1970s, the Cold War divided Japan and China; afterward, Japan increasingly saw its role as a bridge between its Western partners and its modernizing Asian neighbor. Japan's postwar relationship with China came on the heels of President Richard

Nixon's historic trip to Beijing in 1972. In a defining moment in Asia's Cold War experience, Chinese leaders turned away from their Soviet allies and toward a new relationship with the United States and Japan. That geostrategic opportunity was the beginning of a process of post-war reconciliation that many in Japan felt was long overdue.

Beijing's strategic calculus was different. Chinese leaders were interested primarily in limiting Soviet influence in Asia and therefore insisted that Tokyo agree to block any attempt at hegemonic dominance in Asia. Although negotiations on the treaty began in 1974, it was not until 1975 that Japanese negotiators realized that this clause would hinder ratification of the bilateral peace treaty; instead, Japan's leaders worried that Taiwan would be an obstacle.[29] Beijing was willing to leave Taiwan out of the talks, however. In January 1975, the Japanese government produced a tentative draft of a treaty, and in response, Zhou Enlai later conveyed to a leading LDP Diet member the idea that "opposing superpower hegemony" was China's national policy and that he expected Sino-Japanese normalization to offset Soviet "hegemonic" ambitions.[30]

This idea raised all sorts of red flags in the Japanese government. The pro-Taibei groups in the ruling LDP argued that it would harm relations with Moscow, and the Ministry of Foreign Affairs, too, saw the potential damage to Japan's relations with the Soviet Union, by getting in the way of a resolution of its territorial dispute with Moscow. Progressives in Japan were torn between their support for Moscow and Beijing; the Japan Socialist Party favored Beijing, whereas the Japan Communist Party continued to look to Moscow. In the end, factional pressures within the LDP—coupled with intense "people's diplomacy" by the Beijing government[31]—forced Prime Minister Miki Takeo's hand, and the Japanese government agreed to include in the treaty language opposing hegemony. For many, this was a step back from the diplomatic aim of "equidistance" that Japan had crafted to cope with the complex major power relations of that period. Yet, the failure to conclude a peace treaty also began to have serious political costs for Prime Minister Miki, as Japanese businesses and the public wanted the long overdue diplomatic relationship with China to begin.

Japan's opening to China also came on the heels of a significant development in U.S.-Japan relations. Okinawa, Japan's southernmost prefecture, remained under the administration of the United States, and the extended occupation included its free use of the extensive military bases built there during the Korean War.[32] The United States used these bases for its combat sorties in Vietnam, prompting widespread demonstrations on the island that eventually fed into the national antiwar movement. By 1968, the U.S. and Japanese governments had agreed to begin discussing the reversion of Okinawa to Japanese control, and in 1969, the Nixon-Satō communiqué formally began the negotiations for Okinawa's reversion to Japan.[33] Included in the Ryukyu Islands were the small, uninhabited islets, known as the Senkakus to the Japanese, which became the focal point of considerable difficulty in the Japan-China negotiations over a peace treaty.

The negotiations over the reversion of Okinawa led to Taiwanese and then Chinese protests to the U.S. government. At the time, the United States maintained formal diplomatic relations with the ROC, but the Nixon White House—as later become known—was at this time laying the groundwork for its historic "opening" to the PRC in Beijing. In 1970, the ambassador of the ROC presented the U.S. government with his objections to Japanese sovereignty over the Senkakus. Three months later, China's Xinhua news agency issued a statement, interpreted as the official PRC position, that the islands belonged to Taiwan and thus to the PRC.[34] On March 15, 1971, the embassy of the Republic of China in Washington sent the U.S. State Department a *note verbale* outlining its claim to sovereignty over the Senkakus.

The ROC's argument was based on several points: the historical record of a boundary between the disputed islands and the Kingdom of the Ryukyus (later incorporated into the Japanese Empire as Okinawa); the geological features separating the islands from the Ryukyus by the Okinawa Trough at the end of the continental shelf; and the use of these islands by Taiwanese fishermen as traditional fishing grounds. Claiming that the Japanese government did not include the islands as Japanese territory until after China was defeated in the First Sino-Japanese War in 1895 and forced to cede Taiwan and the Pescadores to Japan, the Chinese government asked the United States at the end of its administration of the Ryukyu Islands to return them to the Republic of China. This Chinese scrutiny of the U.S. negotiations to return the Ryukyus to Japanese sovereignty coincided with the now famous secret diplomacy between the Nixon White House and China's top leaders that led to Washington's normalization talks with Beijing.

By mid-April, President Nixon's national security adviser, Henry Kissinger, had requested information on Taiwan's claim, which was provided to him by John H. Holdridge of the National Security Council (NSC) staff. Based on his notes at the time, it seems that Kissinger wanted to explore ways to achieve greater U.S. "neutrality" in the dispute.[35] Until this time, every U.S. administration had referred to Japan's residual sovereignty over the Ryukyu Islands, but a new language in U.S. policy statements suggested a more ambiguous stance on the ultimate sovereignty of the islands. Details of Kissinger's first secret trip to Beijing in July and his later conversations with the Chinese Communist Party leaders regarding these islands remain classified. But the relationship with Taiwan was clearly on the minds of all the president's advisers. Ten days before the Okinawa Reversion Agreement was to be signed in Washington, D.C., between President Richard Nixon and Prime Minister Satō Eisaku, the subject of the island dispute was raised again, this time by the president's economic adviser, who saw the benefit of retaining U.S. control over the islands in order to quell Taiwan's opposition. At the time, the United States was looking for a deal with Taibei on textiles. In the end, President Nixon did not change the agreement to return the Ryukyus—including the disputed islands—to Japan. But the United States did step back from fully endorsing Japanese sovereignty, a position that it had taken since the San Francisco Peace Treaty, and instead adopted a legal position that it was neutral on the ultimate resolution of the competing sovereignty claims over the islands.[36] Japan, too, embraced normalization of diplomatic relations with Beijing, and for decades, the territorial issue settled into the background.

A second moment when Japan and the United States differed over China policy came after the Tiananmen Square confrontation in 1989. Far different from the realpolitik of the Nixon administration, this raised questions about Tokyo's and Washington's interpretations of human rights. The gathering of students and citizens after the death of Hu Yaobang threatened the Chinese leadership and the Communist Party's control. In turn, the deployment of the Chinese military and police to suppress the demonstrations transformed China's image from a modernizing state to an authoritarian regime and began an era of Western human rights activism on behalf of China's dissidents. The United States and other Western nations imposed sanctions on China after its violent repression of the democracy protesters. A month later at the G7 Arch Summit, world leaders roundly "condemned the violent repression in China in defiance of human rights" and called on "Chinese authorities to cease action against those who have done no more than claim their legitimate rights to democracy and liberty."[37]

Unlike many Western states, Japan took time in formulating its response to the events of June 4, 1989. Until that moment, its postwar diplomacy had relied almost exclusively on its own economic development and the support for the economic development goals of others in Asia.[38] The Cold War had been largely in the hands of the two superpowers, with only a supporting role for the allies. Moreover, Japan's leadership in the region emerged as its economy took off. The Japanese economic miracle was emulated across the region, including in China. Economic growth became associated with political liberalization, and democratization movements spread across the Asia Pacific, ousting leaders in the Philippines and South Korea and shaking the governments in other societies in Southeast Asia. Amid these political changes in Asia, the Japanese government sought to focus its foreign policy and economic assistance on the economic development goals of the Association of Southeast Asian Nations (ASEAN).

But the limits of Tokyo's economic leadership were brought home when the Chinese government called out the military to confront student democracy advocates in Tiananmen Square. Equally important, Japan's close support for China's economic modernization also came under scrutiny by the Western states. Media footage of the shocking convergence of student demonstrators and Chinese military tanks in the center of Beijing was broadcast live to a global audience, prompting outrage in Western nations. The United States and European nations called for immediate sanctions against the Chinese leadership in protest of the human rights violations; but Tokyo cautioned the Western nations against an excessively punitive reaction to the use of force, worrying about its repercussions on China's modernization effort. At the time, Japan was China's most generous donor, providing roughly 40 percent of all foreign assistance to China. On a bilateral basis, Japan provided 75 percent of all aid to China, ten times more than the second-highest donor (West Germany). Even so, the International Monetary Fund, the World Bank, and major Western nations imposed severe economic and military sanctions on China.

The Japanese government's immediate response was confused. The prime minister, Uno Sōsuke, announced in the parliament that the students' deaths were "unacceptable on humanitarian grounds" and that Japan would consider whether to cancel or continue its yen loans. In the Ministry of Foreign Affairs, opinion was divided, with some believing that Japan should continue to provide yen loans so that China would not become isolated and others maintaining that Tokyo should follow the lead of the international community.[39] By the end of June, the Ministry of Foreign Affairs had made three different statements about Japan's intentions.[40]

Dissension between the bureaucrats and the ruling party continued into the fall. In the ruling LDP, opinion was strongly opposed to sanctions. The head of the Japan-China parliamentarians' league and a leading LDP politician, Itō Masayoshi, visited Beijing in September and met with senior Chinese leaders, including Deng Xiaoping. Itō argued that Japan's relationship with China was not the same as the U.S. relationship with China and that Japan would not implement the sanctions. He also recommended the dispersal of the third yen loan to Beijing,[41] ¥810 billion over the five years from 1990 to 1995. But the Ministry of Finance and others were in consultation with other nations, and the yen loan was delayed. Japan's efforts to find a compromise between the Western nations and China were already under way, however. In early November, the Japanese finance minister announced that China must make an international apology for the events at Tiananmen Square before Japan could consider resuming the yen loan.

Domestic interests also strongly favored resuming the loans to China. The chairman of Keidanren (Japan Business Federation), Saito Eishiro, argued for continued economic support for China despite human rights concerns over Tiananmen,[42] and by the end of the year, the minister of foreign affairs, Nakayama Tarō, recommended placing priority on helping China succeed with economic reform.[43] For some, the idea that Japan should line up with the Western countries on sanctioning Beijing was not simply a matter of principle but fundamentally impinged on Japan's interests in China. Gotoda Masaharu, a senior LDP leader and vice-chairman of the Japan-China Society, argued for resuming the loans in April after the Chinese government had lifted martial law. This debate continued in Tokyo through the summer as plans for the next G7 Summit meeting in Houston, Texas, were being made.

In the end, the special relationship with Beijing weighed heavily on Japanese decision making. Japan's effort to resolve differences between China and the West came to an end at the G7 meeting in the summer of 1990. Japanese diplomats argued for continuing support for China's economic development in order to modernize the Chinese nation. Yet the prime minister also reminded the United States and other nations that Japan's former prime minister, Takeshita Noboru, had made a political commitment to China and that Japan had a responsibility to keep its promise. While the United States and others continued their economic and military sanctions on China, Japan resumed its yen loan on November 2, 1990.[44] Japan's own interests in the relationship with China prevailed, but so, too, did the idea that in Asia, economic development ought to take precedence over political principles. At the beginning of the 1990s, Japan's leaders were still uncomfortable asserting democratic values or advocating on behalf of human rights. China's behavior would test this proposition in the decades to come.

Cultivating Economic Interdependence

Beyond these broad geostrategic shifts, the postwar settlement for Japan and China largely centered on the economic and cultural benefits of the new relationship. Economic interdependence—and at that time the complementarities of the two economies—was seen as the salve that would heal the wounds of Japan's wartime invasion and subsequent defeat in 1945. Postwar reconciliation was pursued through building strong economic and cultural ties between the

Chinese and Japanese people. Japan's economic ties with China were not a product of diplomatic normalization. Indeed, most of the groundwork had been laid in the years when there were no official state ties. A broad array of Japanese sought to develop strong economic ties with the Communist Party leadership and state-owned enterprises. Since the establishment of the People's Republic of China in 1949, private business leaders had worked independently and in tandem with Japan's political leaders to commence trade with the newly unified Communist government in Beijing.[45]

This economic relationship was in large part a function of postwar Japanese domestic politics. Four organizations were formed specifically to enhance trade with China in 1949, and they reveal the complexity of Japanese sentiment and interest in the newly emerging Communist China. Progressive-left groups, small businesses, and intellectuals sympathetic to the Chinese revolution formed the Japan-China Trade Promotion Association (JCTPA) in May 1949, whose stated purpose was to help Chinese industrialization and to support the Chinese people. Once the Korean War began and Chinese troops crossed the Yalu River, this group's activities were curtailed, and afterward, the JCTPA focused exclusively on trade with China. Another trade association, the Japan Association for the Promotion of International Trade (JAPIT), emerged to facilitate trade between the two Cold War blocs and later included prominent Japanese business leaders. The Japan-China Importers and Exporters Association (JCIEA) was formed in 1955 with Japanese government support, with the purpose of ameliorating the differences between Japan's competitive market and Chinese state-owned monopolies. The JCIEA was largely the brainchild of the Japanese Ministry of Economy, Trade, and Industry (METI) and was designed to harmonize and coordinate Japan's trading relations. Finally, the JCTPA Diet Members League was developed to oversee the negotiations and signature of trade agreements with China. When it was founded in 1949, the league had around ninety members. A decade later, its membership had grown to 360, or roughly 50 percent of Japan's legislators. By the time of normalization, therefore, there was a broad array of knowledge, personal ties, and political support for expanding economic relations with the People's Republic of China.

Once official diplomatic ties were restored, the Japanese government could step into this established network of economic ties to consider how to support China's long-term economic planning. On a visit to China in 1975, Japanese Prime Minister Ōhira Masayoshi outlined Japan's position on providing assistance to China, noting his "heartfelt wish that [Japan's economic assistance] would provide the foundation for building the China of the 21st century." Ōhira cited three principles for Japan's assistance to China: first, Japan would not provide aid to be used for military purposes, so China would not be an exception to that principle; second, Japan's economic assistance to China would not harm the development of any other country in the region, particularly the ASEAN countries, with which Japan maintained a strong bond; and third, the Japan-China relationship would not exclude others.[46] Overseas development assistance (ODA) began in earnest in 1979, and four five-year plans dovetailed with China's economic planning efforts. The Japanese government provided ¥331 billion in loans from 1979 to 1984, ¥540 billion from 1984 to 1989, ¥810 billion from 1990 to 1995, and ¥970 billion from 1996 to 2000.[47] In total, from 1979 to 2011, Japan provided ¥3.65 trillion (US$37.6 billion) in ODA to China, more than 90 percent of which came in the form of yen loans.[48]

For decades, such assistance was indispensable to China's transition to a market economy, and it was designed to complement Beijing's five-year development plans. By the 1990s, ODA to China comprised roughly 10 to 15 percent of Japan's total ODA budget, signaling the priority Japan placed on Chinese economic development. China consistently ranked in the top two destinations of Japanese ODA, while Japan was the number-one ODA contributor to China until 2007 and provided 50 to 60 percent of China's total incoming assistance for more than two decades.[49] China's economic development, however, gradually eliminated the need for Japanese government economic assistance (figure 2.2). Accordingly, on March 17, 2005, Foreign Minister Machimura Nobutaka announced that the yen loans would end by the time of the Beijing Olympics in 2008.[50] In April 2007, Prime Minister Wen Jiabao and Prime Minister Abe Shinzō issued a joint statement noting the "positive role" these loans had played in China's economic development, and Wen expressed China's gratitude.[51] The last yen loans to China were

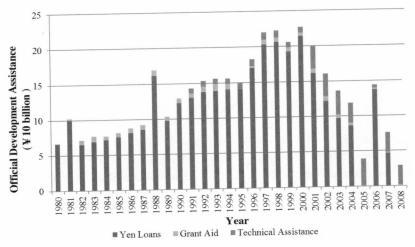

FIGURE 2.2 Japan's official development assistance to China. Data is for Japanese fiscal years (April 1 to March 31). (Ministry of Foreign Affairs, Japan, *Kunibetsu enjyo jisseki* [ODA Results by Country], http://www.mofa.go.jp/mofaj/gaiko/oda/shiryo/jisseki/kuni/index.html. Data from *Diplomatic Blue Book* [1980–1993]; *Japan's ODA Annual Report* [1994–1999]; and *Japan's ODA White Paper* [2001–2012])

disbursed in December 2007, and when President Hu Jintao visited Tokyo in May 2008, he told Prime Minister Fukuda Yasuo that "the Japanese government and people, through ODA, have supported the modernization of China, and for this I give my heartfelt thanks."[52]

As ODA wound down, trade between Japan and China began to take off (figure 2.3). Accordingly, the Japanese government turned its attention from China's economic development toward the resolution of trade disputes. Along with other nations, Tokyo granted Beijing most-favored-nation (MFN) status in 1974 as part of the normalization process. The rapid growth of Chinese imports into the Japanese market in the 1990s, however, created a stream of trade disputes. By the mid-1990s, the Japanese government was increasingly under pressure from domestic producers to prevent Chinese competition in the domestic market. Chinese textiles occupied more than 50 percent of the Japanese market, and Japanese producers demanded import protections. Likewise, agricultural imports from China were rising significantly, prompting Japanese farmers to demand safeguards as well.

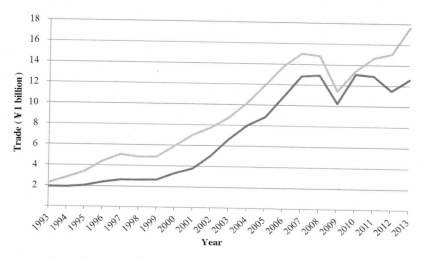

FIGURE 2.3 Japan's trade with China, 1993–2013. (Ministry of Finance, Japan, "Trade Statistics of Japan," http://www.customs.go.jp/toukei/info/index_e.htm)

Garlic, ginger, green onions, shiitake mushrooms, and tatami straw were just some of the products imported from China that threatened Japanese producers.

China's acceptance into the World Trade Organization (WTO) in September 2001 changed the management of trade disputes from bilateral negotiation to third-party adjudication. China had consistently imposed high tariffs on imports from Japan. In 2001, it imposed punitive tariffs on Japanese autos and cell phone exports, and Nakagawa Shōichi, head of a LDP special task force on agriculture and trade, announced that Japan would seek WTO adjudication.[53] The two governments settled the issue through bilateral negotiation, and China lowered the tariffs.[54] Nonetheless, Japanese exports continued to be subjected to Chinese tariff protection. In 2004, Chinese tariffs on foreign semiconductors prompted a serious trade dispute with the United States. Japan again began to consider WTO adjudication, but the United States and China settled their dispute in July 2004, leading the way for a similar resolution for Japan.[55] Eventually, however, Japan relied on the WTO dispute resolution mechanism to cope with its disputes with China, and it did so along with the United States and the European Union. In 2006, these three parties initiated a complaint and asked for WTO adjudication over China's violation of intellectual property rights.[56] In 2010, China's export restrictions of rare earths led Japan to consider similar steps under the WTO, and when export restrictions resulted in a global price increase the following year, Japan initiated consultations with the United States and the European Union, and the three parties filed a WTO complaint in March 2012.[57]

As the Chinese economy grew, Japan's private investors took on a much larger role in the countries' bilateral economic cooperation. For the private sector, the pace of investment in China depended in large part on the development of China's industry. Japan's businesses were chastened by China's inability to follow through on early projects. The first trade agreement negotiated in 1978 by Inayama Yoshihiro, chairman of Nippon Steel and head of the Japan-China Business Association, and supported by the Japanese government, was ambitious—with a goal of Japanese and Chinese exports of $10 billion in the first decade, which was then amended to double or triple that scale. Japanese companies were contracted to build plants and complete other development projects as Japan began to provide yen loans to support Beijing's development. A transition in China's leadership, however, led to a revision of former premier Hua Guofeng's Ten-Year Plan (1976–1985), and Beijing abruptly reduced or canceled Japanese contracts. One of the most symbolic was the cancellation of the Baoshan steel complex, a huge initiative worth ¥398 billion in 1981.[58]

Over the years, Japanese companies continued to be wary of China's economic decision making, but by the early 1990s, Japanese foreign direct investment (FDI) in the Chinese economy had taken off (figure 2.4). Along with Taiwanese and Hong Kong–based investors, Japanese investors were the biggest supporters of Chinese economic transformation and played a critical role in shaping Chinese market reforms.[59] Japanese automakers and other manufacturers led the way in investing in China and, by the end of the 1990s, were concentrating on producing for the burgeoning Chinese consumer market. Over time, FDI from Japan fluctuated, which is attributed to various factors. Yen appreciation as well as other market forces affected FDI trends, as well as Beijing's own economic decisions.[60] Increasingly,

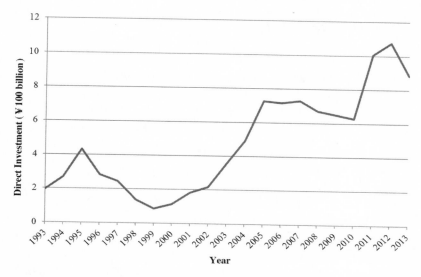

FIGURE 2.4 Japan's foreign direct investment in China, 1992–2013. (Ministry of Finance, Japan, "Foreign Direct Investment," https://www.mof.go.jp/english/international_policy/reference/itn_transactions_in_securities/fdi/index.htm [1992–2004]; "Outward/Inward Direct Investment," https://www.mof.go.jp/english/international _policy/reference/balance_of_payments/ebpfdi.htm [2005–2013])

however, it was the incentives of the China market that became the dominant driver of Japanese corporate investment decisions.[61]

The Limits of Reconciliation Diplomacy

The emphasis on economic cooperation did not diminish the need for political attention to Chinese memories of Japan's invasion of China. There was no Chinese demand for compensation by Japan for war damages during treaty negotiations because Mao Zedong and others had decided against them, but the decision continued to be controversial. Japan refused as well to characterize its postnormalization economic aid to China as compensation for its invasion and pointed to both the San Francisco Peace Treaty and Japan's normalization of relations with the Republic of China as providing the legal basis for the postwar settlement. Yet the impression that postwar Japanese support for Chinese modernization took the place of war damages lingered. Chinese leaders reinforced this notion when tensions arose over the terms of Japan's yen loans to China. While the Chinese leaders who had negotiated the terms of postwar peace with Japan found it expedient to forgo reparations, their successors did not feel constrained in reminding Japan of the price China had paid for Japan's military expansion. Moreover, Chinese citizens, in collaboration with Japanese legal teams and citizen activists, began to use the courts to sue the Japanese government for redress.[62]

In the 1980s, open Chinese criticism of Japanese interpretation of twentieth-century history, especially of the Japanese military's conduct during the war, began to color the relationship. In 1982, the *Asahi shinbun* published an exposé of the Ministry of Education's efforts to rewrite Japanese textbooks. The series prompted a political clash between Japan's conservatives, who wanted the textbooks to have a stronger "patriotic" message, and liberal educators and authors, who sought to portray the suffering caused by Japan's aggression.[63] Prime Minister Nakasone Yasuhiro's visit to the Yasukuni Shrine in 1985 drew especially strongly criticism from China. As a result, Nakasone decided to forgo an appearance at the controversial shrine the following year. From this point onward, Japanese statements of remorse or regret for the suffering of the Chinese people became an integral part of bilateral diplomacy.

High-level state visits provided an occasion for Japanese statements of remorse and a new diplomatic focus on historical reconciliation. Chinese concerns over Japan's "militarism" were put on the back burner, however, when Chinese tanks confronted demonstrators in Tiananmen Square on June 4, 1989. Although Japan halted negotiations on its next five-year yen loan (for fiscal years 1990 to 1995), it played an instrumental role in mitigating calls for sanctions of China by the United States and Europe over Chinese repression.[64] The idea of a high-level state visit to China had been introduced in April that year, when Chinese premier Li Peng raised the possibility of a visit to China by the Japanese emperor.[65] A year later, Japan had yet to resume talks over economic assistance, and General Secretary Jiang Zemin urged that negotiations over the yen loans begin again, stating the importance to China of good relations with Japan.[66] By the summer, Jiang said that he would welcome the emperor if he wished to visit

China, although he noted that the Chinese people could not forget the history of Japanese aggression.[67] The Japanese government's decision to resume yen loans to China was announced at the Houston G8 summit in July 1990.[68] The next year, senior Chinese officials repeatedly asked that the Japanese emperor visit China in 1992 for the twentieth anniversary of Sino-Japanese diplomatic normalization.

Initially, Japanese feelings about the emperor's visit were mixed. The question of how he would be received in China, of course, remained sensitive. In February 1992, China's ambassador to Japan sought to reassure the Japanese by holding a press conference at the National Press Club in Tokyo. Ambassador Yang Zhenya noted that the anticipated visit to China by Japan's emperor would be "a historic achievement" that would take the bilateral relationship to a "new level." The ambassador went on to say, "China is a civilized country, and would never do anything to trouble a foreign leader," yet he thought it "would seem natural for both Japanese and Chinese that the Emperor express his attitude on the unfortunate history of a particular moment in the two countries' relations."[69] In March, Premier Li introduced the possibility to his own people in a public speech when he pointed out the importance of visits by the "highest state leaders" of Japan and China.[70] By the summer of 1992, popular Japanese reservations seemed to have been overcome. A public poll by the *Nikkei shinbun* revealed that around 70 percent of Japanese supported the emperor's visit to China, and only 17.7 percent opposed it.[71] On August 25, the Japanese cabinet approved the visit.

The Japanese emperor and empress traveled to China in late October 1992. After a welcoming ceremony at the Great Hall of the People, China's President Yang Shangkun met with the imperial couple and then hosted a state dinner. There, the emperor spoke first about the long history of relations between Japan and China, dating back to the exchange of emissaries from the eighth to the ninth centuries, including the young Japanese sent to China to study who later returned to share their knowledge of Chinese culture with Japan. He pointed to the long history of Japan's great respect for Chinese culture and experience and praised the contemporary youth exchange programs that brought young Chinese to Japan for study as well. But the emperor then turned to the topic of Japan's war with China. Referring to the "unfortunate era when our country [Japan] caused immense pain and suffering to the Chinese people," the emperor spoke of the "deep sadness" this period caused him; he went on to say that the Japanese people had rebuilt their nation determined never again to wage war and to live in peace with other nations.[72] The emperor toured China, visiting the Great Wall, the Chinese Academy of Sciences, the National Palace Museum, and to Shaanxi, Shanghai, and Xihu. Overall, the visit was a success, and public reaction in both countries seemed positive.[73]

It took another six years, however, for the Chinese to reciprocate the emperor's state visit. Finally, in November 1998, Chinese president Jiang Zemin visited Japan, the first Chinese president to ever do so. Unlike the emperor's visit to China, however, this visit did not encourage greater Japanese support for the relationship with China. Instead, it provoked a sharp decline in popular attitudes toward China and accelerated the diminishing public support for the Chinese government in particular. Like the Japanese emperor's visit, the five-day visit included political meetings, visits to factories and farms to reflect the evolving Japan-China economic interests, and, of course, meetings with Chinese residents and Japanese students.

But the visit began badly. At the state dinner hosted by the emperor and empress of Japan, President Jiang delivered a scolding for Japan's wrongdoing in the war. His speech was televised to the nation, and for many Japanese, both the tone and the fact that it was delivered publicly to the emperor were extremely offensive.[74] Although Jiang remained in Japan for another three days, the Japanese public saw very little of him on television.[75] At the end of his stay, the diplomats issued a joint statement outlining an agenda for Japan-China cooperation, but the legacy of Jiang's trip cast a pall over the bilateral relationship for some time afterward. The shock of his speech at the state dinner may have been amplified by the contrast with the conciliatory tone of a speech given just a month earlier by the South Korean president, Kim Dae-Jung.[76] President Kim had taken a very different tack, seeking to embed the painful Japanese colonization of his country in the twentieth century in a broader sweep of centuries of shared history. Looking back, the 1998 state visit by President Jiang marked the beginning of a decade of repeated tensions between Japan and China and a diplomatic "deep freeze" in the Japan-China relationship.

The Taiwan Straits Crisis

New concerns in Japan about China's growing role in regional security arose after the Cold War ended. The 1990s brought a series of crises in Northeast Asia involving the United States and its allies. The first was the nuclear crisis of 1993/1994 with North Korea, which ushered in decades of regional debate over how to respond to Pyongyang's proliferation of nuclear and missile capabilities. China's role in sponsoring North Korea's nuclear ambitions was suspect, but the crisis that most focused Japan's attention on China's impact on regional security was the 1996 Taiwan Straits crisis. Calls for declaring independence accompanied the election campaign for president in March 1996. The new Democratic People's Party (DPP), led by Chen Shui-bian, criticized the Guomindang for its continued hesitation to pursue sovereignty for Taiwan.[77] Beijing became increasingly concerned about the impact the electoral campaign would have on the "one China" policy, and its opposition to a declaration of independence grew. In July 1995, China even moved missiles for use against Taiwan, threatening force should it declare independence. The Clinton administration reacted by sending a carrier task force to the straits to demonstrate U.S. support for the defense of Taiwan. The standoff between Beijing and Taibei was ultimately defused, but China's willingness to use force over Taiwan reminded Tokyo that the Korean Peninsula was not the only flashpoint in Northeast Asia.

Moreover, this incident also demonstrated the region's changing military balance. Although Japan's security was not directly threatened by either crisis, these regional tensions did raise new questions about Japan's military preparedness and its ability to cooperate with its ally, the United States, in managing the region's security. China was enhancing its military capability, and several aspects of China's military growth concerned Japanese security planners. First, the modernization of China's nuclear force challenged the extended deterrence of U.S. strategic forces as the greater number of nuclear warheads available to Beijing raised the stakes in the region. In fact, the Japanese concern about China's nuclear modernization was sufficient to warrant a halt to ODA when China insisted on testing its nuclear weapons. Two nuclear tests conducted in 1995, one in May and the other in August, drew a Japanese response. In August 1995, Japan cut off most of its grant aid to China, with payments shrinking from ¥7.79 billion in fiscal year 1994 to ¥480 million in fiscal year 1995.[78]

Second, Beijing's reaction to Taiwan's independence movement alarmed Tokyo about Chinese intentions in the region. In the early years of the Cold War, of course, Beijing had confronted the Guomindang regime in Taibei, and both times Washington had responded. These early Taiwan Straits crises preceded normalization, however, and thus the 1996 crisis tested not only the U.S. commitment to Taiwan's defense but also the premise of the "one China" policy that had accompanied diplomatic relations with the PRC. China's growing military capabilities, including the modernization of its nuclear arsenal, raised the stakes for both Washington and Beijing's neighbors. The costs for extending deterrence to Taiwan were mounting, and the benefits to the United States of its relationship with Beijing could be leveraged far differently than in the 1950s. For Japanese strategic planners, the 1996 Taiwan Straits crisis was not only the first indication that Beijing would use force if political change on Taiwan proved inimical to PRC interests; it was also the first open test of how U.S. defense commitments in Northeast Asia would fare against China's burgeoning military power. The 1996 Ministry of Defense White Paper noted what became the chief analytical concern in Tokyo, the shift from "quantitative" enhancements of China's military capability to "qualitative" improvements in its ability to use that military.[79]

Finally, by the end of the decade, Beijing's enhanced maritime power in and around the East China Sea made it clear to Tokyo that its southwestern region was inadequately defended. For most of the Cold War, Japanese military forces had been concentrated in the north; and in the 1980s as the effort to pressure the Soviet Union's Pacific Fleet intensified, Japan's defense of its northern waters around Hokkaido, as well as its Maritime Self-Defense Force deployments in the Western Pacific, played an important role in bottling up the Soviets' strategic naval forces. Throughout the Cold War, it was the U.S. military forces in Okinawa that played the dominant role in defending

Japan's southern islands. When Chinese air and maritime forces started concentrating on the East China Sea, however, Tokyo began to recognize the inadequacy of its own forces in the southwest.

The North Korean and Taiwan crises brought new questions about Japan's military preparedness, and Washington grew more and more concerned about the lack of serious contingency planning in the U.S.-Japan alliance. Because of the constraints of the Japanese constitution, the U.S. and Japanese militaries had no integrated war plans. Unlike NATO and the U.S.-South Korean alliance, there was no provision for a joint command. In fact, beyond a series of exercises between U.S. Forces Japan and the Japanese Self-Defense Forces, there had been little concrete exploration of how the two militaries might operate together in case of a conflict or crisis. A bilateral study group on updating alliance prepared-ness began shortly after the Taiwan Straits crisis in an effort to redress these challenges. A similar policy discussion initiated by the Japanese government in 1978 had produced the first Guidelines for U.S.-Japan Defense Cooperation, which described the roles and missions for the two militaries in defending Japan.[80] As security tensions increased in North-east Asia in the 1990s, the Japanese and U.S. governments recognized the need for an overhaul of these military guidelines for the alliance.

Japan's long-standing limitations on its military were revisited largely in response to the worrisome situation on the Korean Penin-sula. Yet Japanese planners recognized that China could pose an even greater strategic challenge to Japan's defensive force posture. From a broader perspective, drawing the United States more closely into plan-ning for Northeast Asian contingencies made more sense than deal-ing solely with Pyongyang. Thereafter, the focus of the Japanese effort to reconsider the parameters of allied cooperation was on "areas sur-rounding Japan" (shūhen jitai). The Taiwan Straits crisis thus provided both the impetus for Japan to accelerate deliberations with Washington on the guidelines as well as the political stimulus needed to pass leg-islation supporting the alliance's new agenda for military cooperation. In 1997, Tokyo and Washington concluded their talks and announced the revised U.S.-Japan Guidelines for Defense Cooperation.[81]

Tokyo remained sensitive to Beijing's perceptions of the U.S.-Japan alliance, however. Media reports at the time suggested con-siderable differences in the interpretation of Japan's reasons for revising the U.S.-Japan Defense Cooperation Guidelines. The LDP's secretary-general, Katō Kōichi, visited Beijing in July 1997 and met with Chinese leaders, including future president Hu Jintao as well as the defense minister and the vice-minister of foreign affairs. In his meetings, Katō reportedly emphasized that the guidelines were not revised with China in mind; rather, they were aimed primarily at the Korean Peninsula.[82] But a month later the chief cabinet secretary, Kajiyama Seiroku, openly refuted this notion during an interview with *TV Asahi*. Although Katō's comments had prompted quite a stir and some public criticism, Kajiyama clearly stated that the government's interpretation of "areas surrounding Japan" was not limited to any one geographical contingency and that "of course, a conflict between China and Taiwan would be a scenario considered within the guidelines." In fact, he argued that limiting the guidelines to the Korean Peninsula effectively limited the U.S.-Japan alliance and that while the Japanese government had no intention of intervening in domestic affairs, it had serious concerns about China's use of force against Taiwan.[83]

As the domestic debate over the U.S.-Japan Defense Cooperation Guidelines continued, North Korea tested a new, intermediate-range ballistic missile, which passed over Japan. The launch of the Taepodong in September 1998 startled the Japanese public and prompted a renewed debate over Japan's defenses. While politicians pressed for greater independent intelligence-gathering capability, Japanese security planners called for U.S.-Japan cooperation on a ballistic missile defense system. Missile defense had been a topic of discussion between Tokyo and Washington ever since the Reagan administration's emphasis on the development of a "Star Wars" space-based defense system, but the North Korean launch brought home in a very conspicuous way Japan's vulnerability to a such an attack. Even those who had opposed the high-tech weapons system proposed by the U.S. government in the 1980s understood that Japan was now facing neighbors with a growing ballistic missile capability. Of course, Beijing's nuclear arsenal remained a concern, but the openly hostile North Korean government persuaded many Japanese that the time had come to take steps to defend Japan also against long-range missiles.

In 1999, China emerged front and center as parliamentary debate over the legislation to implement the revised U.S.-Japan Guidelines continued. A special committee on the U.S.-Japan Defense Guidelines heard testimony from a variety of experts, with a range of views on whether a Taiwan contingency should be included as part of bilateral military planning. Those who argued for its inclusion emphasized the impact of a Taiwan contingency on Japanese security, and those who argued against it concentrated instead on Taiwan's special relationship with China. Japan's foreign minister, Kōmura Masahiko, and its defense minister, Norota Hosei, continued to insist that "areas surrounding Japan" was not a geographical but a situational concept. In effect, the government of Japan refused to accept any limitation on the alliance's military cooperation. Three laws were amended in accordance with the revision of the U.S.-Japan Guidelines. The most important, the Law on Contingencies Surrounding Japan (Shūhen jitai anzen kakuho ho), allowed Japan's Self-Defense Forces to act with the United States, including rear-area support and search-and-rescue operations, before parliamentary approval, if needed.[84]

Japan's role in Asia Pacific regionalism also underwent a transformation in the 1990s. Its economic leadership in the region was unmistakable, as both the engine of growth for other Asian economies and the lead voice in the regional economic consultations for the Asia-Pacific Economic Cooperation/Commission (APEC). In 1992, the Japanese government strongly supported ASEAN's effort to create a regional security mechanism that would bring together the countries of the region to consider security issues. Regional multilateralism centered on ASEAN, which was initially sponsored and encouraged by Tokyo, a decade later became a new venue for the assertion of Chinese influence.

THE CHANGING BALANCE OF ADVOCACY ON CHINA

As Japan's government agencies began to contend with the various policy adjustments needed to cope with China's economic and military growth, the domestic debate over Japan's foreign policy goals showed signs of change as well.

For much of the postwar period, Japan's China policy seemed to be predominantly in the hands of politicians and business elite. But Japan's political parties took center stage in the debate over normalization. Japan's conservatives in the Liberal Democratic Party were divided over the terms of the peace treaty, with the pro-Taiwan conservatives tempering those in the party who advocated normalization with Beijing. In the years after the peace treaty, the party also divided over the terms of Japanese reconciliation diplomacy. Among opposition parties, the Japanese Socialist Party was the staunchest advocate of close ties between Beijing and Tokyo, and the Buddhist-based Kōmeitō (Clean Government Party), which emerged in the 1970s, also was strongly pro-Beijing. Both these parties were adamantly supportive of Japan's pacifist constitution and reconciliation with China. The second influence on Japan's relations with China was Japan's business elite. Despite some setbacks in its economic ties with China, Japan's corporate leaders welcomed the economic benefits to Japan that accrued from friendly relations and therefore consistently argued for close diplomatic ties.

Over time, domestic interests changed, and policy seemed motivated less by ideological positions or commercial interests. As China increasingly complicated Japanese interests. The standoff between the progressive left's sympathy for Beijing and the conservative right's skepticism of its Communist government gradually gave way to a broader consensus on the importance of China to Japanese policy management. Liberals and conservatives alike recognized the importance of China to Japan's future, although the former were more inclined toward a cooperative approach embedded in regionalism and the latter sought to explore ways to balance Chinese influence with greater U.S.-Japan alliance cooperation.

During the 1990s, outside political circles, the constellations of interests that coalesced around China policy also began to change, as did popular attitudes toward China, creating opportunity for new advocacies and more complex views of China. Virulent nationalists, a minority but a threatening voice in Japan's debate, began criticizing the country's reconciliation diplomacy. Perhaps the most conspicuous consequence was the hesitation of Japan's business community to push for a more cooperative relationship with China. Even though their business interests did not necessarily change as China's economy grew, domestic skepticism of Chinese intentions made advocacy more politically sensitive and, for some outspoken business leaders, drew the unwanted attention of Japan's rightists.

Politicians, Reform, and China Policy

Political reform in Tokyo has greatly affected Japan's diplomacy, including its relationship with China. The conservative Liberal Democratic Party (LDP) lost its ability to command a majority in the House of Representatives in 1993 when Ozawa Ichirō left the party. Japan's postwar single-party dominance, established when the LDP took power in 1955, was over, and coalition governments returned to govern Japan. As Japan's policymakers became concerned about the strategic challenge of China, Japan's politicians were demanding a greater voice in policymaking. Throughout the 1990s, the fluidity of Japanese politics made it difficult to focus on China's rise, as attention remained riveted on the personalities and ambitions of Japan's political elite.

Nonetheless, Japan's political change began to create the foundation for a less ideologically informed debate over China policy. China policy had been a long-standing bone of contention in the divide between the left and the right in Japan's 1955 system. The progressive left, represented most vocally by the Japan Socialist Party (JSP), recommended reconciliation with Beijing and a lessening of Japan's reliance on Washington. The staunchly anti-Communist LDP, in contrast, had advocated a close alliance with the United States during the Cold War and resisted the notion that Japan owed China further apology for World War II. Granted, in the LDP there was a range of opinion on just how much Japan should accommodate Beijing, and many were suspicious of the Chinese Communist Party and its ambitions in Asia. Others in the LDP, such as Katō Kōichi, were more comfortable with the reconciliation effort and the need for Japan to acknowledge wrongdoing in the years leading up to the invasion of China and during the war.

The most dramatic evidence of a blurring of postwar ideological divisions was the coalition formed in 1995 between the LDP and the

JSP that brought a socialist party legislator into the prime minister's office. Prime Minister Murayama Tomiichi argued strongly for reconciliation with China and South Korea, and it was he who crafted the most direct government statement of Japan's responsibility for the war against China:

> During a certain period in the not too distant past, Japan, following a mistaken national policy, advanced along the road to war, only to ensnare the Japanese people in a fateful crisis, and, through its colonial rule and aggression, caused tremendous damage and suffering to the people of many countries, particularly to those of Asian nations. In the hope that no such mistake be made in the future, I regard, in a spirit of humility, these irrefutable facts of history, and express here once again my feelings of deep remorse and state my heartfelt apology. Allow me also to express my feelings of profound mourning for all victims, both at home and abroad, of that history.[85]

This 1995 statement of apology remains in force today as state policy, and both conservative and liberal prime ministers since have endorsed it as the official Japanese apology for its wartime aggression.[86] Yet this formal apology to China did not prove to be a grand resolution for the tensions between Beijing and Tokyo, and did not prevent Chinese president Jiang Zemin three years later from delivering his scalding remarks to the emperor about Japan's lack of remorse.

The five-year tenure of Koizumi Jun'ichirō as prime minister (2001–2006) was characterized by a series of tensions with China and outbursts of Chinese citizen activism against Japanese interests. While Koizumi was seen as the catalyst for some of the more contentious disputes with Beijing, his successors confronted some of the same issues and also had mixed results in their efforts to build a more positive relationship with Beijing. Three of the prime ministers after Koizumi—Abe Shinzō, Fukuda Yasuo, and Asō Tarō—worked hard to mend relations with China, and all were conservative LDP politicians.

The government's ability to negotiate these new influences emanating from China, to shape their impact on Japanese citizens, and to accommodate the growth of China's regional and global power is therefore being affected by not only China's behavior but also the reactions from Japan that are influencing the policymaking process. A careful examination of critical episodes of contention between Japan and China over the past decade reveals a more complex array of interests engaged in forming Japan's China policies than in the past. The pro-China groups in business and in politics still exist, as do the anti-China advocates, individuals, and organized interests. But as diplomats and politicians try to craft a new vision for cooperation that accommodates China's growing strategic influence, Japan's public remains more and more skeptical of the idea of partnering with the current Chinese leadership.

Both China's choices and Japan's own policies helped determine Japanese attitudes toward the Sino-Japanese relationship. More and more Japanese focused on their economic woes and the Japanese government's inability to protect their interests. That is, Japan's vulnerabilities were becoming a source of domestic frustration just as the government was trying to adapt to China's changing influence on Japanese society.

The Limits of Business Advocacy

Japan's private sector, as well, has played a central role in postwar relations with China and has, for the most part, consistently supported maintaining close relations with Beijing. Both of Japan's major corporate associations, the Keidanren (Japan Business Federation) and the Keizai dōyukai (Japan Association of Corporate Executives), frequently analyze and advocate on behalf of business interests in China. Individual firms also have a voice in Japan's understanding of China's rise, and trading companies as well as Japanese manufacturing companies are broadly exposed in the Chinese market.

Political leaders often turn to leading businessmen to help improve relations with Beijing, especially when issues involving historical memory provoke controversy in the relationship. In 2003, for example, the Koizumi cabinet turned to Kobayashi Yotaro, chairman of Fuji Xerox and an executive of the Keizai dōyukai, to lead a new initiative for a more positive relationship with China.[87] The Twenty-First-Century

Japan-China Friendship Commission was established in 2003 by Japanese Prime Minister Koizumi and Chinese President Hu and presented its report to both governments in 2008. Tensions over Koizumi's visit to the Yasukuni Shrine prompted this outreach effort by nongovernmental experts in Japan and China, and even though the binational friendship commission concentrated on supporting the official diplomatic relationship, it could not finish its report and policy recommendations until after the Koizumi cabinet had left office.[88] Other Japanese business leaders were tapped to assist the Japanese government in facilitating official diplomatic relations. A more recent example was the appointment by the new DPJ government in 2010 of the Itōchū Corporation's chief executive officer, Niwa Uichirō, as ambassador to Beijing.

Despite Japan's deep economic interests in China, its business leaders' views on how to manage political tensions between Japan and China have not been unified. Business leaders worried about the impact of Koizumi's visits to Yasukuni on the country's relations with China and so tried to mitigate their impact. The Keidanren's chairman, Imai Takashi, former head of Nippon Steel, joined the political effort to craft an alternative memorial to Yasukuni.[89] Toyota Motor Corporation's chairman, Okuda Hiroshi, who succeeded Imai at the Keidanren, openly expressed his concerns over the visits and urged Koizumi to reconsider.[90] Moreover, Okuda was widely recognized as one of the most significant interlocutors between Hu and Koizumi, repeatedly traveling to Beijing to meet with Hu during the troubled years of the relationship. Nonetheless, Okuda's successor, Mitarai Fujio of Canon, took a different tack and instead, Mitarai publicly echoed Koizumi's interpretation that Yasukuni was a "political issue," implying that business leaders should stay out of it.[91]

The Keizai dōyukai, in contrast, consistently and openly opposed Koizumi's Yasukuni visits. In a well-known exchange via press conferences, the head of the Keizai dōyukai, Kitashiro Kakutaro, and Prime Minister Koizumi disagreed publicly on advocacy by business leaders on political matters.[92] On May 9, 2006, the Keizai dōyukai published a proposal for Japan-China relations, and its chairman openly urged Japan's prime minister to forgo his visit to the Yasukuni Shrine. Kitashiro argued that for the sake of the nation's security, there should be no antipathy between the people of Japan and China.[93] But Prime Minister Koizumi, following up in his press conference, adamantly disputed Kitashiro's logic, dismissing the business leaders' report by quipping, "Politics is different from business."[94]

Prominent business leaders' advocacy of better ties with China has resulted in drawing attention and even threats from marginal right-wing groups that champion the cause of Japanese nationalism. After Kobayashi, head of the Twenty-First-Century Japan-China Friendship Commission, voiced his view in September 2004 that the prime minister should not offend the feelings of the Chinese people by visiting the Yasukuni Shrine, right-wing activists gathered regularly in front of his Tokyo home that fall.[95] In January 2005, the remains of two Molotov cocktails were found there, and police investigating the arson attributed it to right-wing activists.[96] On January 19, Kobayashi received a letter with a bullet inside, which prompted a concerted response by Japan's business elite.[97] Keidanren Chairman Okuda stated, "These acts of terrorism are wrong. If these continue, we cannot comment on political matters."[98]

A different kind of political pressure was placed on Ambassador Niwa Uichirō, the former chairman of Itōchu Corporation who was sent to Beijing in 2010 by the DPJ government. When the island dispute erupted more vehemently in 2012, Niwa gave an interview to the London-based *Financial Times*, speaking out about the Tokyo municipal governor's plans to purchase the Senkaku Islands.[99] He warned that Ishihara's plans could spark an "extremely grave crisis" between Japan and China that would affect business ties. The Noda government came under immediate fire from the Japanese media, and Chief Cabinet Secretary Fujimura Osamu stated that the ambassador was expressing his own "personal view" rather than the government's position. Foreign Minister Genba Kōichiro admonished Niwa in writing the same day.[100] For its part, the LDP criticized Niwa and demanded his immediate resignation. Needless to say, Governor Ishihara echoed the criticism of Niwa's comments, stating that he "was not fulfilling his role of ambassador." At the end of that year, after his retirement, Niwa granted an interview to the *Asahi shinbun*, stating that Governor Ishihara's plans included building a bridge to one of the islands, and he wanted to

warn the Japanese government that there would be severe consequences if this was done. That Niwa felt he had to communicate
with Tokyo via the *Financial Times* reveals his isolation in the government and also the difficulty of managing this intense domestic
political pressure.[101]

Nationalist Activists

On the opposite side of the China debate from Japan's business community were the conservative nationalists who wanted a more distant and less interdependent national stance toward China. Many of
these individuals were anti-Communist and hostile to the Chinese
Communist Party, but some simply wanted a more autonomous
Japan and chafed at the notion of kowtowing to China. In addition,
a small, but dangerous, group of anti-China right wingers in Japan
have been known to use intimidation and, at times, violence against
those whom they perceive as too subservient to "foreign" influence.
Indeed, as noted earlier, several leaders—including both politicians
and business executives—who advocated for closer cooperation and
compromise with China found themselves on the receiving end of
bomb threats and actual physical attacks.

Besides warnings to and, at times, coercive pressure on Japan's
business leaders, marginal right-wing activists turned their attention
to those political leaders who were openly supportive of close relations with China. The most dramatic example of this kind of violence was the August 15, 2006, arson attacks on the home and office of
Katō Kōichi, the former LDP secretary-general, in his home district
in Yamagata Prefecture. On August 29, the Yamagata police arrested
Horikome Masahiro (age sixty-five), who had been found outside
the burning house with self-inflicted stab wounds to his stomach.
He confessed to the crime. Horikome was a member of two fringe
right-wing organizations, one of which—the Dainihon dōhōsha—
was involved in Senkaku Island activism. After his arrest, however,
the leader of Dainihon dōhōsha claimed that Horikome's actions had
nothing to do with his organization's philosophy and mission and
that he had acted alone.[102] This incident finally led Prime Minister
Koizumi to condemn acts of violence and the use of terror to shut

down speech, but at the same time he criticized Japan's media for whipping up nationalist sentiments.[103]

Beyond these marginal activists are new nationalist advocates who are frustrated with the Chinese government and with what they perceive is the Japanese government's inability to defend Japanese interests. In this group are politicians, writers, and other public figures who mobilize demonstrations or speak out in media venues such as Channel Sakura or on blogs that press for a more confrontational approach to China's encroachment on Japanese interests.[104] These newer anti-China nationalists tend to focus on Japan's weakness in the face of Chinese behavior, and the roots of their activism lie in the tensions between Japan and China over historical issues and defense. Japan's political change has also given greater opportunity to these conservative nationalists. Yet on China policy, they have been equally critical of conservative LDP cabinets as they have been of the more recent reformist DPJ governments. The growing use of the media by Japan's politicians, including social media like Twitter, has allowed individual politicians with nationalist sympathies to join these new activists. Channel Sakura regularly features Diet members, and individual politicians use their blogs and Twitter accounts to add to the flurry of anti-China commentary online.

Hardening Public Attitudes Toward China

Besides those groups that have long stood on opposite sides of Japan's China debate, popular feelings about Japan's relations with China have become increasingly important to the policy debate. As frictions over Chinese actions or practices have heated up over the past decade, more and more Japanese have become aware of the ways in which China is affecting their lives, and their perceptions of this country are closely tied to their confidence in their own government's ability to defend their interests.

Over the past decade, pollsters have carefully monitored public concerns about China. The conclusion is striking: Japanese attitudes toward China have become increasingly suspicious and negative. According to Genron NPO, a nonprofit organization that tracked public attitudes in Japan and China in cooperation with the

China Daily from 2005 to 2013, the percentage of Japanese who said they had a negative attitude toward China more than doubled, from 37.9 percent to 90.1 percent. Chinese attitudes toward Japan, too, have become less and less positive, dipping sharply in 2012/2013 when negative feelings toward Japan jumped from 64.5 percent in June 2012 to 92.8 percent in August 2013, a disquieting trend.[105]

Japanese public opinion has also been skeptical of the rewards of Tokyo's diplomacy with Beijing. For example, in 2008, more than half the Japanese respondents claimed that they had not changed their negative perceptions of China, despite the active diplomacy between Beijing and Tokyo designed to improve relations. The reasons for their distrust of China seem to be based on a loss of faith in the Chinese government. Whereas in the past, most Japanese cited ideology (socialism and Communism) as the reason for their dislike of China, increasingly they named the nature of the Chinese government—"absolutist (one-party monopoly on power)" and "hegemonic"—as the reason.[106] In the August 2013 poll following the September 2012 incident with China over the Senkaku Islands, the number of Japanese with negative opinions of China rose to more than 90 percent for the first time, with the island dispute listed as the main reason.[107]

In the 1990s, Japanese policymakers became aware that a rising China was complicating Japan's economic, diplomatic, and security choices. The desire for postwar reconciliation was proving difficult, and the limits of high-level summitry to change popular attitudes were becoming visible. Beijing and Tokyo agreed, however, to seek a new vision for the relationship. For Japanese policymakers, the desire was to find a vision that focused less on apologizing for the past and more on achieving reciprocity and mutual benefit in the future.

The failure to win diplomatic cooperation from China took its toll at home, with the changing perceptions of China's intent—and Japan's vulnerability—influencing a range of domestic actors and advocates. Indeed, the political rhetoric of government critics, and sometimes of government officials themselves, seemed to be shifting to how to say no to China rather than how to find common ground with China.

3

JAPAN'S IMPERIAL VETERANS

After being out of power for three years, Japan's conservative Liberal Democratic Party (LDP) returned to govern at the end of 2012, and controversy over its attachment to the imperial Yasukuni Shrine returned as well. Abe Shinzō, Japan's prime minister and a well-known supporter of the shrine, did not hesitate to state publicly his regrets for not visiting it during his first term in office. Then in April 2013, his deputy prime minister, Asō Tarō, also a former prime minister, became the first high-level member of the Abe cabinet to pay homage to Japan's imperial veterans, immediately drawing criticism from Beijing and Seoul.[1] In protest, South Korea's foreign minister, Yun Byung-se, canceled his imminent visit to Tokyo.[2]

Tensions with China and Korea grew again over the summer as Japan's commemoration of the end of World War II approached. Many in Japan worried aloud that their prime minister would go to the shrine, and diplomats across the region as well as from Washington quietly warned Abe to consider the damage this would do to Japan and regional stability.[3] Abe consequently chose not to go but sent an aide to make an offering on his behalf.[4] Three members of the Abe cabinet, however, did visit Yasukuni on August 15, the sixty-eighth anniversary of Japan's surrender. Afterward, one of them told journalists that "foreign countries" should not interfere in what was essentially a domestic matter. On August 15, 102 members of Japan's parliament visited Yasukuni as a group, as did 175,000 ordinary Japanese, up from 14,000 from the previous year.[5]

Speculation about whether Abe would go to the shrine persisted through the fall. The diplomatic fallout of a prime ministerial visit to the Yasukuni Shrine would be far greater than in the past, as Japan's relations with China already had deteriorated sharply when a dangerous territorial dispute in the East China Sea halted diplomacy in 2012. Relations with South Korea also had soured with the pressure for additional redress for Japan's wartime behavior, including court cases pertaining to sexual slavery and forced labor by POWs. Abe inherited these tensions when he came into office in late 2012, and his personal convictions regarding Yasukuni and Japan's history added yet a new layer of concern about regional relations. Despite his calls for high-level talks with both Chinese President Xi Jinping and South Korea's President Park Geun-hye, Abe found himself watching from the sidelines as both leaders embraced a closer relationship. Most worrisome for Tokyo was South Korea's new emphasis on insisting that Northeast Asian regionalism could proceed only if it were based on a "correct understanding" of history, a barely disguised reference to Japan's conservatives and their perspective on history.[6] On December 26, 2013, Abe thus stunned domestic and international audiences alike by paying an unannounced visit to Yasukuni Shrine to pay his respects to Japan's war dead. As expected, both Beijing and Seoul responded immediately,[7] and for the first time, Washington also expressed publicly its "disappointment" in the prime minister's choice.[8]

Chinese and Korean feelings about Japan's conservatives and their views on Japan's wartime past have been the frame for Japan's diplomacy in East Asia since the 1980s. High-level political visits, however, were only part of the controversy. Since Japan's defeat in 1945, the Yasukuni Shrine has occupied a central role in the debate over war responsibility. The postwar Japanese constitution, drafted by General Douglas MacArthur's Occupation forces, explicitly separated the Shinto religion from the state and transformed Japan's emperor into a symbolic head of state. These reforms were uncomfortable for many Japanese. Accordingly, Yasukuni, as a Shinto shrine, became a rallying point for those who sought to counter the postwar narrative, originating in the Far Eastern War Tribunals, that accused Japan of wrongdoing in the first half of the twentieth century, especially in its prosecution of the wars on the Asian mainland and in the Pacific.

Even though Japanese have been divided over this shrine for much of the postwar period, many chafed at the idea that foreign opinion should restrain Japan from honoring its war dead. Soon after he was elected president of Japan's LDP in April 2001, Koizumi Jun'ichirō told the Lower House of the Diet (parliament) that as Japan's new prime minister, he intended to visit the Yasukuni Shrine "with a full heart" (*magokoro wo komete*) to honor Japan's war dead. Indeed, this was a campaign promise that had helped him win the leadership of his party.[9] When opposition lawmakers challenged the constitutionality of his intended visit—based on the long-standing criticism that visits to Yasukuni by cabinet officials violated article 20's provision for the separation of church and state—he stated unequivocally that an official prime ministerial visit would not violate Japan's constitution.

Koizumi's campaign promise damaged Japan's diplomatic relations with China, with condemnation of his pledge to visit Yasukuni coming from across Chinese society. Official statements began with a Ministry of Foreign Affairs spokesperson, Sun Yuxi, warning that "paying homage to the shrine is in essence an issue of how the Japanese government and Japanese leaders view and deal with the history of aggression committed by Japanese militarists in the past,"[10] a clear message that the Chinese government would interpret Koizumi's visits as an endorsement of militarism. Chinese Foreign Minister Tang Jiaxuan also told visiting Japanese Diet members of the LDP, the Kōmeitō (Clean Government Party), and the New Conservative Party that the Chinese people and the people of all Asian nations who had suffered from Japanese aggression would never accept Japanese leaders' visits to Yasukuni.[11] China's new ambassador to Tokyo, Wu Dawei, used his initial courtesy call on Prime Minister Koizumi to convey in person the depth of the Chinese sentiment.[12] Yet this did not stop Japan's prime minister from visiting the shrine. Koizumi remained in office for five years and visited Yasukuni each year, making official meetings between Koizumi and Chinese leaders more and more difficult. By the end of 2005, Chinese officials were publicly stating that it was "impossible" to hold bilateral talks between Koizumi and China's leaders at significant Asian multilateral events because his shrine visits had "severely damaged the feelings of the Chinese and other Asia peoples."[13]

Chinese sentiments were not conveyed solely by government officials. A broad range of Chinese groups organized to demonstrate their anger at Koizumi's annual visits to the shrine, showing little appreciation for the prime minister's efforts to assuage Chinese concerns by avoiding August 15. In the summer of 2001, students rallying at Tsinghua University delivered statements of protest to the Japanese embassy and burned Japanese flags. In addition, scholars from China, Japan, and South Korea, along with local residents, gathered at the Memorial Hall of the Nanjing Massacre to protest Koizumi's first visit to Yasukuni on August 13, 2001, only two days before the Japanese nation officially marked the end of World War II. Over the years, demonstrations grew in intensity and in 2005 ultimately resulted in attacks against Japanese companies and consulates in China.[14] The antipathy against Koizumi reached a crescendo in the Chinese media during his final year in office, during which charges against his "failure to properly understand history" were frequent.

Koizumi often expressed his deep appreciation for Japan's historic defeat and the human toll it took on his country, and he tried to get China's agreement that the costs of war had been high for both the Japanese and the Chinese people. When he visited the Chinese war museum at Marco Polo Bridge, located nine miles (15 km) southwest of Beijing, he stated, "I looked at the various exhibits with a feeling of heartfelt apology and condolences for those Chinese people who were victims of aggression."[15] Although he was the second Japanese prime minister to visit the Marco Polo Bridge, he was the first conservative leader to do so.[16] Like other conservatives before him, Koizumi sought to balance Japan's diplomacy with China against his desire to pay homage to those who died in World War II. But his apology did not assuage Chinese concerns about the shrine's significance.

Despite his campaign promise to veterans' families, Koizumi seemed ambivalent about how best to gain Chinese acceptance. China's reaction clearly influenced his decision. Only a few weeks before he stepped down as Japan's prime minister, Koizumi donned formal wear and officially paid his respects on August 15 to those who had fought and died for imperial Japan. He thereby left it to his successor, Abe Shinzō, in his first stint as prime minister in 2006, to find a way to thaw the country's relations with Beijing.

THE CONTROVERSY: PRIME MINISTERIAL VISITS TO THE YASUKUNI SHRINE

In 1982, the Japanese government created a secular ceremony to commemorate the end of the war, with the families of Japan's imperial veterans and the emperor and empress participating. In addition, Japan's political leaders had long visited Yasukuni during the annual Shinto celebrations in the spring and autumn to avoid political controversy as they paid their respects to those who had died in the name of the Japanese emperor. They visited in their private capacity—a practice mandated by U.S. Occupation authorities in the immediate aftermath of the war and continued once Japan regained sovereignty. By 2001, therefore, Koizumi's interest in the shrine seemed somewhat anachronistic in Japan's domestic politics, but it was his willingness to take this stance knowing full well that it would attract criticism from Japan's neighbors that distinguished him from his predecessors.

Three factors made Koizumi's visits controversial. First was the frustration among Japan's conservatives with what many saw as Chinese intervention in the effort to legitimize the shrine; second was the inclusion in the Yasukuni Shrine of those deemed class-A war criminals during the Tokyo War Crimes Tribunals; and finally was the unresolved question in Japan about just what kind of state support ought to be given to Japan's veterans and their families. The Yasukuni Shrine was closely associated with the calculus of Japan's war responsibility, and its worst crisis of identity, the inclusion of those class-A war criminals in the late 1970s, coincided with Japan's debate over normalizing its relations with China. By the twenty-first century, however, the Yasukuni Shrine was no longer simply a place to honor Japan's war dead, but a site for rejecting foreign criticism of its history in the twentieth century.

The U.S. Occupation of Japan and the Yasukuni Shrine

Since the time of Japan's defeat in August 1945, foreign objections have framed the country's internal debate about the Yasukuni Shrine. To the U.S. Occupation authorities, any institution that glorified war and the emperor would interfere with Japan's postwar democratization, and this defined the place of the Yasukuni Shrine in Japan's postwar politics.

From the Meiji Restoration onward, those who died in the military service of the Japanese emperor were enshrined at Yasukuni, to become deities as a spiritual reward for services to the nation's divine ruler. Since its creation in 1869, Yasukuni has enshrined more than 2.46 million Japanese. The majority of them perished in Japan's multiple mid-twentieth-century conflicts (the wars of World War II): 2.1 million in the Greater East Asian War (the Asia Pacific theater of World War II); 191,250 in the Japanese invasion of China; and 17,176 in the Manchurian Incident.[17]

After World War II ended, the Tokyo War Crimes Tribunals were immediately organized to determine who was responsible for leading Japan's Imperial forces in their expansion into Asia. These trials, like the Nuremburg Trials in Germany, were designed to hold accountable those at the state's highest level (class-A war criminals) who had direct responsibility for leading Japan to war. Hundreds of Japanese were tried in the Far Eastern War Tribunals, in courts in Japan and also across Asia in the territories that the Japanese military had occupied in its move across the region. This was the first step in the Occupation's effort to "demilitarize and democratize" Japan.

Because the Yasukuni Shrine was emblematic of Japan's pursuit of imperialism, it was part of this demilitarization effort. Immediately after General Douglas MacArthur, who was in command of the postwar Occupation of Japan, landed at Atsugi Airport on August 30, 1945,[18] Japanese authorities had to begin disbanding the military and bringing to a close the structures of colonial rule in China and on the Korean Peninsula.[19] The most pressing and immediate responsibilities of the Japanese state were therefore a result of Japan's war with, and over, China. The priority of Japan's leaders from the time of surrender on August 15, 1945, was bringing home the 6.6 million Japanese who were abroad.[20] Half of them were Imperial Army and Navy personnel, and the other half were civilians mobilized in support of Japan's colonial enterprise. Most of them were on the Asian continent, spread across Manchuria, the Korean Peninsula, and China. In addition were those who could not be brought home: the Japanese soldiers who had been captured by the Soviets, and the many civilians—including Japanese children—left behind in the confusion of the Japanese retreat from China.

While honoring the historical position of Japan's Emperor Hirohito, General MacArthur was quick to demonstrate to the Japanese people the diminished status of their divine ruler. He summoned the emperor to the U.S. General Headquarters (GHQ) on September 27, 1945, and in a photograph taken during his visit, MacArthur, dressed in khakis, towers over the formally dressed, diminutive emperor. The public release of this photo to the Japanese people spoke volumes about who now was in command of Japan.[21] The Shinto religion, militarism, and the emperor all were linked to the status of Yasukuni in the prewar years, and thus Yasukuni, too, had to be reformed if the Occupation reforms were to be successful. But it was Yasukuni's connection to the Japanese emperor that in fact ultimately saved it.

The transition from an imperial Japan at war to an occupied Japan dismantling its empire was chaotic and uncertain. Yet even as they were being disbanded, Japan's Imperial Army and Navy—as well as the emperor himself—began the process of honoring those who had fought and died. The Imperial Army and Navy had a prominent role in the management of Yasukuni, as Japan's military memorial, with the army taking the dominant role in the shrine's operations. Immediately after the war ended, army officers began to tackle the myriad challenges associated with demobilization, and the treatment of Japan's war dead was high on their priority list. With the army and navy scheduled to be disbanded on November 30, 1945, and with the Occupation authorities focused on ending state Shinto, Yasukuni's fate was uncertain. Those who had returned from war felt an obligation to honor those who had not returned and wanted them to receive the emperor's acknowledgment of their service to the country. After some difficult conversations between the army and Yasukuni officials over how to handle this unprecedented number of war dead—as well as the sense of urgency that they needed to act before the army was dismantled—the decision was made to hold a mass ceremony on November 20, 1945, to enshrine Japan's Imperial Navy and Army war dead.[22] In attendance were GHQ officials as well as Emperor Hirohito. Prime Minister Shidehara Kijūrō, Army Minister Shimomura Sadamu, Navy Minister Yonai Mitsumasa, and other members of the cabinet attended, as did fifty unit commanders of the Imperial Army, twenty-four commanders of the Imperial Navy, forty of Japan's leading civilian bureaucrats, and 1,100 members of the aristocracy—all dressed in civilian clothing, a demonstration of the transition to civilian rule that already was under way.[23] Occupation authorities later prohibited Japan's leaders, including the emperor, from making visits there, and only late in the Occupation did U.S. officials permit Japanese authorities to visit in their "private" capacity.

The shrine was emblematic of what Japan needed to be rid of: the fusion of imperial rule, state-sponsored Shintoism, and the militaristic impulses that had set Japan on its path to war. The Japanese government shifted quickly in August 1945 to reorganize for the Occupation. The government organized a commission to manage Japan's postsurrender policies and initially assigned the Imperial Army and Navy to plan for the repatriation of military personnel.[24] In June 1946, at the directive of the Occupation authorities, the army and navy offices were combined into one demobilization agency, with army and navy personnel processed in two separate divisions. A year later, this agency was disbanded, and the functions associated with Japan's veterans were handed over to the civilian Health and Welfare Ministry (Kōseishō).[25] The Japanese government then created within the Kōseishō a new agency, the Repatriation and Veteran's Relief Agency, specifically to handle all administrative tasks associated with Japan's veterans and their families. By 1952, as the Occupation drew to a close, this agency had completed the bulk of its assignment. The majority of Japanese army and navy personnel had been brought home; studies of those yet to be found had been concluded; and the group repatriation of Japanese soldiers held in prison camps by the Soviet Union had been completed. The agency was dismantled, and a smaller bureau was created within the Kōseishō proper to continue providing support to Japan's veterans and their families.

The Yasukuni Shrine survived the U.S. Occupation's reform efforts despite the GHQ's early interest in shutting it down. The shrine's unique status as a war memorial was what drew U.S. sanctions, as Occupation authorities saw it as a dangerous tool for inculcating loyalty to the emperor and glorifying war. A directive issued on December 15, 1945, dissolved the institutions associated with state Shinto, and on May 3, 1947, Japan's new postwar constitution provided for the separation of church and state (article 20),[26] a principle opposed to the Shinto Yasukuni Shrine as a national memorial.[27]

When Japan regained independence in 1952, there was an opportunity to reconsider this aspect of the postwar settlement. The Diet debated the status of those convicted in the Tokyo War Crimes trials and concluded that the tribunal's verdicts would not be challenged. Nonetheless, these convicted individuals could not be punished or otherwise discriminated against under Japanese law. They were free to return to their normal lives. Moreover, the new constitution drafted by the Americans was broadly supported by Japanese who opposed a return to Japan's prewar society. Whether it was article 20's separation of church and state or article 9's proscription on the use of force to settle international disputes, the constitution became the defining statement of a new Japan—a democratic Japan that eschewed its early-twentieth-century imperial past.

Yasukuni survived, however. From 1952, the Kōseishō identified individuals in the Imperial Army and Navy who died in war and compiled lists with their personal data to allow the Yasukuni Shrine to conduct the full enshrinement ceremony. Early on, the Japanese government decided to send to Yasukuni for enshrinement the names of those designated as class-B and -C war criminals. But the Kōseishō waited until February 8, 1966, to send the class-A war criminals' names to the shrine. It was another decade before Yasukuni Shrine officials decided to hold the ceremony to enshrine these fourteen war criminals, and it was done without public acknowledgment. The circumstances and responsibility for the decision to enshrine Japan's class-A war criminals remained secret until the Yasukuni priest who oversaw their inclusion went public in 1992. Another decade or so later, a diary kept by a confidant of the emperor revealed that the emperor himself had ended his visits to Yasukuni over the enshrinement of the fourteen class-A war criminals.[28]

The Japanese government was directly involved in managing veterans' affairs, and it was bureaucrats, not politicians, who were responsible for identifying those who would be interred in the Yasukuni Shrine. A civilian Japanese government agency, the Repatriation and Veterans' Relief Bureau, made some of the most controversial decisions regarding Japan's war dead—and their postwar memory. This bureau took on the task of consulting with Yasukuni Shrine officials on the names of those to be included in the shrine's rosters of war dead (*gōshi*).[29] In the prewar era, the army and navy had identified those who died in the service of the emperor. But after the war, civilians took over that responsibility. This shift from military to civilian authority over veterans' affairs was a nominal one, however, since those who staffed the new Kōseishō were World War II veterans themselves. The first leader of the Repatriation and Relief Bureau, Tanabe Shigeo, had been the deputy director of the agency that preceded it. But it was his deputies, former army officer Miyama Yōzō and Hatsumi Eigorō of the Imperial Navy, who had the direct connection with Japan's veterans[30] and were seen as successors to the prewar organization that had handled Yasukuni's rosters.[31]

Thus, Japan's prewar memorial for military service continued to have a close association with the emperor, as his new status in the postwar period did not prevent him from honoring those who had served and died for him during the war. But the Shōwa emperor himself stopped visiting the shrine after the late 1970s when those who sought to revive Yasukuni's place as a rallying point for nationalism began to emerge in Japanese politics.

The Policy Challenge

State policy regarding the care of Japan's World War II veterans was a deeply contested policy arena. The state provided financial support to veterans and their families and sought to honor the memory of those who had died. The postwar Japanese constitution, drafted under the Occupation and promulgated in 1949, redefined the relationship between Japan's civilian leaders and their military and also clearly distinguished between the state and the Shinto religion. The status of Japan's imperial veterans had been a sensitive issue in its diplomacy from the start, as foreign dignitaries refrained from visiting the controversial shrine. But this was a minor issue compared with the increasing entanglement of Japan's war dead with its diplomacy in the late 1970s when Tokyo and Beijing formally restored diplomatic ties.

Most Japanese had lost family members, friends, and loved ones in the war. By 1945, millions of Japanese had died, many of whom were civilians who had had no direct role in Japan's military or government. Moreover, the atomic bombing of Hiroshima and Nagasaki had profoundly changed public opinion in Japan over the costs of war and the use of military force. Accordingly, few Japanese sought to revise the 1947 constitution that prohibited the use of force to settle international disputes, and although some conservatives chafed at the foreign origin of the document, most Japanese continued to support this ideal of self-restraint in the development and use of military power.

In the meantime, the policy of the United States shifted as the Cold War took hold. The Korean War—and the beginning of the Cold War standoff that shaped so many of Japan's postwar policies—led to the United States' interest in reviving Japan's military capability. The San Francisco Peace Treaty that ended the occupation of Japan restored Japanese sovereignty, but accompanying that treaty was a new bilateral security treaty with the United States, a treaty that provided for the continued presence of U.S. military forces on Japanese soil. By 1954, a new Japanese military had been formed, although it was limited to the mission of defending Japan.[32] This Self-Defense Force (SDF) was not to be the military of old but a new postwar military that, in accordance with article 9 of Japan's constitution, would no longer use force to settle international disputes. For those whose family members had died in the war that ended in 1945, this new military must have unearthed complex emotions. National sentiments about Japan's military leaders and their decisions during the war endured and become even more complex in Japan's domestic political debate as the years unfolded.

The Japanese government faced several policy challenges associated with the military veterans. The first, and most immediate, was financial support for the veterans and their families.[33] In the first years after the war, all Japanese suffered from economic hardship, and because the wives and children of Japan's imperial war dead had virtually no state support, a nationwide association was established to champion their cause. Along with Japan's economic growth, the pensions awarded to imperial veterans and their families were given fuller attention. Then, given the new status of the SDF, Japan's postwar military also had to contend with popular ambivalence about honoring those who had died while in uniform. Court cases challenging the inclusion of imperial as well as SDF members in Yasukuni limited the state's behavior. Finally, by the 1980s, successive Japanese governments had to balance their desire to memorialize their military with the increasing number of protests from China. Managing relations with China after 1978 was one of Tokyo's highest foreign policy priorities, but despite the economic benefits of good relations with Beijing, its China policy was still a cause for dissension, even in Japan's ruling conservative party. No issue intensified that split more than the question of war memory.

DOMESTIC INTERESTS AND ACTIVISTS

The domestic interests that shape state policy surrounding the Yasukuni Shrine have straddled several generations, from the wartime generation to those who reconstituted Japanese politics in the early decades after the war to those who entered the debate that erupted over Koizumi's visits as prime minister. Two interest groups, the Izokukai and the LDP, influenced the debate over the Yasukuni Shrine and played a role in Koizumi's decision to visit it. But by the time he left office, their activism seemed to have been weakened rather than strengthened. Neither of these two interest groups today overwhelmingly supports the idea of future prime ministerial visits. Furthermore, the advocacy group that represented Japan's World War II veterans and their families is shrinking, along with their support of the shrine.

The Nippon izokukai

The group representing Japan's war dead, the Nippon izokukai,[34] was formed in 1947 as the Japan Bereaved Family Welfare Federation

(Nihon izoku kōsei renmei) and is composed of those who lost family members in the war. Its membership included 1.5 million Japanese, the largest organization of its time. The Izokukai is an umbrella organization of local chapters from each of Japan's prefectures. Formed in response to the U.S. Occupation's termination of pensions to Japan's prewar military, the Izokukai after 1952 became a nationwide organization. It identified its goals as, first, ensuring the honor and the memory of those who died serving their country and, second, improving the care and social welfare of the families left behind.[35]

It was the second goal that occupied much of the Izokukai's attention in the early decades after the war: advocating for the millions of parents, widows, and children left behind, which gave it a unique place in postwar politics. After the U.S. Occupation ended, the government of Japan revised its pension law and crafted a new, supplementary pension law for those who had died or were wounded in World War II.[36] By the early 1960s, when Japan's economy was growing, additional government subsidies to the wives of Japan's war dead were granted. Starting in 1963, these payments were given to "console the wives of those lost in war for their emotional suffering." According to the Izokukai's records, Japan's widows were given lump-sum payments of ¥200,000 in 1963, ¥600,000 in 1973, and another ¥1,200,000 in 1983, all issued in Japanese government bonds.[37]

The LDP-led government expanded state support for family members of Japan's war dead, and the Izokukai continued to play a key advocacy role. Four years after the special consolation funds for Japan's war widows were established, a similar consolation fund was set up for the parents and grandparents of those who had died in World War II. These payments also were in government bonds, but in five-year issues. The Izokukai argued that "the pain of losing children and grandchildren only deepened over time," and thus these payments, as well, grew every five years. The Izokukai's records reveal that in 1967, the Japanese government's payments to these family members were ¥100,000; in 1973, ¥300,000; in 1978, ¥600,000; and in 1983, another ¥600,000. Finally, in 1965 the Japanese government created a special sympathy fund for the children and siblings of deceased veterans who did not qualify for pensions or other types of government support. On the twentieth anniversary of the end of the war, 1965, this group received ¥30,000 bonds; on the thirtieth anniversary, 1975, it received another ¥200,000; and on the fortieth anniversary, 1985, it received ¥300,000, all in ten-year-issue Japanese government bonds.[38]

The close relationship between the Izokukai and the LDP created a fairly seamless lobby for the families of Japan's veterans. By the 1980s, the Izokukai was firmly enmeshed in the Japanese government's policymaking on veterans' affairs.[39] Yet the early postwar years were marked by political protest and contention between the families of Japan's war dead and the Japanese government. Sit-ins in front of the home of Prime Minister Yoshida Shigeru were frequent, and hunger strikes by widows at the Yasukuni Shrine were common. The Izokukai was the leading supporter of the impoverished families of Japan's war dead and repeatedly demonstrated for greater government attention to the plight of those who had been shunned and ignored in the early postwar years.

All but one of the chairmen of the Izokukai were politicians, and some served as ministers in the cabinet (table 3.1).[40] In his preface to the forty-year history of the Izokukai, the then chairman, Hasegawa Takashi, who had been elected to the Diet's Lower House in the first postwar election of 1953, asks, "Who thought we would lose the war?" and goes on to describe the social need for the Izokukai to advocate on behalf of the bereaved families.

Perhaps as important as Izokukai's role as a policy advocate for Japan's veterans was its political role as a major source of votes for the LDP. By the early 1970s, the Izokukai was central to the LDP's electoral fortunes. Along with the Japan Physicians' Association, which was flush with funds for political activities, and the agricultural cooperatives, which delivered the farm vote, the Izokukai, with its ability to mobilize the family members of Japan's war dead, was one of the three main pressure groups on the LDP.[41] The sustained pressure by the widows of Japan's World War II veterans during electoral campaigns shows that they were keenly aware of their political clout. On November 8, 1972, for example, 5,700 widows gathered at the indoor sumo ring at the Yasukuni Shrine to meet with about two hundred Diet members. As each Diet member invoked the honor of their long-dead husbands, the widows stood up one by one to state their case. The head of the Izokukai's women's group,

TABLE 3.1 Izokukai Leadership

Tenure	Name	Background
1948–1953	Nagashima Ginzo[a]	House of Lords
		House of Councillors (LDP)
1954–1961	Takahashi Ryūtarō	House of Lords
		House of Councillors (LDP)
		Minister of International Trade and Industry
1961–1962	Yasui Seichiro	Governor of Tokyo
		Governor of Niigata Prefecture
1962–1977	Kaya Okinori	House of Representatives (LDP)
		Minister of Justice
		Minister of Finance
1977–1985	Murakami Isamu	House of Representatives (LDP)
		Minister of Posts and Communication
		Minister of Construction
		Director-General of Hokkaido Development Agency
1985–1992	Hasegawa Takashi	House of Representatives (LDP)
		Minister of Labor
		Minister of Transport
		Minister of Justice
1993–1996	Hashimoto Ryūtarō	House of Representatives (LDP)
1996–2002	Nakai Sumiko	First leader promoted from within the Izokukai organization
2002–2012	Koga Makoto	House of Representatives (LDP)
		Secretary-General of the LDP
2012–present	Otsuji Hidehisa	House of Councillors (LDP)
		Minister of Health, Labor, and Welfare (Koizumi cabinet)
		Vice President, House of Councillors

[a]Nagashima Ginzo was the first and only president of the Nippon izoku kōsei renmei, which later became the Nippon izokukai.

Source: Compiled from media sources, including the *Asahi shinbun, Nikkei shinbun, Yomiuri shinbun,* and *Mainichi shinbun.*

ninety-four-year-old Fujita Mie, who had lost her husband in China, noted to reporters that the meeting was quite lively: "After all, the politicians need votes for the upcoming Lower House elections next month." She also claimed that one of the benefits of losing the war

was that women in Japan now had the right to vote and could influence the outcome of Japan's elections.[42] Japan's war widows were a
formidable political force.

The Izokukai became even more important in the 1990s when the
LDP's political fortunes became less secure and the party's internal
competition for votes from party members became fiercer. By this
time, the LDP had become a party sustained primarily by interest groups rather than individuals. In the run-up to the September
1999 party leadership race, the LDP surveyed its supporters, and the
published results were revealing. More than 70 percent of the LDP
party members and friends of the party belonged to these support
organizations. Even more troubling, ten of the eleven organizations
(with more than 100,000 members) in the 1999 party leadership race
were under the control of Upper House members who supported the
reelection of Obuchi Keizō as prime minister. This revelation to the
LDP of the importance of organization votes led it to revise its internal rules for selecting party leaders.[43] For individual politicians, like
Koizumi in 2001, the Izokukai's vote could make or break a run at the
leadership of the party and the prime minister's office.

The LDP and Prime Ministerial Visits

The ruling LDP also fought hard to transform the Yasukuni Shrine
into a legitimate national memorial for Japan's veterans, but many
Japanese—including some in the LDP itself—opposed the idea of
making the prewar state Shinto shrine into a national memorial to
Japan's war dead. The Liberal Democrats first focused on a legislative
effort to legitimize—and fund—what was already de facto government sponsorship of the shrine's activities. In the 1960s, the LDP
presented a bill that would give Yasukuni the status of a national
war memorial. Objections came not only from opposition parties
but also from religious groups in Japan that wanted to block any
religious entity from gaining state support, and preference, in Japan.
Article 20 of Japan's constitution was the main weapon used to
defeat the LDP's efforts to nationalize the shrine. Four efforts were
made to turn this bill into law, yet each time the ruling party's efforts
were defeated in the Diet. In 1974, the law was put forward for the

last time and again was resoundingly defeated. Yasukuni was given no access to government funds.

Then Japan's ruling party changed tack. Prime Minister Miki Takeo visited Yasukuni in 1975 as part of a new LDP strategy to overcome domestic opposition. State visits would be the LDP's fallback position. If it could not provide a special legal status for Yasukuni, regular visits by Japan's state leaders would legitimize the shrine as Japan's national war memorial. Three years later, another moderate LDP leader, Prime Minister Fukuda Takeo, moved this effort further, signing the register at Yasukuni as the prime minister of Japan (*naikaku sōri daijin*). But the Fukuda cabinet initially refused to argue that this was appropriate under Japan's constitution. In response to questioning in the Upper House, Chief Cabinet Secretary Abe Shintarō explained that the prime minister felt that all Japanese citizens had a right to pay their respects at the shrine, if they chose, and that because cabinet members had to use state vehicles for security reasons, even when they were off duty, they were correct in clearly identifying themselves as officials of the Japanese state.[44]

The tenor of the public debate soon changed dramatically. Two months after Fukuda made his visit in August 1978, the Yasukuni Shrine enshrined the fourteen class-A war criminals. Only in recent years has there been an effort in Japan to clarify the circumstances under which this decision was made. For years, this moment in Yasukuni's history was seen as suspicious, yet too sensitive to discuss, in part because of the close relationship between Yasukuni and Japan's imperial family. The leaders of Yasukuni themselves were advocates for the shrine's role in memorializing Japan's war dead. Moreover, through the efforts of the Kōseishō, the Japanese government was quietly complicit. Thus, Yasukuni was not simply an object of ideological difference. As Japanese society divided over the question of war responsibility, shrine officials quietly went about interring those who had fought and died in the war. In the late 1970s, however, this all changed when the media reported that shrine officials had interred the class-A war criminals at Yasukuni. Even Japan's emperor took umbrage at the decision, and according to a diary kept by a member of the Imperial Household staff and a confidant of the Shōwa emperor himself, the emperor thought that the blame rested squarely on the shoulders of the head of the Yasukuni Shrine, Matsudaira Nagayoshi.

At the time, however, media accounts were spotty, and no official statement was made, by either the shrine or the Japanese government. Then, on April 19, 1979, the *Asahi shinbun* made public the inclusion of the class-A war criminals in Yasukuni. It was widely assumed that there was a politically motivated—and, more troubling, a government-supported—effort to resurrect the reputations of these fourteen individuals who had been formally charged with and convicted of war crimes. No one at the time, though, was willing to be openly associated with the inclusion.

The LDP was not blamed directly, and in fact, the Yasukuni priest came forward in 1992 to explain that it was his personal decision. Matsudaira Nagayoshi had assumed the position of head priest of the Yasukuni Shrine in 1978. He was not trained in the Shinto faith but had been an Imperial Navy officer, who joined Japan's Ground Self-Defense Forces after the war. His father, Matsudaira Kenmin, had been head of the Imperial Household Agency in the immediate postwar period, and the younger Matsudaira later talked about his decision to join the ground forces instead of the navy as being influenced by his early experiences watching his father contend with "red flag–waving protestors who were storming the Imperial Palace." Wanting to defend the emperor, he thought it better to stay in Japan than "to float out in the open ocean." He explained his decision to include the class-A war criminals in an article in *Shokun* magazine in December 1992:

> Even before I became the Head Priest, I had thought that Japan would never recover its spirit until it countered the historical view created by the Tokyo War Crimes Trials that "everything about Japan was bad." Soon after I took over Yasukuni Shrine, I examined the files and realized there had been an inquiry to the acting head of the shrine about what Yasukuni Shrine intended to do about the Class-A war criminals. Since I assumed my position in July 1978, and the next annual opportunity for enshrining souls was in October, I asked my subordinates if we would be able to complete the full process of getting the paperwork in

order in time. This was just before the beginning of September. I was told we would make it, and so along with over a thousand others, I decided to include the souls of the fourteen Class-A war criminals . . . my reason for doing this was simple. At the order of the Emperor on the 15th of August 1945, we stopped fighting. But aggression against us did not stop on August 15th. The USSR continued its invasion into our northern islands, and we dealt with it as best we could. But we lost many lives. On September 21, we signed our surrender documents, and the occupation of Japan began. . . . [T]he occupation ended with the signing of the San Francisco Peace Treaty seven years later. . . . Japan was free to determine the status of its citizens, and legally they were the same as any other Japanese. Their families suffered terribly . . . the Japanese government had provided us with the names, and there was no obstacle to including them in Yasukuni Shrine.[45]

Not all the priests at the Yasukuni Shrine shared Matsudaira's views, and indeed, some were outspoken opponents of the inclusion. Nonetheless, the shrine has stopped short of offering to remove these fourteen souls.

Initially, the LDP did not step back from its effort to legitimize annual visits by the prime minister.[46] After the *Asahi* report, Prime Minister Suzuki Zenkō visited the Yasukuni Shrine on August 15, 1980, and took a number of his cabinet members with him. On November 17 that year, Miyazawa Kiichi, the chief cabinet secretary, issued a statement in the Lower House that revealed the government's reluctance to endorse visits to Yasukuni by Japanese cabinet ministers. Nonetheless, Miyazawa did not go so far as to suggest a government position on the constitutionality question. Rather, he simply urged the ministers to curtail their visits because of the controversy surrounding the constitutional question.[47]

Prime Minister Suzuki returned to Yasukuni in 1981 and 1982. On March 31, 1982, Justice Minister Sakata Michita argued in the Lower House Justice Committee that the constitution did not in fact prohibit the prime minister or his cabinet ministers from visiting Yasukuni, and in the following month, on April 22, during the annual spring festival, about one hundred Diet members, led by Minister of Finance

Takeshita Noboru, visited the shrine. On August 15 that same year, Prime Minister Suzuki and the majority of his cabinet visited Yasukuni as well but refused to answer questions about whether they were visiting in their "personal" or their "official" capacity. The annual visits of the prime minister and his cabinet finally seemed to be regular—and relatively accepted—events (table 3.2).

China's leaders, however, began to take notice. On September 1, 1982, the chairman of the Chinese Communist Party, Hu Yaobang, noted in the twelfth National Congress that he was concerned about recent efforts by some in Japan to "beautify Japan's past aggression."[48] A couple of months later, Nakasone Yasuhiro assumed the prime minister's position, and emotions ran high in Tokyo and Beijing in anticipation of his possible visit to the Yasukuni Shrine. Although Nakasone had strong ties to the leaders of the Chinese Communist Party, he wanted to revise his party's resigned acceptance of "questions" about the constitutionality of official cabinet visits to Yasukuni. His advocacy for Yasukuni was linked to other positions he held on revising Japan's constitution and ending its postwar self-restraint. The LDP was becoming more assertive on issues related to Japan's military and its constitution, and state visits to Yasukuni were included on the agenda by those who wanted Japan to end its hesitancy over the past. Accordingly, Prime Minister Nakasone visited the shrine on August 15, 1984, taking with him fifteen of his cabinet's twenty members.

At the time, Nakasone had considerable support from his party. In addition to the prime minister and his cabinet, a delegation of more than 140 Upper and Lower House LDP politicians visited the shrine, organized under the leadership of Shin Kanemaru in the "Let's Visit Yasukuni Shrine Together Committee."[49] The LDP's push to gain acceptance in Japan for Yasukuni's role in memorializing World War II veterans was gaining momentum, and despite the opposition parties' criticism, the LDP went forward with its restatement of its party position on the constitutionality question. The cabinet also launched a study of the "Yasukuni visit problem" as public debate intensified.[50] Believing that public opinion was increasingly on their side, the Nakasone cabinet returned again to the Yasukuni Shrine the following year.

The LDP was ready to declare victory in its effort to make annual state visits to Yasukuni, but in the days leading up to August 15,

TABLE 3.2 Prime Ministers' Visits to the Yasukuni Shrine

Prime Minister	Year	Date	On August 15?
Miki Takeo	1975	April 22	No
Miki Takeo	1975	August 15	Yes
Miki Takeo	1976	October 18	No
Fukuda Takeo	1977	April 21	No
Fukuda Takeo	1978	April 21	No
Fukuda Takeo	1978	August 15	Yes
Fukuda Takeo	1978	October 18	No
Ōhira Masayoshi	1979	April 21	No
Ōhira Masayoshi	1979	October 18	No
Ōhira Masayoshi	1980	April 21	No
Suzuki Zenkō	1980	August 15	Yes
Suzuki Zenkō	1980	October 18	No
Suzuki Zenkō	1980	November 21	No
Suzuki Zenkō	1981	April 21	No
Suzuki Zenkō	1981	August 15	Yes
Suzuki Zenkō	1981	October 17	No
Suzuki Zenkō	1982	April 21	No
Suzuki Zenkō	1982	August 15	Yes
Suzuki Zenkō	1982	October 18	No
Nakasone Yasuhiro	1983	April 21	No
Nakasone Yasuhiro	1983	August 15	Yes
Nakasone Yasuhiro	1983	October 18	No
Nakasone Yasuhiro	1984	January 5	No
Nakasone Yasuhiro	1984	April 21	No
Nakasone Yasuhiro	1984	August 15	Yes
Nakasone Yasuhiro	1984	October 18	No
Nakasone Yasuhiro	1984	January 21	No
Nakasone Yasuhiro	1985	April 22	No
Nakasone Yasuhiro	1985	August 15	Yes
Hashimoto Ryūtarō	1996	July 29	No
Koizumi Jun'ichirō	2001	August 13	No
Koizumi Jun'ichirō	2002	April 21	No
Koizumi Jun'ichirō	2003	January 14	No
Koizumi Jun'ichirō	2004	January 1	No
Koizumi Jun'ichirō	2005	October 17	No
Koizumi Jun'ichirō	2006	August 15	Yes
Abe Shinzō	2013	December 26	No

Source: Compiled from media sources, including the *Asahi shinbun, Nikkei shinbun, Yomiuri shinbun,* and *Mainichi shinbun.*

1985, the mood on the grounds of the shrine was becoming contentious. Two hundred uniformed police were mobilized to protect the prime minister and his cabinet. Shouts could be heard of "banzai" and "arigatō" from applauding supporters—and jeers of "Nakasone, go home!" from opponents. Yasukuni Shrine had become the venue for vehement and noisy demonstrations rather than a place of quiet commemoration of those who had died in Japan's wars. When he emerged from paying his respects, Nakasone himself sought to explain his motivations to the press waiting for him, saying that he avoided all religious activities such as bowing and clapping in reverence to the gods, being blessed by the priests, or drinking the sacred wine. He argued that by staying within the boundaries of Japanese custom and social conventions, he was not violating the constitution.

Nakasone had consulted with the Cabinet Legal Affairs Bureau on the constitutionality question before his visit, and he believed that as long as he did not perform any religious act, he would not violate article 20's call for the separation of church and state. Nakasone felt strongly that Japan's prime minister ought to honor the heroes who died in World War II, and he blamed his predecessors for avoiding official visits. He had served in the war and had lost soldiers under his command. His brother had died in the war as well. Later, he recalled that he was deeply affected by the young men, the youth league of the Izokukai, who were carrying out a hunger strike in order to encourage his visit.[51] Nakasone was committed to the notion that Yasukuni was the proper place to honor Japan's war dead. Moreover, the prime minister's audience was not China or Korea, but those in Japan who supported the postwar reforms embodied in the nation's constitution. It was his critics, who argued that the constitution prohibited state visits to Yasukuni, that he sought to mollify—and they were Japanese, not foreign.

Nonetheless, even Nakasone, who had long argued that the Japanese constitution had been imposed during the U.S. Occupation and who decried the stigma of the class-A status attached to Japan's prewar leaders, stopped visiting the Yasukuni Shrine in the face of the vehement Chinese criticism that followed his 1985 visit. Indeed, the Chinese government warned Nakasone the day before he went to the shrine that a prime ministerial visit would "seriously hurt the feelings" of the people of Asia who were victims of Japanese aggression.[52] In the days after his visit, senior Chinese leaders reiterated this warning. China's vice-premier, Yao Yilin, publicly criticized Nakasone for his visit, and then General Secretary Hu Yaobang, who had a close personal relationship with Nakasone, told a visiting delegation of Japanese Socialist Party members that the prime minister had "hurt the feelings of the people of China."[53]

On August 14 the following year, Chief Cabinet Secretary Gotoda Masaharu announced that Prime Minister Nakasone and other state ministers would not visit the shrine. Gotoda issued a formal statement expressing the reasons for the Nakasone cabinet's decision:

On August 15, 1985, the "day to express mourning to the war dead and pray for peace," which was a milestone in history as the fortieth anniversary of the end of the war, the Prime Minister made a so-called official visit to Yasukuni Shrine together with like-minded Ministers, in response to the strong requests of the people and bereaved families over many years. The objective was to mourn for the people in general who became the victims of war for the sake of their homeland and their comrades and to renew Japan's determination for peace of Japan and the world. It was unrelated to any individual deities enshrined at Yasukuni. The related statement by the Chief Cabinet Secretary on August 14, 1985, remains true today, and there has been no change at all in the Government's opinion expressed in that statement.

However, for such reasons as the enshrinement of the so-called "class-A war criminals" at Yasukuni Shrine, criticism of the official visit last year has been raised by the peoples of neighboring countries who experienced tremendous suffering and damage as a result of Japan's acts in the past, questioning whether the Ministers worshipped these "class-A war criminals" who were responsible for such acts of Japan. In addition, it is even possible that they came to misunderstand and mistrust Japan's remorse on the past war and the determination for peace and friendship, which were expressed on various occasions.

This would not be either the interest of Japan, which hopes to promote friendship with other nations, or the ultimate wish of the war dead.

Gotoda hedged somewhat on whether visits should be made by Japan's future prime ministers, however, when he concluded,

As I have repeatedly made clear, since the official visit has not been an institutionalized practice, whether it should be conducted or not should be judged on each occasion. It is thus natural that this decision itself does not deny or abolish official visits themselves. The Government intends to maintain good international relations and to continue to make its maximum effort to improve the situation.[54]

Nakasone's decision to cease his official visits frustrated those who felt that Yasukuni deserved the imprimatur of Japan's highest elected leader. On August 15, the Izokukai delivered its verdict on Nakasone's decision. The chairman, Hasegawa Takashi, issued a scathing protest: "Neither god nor man will forgive [Nakasone's] submission to Chinese intervention in our affairs." More to the point, Hasegawa bluntly stated that the prime minister would be responsible for the Izokukai's response, beginning with the removal from the LDP party membership of the 160,000 members of the organizations associated with veterans' affairs.[55]

The Izokukai did not follow through with this threat, but the sensitivity of its membership to Nakasone's perceived betrayal of their interests in favor of Chinese sentiment continued to inform their relationship with subsequent LDP party leaders. More broadly, with this episode in the Japan-China relationship, the narrative of Japan's conservative elite—including even those, like Nakasone, who had strong nationalist credentials—was that they had bowed to Chinese criticism. The Izokukai subjected successive LDP leaders to scrutiny over their intent to visit the shrine. More than a decade later, another prime minister, Koizumi Jun'ichirō, revived this question of state visits to Yasukuni, seeking to end the legacy of submitting to Chinese criticism.

Koizumi's official visit to the Yasukuni Shrine on August 15, 2006—the first since Nakasone's visit more than twenty years earlier—was therefore a triumph for many of Japan's conservatives, including the Izokukai. The photographs of Japan's prime minister in full formal wear, flanked by the priests of Yasukuni paying homage to those who lost their lives in the service of the emperor, was the culmination of a half century of political effort to legitimize this controversial emblem of Japan's modern nationalism. By the time Koizumi visited the shrine, more Japanese thought he was right to do so than at any point earlier in the postwar era. Koizumi's willingness to "stand up" to China clearly earned him public support, even if many Japanese remained ambivalent about whether the shrine should be a national memorial to Japan's war dead.

Although China's reaction to the Japanese debate over its past has been very critical, visits to Yasukuni by Japan's political leaders have not always occasioned the same intensity of diplomatic friction. For instance, when Prime Minister Miki Takeo visited Yasukuni on August 15, 1975, the Chinese media and government paid no attention, even though Japan and China had begun negotiations the year before on the peace treaty that would fully normalize their bilateral relations. Miki's continued adherence to the norm of visiting in his "private" capacity undoubtedly placated his critics.[56]

But when the well-known conservative nationalist, Nakasone, visited the Yasukuni Shrine on August 15, 1985, in formal dress and with the explicit intent of demonstrating the full trappings of a prime ministerial visit to honor Japan's war dead, China reacted strongly. Diplomatic ties suffered, and Nakasone stepped back, irritating conservatives at what they perceived as Japan's weakness in the face of Chinese criticism. Unlike his predecessors, Koizumi seemed unconcerned about—or indifferent to—Chinese criticism. Indeed, he openly stated that he would go to Yasukuni even if his close friend, President George W. Bush, asked him not to, asserting that he would stand up to the pressures of any foreign criticism.[57]

The controversy that erupted when Koizumi became prime minister was not fed by new sentiments. In fact, Chinese criticism in the early twenty-first century sounded much like the criticism of U.S. Occupation authorities in the immediate aftermath of Japan's defeat.

Over the half century since Japan's defeat and occupation, strong emotions—and political differences—repeatedly bubbled up over the unresolved question of war responsibility. Although Japan's conservatives and their progressive opposition differed in their interpretation of their country's past, their real issue of contention was the need for Japan to apologize for its conflicts with its Asian neighbors during the twentieth century. The Japanese emperor's visit to China in 1992 had also produced support in Japan for reconciliation, and an apology, for the country's past aggression. Political change in the 1990s, in addition to the passage of time, had dulled the sharpness of this divide and provided the opportunity for compromise. After losing power in 1993, the LDP regrouped to form a governing coalition with its postwar political rival, the Japan Socialist Party (JSP). The JSP's leader, Murayama Tomiichi, became prime minister in this coalition government and, in 1995, issued as official state policy the most forthright apology to date for Japan's pursuit of war in China and beyond. Although Murayama's apology continues today to define Japan's remorse toward its neighbors for the conflicts, it still remains a bone of contention among a minority in the LDP.

Koizumi brought new political support to the floundering LDP, and with his leadership, the conservative party recovered its popularity in Japan. In coalition with the Kōmeitō, the LDP had a majority in Japan's Lower House election in 2005. By the end of Koizumi's time in office, the LDP and the Kōmeitō had gained a two-thirds' majority in the Lower House, opening the way for considerable legislative advantage. But the Yasukuni Shrine issue continued to cleave rather than unite Japanese politics. Despite being part of the ruling coalition, the Kōmeitō was adamantly opposed to the prime minister's Yasukuni Shrine visits. Moreover, the new Democratic Party of Japan (DPJ), formed in 1998 and composed of a number of former LDP politicians as well as former members of the Japan Socialist Party, took the position early on of openly opposing shrine visits.

THE NEW POLITICS OF YASUKUNI

In 2001, Prime Minister Koizumi emerged to lead an LDP very different from the party that Nakasone had led two decades earlier. Conservatives in the LDP had long been frustrated by Nakasone's decision—in the face of intense Chinese pressure—to step back from the prime ministerial visits to the Yasukuni Shrine that were becoming routine in the mid-1980s. China's increasingly harsh criticism of Japan—and its accusation that Japan had "returned to militarism"—rankled many in Japan, even those not in favor of the Yasukuni Shrine. But in Japan, views on the shrine remained divided.

Koizumi's Calculus

There is no doubt that Koizumi's promise to visit the Yasukuni Shrine reflected both his own personal convictions and his political ambition. In February 2001, Koizumi made a well-publicized visit to the Chiran Peace Museum for Kamikaze Pilots (Chiran tokkō heiwa kaikan) in Kagoshima Prefecture, a museum made famous by Japanese actor Takakura Ken's portrayal in the movie *Hotaru* of a kamikaze pilot who survived the war. At that time, Koizumi was the head of the powerful Mori faction, and although the public was increasingly critical of Prime Minister Mori Yoshirō, Koizumi remained a force to be reckoned with. The press corps following Koizumi to the museum wrote about the tears he shed while reading the letters and viewing the photos of the young men sent off to fight in Japan's desperate attempt to fend off the U.S. invasion of its home islands. It was this visit that one reporter described as the catalyst for breaking the sixteen-year silence that followed Nakasone's visit in 1985.[58]

Despite the belief that Koizumi came into office committed to make an official visit to the shrine, there is clear evidence that his thinking evolved over his five years in office. Initially he seemed to want to find a way for Beijing to accept Japan's need to memorialize its war dead. In his first year in office, Koizumi was careful to temper his campaign statements, reaching out to critics in both China and Japan. His efforts to reach out to Chinese leaders seemed to be making some headway, and in October 2001, he visited the Marco Polo Bridge, site of the Japanese military's initiation of its conflict with China. Clearly stating his apology (*owabi*) and regret (*aitō*) for the "sacrifice of Chinese lives" caused by Japan's invasion (*shinryaku*), Koizumi laid a wreath at the memorial and visited the museum that chronicled Japan's initiation of war with China.[59] In addition to his remarks on Japan's past war with China, Koizumi took the opportunity to raise the issue of global terrorism, citing the need for Japan and China to cooperate in their response. In conclusion, Koizumi went a step further, arguing that the wartime legacy should not be a barrier to building stronger ties between Japan and China: "I want to build a strong relationship of friendship between Japanese and Chinese, as strong as the bonds of friendship between the American and Japanese people."[60] Yet in his meeting with Hu Jintao, the Chinese leader clearly stated that visits to the Yasukuni Shrine would represent a return to Japan's past "militarism," as it would mean honoring those deemed war criminals at the end of the war.[61]

In Japan, Koizumi's campaign promise created great controversy, and he took time in considering his options. He did not visit Yasukuni on August 15 during his first year in office. Rather, he spent 2001 reaching out to those in the country most affected by the Japanese military's actions in World War II. In June, at the ceremony commemorating the Battle of Okinawa, and again on August 15, at the site of the memorial to Japan's unknown soldiers at Chidorigafuchi, Koizumi pledged that Japan would not return to the path that led to war. As he did during his visit to the Marco Polo Bridge in China, Koizumi sought to reassure his critics that honoring Japan's war dead in no way signified a return to past policies. The media dubbed the efforts Koizumi's "tour for the repose of the souls" (*chinkon no tabi*) of those who died in war.[62]

Nonetheless, Koizumi did not avoid visiting the controversial shrine and at times seemed irritated at foreign criticism of his visits. In April 2002, even though the South Korean ambassador openly warned the prime minister against visiting, Koizumi went the following day.[63] China's foreign minister, Tang Jiaxuan, told senior LDP leaders Nonaka Hiromu and Koga Makoto (also the head of the Izokukai) during their visit to Beijing that he personally hoped that August would be peaceful. Koga had said publicly that he did not want to be constrained by China, as 2002 was the fiftieth anniversary of the Izokukai's formation. But in the meeting, he reportedly stated that as the head of the Izokukai "and as a politician," he felt a need to consider this decision carefully. Koizumi said he would think it over, and ultimately he did not visit the shrine.

There were more signs that some sort of compromise with Beijing had been found. Koizumi continued to avoid the August 15 date and markedly toned down his public commentary when he did visit.[64] When the two leaders met on the sidelines of the Asia-Pacific Economic Community (APEC) meeting in St. Petersburg, Russia, in October 2003, Hu noted that China's leaders were ready "to work with Japan to promote the friendly cooperative relations between the two nations," and he agreed with Koizumi to establish what became the Twenty-First Century Committee for Japan-China Friendship.[65] A year later, at the November 2004 APEC meeting in Santiago, Chile, Hu claimed the relationship had made great achievements in the thirty-two years since normalization, "thanks to the relentless efforts of several generations of leaders and governments of the two countries and people of insight."[66] Yet he also cautioned that the "root cause for the difficulties of the bilateral political relations" was visits to the Yasukuni Shrine by Japanese leaders.

Ultimately, Koizumi made little headway in persuading Chinese leaders that the Yasukuni Shrine was an appropriate venue for commemorating Japan's war dead. China's leaders did seem to acknowledge that both Japanese and Chinese soldiers who had lost their lives must be remembered. But Yasukuni's military associations proved a step too far. Diplomacy faltered and then ground to a halt. By their next meeting in April 2005 in Jakarta for the Asia-Africa Summit, Hu had changed his tone and instead claimed that "China-Japan relations faced great difficulties at present and the leaders of the two nations needed to handle it seriously."[67] Koizumi went to Yasukuni anyway in October 2005, although he toned down his dress and his behavior, made no official statement, and did not hold a press conference.[68] None of this had any effect on Chinese views. The downturn in diplomatic relations with Beijing continued until Koizumi left office.

In fact, it was only on August 15, at the very end of his tenure as prime minister, that Koizumi chose to make his official visit to the Yasukuni Shrine. While in hindsight his tenure in office seems stable, at the time it was by no means clear that his government would last for five years, given his broader policy goals and the tumultuous politics surrounding his effort to restructure the LDP and Japan's government. Thus when he called a snap general election in 2005, the LDP could easily have lost its grip on power. Indeed, despite all the media attention, Koizumi's visit to the shrine on August 15 seemed to be an option that he considered only in 2006 when his time in office was drawing to a close. The fact that it was by no means certain that he could count on being in office each year discounts the idea that the visit was his top priority. Koizumi sought alternatives, ordering his cabinet to consider the construction of a new, secular memorial, an option with strong advocates even in the LDP.

An Alternative Memorial

The idea of constructing an alternative, secular memorial where Japan's leaders, as well as foreign dignitaries, could honor those Japanese who died in the service of their country has long been seen as the solution to the divisive politics of the Yasukuni Shrine. The practical problem of how to memorialize those who could not be identified created the first opportunity to construct an alternative memorial. Since the Yasukuni Shrine could not accept them, the Japanese government had to come up with a means of honoring its unknown soldiers. In 1959, Chidorigafuchi was created for precisely this purpose and remains today the memorial to Japan's unknown soldiers. Moreover, in 1963 the government established an annual ceremony in April honoring Japan's war dead, which included the participation of the emperor and empress as well as Japan's cabinet. On April 13, 1982, the cabinet declared August 15 as the national day of mourning for Japan's war dead, and the national ceremony was moved to Japan's Budōkan, located across the street from the Yasukuni Shrine.[69]

The LDP had begun to seriously consider constructing a new alternative memorial after Nakasone's visit to Yasukuni in 1985 occasioned such intense protest. Even within the LDP, there was growing discomfort with the controversy caused by the inclusion of class-A war criminals. But the tensions with China and South Korea offered an even more persuasive reason for exploring the idea of constructing a new national memorial. Nakasone's cabinet secretary at that time,

Fujinami Takao, began the conversation in the party on the problem of including the fourteen class-A war criminals but reached no conclusion. Again, under Prime Minister Obuchi Keizō, his chief cabinet secretary, Nonaka Hiromi, continued to explore options for an alternative memorial that might offer a way forward. In a press conference in August 1999, Nonaka suggested removing the class-A war criminals (*bunshi*) and designating Yasukuni as a secular nonprofit entity (*junwaku na tokushuhōjin*).

Early on, Prime Minister Koizumi seemed receptive to the idea of a new memorial, one that foreign dignitaries and others would have no problem visiting. As anticipated, Koizumi's first visit to Yasukuni on August 13, 2001, inflamed public sentiments in China and Korea, and this prompted an effort by his chief cabinet secretary, Fukuda Yasuo, to continue looking for alternatives. In December of that year, Fukuda formed a private study group to explore ways to ameliorate the diplomatic impact of honoring Japan's war dead. On December 14, the Koizumi cabinet's Advisory Group on a Vision for a National Memorial for Condolences and Peace announced:

> As Japan looks ahead to the twenty-first century, and in light of the fact that it will celebrate the fiftieth anniversary of the peace treaty next year, it is a good opportunity to have a wide-ranging debate on the vision of a national facility that allows all Japanese to sincerely memorialize those who have died for their country and where we as a nation can pray for peace. At this time, under the guidance of the chief cabinet secretary, we will convene a group of experts with deep insights and knowledge to advise us on this issue.[70]

The participants included a number of senior academics, such as the former president of the University of the Ryukyus in Okinawa, the head of Japan's leading business association, and other public intellectuals. The advisory group convened ten times and broke out into smaller working groups to complete their work over the summer. The group considered why such a memorial would be necessary and decided that it should be a place where everyone could go without hesitation. It also concluded that a new memorial would not be intended to replace other memorials in Japan, including the Yasukuni Shrine. In March 2003, Fukuda's private advisory group met with Koizumi, and at that meeting, the prime minister seemed ready to support the effort to build a new site.[71]

Outside the cabinet, however, Fukuda's report drew heavy criticism. Deep discord emerged in the LDP over the initiative; the Izokukai, as well, voiced strong opposition. The Izokukai, led by the LDP secretary-general, Koga Makoto, stated that a new site would diminish (*keigai*) the significance of the Yasukuni Shrine and that they were strongly opposed. Moreover, by this time, Koizumi had made his annual Yasukuni Shrine visit on New Year's Day, a traditional time for Japanese to visit Shinto shrines, in an effort to attract as little criticism as possible. Then, as the Upper House election in July approached, the LDP's electoral concerns took precedence. It was not the right moment to alienate the Izokukai.

Despite his effort to keep Yasukuni from becoming a major issue in 2004, Koizumi's January visit did attract criticism and prompted a chorus of calls for seriously considering an alternative site for Japan's war memorial. The LDP's coalition partner, the Kōmeitō, was unhappy, as were some in Koizumi's own party. The head of the Kōmeitō, Kanzaki Takenori, argued publicly on January 6, 2004, for the government to move forward quickly with the construction of an alternative site. Kan Naoto, leader of the opposition DPJ, also called for an alternative memorial. Korean and Chinese officials reacted to Koizumi's visit, and the South Korean ambassador in Tokyo called on the Japanese government to build a site where anyone could go to honor Japan's war dead.[72]

Ultimately, Koizumi himself suggested that even if a new memorial were built, he would still visit Yasukuni. Thus Korea and China still would be offended, so an alternative site would not resolve Japan's diplomatic problem. This effectively ended Fukuda's effort to generate support for an alternative memorial. At a press conference held on January 6, 2004, to announce the government's decision not to pursue a new memorial, Chief Cabinet Secretary Fukuda noted, "It would not be right to make the effort to build a new memorial if there were still people willing to throw stones at it in protest. A new memorial should be built when there is broader public understanding/

acceptance of the idea."[73] Fukuda later looked back at this effort as time well spent. Today the plan remains "on the shelf" in the cabinet office, ready for the time when the Japanese people are ready to move forward.[74]

The Izokukai's Dilemma

Opinions in the Izokukai were complex. Although Koizumi had promised to visit the shrine on August 15, he seemed unable to do so in 2001. Moreover, to many families, the political controversy surrounding these visits seemed misplaced. Rather than resolving the "Yasukuni problem," the turmoil over Koizumi's pledge to visit appeared only to make matters worse. By the following year, a more nuanced perspective emerged from the Izokukai. The new chair, the former secretary-general of the LDP, Koga Makoto, articulated the organization's concerns on August 9, 2002, in an interview with the *Asahi shinbun*. The annual commemoration of the end of the war was only days away. When asked for his view of the proposal to remove the class-A war criminals from the shrine, Koga carefully replied that he had no particular position on the subject, yet he did think it odd that the Yasukuni Shrine would refuse to accommodate a request, should one be made, by a family member to have a relative removed from the shrine.[75]

Koga's articulation of this approach—what came to be referred to as a family's voluntary request for removal from Yasukuni (*jiha-tsuteki bunshi*)—was not the first time that members of the Izokukai expressed concern over the politicization of the treatment of their family members. A similar effort undertaken in 1985 by one of the children of a class-A war criminal revealed the complexity of this issue even for the families of those in the class-A designation. Itagaki Tadashi, a son of the prewar minister of war Itagaki Seishirō, tried to persuade the Izokukai and the Yasukuni Shrine to reverse (*torisage*) the inclusion of the fourteen class-A war criminals in the shrine. At the time, Itagaki was an LDP member in the Upper House, and he initiated a conversation over who had the right to say who should be in Yasukuni. In his interview with the *Asahi,* Koga noted that he would like to talk with Itagaki to learn more about the circumstances at the time so as to better understand how to approach a resolution to this issue.[76] Koga himself was a son of a World War II veteran and, like most family members, had a personal desire to de-politicize the issue. His hope was that Japan's emperor could once again visit Yasukuni and thus pay due respect to his father and those who had died for imperial Japan.[77] Publicizing the differing views held by family members on the inclusion of the class-A war criminals suggested the possibility of some movement in resolving the impasse at Yasukuni.

But Yasukuni Shrine officials opposed Koga's support for family discretion over inclusion in the shrine. Tensions between the shrine and Koga intensified, and he resigned from Yasukuni's board. This break between the leadership of the Izokukai and the management of the Yasukuni Shrine revealed the fraying alliance among those who had long sought greater public acceptance of the shrine's role as a national war memorial. As Japan's media debate over Yasukuni continued, the window of opportunity for Prime Minister Koizumi to visit the shrine was closing. He had made it clear that he intended to step down from his post in September 2006 when the next LDP party leadership election was scheduled. By the summer of 2006, the debate over who would run to replace him was in full swing. His chief cabinet secretary, Abe Shinzō, was widely seen as the front-runner, although his conservative credentials were a source of discomfort for some in the party. Fukuda Yasuo, chief cabinet secretary during the early Koizumi years and a more moderate party leader, also was supported as a contender.[78] In the media, the prospect of Koizumi's visit to Yasukuni on August 15 loomed large. Would he or wouldn't he? Koizumi's promise to step down from the post of prime minister in September meant that he had only one more opportunity to fulfill his promise to visit the Yasukuni Shrine on August 15.

As anticipation mounted, a banner headline on July 20, 2006, on the front page of the *Nikkei shinbun*, Japan's renowned business daily, drew national attention: "The Showa Emperor Displeased Over Inclusion of Class-A War Criminals."[79] For days, the *Nikkei*'s report of a memo taken by the then head of the Imperial Household Agency, Tomita Tomohiko, on his conversation with the Shōwa emperor, consumed the nation's attention. Discovered among the papers held by Tomita's widow, this account of a private conversation with the deceased emperor, who reigned from 1926 until his death in 1989, clarified the reason that he had ended his visits to Yasukuni:[80] He had disapproved of Head Priest Matsudaira's inclusion of the fourteen class-A war criminals in the Yasukuni Shrine. The final visit of the Shōwa emperor and empress to the shrine was in November 1975. Japan's current emperor, the Shōwa emperor's son, has never visited the Yasukuni Shrine.[81]

The *Nikkei*'s story sent shock waves throughout the country, and suspicions about who was behind this very timely revelation led to the creation of an expert group to ascertain whether the memo was real. In fact, the memo only confirmed what many in Tokyo already assumed to be true.[82] The end of the emperor's visits to Yasukuni did suggest that the class-A inclusions offended him. Matsudaira himself had already written about the inclusion, and few wondered about his commitment to proceed. He was not, after all, a religious man. The National Diet library also released its history of the Yasukuni Shrine, although it did not reveal the decision making associated with the inclusion. Ascertaining who was responsible for deciding to include the class-A war criminals was, after all, only one footnote in the story of Yasukuni's past. The broader context of Japan's postwar cleavages over the issue of war responsibility was the more important refrain. The U.S. Occupation authorities and the Allied justices at the Tokyo War Crimes Trials had identified all the protagonists, but the Japanese people had not yet decided whom they thought was responsible and how that assignment of responsibility should inform their postwar lives.

For all the debate and criticism of Koizumi's decision to visit the Yasukuni Shrine on the day the war ended for Japan, the energy dissipated from this issue once he donned his formal tuxedo and paid his respects on August 15, 2006. The anticipation during the years he was in office was palpable, and by the summer of 2006, it was clear that if he were going to fulfill his promise to Japan's war dead and their families, then this was the year it would have to happen. Photographs of Koizumi's visit were on the front page of every Japanese newspaper.[83] Like Nakasone before him, he did not perform the traditional Shinto ritual of bowing and clapping to summon the gods.[84] Yet he walked resolutely and calmly through the crowds and media cameras that lined the shrine's perimeter. The world watched him, as did virtually every Japanese household. Koizumi left office three weeks later, having fulfilled his promise to the families of Japan's war dead to honor their relatives at Yasukuni. His decision did more than that, however. Sixty years or so after the nation's defeat, it opened up a debate over Japan's war responsibility. It was a debate that many Japanese who had not been participants in that war had shied away from for personal or political reasons, but it was a debate long overdue.

The Accelerating Debate in 2006

Koizumi was not unaware of the need to confront the divided public opinion over Yasukuni and the limits imposed by the postwar constitution on the state's sponsorship of the former imperial shrine. Nor was he unaware of the consequences this would have for Japan's diplomacy, particularly its increasingly tumultuous relationship with China.

China's influence in instigating this debate was considerable, and the challenge of balancing Japan's diplomacy with the desire to formally honor Japan's war dead only intensified as China's influence in international politics grew. The less than transparent inclusion of the class-A war criminals certainly did not serve the cause of those who wanted to more openly acknowledge that Yasukuni was the proper place for honoring veterans. Also, the inclusion of these war criminals coincided with Japan's diplomatic opening to China, making for intense feelings on both sides. By the late 1970s when Japan and China began to negotiate the terms of their diplomatic relations, a new push got under way in Japan to resuscitate the reputations of its class-A war criminals. Only afterward, after the Japanese themselves began to reckon with their own ambivalence over who was responsible for the country's war and defeat, were alternatives to the Yasukuni Shrine considered. Although China's complaints started this process, they also complicated the way forward for those who pushed for the construction of a new, secular Japanese war memorial. Again, though, it was foreign pressure that was dictating Japan's choices and limiting the nation's ability to honor those who had died fighting for the emperor.

Koizumi's campaign promise to visit the Yasukuni Shrine on August 15 in his official capacity as Japan's prime minister was the catalyst for serious debate in Japan. Despite the many narratives surrounding the Yasukuni Shrine, none was more riveting than the question of Japan's postwar commitment to an open and transparent government. The 1978 inclusion of class-A war criminals was not simply about war responsibility; it also raised the specter of conspiracy and malign intent, a hint of the atmosphere of the prewar machinations that had led to coups, palace intrigue, and ultimately the downfall of Japan's early efforts at democracy. Koizumi's head-on articulation of his intentions brought back to life all the ghosts of Japan before the war.

At the same time, Koizumi articulated a very contemporary response to China's growing influence on Japan's choices, as well as the growing intolerance of what many Japanese saw as a tactical effort by the Chinese government to turn international opinion against their country. The Chinese government's reaction to Prime Minister Nakasone's visit in 1985, and Nakasone's subsequent avoidance of Yasukuni, cemented the idea that Japan's political leaders were curtailing their commitment to Japan's war dead on account of China's reaction. Thus, for those interests that had long sought to support Yasukuni, Koizumi's public promise was interpreted as a willingness to end China's influence on a domestic decision about Yasukuni. The Koizumi years brought to a head the long-standing Japanese debate over Yasukuni, and while many opponents feared this would revive the shrine in national life, instead the debate revealed that public sensitivity to China, rather than a domestic embrace of the controversial shrine, was driving the conversation.

Between 2001 and 2006, Koizumi made six visits to Yasukuni Shrine. Each year, the media speculated whether this year would be the one when Japan's prime minister would make a state visit on August 15, thereby sanctioning Yasukuni as the official site commemorating the end of World War II.[85] A national debate over Yasukuni emerged from within the LDP and the Izokukai to engage a wide variety of Japanese voices, and as each year passed, the tensions and emotions seemed to rise as Koizumi put off fulfilling his campaign promise to the Izokukai. During these years, the alliance of the LDP, the Izokukai members, and the Yasukuni Shrine leadership was sorely tested. Indeed, long-standing differences within the LDP ranks reemerged, as did differences within the Izokukai itself as to whether or not this effort to get Japan's prime minister to visit was indeed the best strategy for honoring their family members.

Another influence on Japan's domestic debate over Yasukuni was the court cases and judgments issued over the constitutionality question. Legal cases regarding the Yasukuni Shrine had long focused on the process of interring individuals, and many Japanese (and, later, Korean) families argued that they did not want their relatives included on Yasukuni's rosters, owing to religious or other reasons. Once interred, however, the Yasukuni Shrine argued that individual souls could not be removed. District courts across Japan also heard cases brought by families of postwar Self-Defense Force members who objected to their inclusion in Shinto ceremonies at the regional shrines associated with Yasukuni. Once Koizumi began to visit Yasukuni as prime minister, another round of court cases associated with the constitutionality question were initiated. From 2004 until he left office in 2006, at least seven cases were heard regarding the constitutionality of the prime minister's visits. Five were heard at the District Courts (two in Osaka and one each in Fukuoka District Court, Chiba District Court, and Matsuyama District Court); and two appellate courts (Tokyo and Osaka High Courts) heard cases related to the shrine. On September 30, 2005, the Osaka High Court ruled that Prime Minister Koizumi's visits to Yasukuni were indeed a violation of article 20-3 of the Japanese constitution, although it did not rule on any damages for the plaintiffs.

In addition, open feuding between Japan and China on trade issues resulted in even greater tensions. Incidents of violence against Japanese nationals in China escalated, and the strained atmosphere in diplomatic meetings between Japanese and Chinese leaders contributed to the chill in the bilateral relationship. Although Koizumi's decision to visit Yasukuni was not the only reason for this downturn in the Japan-China relationship, it was an easy focal point and one with which the citizens of both countries could take issue.

China and the Yasukuni Shrine

China's feelings about Yasukuni have been an important part of the domestic politics of memorializing Japan's war dead since the 1980s, when the Chinese government began to signal its opposition to the conservatives' effort to legitimize prime ministerial visits. China's response to Prime Minister Nakasone's visit in 1985 struck a resonant chord in Japan, and even Nakasone himself set aside his ambition to set things right for those who had lost their lives in World War II. Yet by the time Koizumi made his public promise to visit the shrine, Japanese sentiment was shifting. Instead of finding common cause in Japan, Chinese statements brought resentment. The Japanese public was tired of the constant charges of a "resurgence of Japanese militarism," and Koizumi's willingness to ignore Chinese criticism earned him support. While it is difficult to pin down exactly what prompted him to make his stand on Yasukuni—instead of on one of the many other issues of dispute between Japan and China—it was the fact that he took a stand that seemed to matter most.

A small group of conservatives saw the growing public discomfort with a rising China as an opportunity to reinvigorate nationalist sentiment. For those with a direct interest in supporting the Yasukuni Shrine, of course, this allowed for a greater public awareness of and interest in the shrine's status. The renovation of the Yūshūkan (the war history museum at Yasukuni) presented a modern and seductive revisionism of Japan's prewar history, a glorification of the Yamato spirit, and a seriously impaired sense of historical determinism that led to Japan's twentieth-century militarism.[86] The flare-up of the neo-nationalist response to China's criticism of Prime Minister Koizumi's stated intention to visit Yasukuni revealed a new populist interpretation of the shrine that had a certain appeal to a younger generation who knew little about the details of Japan's wartime history. For a variety of reasons—far removed from the politics of the Yasukuni Shrine visits—the upsurge in popular support for Koizumi and his political reform agenda boosted the LDP's legislative majority in 2005, creating the political foundations of a conservative push to implement its long-held agenda.

Within the LDP, however, Koizumi's position on the shrine was seen as unusual and somewhat detached from mainstream views. Others in his cabinet, including his chief cabinet secretary, Fukuda, did not share his enthusiasm, nor did Koizumi attempt to claim that his position represented that of his party. The debate that erupted in 2006 in effect revealed that the conservatives had lost their battle to win popular support for their cause. Instead, Koizumi's successors—with the notable exception of Abe Shinzō—stepped back from the Yasukuni issue, arguing for various other solutions to Japan's need for a national war memorial. Later, when Abe, who publicly supported the neonationalist impulses that Yasukuni inspired, began his tenure as prime minister in 2006, he initiated the blueprint of reconciliation that diplomats in Japan and China had earlier prepared in anticipation of Koizumi's resignation. Abe's "don't ask, don't tell" position in his discussions with his counterparts in Beijing accordingly enabled both countries to step back from the high-wire politics of the Yasukuni Shrine visits.

Chinese criticism of Yasukuni also has shaped Japan's own, domestic debate about the Yasukuni Shrine, but perhaps not in the way that many in Beijing would have preferred. Instead, the increasing Japanese public sensitivity to China's criticism of Japan and the Japanese people, as well as the Chinese people's violent behavior toward Japanese citizens during demonstrations, provides a better context for understanding this greater receptivity to revisionist views of Yasukuni. The public mood in Japan has turned against China, especially the Chinese government.

Because Beijing attributed the "freeze" in the Sino-Japanese relationship to Koizumi, when he left office, Sino-Japanese diplomacy returned to defining the terms of reconciliation, although by now the bilateral relationship was increasingly less about history and more about broader currents of change. Trade disputes, particularly over agricultural and resource imports to Japan; maritime tensions; and China's emerging regional ambitions revealed the new competitive dynamics in the Sino-Japanese relationship.

THE FUTURE OF THE YASUKUNI SHRINE

Domestic activism on behalf of Yasukuni no longer belongs solely to those who represent Japan's World War II veterans and their families. The Izokukai's political clout now is less than it once was. Fewer families now want it to advocate on behalf of their economic interests. Indeed, the generation with family members directly related to Japan's imperial veterans is passing away. But the Izokukai is still one of the top-ranking organizational supporters of the LDP, and it can mobilize its membership on behalf of those legislators that it thinks will work for its cause. A decade or more ago, the Izokukai had 137,000 LDP party members, coming in seventh in the overall ranking of organizations making up the party membership.[87] But newer interest groups, such as postal workers, doctors, and nurses, are overshadowing veterans' organizations with almost double the number of party members that the venerable Izokukai has.[88]

The status attached to those convicted of war crimes remains an integral part of the debate over Yasukuni. The fate of incarcerated war criminals was legally resolved in the Japanese Diet in the years immediately after Japan regained its independence. In accordance with article 11 of the San Francisco Peace Treaty, the Japanese government had to consult with the governments that imposed the sentences.[89] The United States, in particular, was instrumental in approving the establishment of a clemency and parole board for Japanese war criminals.[90] From 1952 through the early 1960s, this board oversaw the process of determining parole, release, and pardon for those who remained in custody.[91] Yet the question of who ought to be assigned responsibility for the war itself proved more difficult to address, and as the debate over Koizumi's visit to Yasukuni demonstrated, the country remained divided over who was to blame, even after Koizumi left office.

On the surface, it seems that interest in debating the place of Yasukuni in Japan's postwar politics is backed by a resurgence of popular support for the conservative revisionist agenda, but opinion polls continue to track deep divisions in the Japanese public. Indeed, Koizumi himself also seemed to hesitate, as his annual visits avoided the formal sanctioning of a prime minister's visit on August 15. His views of Yasukuni did, however, renew interest in the question of Japan's war responsibility. Across Japanese society, there has been a growing willingness to openly discuss what has long been too sensitive a topic for most Japanese and to debate Koizumi's decision in the context of evolving ideas of Japan's contemporary politics. Competing visions of Japan's wartime history are thus being created that seek to inform and engage public opinion. Editorialists on both the conservative and the progressive ends of Japan's political spectrum have discussed their differing views of the country's war responsibility.[92]

For example, Watanabe Tsuneo, editor of the conservative *Yomiuri shinbun*, Japan's most widely circulating newspaper, wrote a series of articles asking the long postponed question of who was responsible for Japan's disastrous war.[93]

The domestic political forces that had motivated the push toward recognition of the Yasukuni Shrine as Japan's preeminent war memorial have clearly lost their momentum. The Izokukai members are growing older and dying, and their children's desire is not to encourage nationalism. In LDP leadership races after Koizumi, the Izokukai backed the person most likely to resolve the tensions over Yasukuni rather than the person who promised to visit. Even Abe Shinzō, perhaps the most ideologically driven conservative leader, set aside his personal desire to visit the shrine as he made rapprochement with China his top diplomatic priority in 2006. But just a year later, 2007, the Izokukai backed Fukuda in the leadership race to replace Abe, despite Fukuda's role in advocating a new alternative memorial. His opponent, Asō Tarō, put forward his idea of making Yasukuni a state memorial but eradicating its status as a religious shrine. Likewise, in the 2008 LDP leadership race to succeed Fukuda, two of the next-generation LDP leaders—Ishiba Shigeru and Ishihara Nobuteru—openly stated they would not visit Yasukuni, and only one, Koike Yuriko, made Yasukuni Shrine visits a part of her platform. Fewer and fewer cabinet members visited Yasukuni in the years following the Koizumi cabinet. Only one cabinet member from Prime Minister Abe's 2006 cabinet visited, despite Abe's well-known sympathies with Yasukuni's cause. Likewise, few cabinet members visited the shrine under the next two LDP prime ministers: three Fukuda cabinet ministers visited on August 15, 2008, and one Asō cabinet minister visited on August 15, 2009.

The arrival of a new ruling party in the fall of 2009 seemed to signal an end to the high-stakes political activism on behalf of the Yasukuni Shrine. The DPJ as a party did not support the idea of state visits to Yasukuni. No cabinet ministers in the first two DPJ cabinets visited the shrine to commemorate the end of the war on August 15, although three parliamentary secretaries did.[94] The DPJ's third prime minister, Noda Yoshihiko, generated concern in China and South Korea, however, because of his role in an opposition critique of Koizumi.

In October 2005, Noda filed in the legislature an official question for Koizumi, then the prime minister, on his ambivalent statement on the class-A war criminals. He was asked to clarify the Japanese government's position that these individuals were not to be punished under Japanese law.[95] Once he became prime minister, Noda's defense of the postwar legal position of those indicted by the Far Eastern War Tribunals raised speculation that he was sympathetic to Yasukuni, and indeed when Noda was finance minister in the Kan cabinet, he refused to make a statement on visits to the shrine. As prime minister, however, he was clear. In a press conference on September 2, 2011, only a few days after his election, he reiterated the DPJ's position on official state visits to the shrine and said he would include international politics in his consideration of this issue. Noda also made it clear that his 2005 question on class-A war criminals was made in his capacity as an individual politician and that he sought clarification of the government's legal stance.[96]

The changing politics of Yasukuni are due largely to generational change. Yasukuni's place in the postwar debate over Japan's national memory has been diminishing in large part because those who wanted most for their loved ones to be commemorated by Japan's postwar leaders are passing away. Today it is their children and grandchildren who are carrying on the campaign to honor their family members at Yasukuni. Although some conservatives continue to use Yasukuni to their electoral advantage, few openly advocate honoring the class-A war criminals who were surreptitiously enshrined in the late 1970s. Even the Izokukai, the most ardent constituency supporting the Yasukuni Shrine, is not consistent on idea of prime ministerial visits.

Yasukuni thus remains a lightning rod for those who want to challenge foreign criticism of Japan's past. Within Japan's conservative party, many younger politicians use their visits to Yasukuni to burnish their conservative credentials, and it remains a rallying point for those who resent Chinese and South Korean criticism of Japan and its interpretation of its twentieth-century history. Indeed, in his return to power in late 2012, Abe Shinzō raised the possibility of yet another round of Yasukuni nationalism. When in response to Deputy Prime Minister Asō Tarō's visit to the shrine in April 2013, the South Korean foreign minister, Yun Byun-se, canceled his visit to

Tokyo, 168 LDP Diet members marched to the Yasukuni Shrine, the largest group of sitting legislators ever to visit there.[97] Abe's own visit in December 2013 invited ever greater criticism from Beijing and Seoul, but it also became a bone of contention with Washington. As Japan's regional relations have deteriorated, the costs of Yasukuni nationalism have risen. Geostrategic change has turned revisionist sentiment in Japan into a strategic risk. Both inside and outside Japan, the Yasukuni Shrine is thus seen not only as a memorial to Japan's imperial veterans but also as a symbol of defiance by Japan's conservative politicians.

4

A SHARED MARITIME BOUNDARY

On August 1, 2013, a stern-faced Yamamoto Taku, head of the Liberal Democratic Party's Resources and Energy Strategy Study Group, visited the prime minister's office. For nearly a month, reports that China was building a new drilling site for gas in the East China Sea had plagued policymakers. Yamamoto urged Prime Minister Abe Shinzō to demand that Beijing dismantle this new site and refuse to allow China to build anywhere near the Japan-China median line.[1] Chief Cabinet Secretary Suga Yoshihide also publicly decried Beijing's "unilateral" actions as violating a bilateral understanding reached five years earlier.[2] In addition, the Japanese government lodged repeated formal protests, but with diplomatic relations between Tokyo and Beijing frayed yet again over their territorial dispute, this new evidence that China was moving ahead with its own plans for drilling in the East China Sea only exacerbated the deep frustration in Tokyo over its inability to reach a compromise on the shared maritime boundary.

China's drilling for gas in the area near the median line had been a source of frustration in Japan for many years. In 2005, China had already begun drilling on the gas field that straddles the median line, highlighting the cost of their differences over how to define their overlapping exclusive economic zones (EEZs). Chinese officials refused to accept Japan's suggested median line. Although Beijing did agree in 2008 to jointly develop energy resources in the East China Sea, it did not follow through with the implementation treaty. In response to this latest round of Japanese protest again Chinese drilling, Beijing denied that there had been any mutually agreed-on ground rules for exploiting seabed resources in and around that area, suggesting that Japan and China remained far apart in defining their shared interests in the East China Sea. To make matters worse, Reuters reported on July 17, 2013, that the China National Offshore Oil Corporation (CNOOC), Beijing's state oil company, had plans for seven new gas fields, two of which were on or near the median line.[3] When questioned by a *Nikkei shinbun* journalist at a press conference on August 20 in Hong Kong, a senior CNOOC official refused to confirm that this was indeed his company's plan.[4] Today, the potential for energy resources in the East China Sea dominates the headlines over the maritime boundary dispute between Japan and China.

In the past, it was fishermen who urged the Japanese government to come to the bargaining table with China. Japanese and Korean trawlers sought tuna and other deepwater fish in the northern waters, while Taiwanese and Japanese fishermen competed in the south. Chinese fishermen initially stayed closer to shore, but as their boats got bigger and the demand for fish increased, China's fishing trawlers spread farther out into the East China Sea and closer to the Japanese, Taiwanese, and Korean shores. Incidents involving fishing boats of all nations have resulted in government protests and carefully renegotiated fisheries agreements.

Future access to resources is paramount. Japan has staked an expansive claim to its EEZ, and China has invested heavily in reaping the East China Sea's marine and submarine resources. Moreover, Japanese and Chinese mariners share these waters with Korean and Taiwanese ships, and all four nations lay claim to the prospective oil and gas fields thought to be in the seabed below. Policing the East China Sea are the coast guards, fisheries, and seabed research agencies as well as the navies of all four nations. Whether or not the potential resource benefits of the East China Sea will be realized, the enhancement of national maritime forces in this sea makes the contest over legitimate boundaries increasingly fraught.

Japan's maritime boundaries have been complicated by a long-standing island dispute, with China's claim to an EEZ based on its continental shelf changing the importance of the Senkaku Islands in the broader bilateral contest over the East China Sea. The boundary claim and the territorial dispute have now become linked. As a consequence, the economic interests that have been affected by the inability of Tokyo and Beijing to negotiate a compromise on the resources of the East China Sea have now been joined by political activists organized around defending Japanese sovereignty over the islands.

THE CONTROVERSY: CHINA'S MARITIME CLAIMS AND JAPAN'S EEZ

Japan had negotiated its interests in the East China Sea bilaterally with its maritime neighbors until the UN Convention on the Law of the Sea (UNCLOS) changed the terms of maritime boundaries in 1996.[5] Since then, Tokyo and Beijing have taken very different positions on their interpretation of their EEZs' boundaries. Given that only 360 nautical miles across the East China Sea separate Japan and China, neither can claim as their exclusive economic zone the full 200-nautical-mile area extending from their coastlines. Rather, their maritime boundaries must be negotiated according to the UNCLOS. Japan has proposed a median line dividing the East China Sea roughly in half, which China has refused to accept. Instead, it claims that its territorial waters extend to the edge of the continental shelf and that therefore its EEZ begins where Japan's territorial waters end.

Further complicating the differences between Japan and China over their maritime boundaries is the territorial dispute that dates back to the early 1970s. Japan claims full sovereignty over the Senkaku Islands, a claim that China and Taiwan contested in 1971. In the negotiations leading up to the 1978 Treaty of Peace and Friendship, both governments finally had to agree to disagree. At the time, during a visit to Japan, Deng Xiaoping announced his now well-known formula for managing their differences: "We call it Tiaoyu Island, but you call it by another name. It is true that the two sides maintain different views on this question. It doesn't matter if this question is shelved for some time, say, ten years. Our generation is not wise enough to find common language on this question. Our next generation will certainly be wiser. They will surely find a solution acceptable to all."[6] It was the broader relationship with

Japan that Deng and his contemporaries were interested in, and economic relations were at the top of his agenda. Japanese leaders, too, for the sake of the greater benefits of the relationship with China, sought to minimize the friction over the island dispute and keep at bay those in Japan who wanted to highlight it. Although they concluded a fisheries treaty in 1975, the two governments set aside the matter of the disputed island waters. Energy development plans, already deemed technically difficult because of the deep waters near the islands, also were set aside in the interest of peaceful diplomatic relations.

When a new international maritime regime came into force in the late 1990s, however, the bilateral management of the maritime boundary between Japan and China in the East China Sea drew attention to the sovereignty dispute and complicated their discussions on how to share the East China Sea.[7] The UNCLOS's establishment of EEZs and the resource rights of coastal states introduced a new dimension to the bilateral discussion over how their common maritime boundaries were to be shared (figure 4.1). China claimed the rights to waters above its continental shelf (figure 4.2), but Japan argued for the negotiated median line that the UNCLOS recommended. Taiwan also has significant interests at stake, although it has been unable to ratify the UNCLOS because the United Nations does not recognize it as an independent state.

Beginning in the late 1990s, Japan and China increased their research and undersea survey activities in order to build a case for their claims. China's continental shelf approach meant that it was sending research ships closer to Japanese territorial waters, and other maritime interests followed these boundaries as well, including fishing boats and, increasingly, Chinese naval vessels.

Japan's research and survey activities were conducted across a variety of national government bureaucracies. The Ministry of Education, Culture, Sports, Science, and Technology (MEXT), as well as the Ministry of Economic, Trade, and Industry (METI), expanded their marine research and seafloor surveys, respectively, in the wake of the UNCLOS.[8] Japan's Ministry of Agriculture, Forestry, and Fisheries (MAFF) also conducted research on fisheries stocks in the waters surrounding Japan, including the East China Sea.[9] Japan upgraded its maritime research and survey capabilities, and all agencies with maritime interests were funded to improve and expand their fleets (table 4.1).

TABLE 4.1 Japan's Ocean Protection and Research Vessels

Ministry/Organization	Ship Purpose	Number
Japan Agency for Marine-Earth Science and Technology (MEXT)	Research	4
	Manned research (submersible)	1
	Oceanographic research	1
	Deep-sea drilling	2
	Support	1
Total		**9**
Japan Oil, Gas, and Metals National Corporation (METI)	Three-dimensional seismic survey	1
	Seafloor resource research	1
Total		**2**
Fisheries Agency (MAFF)	Fishing survey	2
	Fishing management	6
Total		**8**
Fisheries Research Agency	Research	8
Total		**8**
Ministry of the Environment	Cleaning	2
	Cleaning and oil collection	8
	Research, observation, and cleaning	2
Total		**12**
Japan Meteorological Agency (MLIT)	Research	8
Total		**8**

Sources: "Research Vessels," Japan Agency for Marine-Earth Science and Technology (JAMSTEC), Ministry of Education, Culture, Sports, Science, and Technology (MEXT), http://www.jamstec.go.jp/e/about/equipment/ships/index.html; "Annual Report 2012," Japan Oil, Gas, and Metals National Corporation (JOGMEC), Ministry of Education, Trade, and Industry (METI), 2012, http://www.jogmec.go.jp /content/300075892.pdf; "Suisanchou shozoku senpaku" [Ships Belonging to the Fisheries Agency], Fisheries Agency, Ministry of Agriculture, Forestry, and Fisheries (MAFF), http://www.jfa.maff.go.jp/j/koho/senpaku.html; "Fisheries Research Vessels," Fisheries Research Agency, http://www.fra.affrc.go.jp/english/vessels. html; "Mizu, dojō, jiban, kaiyō kankyō no hozen" [Environmental Preservation of Water, Soil, Ground, and Ocean], Ministry of the Environment, http://www.env. go.jp/water/; and "Oceanographic and Marine Meteorological Observations by Research Vessels," Japan Meteorological Agency, Ministry of Land, Infrastructure, Transport, and Tourism (MLIT), 2013, http://www.data.kishou.go.jp/kaiyou /db/vessel_obs/data-report/html/ship/ship_e.php. All sites were last accessed on October 2, 2013.

FIGURE 4.1 Maritime claims in the East China Sea. (Geographic data from NGA Pentagon Geospatial Analysis, July 2011. Original artwork courtesy of Martin Hinze)

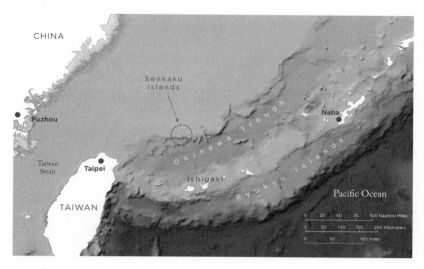

FIGURE 4.2 Topographical map of the East China Sea. (Topographical data from Google Earth. Original artwork courtesy of Martin Hinze)

The Senkaku/Diaoyu Islands

The increasing number of China's maritime activities brought to the fore its territorial dispute with Japan. Before the UNCLOS, the two countries' negotiations over fisheries and energy resource development in the East China Sea had dealt with the dispute by simply excluding the area near the Senkaku Islands (south of 27°N), so as to avoid the unresolved claims that each had on these islands. Interests in the areas north of 27°N could be deliberated, and resolutions to disputes and resource claims could be worked out.

But for Japan, the island dispute remained contentious. Even in the final negotiations over the 1978 treaty, there was deep disagreement in the Liberal Democratic Party (LDP) on the terms of peace with China, and diplomats in the Japanese Ministry of Foreign Affairs were hard-pressed to de-link this sovereignty dispute from the overall normalization negotiations.[10] To make matters worse, in May 1978, a flotilla of Chinese fishing vessels appeared near the Senkaku Islands, feeding concerns about Beijing's intentions in an already sensitive debate in the ruling party over bilateral talks.[11] Negotiations in

Beijing between Deng Xiaoping and the Japanese foreign minister, Sonoda Sunao, attempted to resolve the territorial issue, but they had little success. Japan's ambassador to China, Satō Shōji, persuaded his counterparts in the Chinese Ministry of Foreign Affairs to agree that this problem would be handled separately from the broader interests and spirit of the Japan-China joint communiqué, ultimately leading to Deng Xiaoping's famous October 1978 statement about leaving this problem to future generations.[12] Even though Japanese leaders did not use Deng Xiaoping's idea of placing this on the shelf for the time being, they did not publicly oppose it.

At the time, Japan's diplomacy was not guided solely by the effort to normalize relations with China. Japan's diplomatic opening to China coincided with the reversion of Okinawa to Japan, thus linking the negotiations over contested sovereignty claims and the terms of the postwar peace between Japan and China to the U.S.-Japan alliance. On May 15, 1972, the United States relinquished its control over Okinawa, and four months later, Tokyo and Beijing issued their historic joint communiqué announcing their desire to normalize diplomatic relations. No mention was made in the communiqué about the territorial dispute. Rather, its focus was on Japan's recognition of the People's Republic of China (PRC) as the country's only legal government.[13] Not for another six years were the terms of diplomatic normalization agreed on and a peace treaty concluded.

The restoration of Japanese sovereignty over its southwestern islands required rebuilding ties between the national and local governments. Article 3 of the San Francisco Peace Treaty had allowed the United States to continue its administration of this Japanese territory until Washington and Tokyo signed the reversion treaty in 1971. Several years earlier, though, local Okinawa government officials had begun planning for this transfer of authority, conducting surveys in preparation to reclaim administrative jurisdiction over their islands. On May 10, 1969, Ishigaki City, the municipality that included the Senkaku Islands, conducted a land survey (*hyōshiki*) of the five islands as its administrative district. In August the following year, the Ryukyu government (still under U.S. administration) included the Senkaku Islands in its territorial map.

A month later, a ship attached to the Taiwan Marine Training Center put up a Taiwanese national flag on the Senkakus and claimed them as Taiwan's territory. The Ryukyu government consulted with both the U.S. and Japanese governments and, with their approval, removed the flag. Then the following spring, on April 20, 1971, Taiwan officially claimed the Senkakus as its territory, and on December 30, 1971, China's Foreign Affairs Department followed suit. This was the first time that Beijing had officially claimed these islands, but just as important to the territorial claim was that the Chinese government was protesting the United States' role in a territorial dispute between China and Japan.[14]

China's claim quickly brought a response from the Japanese government. On March 8, 1972, Japan's Ministry of Foreign Affairs issued the following statement regarding China's claim: first, the Japanese government confirmed that in 1895 (the twenty-eighth year of Meiji), the Senkaku Islands were included in Japanese territory. At the time, these islands were uninhabited and not under the control of imperial China. Second, Japan was ceded Taiwan and the Pescadores Islands in the Treaty of Shimonoseki following the Sino-Japanese War, but the Senkakus were not included at that time as part of either. Third, as a result, the Senkakus were not included in the territory that Japan was forced to give up under the terms of the San Francisco Peace Treaty at the end of World War II. Rather, they were included in the territory identified as Japanese sovereign territory and returned to Japanese sovereignty in the Okinawa Reversion Agreement. Fourth, because China does not include the Senkakus as part of Taiwan, because to date China has not protested the inclusion of the Senkakus as part of the U.S. administrative territory, and because Chinese maps clearly put the Senkakus in Japanese territory means that these recent Chinese claims have no basis in international law.[15]

These conflicting claims to sovereignty over the Senkaku Islands were amplified by the UNCLOS negotiations. Before the UNCLOS, maritime boundaries were defined as being within twelve nautical miles of a nation's coastline.[16] With the UNCLOS's extension of EEZ claims, however, the sovereignty claims of the Senkakus took on new significance. Although the Senkakus themselves are uninhabited, their location about 99.4 miles (160 km) southwest of Naha,

Okinawa, in the waters off the continental shelf, made them valuable markers for all three nations trying to claim their sovereign rights in the East China Sea.

Feelings about the Senkakus ran high both inside and outside the Japanese government, with the call for a more assertive demonstration of Japanese sovereignty coming most strongly from within the LDP itself. Activists who saw the territorial dispute as a powerful focal point for nationalist activism periodically challenged the terms of this compromise. Likewise, although government leaders in both Tokyo and Beijing tried to keep the activists quiet, by the 1990s, Japanese, Taiwanese, and Chinese citizens—fishermen, nationalists, and even self-proclaimed "refugees" who sought asylum from the PRC— began to challenge their approach to managing the dispute.

The Increase in China's Maritime Activities

After ratifying the UNCLOS, China's interest in the maritime region around Japan grew. The convention also changed Japan's thinking about its maritime territory, although it took years for the country to respond to the UNCLOS's determination of EEZ boundaries and to consider what this new international maritime regime meant for Japanese maritime policy. Until a 4,420-ton Yanbing-class Chinese ship was observed circling Japan in May 2000, there seemed to be little official Japanese government attention paid to China's maritime presence in Japan's new EEZ waters.

Japanese media reports at the time raised concerns about Chinese intentions.[17] At the Japan-China foreign ministers' meeting in August 2000, the two countries agreed to create a prior-notification framework for these sorts of maritime activities, and Japan's ambassador to China, Tanino Sakutarō, met with Vice-Minister of Foreign Affairs Yang Wenchang to ask that China halt its surveillance activities in Japan's EEZ.[18] A few days later, Japan's vice–foreign minister, Kawashima Yutaka, formally complained to China's ambassador to Japan, Chen Jian, about the research activities of another Chinese ship, and the two governments hastened their discussion of a prior-notification framework. In October, Prime Minister Mori Yoshirō and Premier Zhu Rongji agreed to accelerate these talks so as to complete them by the end of the Japanese fiscal year (March 2001), before the Japanese yen loan to China (¥20 billion) was to be disbursed. On February 13, 2001, the Japanese and Chinese governments agreed to notify each other two months in advance regarding maritime activities in "adjacent seas" and to provide information on the purpose, research details, site, and time frame for research.[19]

Japanese waters continued to be a popular destination for Taiwanese and Chinese fishermen, with a new fisheries treaty managing their interactions. The extension of EEZ boundaries after the UNCLOS was ratified did change the fishermen's behavior. For example, the number of Chinese fishing boats observed in Japan's EEZ jumped from 6,099 in 1998 to 16,355 in 2004 (table 4.2), but the number of Chinese fishing boats observed in Japan's territorial waters declined from 1,893 in 1998 to 390 in 2004. Thus, the Japanese Coast Guard (JCG) had cause to inspect fewer vessels, and arrests of Chinese fishermen fell as well.

TABLE 4.2 Chinese Fishing Vessels in Japanese Waters

Year	Observed (Territorial)	Observed (EEZ)	Inspections (Territorial)	Inspections (EEZ)	Arrests (Territorial)	Arrests (EEZ)
1998	1,893	6,099	62	0	3	0
1999	1,951	17,638	34	2	3	0
2000	561	9,981	50	16	11	3
2001	249	10,460	2	7	0	6
2002	346	7,621	53	3	0	0
2003	274	23,604	72	0	0	0
2004	390	16,355	19	2	0	0
2005					0	0
2006					0	0
2007					1	0
2008					0	1
2009					0	1
2010					1	0
2011					3	3
2012					0	1
2013					0	3

Source: Japan Coast Guard, "Annual Reports, 1999–2013," http://www.kaiho.mlit.go.jp/info/books/.

After a new Japan-China fisheries agreement went into effect in 2000, the JCG inspected sixty-six Chinese fishermen in Japan's EEZ and territorial waters and made fourteen territorial arrests that year. But this turned out to be an exceptionally high rate of interaction between the JCG and Chinese fishermen. After 2000, arrests of Chinese fishermen were rare, with only one in Japan's territorial waters in 2007 and one in 2008 and 2009 in its EEZ. More arrests came after the 2010 fishing trawler incident, however. JCG records show that from 2003 to 2013, few Chinese ships were detained. In fact, Korean and Taiwanese ships were detained more often than Chinese vessels (table 4.3). Similarly, the Japan Fisheries Agency reported that it had detained far fewer Chinese than South Korean ships (table 4.4). In

TABLE 4.3 Foreign Fishing Vessels Taken into Custody by the Japan Coast Guard

Country	Waters	2003	2004	2005	2006	2007	2008	2009	2010	2011	2012	2013	Total
Korea	Territorial	2	0	3	0	3	0	0	0	0	0	0	8
	EEZ	3	5	5	2	1	0	0	0	2	5	3	26
	Total	5	5	8	2	4	0	0	0	2	5	3	34
China	Territorial	0	0	0	0	1	0	0	1	3	0	0	5
	EEZ	0	0	0	0	0	1	1	0	3	1	3	9
	Total	0	0	0	0	1	1	1	1	6	1	3	14
Russia	Territorial	0	1	0	1	0	0	0	0	0	0	0	2
	EEZ	0	0	0	0	0	0	0	0	0	0	0	0
	Total	0	1	0	1	0	0	0	0	0	0	0	2
Taiwan	Territorial	2	1	0	0	0	0	1	1	0	0	2	7
	EEZ	0	0	2	2	0	1	0	1	1	1	1	9
	Total	2	1	2	2	0	1	1	2	1	1	3	16
Other	Territorial	0	2	0	1	0	0	0	0	0	0	0	3
	EEZ	0	0	1	0	0	0	0	0	2	0	2	5
	Total	0	2	1	1	0	0	0	0	2	0	2	8
All	Territorial	4	4	3	2	4	0	1	2	3	0	2	25
	EEZ	3	5	8	4	1	2	1	1	8	7	9	49
	Total	7	9	11	6	5	2	2	3	11	7	11	74

Source: Japan Coast Guard, "Annual Reports, 2004–2014," http://www.kaiho.mlit.go.jp/info/books/.

TABLE 4.4 Foreign Fishing Vessels Seized by Japan Fisheries Agency

Country	2001	2002	2003	2004	2005	2006	2007	2008	2009	2010	2011	2012	2013	Total
Korea	17	25	23	14	9	8	11	18	12	13	11	5	9	175
China	3	12	12	5	2	1	1	2	3	1	0	2	6	50
Russia	0	1	0	2	0	0	0	0	0	0	0	0	0	3
Taiwan	1	0	0	7	5	1	1	0	2	5	1	4	4	31
Other	0	0	0	1	0	0	0	0	0	0	0	0	0	1
All	21	38	35	29	16	10	13	20	17	19	12	11	19	260

Note: Seizures allude to confiscation of vessels or arrest of ship captain or ship employees.
Source: Japan Fisheries Agency, Ministry of Agriculture, Forestry, and Fisheries, http://www.jfa.maff.go.jp.

all, 175 South Korean fishing vessels were detained from 2001 to 2013, compared with 50 Chinese fishing vessels.

The more serious problem for Japan was the growing number of incidents of Chinese maritime research in Japan's EEZ (table 4.5). China's increasing survey and research interest in and around Japanese waters was widely reported in the media. Pressure on the Japanese government to take a more assertive stance toward Chinese activities intensified when, on October 19, 2003, a Chinese ship was found echo-sounding well within Japan's territorial waters around the Tokara Islands near Kagoshima.[20] Beijing had ignored the newly negotiated 2001 agreement to provide two months' notification of maritime activity in adjacent seas, which led to even stronger advocacy in Tokyo for a more comprehensive policy response to Chinese maritime activities.

Equally troubling was the Chinese drilling activity in the East China Sea's natural gas fields. Although the East China Sea is home to significant, if unexploited, energy resources, technology and cost have prohibited their full development. International oil companies backed by national government funds have begun exploration, but because of the deep waters under the continental shelf, the commercial rewards have been limited. In 2003, the Japanese government declared that a "median line" based on equal distances from the Japanese and Chinese coastlines could serve as an appropriate dividing

TABLE 4.5 Chinese Research Ships in the East China Sea

Year	Ships Observed Entering Japan's EEZ	Ships Receiving Special Action[a]
1997	4	4
1998	16	14
1999	33	30
2000	24	20
2001[b]	13	5
2002[c]	12	4
2003	11	9
2004	14	15
2005	2	0
2006	19	4
2007	11	1
2008	8	2
2009	11	1
2010	22	3
2011	19	8
2012	[d]	5

[a]The phrase "irregular action" (*tokui na kōdō*) is used by the Japan Coast Guard (JCG) to include actions conducted without prior notification or different from those described in prior notification, or ships that had repeatedly entered Japan's waters.

[b]In 2001, Japan and China agreed to notify each other in advance of sending ships for scientific research near their respective coastal waters. Both countries began using this agreement in February of that year.

[c]Following the agreement, these numbers do not include the total number of ships that entered Japan's EEZ but instead represent cases in which either advance warning was not given or the information provided differed from the route the ship took. These numbers include cases in which the JCG dispatched patrol ships and/or aircraft to compel the ships to turn around as well as cases in which Japan protested the intrusion through diplomatic routes.

[d]The total number of Chinese research ships observed entering Japan's EEZ is not included in the JCG's "Annual Report," but the number of Chinese ships receiving special action (5) is included. Instead, the 2013 edition included a special feature regarding the number of times that Chinese ships were observed entering Japan's EEZ near the Senkakus from September 2012 to March 2013, a total of 405 times, including 113 times in which ships entered Japan's territorial waters. The 2014 edition did not list either number, but expanded the special feature on Chinese ships entering Japan's EEZ near the Senkakus. Therefore, 2013 numbers are not included in this table.

Source: Japan Coast Guard, "Annual Reports, 1998–2013," http://www.kaiho.mlit.go.jp/info/books/.

line for the East China Sea. China, however, took a different tack, arguing instead that its EEZ was based on the extension of the continental
shelf. According to Beijing, that extension ended somewhere near the
Okinawa Trough, a deep undersea trench 868 miles (1,398 km) long,
located on the southeastern edge of the Ryukyu Island chain. Japan's
declaration of a median line, however, seemed to accelerate China's
efforts to exploit the undersea gas fields nearby, which extended into
Japan's EEZ claims, straddling the median line on both sides. Not long
after Japan made public its median line claim, drilling activities on the
Chinese side of this line began (figure 4.3).

After reports of Chinese drilling at the Shirakaba/Chunxiao gas
field, Japan's minister for economy, trade, and industry (METI),
Nakagawa Shōichi, took steps in June 2004 to counter China's activities. This field is only 2.5 miles (4 km) on the Chinese side of the
median line, and thus a Chinese effort to develop the gas would,
in Nakagawa's words, "siphon off, like a straw," the gas resources in
the seabed on Japan's side of the line.[21] Bilateral talks between the
Japanese and Chinese governments in October that year yielded
no information from Beijing about China's activities there, and
the Chinese government denied any knowledge of reports that a
Chinese company had set up concessions in Japanese waters. Nakagawa was an ardent critic of Chinese behavior in the East China
Sea and argued for a concerted and active Japanese response. In his
position as the minister of METI, he began to take steps for Japan's
exploration of the Shirakaba/Chunxiao gas field, announcing that
if China continued to exploit these resources without coming to an
agreement with Japan, Japan would proceed as well. Nakagawa then
issued permits for drilling and concessionary rights to Japanese
petroleum corporations.[22]

Commercial profits from the Shirakaba/Chunxiao gas field were
not an adequate incentive, however. Moreover, the oil companies'
concerns about a possible Chinese military response to drilling
introduced even more caution. On July 14, 2005, Teikoku sekkyu
announced in a press release that although it had secured drilling
rights, the safety of its drilling team was a major concern, and thus it
would be consulting carefully with the Japanese government before
beginning to drill the wells.[23] Japan's petroleum companies (Japan

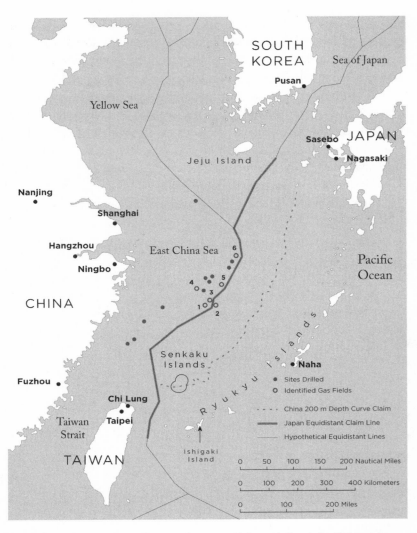

FIGURE 4.3 Gas fields in the East China Sea: (*1*) (Japan) Shirakaba /(China) Chunxiao; (*2*) Kusunaki / Duanqiao; (*3*) Kashi / Tianwaitian; (*4*) Pinghu; (*5*) Kikyo / Canxue; (*6*) Asunaro / Lungjing). (Geographic data from NGA Pentagon Geospatial Analysis, July 2011. Original artwork courtesy of Martin Hinze)

Petroleum, Teikoku Oil, Fuyu Petroleum Development Corporation, and Uruma Resources Exploration Corporation) estimated the natural gas reserves there as being the equivalent of 180 million barrels, a small find compared with other development projects, such as the two fields at Sakhalin, which were estimated at 9.52 billion barrels.[24] Yet even for Japan's oil and gas industry, the idea that China would simply take what it wanted from the seabed just off Japan's coastline was hard to stomach. Accordingly, Japan began to adjust its strategic approach to maritime policy. The exploitation of resources was one area in which both sides stated they had shared interests. Finding a way to negotiate those interests was thus the means to avoid direct confrontation between Japanese and Chinese citizens and commercial interests in the East China Sea.

The Policy Challenge

In the early decades of their postwar relationship, Tokyo and Beijing expended considerable diplomatic energy ensuring that their differences over maritime domains and their different understanding of legitimate activities there would not interfere. The first issue that confounded diplomats was the territorial dispute over the Senkaku/Diaoyu Islands. While negotiating the treaty, the islands remained an issue on which neither side was willing to compromise. At the time, Chinese and Japanese political leaders eventually concluded that the only way forward was to set it aside, resulting in the countries' literally working around the waters surrounding these islands. These unregulated waters, therefore, continued to hold the prospect of confrontation, and this solution worked only as long as both governments agreed to downplay the dispute.

The undersea topography and the technical challenges of drilling have thus far limited China's exploration in the East China Sea, but Korean and Japanese companies already have surveyed and tested some of the seabed under their territorial waters. More recently, the Japanese and Chinese governments have discussed joint development in parts of the East China Sea yet to be explored. But this vision has thus far failed to come to fruition and instead has become a source of

bickering and aggravation as China has begun unilaterally developing gas fields in one of the areas identified for cooperation.

The second issue is that the Japanese government has had to
reconsider its maritime concerns within the framework of the newly
established international law governing maritime claims. From the
mid-1990s onward, the UNCLOS offered a new venue for articulat-
ing, advocating, and defending Japan's approach to establishing a
maritime boundary with China across the East China Sea. Yet it also
created a way for Beijing to expand its claim using the continental
shelf as its basis for extending its EEZ waters right up to Japan's territorial waters off Okinawa, and from the late 1990s onward, China has
been mapping and traversing the waters around Japan.

Once both states ratified the UNCLOS in 1996, surveys of the seabed topography and other scientific assessment intensified.[25] More
and more research vessels were populating the East China Sea. In
addition, China started constructing oil and gas fields just west of
the median line stipulated by Japan, which Japan argued could be in
violation of the UNCLOS. With no data provided by Beijing to clarify
its activities and intentions, the Japanese began to conduct their own
exploratory efforts on the gas fields east of the median line. According
to the Ministry of Foreign Affairs, this exploration continued until
June 2005,[26] prompting both governments to initiate consultations on
the East China Sea. Here again, the two countries disagreed on their
maritime boundaries, with China suggesting that any joint effort to
develop resources focus on the region between Japan's median line
and the Okinawa Trough, where, Beijing claimed, the continental
shelf ended.

Repeated discussions proved unproductive, and Japan argued that
China should halt any development activities pursuant to article 74:3
of the UNCLOS. This article stipulates that parties to a boundary dispute not act in a way that would "jeopardize or hamper the reaching
of a final agreement" on the dispute. But without cooperation from
China, Japan had to build its case for review at the UN Commission on the Limits of the Continental Shelf (CLCS). In 2008, Japan
and China seemed to have finally reached consensus on their joint
development agreement, but its implementation proved elusive. In
November of that year, Japan submitted to the CLCS its challenge

to the scientific merit of China's continental shelf claim,[27] and China followed suit, with added data in support of its claim, in May 2009.[28]

Finally, the Japanese government also had to contend with pressures from within Japan. Activism in support of Japan's sovereignty over the Senkaku Islands came from nationalist groups that asserted their rights to land on the Senkakus and to demonstrate Japan's control over them. Local government desires for active use of the islands notwithstanding, these activists were decidedly critical of China and of the Japanese government's low-key management of the issue.

Citizen activism by groups in Taiwan and China became an additional complication for the Japanese government's strategy of downplaying its differences with Beijing. As boatloads of Taiwanese and Hong Kong Chinese arrived in Senkaku waters, activists in Japan became even more frustrated with the government's approach. Far from Tokyo, local politicians and activists, wanting the government to abandon the compromise in the 1978 treaty, struggled to push the issue of Japanese sovereignty into the national spotlight, and symbolic efforts to demonstrate Japan's sovereignty, such as placing a lighthouse on the largest island, were designed to force Tokyo's hand.

DOMESTIC INTERESTS AND ACTIVISTS

The legal debates over the UNCLOS were too arcane for most of the Japanese public, and thus the differences with China over interpretation did not foster broad civic activism. But the economic implications of control over EEZs clearly attracted attention at home.

Two commercial constituencies were particularly affected. First, fishermen had long wanted Beijing to work more closely with them in resolving disputes. National industry representatives had engaged in discussions with China since the early 1950s, even though Japan had no formal diplomatic relations with Beijing at that time. The Japanese fisheries industry has changed significantly since then, however, and today fishermen are becoming a smaller and smaller portion of Japan's workforce. Fewer fishermen and more competition for fish make negotiations over fisheries today more a political than a commercial exercise.

Second, commercial oil and gas interests took an active part in the discussions about potential energy resources in the East China Sea seabed. South Korea and Taiwan decided to collaborate after the United Nations sent a team of geologists to survey the area, and their study revealed the potential for considerable hydrocarbon resources under the seabed. To date, joint development projects with South Korea have yielded little, but the unexplored areas along the median line with China drawn by the Japanese government in the East China Sea continue to offer hope of discovery. The technical challenges for exploiting oil and gas from deepwater drilling, however, make this as yet an unrealized source of commercial gain. Furthermore, the failure of Japan and China to implement a joint development initiative suggests that a cooperative solution to contending claims in the East China Sea continues to depend on the overall health of their bilateral relationship.

A more contentious set of interests involved in the East China Sea is the wide variety of activists and advocates who have coalesced around Japan's sovereignty dispute over the Senkaku Islands. The islands are privately owned, and the family that owns them has thus far stayed out of the public eye. Nonetheless, others have entered into the debate over the islands, which now has become part of the debate over Japan's maritime agenda with China. Nationalist activists, both individual politicians and smaller groups with clear right-wing tendencies, have always been fond of the Senkaku issue as a platform for anti-China rhetoric. After the conclusion of the 1978 peace treaty, the Japanese and Chinese governments were able to negotiate around this territorial dispute, but the interests in Japan that organize around this issue have tried to propel it more forcibly into the center of the country's politics. Fishermen, oil interests, and nationalists all have looked to the Japanese government to push harder in defending its maritime rights.

Negotiating Access to East China Sea Resources

Long before the two governments normalized their relations in the 1970s, private associations of Japanese and Chinese fisherman sought to address the dangers of their interactions in the East China

Sea. Japan's fishermen began this nongovernmental dialogue in the hope of ending the random attacks and confiscations of their boats by China. On December 7, 1950, a Chinese ship suddenly shot at a Japanese fishing trawler operating in the western region of the East China Sea. China then seized four more Japanese vessels in the same month, and these seizures continued into the following year. Chinese authorities captured seven Japanese fishing boats in February, nine in March, four in April, and two in May. The rationale for these seizures was the boats' violation of Chinese territorial waters, damage to coastal fishing, and suspicion of spying.[29] The Korean War had begun, and many in Japan saw Chinese behavior as driven by the new Cold War divisions in Northeast Asia.

For seven years after the end of World War II, Japanese fishermen who needed help in getting their boats back from China had to refer their cause to the U.S. Occupation authorities. This was complicated by the fact that Washington had formal relations with Chiang Kai-shek and his Guomindang government, which were in a bloody civil war with the Chinese Communist Party. When the Communists took power in China in 1949, the United States did not recognize their government, but after the Occupation ended three years later, Japanese fishermen could initiate direct contact with Beijing. Japanese companies made the first move, concluding an informal trade agreement,[30] and Japan's fishermen adopted a similar approach. The major Japanese fisheries groups—the All-Japan Marine Association (Dai nippon suisankai), the All-Japan Seaman's Union (Dai nippon kaiin kumiai), and the Japan Far Seas Trawler Fisheries Association (Nihon enyōkai gyogyō kyōkai)—gathered to consider how to approach China and wrote a letter to Beijing asking for a dialogue on resolving the fisheries disputes. By the following year, conditions seemed more conducive to a discussion between Chinese and Japanese fishermen. China's premier, Zhou Enlai, told a group of visiting Japanese Diet members and academics that China would be ready to discuss the fisheries' concerns and suggested that a group of Japanese fisheries representatives come to Beijing to meet with their counterparts.

Japanese fishermen then created the Japan-China Fisheries Consultative Association,[31] and on January 13, 1955, the first meeting between Japanese and Chinese fishermen opened in Beijing. This was the mechanism for establishing a basic understanding of how Japanese and Chinese fishermen could share the East China Sea. Ultimately, they agreed to six fishery areas—areas that were far from Chinese military–controlled waters and outside China's own exclusive coastal fisheries regions—where Japanese fishermen could fish according to agreed-on rules that would protect fisheries stocks. This agreement went into force on June 13, 1955, and was extended annually twice more. Since the Japanese Fisheries Association delegation wanted to find some accommodation and assistance for those Japanese fishermen who ran into trouble with China, these agreements generally conformed to terms acceptable to the Chinese authorities. Nonetheless, they provided a framework that created some predictability in the way that such incidents would be managed.

Politics intervened, however, in June 1957. Prime Minister Kishi Nobusuke, an ardent supporter of Taiwan, took office, banned any direct negotiation with mainland China, and instead called for its liberation from Communist rule. Thus, the tenuous relations between Japan and China were interrupted, and this political hostility effectively ended their fisheries agreement. But Japan's fishermen continued to worry about the dangers of their operations in the East China Sea and the Yellow Sea if the fisheries were unregulated, and they lobbied visiting Japanese Diet members and other visitors to Beijing to recommend restarting the fisheries talks. In January 1963, the head of the Japan-China Fisheries Consultative Association, Hiratsuka Tsuneji, took another delegation to Beijing and succeeded in gaining China's agreement to another round of talks. A second fisheries agreement was concluded and put into force by the end of the year, and it lasted until the Japanese and Chinese governments began to normalize their postwar diplomatic relations a decade later.

The formal fisheries agreements reflected important differences between Tokyo and Beijing. Japanese fishermen were restricted from operating in broad areas of China's coastal waters. But after Prime Minister Tanaka Kakuei's historic visit to Beijing in 1972, preparatory talks between the governments began. Official negotiations started in May 1974, with representatives from the Japanese Fisheries Agency meeting with their counterparts from China's Fisheries Bureau. As with the private-sector talks that preceded them, the two governments disagreed completely on how to handle China's desire to exclude its three military maritime regions from any fisheries activities and also on the procedural contents of joint regulatory guidelines.[32] China argued for its sovereign right to determine its own military and defense needs and to designate maritime regions that would be off limits. Japan contended that China's prohibition unilaterally and arbitrarily violated international law by prohibiting the transit of fishing boats in the open sea.

Similarly, China and Japan disagreed on acceptable procedures for regulating fishing. The Japanese Fisheries Agency wanted to continue the precedent set by the private associations' agreement of limiting fishing according to maritime region and limiting the number of boats operating in any given time period in order to maintain the fisheries' limits. China, however, argued that in addition to restricting the number of boats at any given time, limits should be placed on the horsepower of the fishing boats in any given area. Moreover, China claimed the right to further restrict the areas open to Japanese fishermen in order to protect fish species. Japan strongly protested this approach as too harsh and damaging to the interests of its trawlers. Ultimately, three rounds of intense negotiations—a total of 120 days—took place before an agreement was reached.

The Japan-China Fisheries Agreement covered the Yellow Sea and most of the East China Sea. Both governments decided to focus on only the East China Sea 27 degrees north latitude in order to avoid the disputed territory around the Senkaku Islands. Moreover, the two negotiating teams agreed to disagree in the treaty, and differing views between China and Japan were referenced only in the memorandum of understanding (MOU) that accompanied it. Zones of exclusion also were included in a MOU and referenced as requests made by China. Japan's note stated that it could not acknowledge the Chinese exclusions but that to protect resources, it would make every effort to minimize Japanese fishing in the areas suggested. Article 4 of the bilateral fisheries agreement, which went into force in December 1975, also referred to a note that gave continued responsibility to the national fisheries associations in helping ensure safe fishing operations in the waters between the two countries.[33]

Updates of the bilateral fisheries agreement retained the essence of this compromise between Tokyo and Beijing until Japan's access to fisheries resources in the East China Sea had to be reconsidered in light of the UNCLOS.[34] Announced in 1982, the UNCLOS took years to emerge as the basis of East China Sea deliberations, but when China ratified the convention in 1996, the stage was set for reconsidering how to organize the variety of fisheries interests at stake there. Once China, Japan, and South Korea declared their new overlapping EEZs, Tokyo and Beijing began discussing how this would shape their understanding of acceptable fisheries activities.

Japan's reliance on the East China Sea for fishery resources has diminished considerably, however. Before World War II, the East China Sea was a crucial location for Japanese fishermen, and many of Japan's postwar fisheries policies reflected this importance. Since then, fish stocks have been dwindling in the East China Sea, and over the last thirty years, Japan's share has been far smaller than it once was. In 2008, Japan's overall catch was 4.37 million tons, less than half that in 1979 (9.477 million tons), with only 12.2 percent from the East China Sea. Moreover, only 185,465 Japanese fishing vessels were registered, down from the 325,739 in 1979. Fewer than 10,000 fishing boats operate out of the southern prefectures of Kagoshima (6,446) and Okinawa (3,035), where the bulk of East China Sea fishing would be located. Japan's trawling industry—once the mainstay of Japanese fisheries—operates far fewer ships in the East China Sea today, most having moved into the Pacific and other global waters. Only 35 percent of Japanese fishing in the East China Sea is net fishing (186,266 tons), with the remainder of fishing in these waters from smaller boats: line fishing for tuna, sea bream, bonito, mackerel, sardines, saurel, tilefish, and blowfish (354,842 tons), some of which is in Japan's coastal waters rather than international waters.[35]

Furthermore, as an interest group, Japan's fishermen represent a far smaller share of the nation's economy. In 1979, 467,790 Japanese were working in the industry, whereas in 2008, there were only 221,910. Of these, 141,000 of these were self-employed, and the majority of them were older than sixty. That said, however, more fishermen are working in the East China Sea than in any other region. Both communities along the less industrialized coastline that borders the East China

Sea and those in the Bonin and Ryukyu Islands have long depended on fishing for their livelihood. The Ministry of Agriculture, Forestry, and Fisheries estimated that of the 211,810 fishermen in the industry in 2008, roughly 25 percent were operating in the East China Sea. Finally, the earnings from fishing in the East China Sea did not outweigh the complications of fishing in this area, as only 10 percent of Japanese fisheries sales are generated from East China Sea waters.[36]

Japanese claims against China for the mistreatment of their fishermen in Chinese coastal waters have all but disappeared today, as few Japanese ships operate close to China's coast. Instead, it is the Chinese government that lodges protests against Japan for the JCG's treatment of Chinese fishing vessels.[37] Other fishermen in the East China Sea, however, challenge Japan's maritime boundaries and its fishing stocks. Taiwan's fishermen operate in roughly the same southwestern waters as Japan's fishermen do, and they often are more assertive in their competition with Japanese fishermen than Chinese fishermen are.[38]

Today, Japan's resource claims against China in the East China Sea are less about fish and more about gas and oil. The discovery of potential seabed deposits in the late 1960s led to intense rivalry over maritime territorial claims between Japan and both of its Chinese neighbors, the People's Republic of China (PRC) and Taiwan. At the time, it was Taiwan that first challenged Japan's claim to the Senkaku Islands; it was the Japanese economy that was rapidly expanding, with unprecedented double-digit growth rates; and it was Japan's global search for oil that was the center of international media attention.[39]

In 1968, a multinational group of surveyors from Japan, South Korea, and Taiwan, under the auspices of the United Nations Northeast Asia Economic Commission, conducted a geophysical study in the East China Sea and the Yellow Sea.[40] Their conclusion, not published until more than a year later, was that the continental shelf of the East China Sea held considerable oil and gas reserves and also that "[a] high probability exists that the continental shelf between Taiwan and Japan *may be one of the most prolific oil reservoirs in the world*" (italics added). The scientists went on to say, however, "[It] also is one of the few large continental shelves of the world that has remained untested by the drill, owing to military and political factors, as well as to a lack of even reconnaissance geological information such as provided by this short survey."[41]

Once the survey results were made public, the governments of Japan, South Korea, and Taiwan all began to consider exploiting these resources and hired private oil companies to start testing the sites.[42] For Tokyo, the prospect of finding an oilfield comparable to those in the Middle East created great excitement. Japan's prime minister, Satō Eisaku, created an advisory committee made up of scientists and local Okinawa experts to consider how Japan ought to proceed.[43] Early Japanese government surveys of the waters off Okinawa were positive, and media reports confirmed the existence of sediment a mile and a half deep and 90 to 150 miles wide, an indication of plentiful oil resources.[44] Okinawans became giddy with anticipation that they might become Japan's oil-rich prefecture.

Meanwhile, the Japanese government announced that it would be interested in joint development with its neighbors, and while it would not discuss its sovereignty over the islands, it would be happy to negotiate in regard to the continental shelf. Tokyo was looking to work with Seoul and Taibei. On December 21, 1971, bankers and business leaders from all three countries met in Tokyo, and Prime Minister Satō's brother, the former prime minister Kishi, presided over the discussion. China strongly protested on December 30, 1971,[45] laying out its historical claim to the Senkaku Islands dating back to the Ming dynasty.

Beijing also lodged a protest with Washington for its complicity with Tokyo. The extended U.S. Occupation of the Ryukyu island chain (present-day Okinawa Prefecture) was coming to an end. Washington included the Senkaku Islands in the territory that it administered after the war and even used some of them as bombing ranges for the U.S. military stationed in Okinawa.[46] Despite this, the U.S. government did not take a position on the PRC's announcement in December 1971 that it claimed the islands as Chinese territory. Taiwan had already outlined the basis of its sovereignty claim on March 15, which had been fully communicated to the Nixon administration. At the time, Nixon and his national security adviser, Henry Kissinger, were pursuing their own diplomacy with Beijing, and the Senkaku sovereignty claims must have complicated an already complex diplomatic strategy. But it was Washington's relationship with Taibei that determined the internal U.S. government debate over what to do about the Senkakus.[47]

By April 1971, the State Department worried that the search for oil in and around the Senkakus and the attendant sovereignty dispute among Japan, Taiwan, and mainland China would lead to conflict in the region. China's warnings increased, and in a surprise announcement by a State Department spokesman, U.S. oil companies involved in the search for oil were told that their involvement was "inadvisable," as the rising tensions over the territorial dispute might increase the risk of seizure.[48] On April 9, the Pacific Gulf Corporation withdrew its research ship, which had been working under contract from Taiwan.[49] There also were domestic pressures on the U.S. government. Chinese and Chinese Americans in the United States were increasingly outspoken in defense of Chinese sovereignty claims over the Senkaku Islands, and they mobilized a nationwide protest effort. Demonstrations took place on April 10 and 11 in major U.S. cities across the country, focusing their anger at not only Japan and the United States for colluding against Chinese interests but also the government of Taiwan for not effectively defending Chinese interests.[50] Indeed, after the demonstrations Chiang Kai-shek instructed his ambassador to raise the Senkaku issue with President Richard Nixon.[51]

Private Islands, Nationalist Cause

Japan's territorial dispute with China and Taiwan over the Senkaku Islands has long motivated nationalists, who saw too much compromise by the Japanese government in the normalization of relations with Beijing. Tensions over Taiwan complicated Tokyo's effort to negotiate a peace treaty with Beijing and raised deep suspicions over the interactions with Chinese fishing boats in the East China Sea, particularly near the Senkaku Islands. In 1978, the Japanese government faced its first real test by Chinese vessels in the waters surrounding the Senkaku Islands. The Maritime Safety Agency (MSA, the predecessor of today's Japan Coast Guard) patrol vessel *Yaeyama*, attached to the Eleventh Regional District in Naha, reported in the early morning of April 12 that Chinese fishing vessels had entered

Japan's waters near the islands. When the *Yaeyama* ordered these vessels to leave, they responded with pistol fire and displayed signs that read "This is China's territory!" For some time, these fishing vessels continued to go back and forth across the maritime boundary. The Japanese government immediately lodged a protest with the PRC embassy in Tokyo and requested that the vessels leave Japanese waters. But the embassy responded by citing its government's 1971 diplomatic statement to the effect that the Senkakus were islets attached to the province of Taiwan.

The Chinese vessels prompted a heated political debate in Tokyo over the Chinese government's intentions. A group of Socialist Democratic Federation Diet members, led by Den Hideo, went to Beijing and met with Vice-Premier Lin Biao, who asserted that this incident was unintentional. Conservatives in the LDP were skeptical, however, with few believing the Chinese government's claim, given the crucial timing of the bilateral negotiations on normalization. The perception that Japan was being tested by China on the territorial issue was shared by many in the LDP and exposed the cabinet of Prime Minister Fukuda Takeo to considerable scrutiny by party conservatives concerning its approach to the normalization process.[52] The Senkaku issue thus exacerbated cleavages within the LDP, intensifying contention over the future leadership of the party.[53]

Rumors flew in Tokyo, some even suggesting that Foreign Minister Sonoda Sunao, a well-known "friend of China," may have known in advance that this was going to happen. The prime minister's supporters, however, were reportedly more inclined to believe that there was a deeper purpose for the arrival of these fishing vessels. By some accounts, this large Chinese fishing presence was in fact an amphibious landing exercise aimed at "liberating" Taiwan. According to media reporting at the time, more than three hundred ships participated, including fuel transport ships and other ships that would not normally be accompanying a fisheries expedition.[54] Others suggested that this was aimed instead at demonstrating China's ability to land on the Senkakus themselves. "Powerful LDP politicians" were anonymously said to consider an even bigger context for Chinese action: Beijing was in fact trying to push Washington to abandon Taibei. According to this version of Beijing's motive, for the first time Taiwan had given the Soviets permission to transit the Taiwan Straits, and China wanted the United States to understand how Taiwan's behavior complicated the strategic balance in the region. Accordingly, the Chinese were not testing the Fukuda cabinet but testing Washington's understanding of the region's dynamics.

In the wake of the incident, the LDP chose to continue its support of treaty negotiations with Beijing but also to exert physical Japanese control over the Senkaku Islands. On April 20, Chief Cabinet Secretary Abe Shintarō, Abe Shinzō's father, discussed in the LDP the options for responding to the incursion of Chinese fishing vessels, arguing that Japan needed some facilities there. Citing examples, he noted that a port used for shelter by Okinawan fishermen could be refurbished and a lighthouse constructed.[55] Similarly, Nakasone Yasuhiro, then the party chairman for International Affairs and Communications and a future prime minister himself, pointed out at a leadership meeting that he was opposed to proceeding with negotiations without taking a stand on the Senkaku issue.[56] He had long been cautious about negotiations with Beijing and pressed for a demonstration of Japan's effective control (*jikkō shihai*) of the islands. This concern over Japanese control of the Senkakus resulted in a decision to construct a government heliport on the largest island, Uotsurijima.[57]

Meanwhile, the Japanese and Chinese diplomats agreed to move forward with their negotiations over a peace treaty, which was concluded in August 1978. But this did not end the tensions over the islands. The Okinawa Development Agency began planning the construction of the heliport on Uotsurijima.[58] The MSA wanted to use its helicopters to transport local government survey teams across the almost 100 miles (160 km) from Ishigaki Island to the Senkakus. By ship, this would be a six- to ten-hour voyage, depending on the weather. The seas around the islands are very rough, with the waves in winter making it impossible to land. Helicopters could provide more predictable access to the islands, and the MSA believed that it would require only a provisional heliport, with no fuel tanks or other support needed.

On March 31, the MSA completed its survey of Uotsurijima[59] and announced its development plans for the Senkakus. The following day, the Chinese government officially protested Japan's effort to build a heliport,[60] and the MSA abandoned its plans and resumed access to the islands by ship. For decades, the Japanese government took no further action until the increase in Chinese maritime activities in and around Japanese territory forced a new debate over how to demonstrate Japanese control of the Senkaku Islands.

Local fishermen also lobbied for the construction of a lighthouse on the Senkakus. Activists from Nihon seinensha (a right-wing group associated with Sumiyoshi rengōkai, a Japanese mafia organization), collaborated with an Ishigaki fisherman and filed an application with Japan's Eleventh Regional Maritime Safety Headquarters in Naha, Okinawa. The application asked the MSA for official approval for an internationally recognized navigational aid. Although the coast guard's regional headquarters routinely issued permission in regard to requests like this, the controversy over the Senkakus prompted the Naha coast guard to send this on to Tokyo. A year later, the Japanese media reported that the Seinensha had succeeded in building a lighthouse on Uotsurijima—with the permission of the island's owners—and had registered it in Ishigaki City.[61] The Seinensha then approached the MSA to register the lighthouse internationally.

The governments of both Taiwan and the PRC denounced the Seinensha's construction of a lighthouse. Taiwan's President Lee Teng-hui promised to respond, while the Chinese Foreign Ministry's spokesperson claimed that the lighthouse violated China's sovereignty and urged the Japanese government to prevent this type of activity.[62] The construction of this lighthouse, and the effort to gain international registration for it, set off activists in both Hong Kong and Taiwan. Over the next decade, the Japanese coast guard faced repeated episodes of protest, with vessels from both Hong Kong and Taibei carrying activists to the waters off the Senkaku Islands.

The Seinensha again ruffled feathers on July 14, 1996, when it returned to the Senkakus. Seven members landed on Kitakojima and spent the night there building another lighthouse. Again, the governments in Taibei and Beijing protested, but it was Taiwanese fishermen who acted. Associations of fishermen in east and north Taiwan joined forces to launch a protest. Their plan was to send more than two hundred fishing boats to the Senkaku waters in early August. The Seinensha requested that the Ishigaki branch of the MSA list the new lighthouse as an official "aid to navigation."[63] The head of the Ishigaki City assembly joined in the fray, calling on the MSA to act in the face of Taiwan's sovereignty claim. Two days later, a Taiwanese TV reporter landed on the island. The Chinese government and media saw this activism as condoned by the Japanese government and called on Tokyo to control it. Hong Kong media tried to reach the Senkaku Islands also, but the Japanese coast guard prevented them from landing. In September 1996 alone, the media and activists made four attempts to land on the Senkakus.

The televised interplay between Japanese- and Taiwanese- and Chinese-based activists broadened the domestic interest in the territorial dispute in all three countries. New groups saw an opportunity to join this rising wave of protest and sovereignty advocacy. The People's Liberation Army newspaper, *Guofangbao*, carried an essay lambasting Japan and asserting China's claim to the Diaoyu Islands.[64] Rallies were held in Hong Kong. The Seinensha, with the permission of the islands' owners, requested approval from the MSA to return to the Senkakus to repair the lighthouse.

The Japanese government told Chinese authorities that it was difficult to stop activities that were sanctioned by the island's owner. On September 13, 1996, Chief Cabinet Secretary Kajiyama Seiroku stated that Japan was not in a position to approve or disapprove building a lighthouse on private property but that the government would monitor the situation. On September 25, however, after considerable Japan-China consultations on the protests, Kajiyama restated his government's position. The Japanese government intended to withhold its permission for the Seinensha's request to repair the lighthouse. The very next day, five Hong Kong activists aboard a freighter in Senkaku waters jumped overboard after being stopped by the JCG. One drowned, and another was rushed to the hospital in Yaeyama for treatment. It was the leader of the Hong Kong activists who died, and twenty thousand people gathered in a sympathy rally days later. Despite Japanese and Chinese government efforts to dampen the sovereignty activism, the situation was getting more and more difficult to contain.

The status of these islands as private property clearly compounded the Japanese government's difficulties. Access to the islands was the owner's prerogative. The Seinensha had developed a relationship with the owner's family, although the exact details of that relationship are unclear, and this facilitated the organization's access to the islands. Even more worrisome, if the islands were sold to activists, there would be no means by which the national government could assert control. Ownership of the islands had been transferred around the same time that Japan and China were normalizing their diplomatic relations. Since the Meiji era, an Okinawan family had owned these islands, and in June 1972, the elderly owner, Koga Zenji, was interviewed in *Gendai* magazine. Koga, a resident of Okinawa whose father had used the Senkaku Islands to build a small business in the late 1800s, told the story of his father's exploration of the islands and of the early Okinawan government's interest in claiming them for Japan.[65] Eleven years after Koga's father reported his discovery of these uninhabited islands, the Meiji government finally claimed them for Japan and, as a reward for his early exploratory efforts, gave him a thirty-year leasehold over their use. He experimented with various ventures, including collecting bird feathers and guano and constructing a dried bonito factory, which, according to his descendant's account, employed enough people to support a population of around two hundred on Uotsurijima. Koga described the Senkakus as a "treasure house of seabirds" (*umidori no hōko*). The products made from the bird feathers were sold in Europe, while the residents of Taiwan purchased the guano, used as fertilizer. At the time, Uotsurijima had a port that could accommodate ships of up to fifteen tons. When Koga died at the age of sixty-three in 1918, his son Zenji took over the businesses, and when the Meiji-era thirty-year lease expired eight years later, he petitioned the Japanese government for purchase of the islands. In 1932, the four islands of Uotsurijima, Kumebajima, Kitakojima, and Minamikojima became the private property of Koga Zenji.

The politics of Senkaku ownership became more conspicuous after Koga Zenji died. He and his wife, Hanako, had no children and promised to sell the islands to his close friends, the Kuriharas. Before his death, in March 1978, Koga sold two of the small islands (Minamikojima and Kitakojima), and his wife inherited Uotsurijima, which she sold to Kurihara Kunioki on April 25, 1978. At the time, Kurihara, who lived in Saitama Prefecture, outside Tokyo, was thirty-six years old, and his family's company ran a wedding hall and a real estate business. A *Mainichi* newspaper report in 1990 suggested that after Koga's wife died in 1988, Ishihara Shintarō, a well-known conservative nationalist and then an LDP member of the Lower House, made an offer to the family to buy the islands.[66] According to a member of the Kurihara family, offers also were received from Japanese oil interests and similarly refused, in order to keep the islands from someday ending up in China's hands. The original owner, Koga Zenji, apparently had requested that the islands be kept in their natural state,[67] and the Kurihara family wanted to honor that request. The diplomatic management of these islands, therefore, rested solely on the Kurihara family's continued ownership.

Military tensions regarding the Taiwan Straits in 1996 only heightened the Japanese government's concern. From October 1 to 3, the Chinese PLA Navy's East Fleet conducted exercises in the waters northwest of the Senkakus, and Taiwan sent its navy to observe. Around this time, both the Japanese and Chinese governments reportedly took steps to quiet sovereignty activists. On October 3, the Japanese government arrested a senior adviser of the Seinensha for possession of guns and ammunition. According to the *Yomiuri*, around this time also, the Chinese Communist Party issued an internal memo seeking to limit protest activities surrounding the Senkakus.[68] But within days, fifty ships carrying protesters from Taiwan, Hong Kong, and Macao approached the Senkakus, and four people landed on Uotsurijima raising both the Taiwanese and PRC flags. As the Chinese and Japanese governments tried to control the situation, Etō Tōyōhisa, leader of Seinensha, held a press conference at the Foreign Correspondents Club of Japan and announced that the purpose of building a lighthouse on the Senkakus was to secure safe navigation in the East China Sea. He pointed out that it was the Japanese government that should build a lighthouse and protect the islands from those who sought to wrest sovereignty from Japan. The next day, Japan's chief of staff of the Air Self-Defense Force (ASDF) warned that he would respond to the Taiwanese activists attempting to land by air on the Senkakus in the same way that Japan's ASDF treated any other violation of Japan's air defenses, thereby foreshadowing a much more serious confrontation with the PRC more than a decade later.

Public statements by the Japanese and Chinese governments regarding the intensifying activism revealed no real change in their positions on the sovereignty of the Senkaku Islands. Chinese authorities repeatedly argued that the two nations had agreed to shelve this issue and urged the Japanese government to respect that approach to their relationship. Japan's government, however, denied that any such agreement existed and refused to acknowledge that there was a territorial dispute at all. Pressure was building on the government to be more forthright in protecting its sovereignty as Taiwan- and Hong Kong–based activists challenged Japanese sovereignty over the islands. The Japanese government deferred to the islands' owner but also sought to prevent the Seinensha activists from provoking Chinese anger. A decade later, though, this delicate balancing act became impossible to sustain when PRC activists began to challenge Japan's control of the islands and Japanese activists directly engaged the owner in an effort to sidestep government control.

NEGOTIATING NEW POLICY FRAMEWORKS

While the bilateral management of their territorial dispute was becoming more and more difficult, Japanese and Chinese diplomats also got caught up in the new international UN Convention on the Law of the Sea (UNCLOS). Its ratification in the mid-1990s created a new framework for considering Japanese and Chinese maritime interests, as well as a new cause for disagreement. The recognition of EEZs meant that the placement of the maritime boundary in the East China Sea was subject to negotiation between Tokyo and Beijing, and the competition over the resources there was bound to result in contention. The UNCLOS thus challenged the bilateral compromise over fisheries that China and Japan had made in the past and raised new competitive dynamics, especially in regard to seabed resources. Furthermore, this competition brought a rethinking of Japan's own maritime ambitions. As the contention grew, Beijing and Tokyo did find their way to collaborate on a joint resource development plan, but they failed to agree on an implementation treaty.

Japan's New Oceans Law

On February 4, 2004, the LDP's Special Committee on Maritime Policy and the Joint Diet Member's Conference on Maritime Issues announced that maritime policy was a critical component of Japan's future development, given the resources that might be found under the seabed. Developing a comprehensive maritime policy, the committee concluded, ought to be a "national project."[69] The competition with China over claims to the seabed resources depended on Japanese justification for its EEZ claim. China already had indicated that it rejected the idea of drawing a median line in the East China Sea and instead decided to base its EEZ claim on the continental shelf, which was close to the territorial waters of its East China Sea neighbors.[70]

As China had done, Japan updated its topographical surveys of the seabed under its surrounding waters, and its fiscal year 2004 budget allocated to survey Japanese waters was seven times higher than that of the previous year. China and Japan began to amass scientific data to support their competing claims. Under the UNCLOS, provisions had been made to allow land features equivalent to a continental shelf to be considered as cause for extending the two-hundred-nautical-mile limit for claiming the seabed. The onus for providing the supporting documentation of these underwater land features fell on the coastal states, and the deadline for providing evidence for such claims was May 2009.

Beyond the intricacies of the UNCLOS negotiations were broader reasons to develop a Japanese maritime strategy. Domestic concerns were rising over Chinese behavior in and around Japanese waters. Chinese activists began to join the sovereignty protests, and alarm bells were triggered in Japan when a group of Chinese activists landed on the Senkaku Islands on March 24, 2004. The JCG arrested seven Chinese who had landed on Uotsurijima, the first time that PRC citizens had set foot on the Senkakus. Beijing protested the arrests and warned Japan not to harm the activists. Prime Minister Koizumi Jun'ichirō calmly acknowledged that following the law was the right thing to do in "a law-abiding country" and then sent them home two days later.[71]

A second and more ominous Chinese incursion into Japanese waters that year created media frenzy in Tokyo. On November 10, Japan's Maritime Self-Defense Force (MSDF) discovered a Chinese Han-class submarine in Japanese waters. The appearance of a Chinese submarine in such proximity to Japan provoked a public outcry. The PLA Navy's purpose remains unclear, but its submarine's transit of the strait between the islands of Miyako and Ishigaki in the Okinawa island chain added public support for the new legislation concerning Japan's maritime strategy. Prime Minister Koizumi ordered the director-general of the Defense Agency, General Ono Yoshinori, to dispatch the MSDF to defend Japanese waters.[72] This was only the second time since the end of World War II that Japan had issued a maritime security order to its navy,[73] and the MSDF tracked the Chinese submarine for more than a day until it finally surfaced. The incident received intense real-time media coverage, and the interaction between the two navies was broadcast live on Japanese television. Under international law, the submerged transit of sovereign waters by a foreign submarine signaled hostile intent, and military analysts could not help but wonder whether this was a deliberate test of Japan's own military readiness.[74]

The proliferation of Chinese-Japanese interactions in waters around Japan, and the seemingly abandoned moratorium on ruffling nationalistic feathers over the Senkaku/Diaoyu dispute, concerned many in Japan, including the Sasakawa Peace Foundation's president, Sasakawa Yōhei. The LDP Policy Research Council, led by Upper House member Takemi Keizō, began to work with the support of the Sasakawa Foundation to draft the conceptual framework for Japan's strategy. Takemi argued that since the UNCLOS became effective in 1994 and Japan ratified it in 1996, Japan had made virtually no progress in undertaking the kinds of policy changes that would be required for maritime management. Compared with Japan's neighbors, Japan lagged far behind.[75] Joining forces with the Sasakawa Peace Foundation, Takemi reached out to others in the LDP as well as the bureaucracies for greater study of Japan's existing maritime interests. Takemi's assessment was that government inertia was a large part of the problem.[76]

Japan's lack of a maritime strategy up to this point was blamed on the diffusion of government authority. Too many bureaucracies were handling different aspects of Japan's maritime concerns. Rather than a centrally organized agency charged with overseeing Japan's strategic interests, policy related to maritime issues was divided among four bureaucracies, each assigned to different pieces of the overall maritime pie.[77] Thus, even when the time came for the Ministry of Foreign Affairs to negotiate with China on the gas fields under the East China Sea, the requisite scientific knowledge was inaccessible to Japan's diplomats. Takemi also noted the lack of political leadership that could bring all these bureaucracies together. But he reserved his strongest criticism for the lack of urgency felt by Japan's diplomats, a failing that, he observed, was due to their oversensitivity to the neighboring countries'—specifically China's—sensibilities.[78]

Growing concern about Chinese maritime activities changed the Japanese calculus, and advocates for policy reform focused on several layers of initiative. Within months of its formation, Takemi's Maritime Interests Working Group had formulated its proposals, and one of its most urgent recommendations was convening a cabinet-level meeting to discuss Japan's maritime interests. The Nippon Foundation, headed by Sasakawa, presented its policy recommendations to Koizumi's chief cabinet secretary, Abe Shinzō, on November 18, 2005. With Ministry of Foreign Affairs talks with China on gas field development stalled, the committee agreed to push for enactment of the Basic Act on Ocean Policy in 2006. On April 24, 2006, Ishiba Shigeru of the LDP and Kuribayashi Tadao of Keio University, an expert on international maritime law, assumed cochairmanship of a study group on the new ocean policy legislation, and on June 29, the LDP's coalition partner, the Kōmeitō, established a project team under the leadership of Takano Hiroshi.

The new basic law on maritime issues had broad support among Japan's political parties, and the effort to legislate a new approach to managing Japan's ocean interests immediately gained legislative approval. On December 6, the LDP's Special Committee on Ocean Policy, chaired by Ishiba Shigeru, confirmed that it would submit legislation at the next regular Diet session, and a number of government officials as well as the Kōmeitō's leader, Ōta Akihiro, voiced approval of the bill. On December 19, sixteen Democratic Party of Japan (DPJ) lawmakers, including one of the party's leading foreign policy experts, Maehara Seiji, announced an alliance in support of the Basic Act on Ocean Policy. Consultations among the LDP, Kōmeitō, and DPJ Diet affairs heads led to an agreement on a supraparty bill on March 27. The Lower House passed the bill on April 3, 2007.[79] With the impending visit of China's premier, Wen Jiabao, however, the Upper House of Japan delayed passage of the bill in an effort to avoid any bad feelings during his visit.[80]

The following six basic principles outlined in Japan's new oceans law reflected a new vision for maritime Japan:

- Harmonizing maritime development and use with protection of the marine environment.
- Ensuring maritime security.
- Cultivating and enriching scientific expertise on oceans.
- Developing a healthy marine industry.
- Ensuring comprehensive management of the oceans.
- Coordinating with international efforts to manage the world's oceans.[81]

This plan to realize a "new maritime Japan" was designated as a national strategy, and a new office for maritime affairs was created in the prime minister's office. A minister for ocean affairs was to be appointed, and a new plan for implementing the basic oceans law was crafted in 2008.[82] The following year, this plan was announced, and the year after that, additional laws were drafted to cope with piracy and with the protection and management of Japan's islands.

The Elusive East China Sea Agreement

Discussions between Japan and China over the East China Sea began anew in 2006 as the diplomatic reconciliation effort unfolded after Prime Minister Koizumi left office. The new diplomatic initiative to develop a "mutually beneficial relationship based on common strategic interests" provided the political mandate for a renewed focus on the East China Sea and its resources. When Premier Wen Jiabao arrived in Tokyo in April 2007, Prime Minister Abe Shinzō raised the issue of finding an approach to joint resource development in the East China Sea that would be acceptable to both countries. Diplomats were assigned to find out which areas of the East China Sea would be appropriate for cooperation and to decide how to cope with Chinese drilling in the Shirakaba/Chunxiao gas field.

The mood in Tokyo was optimistic. Wen's visit had been a great success, and his message of Chinese goodwill delivered in a powerful speech in the Japanese Diet was persuasive. Moreover, China was a year away from the 2008 Olympics in Beijing, and this moment was seen as the best opportunity for breaking through the long-standing bilateral stalemate over sharing resources in the East China Sea. Even at this high point of political reconciliation, however, Tokyo and Beijing found it difficult to define an acceptable plan for resource development. Repeated efforts to find common ground resulted in only intermittent progress.[83] In the absence of a negotiated resolution of the maritime boundary, Japan had long pressured Beijing to halt its development of the Shirakaba/Chunxiao gas field, but to no avail. Moreover, the deployment of Chinese naval vessels in the area near the Chinese drilling site had also provoked a Japanese protest. Tokyo therefore proposed designing a joint development plan to offset these differences in the interpretation of maritime rights in order to halt any further exploitation of resources until a firm decision could be reached on the interpretation of the UNCLOS. Beijing was not enthusiastic about halting its drilling.

Nonetheless, an agreement was drafted in time for the summit meeting between China's president, Hu Jintao, and Japan's prime minister, Fukuda Yasuo, during Hu's visit to Tokyo in May 2008. For the first time, it seemed that Tokyo and Beijing had achieved a breakthrough and identified common interests in exploiting the energy resources that lay under the seabed in the East China Sea. Hu Jintao's visit to Tokyo demonstrated the progress made in restoring a positive diplomatic atmosphere between Japan and China, and this momentum made it possible to craft a political understanding that a vision for cooperation in the East China Sea would bridge the period during which their divergent claims could be considered under the

UNCLOS. Dubbed the "Sea of Peace, Cooperation and Friendship," the East China Sea was to become a place of cooperation in developing new energy resources and sharing in the exploitation of proven existing resources such as the Shirakaba/Chunxiao gas field.

The real work of ironing out the details of this vision came in the weeks after the Hu-Fukuda summit. A month later, in a joint press conference on June 18, 2008, Minister of Foreign Affairs Kōmura Masahiko and Minister of Economy, Trade, and Industry Amari Akira announced the details of the agreement.[84] Japanese companies would be invited to participate in the Chinese gas field development already under way at Shirakaba, but the real attraction was in the northern region of the East China Sea where significant hydrocarbon deposits were thought to lie. Despite Japan's protest of Chinese activities at the Shirakaba/Chunxiao gas field, it was really the northern region— and the promise of potentially extensive energy resources there—that was the commercial attraction for Japan. Needless to say, the political achievement of doing this jointly with China was a tremendous accomplishment, especially given the contention over the maritime boundary during the decade since the UNCLOS was ratified.

Japan and China agreed to work together on two areas along the median line recognized by Japan in the East China Sea. In the Shirakaba/Chunxiao gas field, which is on both sides of the median line, China would allow Japanese commercial investment and farming of the gas from its side of the line, and Japan, although it has no wells on its side, would, in principle, agree to similar participation by Chinese firms. In an area farther north, in some of the deepest waters of the East China Sea where exploratory drilling had not yet started, Japan and China agreed to work jointly to explore and develop these potential resources under the seabed. Japanese technology and investment would be needed, as deep drilling remains prohibitively expensive, but the expectation was that the time would come when that would not be the case. Despite this hard-won compromise, the Fukuda cabinet was roundly criticized in Tokyo for giving up too much to China, and public opinion was ambivalent on the overall accomplishments of the Hu-Fukuda summit.

The diplomatic accomplishment of the Hu-Fukuda summit was quickly overshadowed by the Great Sichuan Earthquake of May 12,

2008, which occurred just after President Hu returned home from Tokyo. The earthquake left more than 65,000 dead in China. Fukuda immediately organized Japanese assistance, and Hu quickly gave permission for Japanese search-and-rescue teams and logistical support to enter China.[85] For whatever other difficulties Japan and China had in convincing their publics of the merits of their diplomacy, the Hu-Fukuda summit undoubtedly allowed the two leaders to work together in response to the disaster.

When the LDP left office in the fall of 2009, the implementation treaty for the joint resource development plan for the East China Sea had yet to be completed. As media reports circulated in Tokyo that China had begun again to extract gas from the Shirakaba/Chunxiao field, tempers flared. Tensions between the new DPJ government's foreign minister, Okada Katsuya, and his Chinese counterpart, Yang Jiechi, erupted in January 2010 over the lack of progress on the East China Sea agreement.[86] The DPJ government's relationship with Beijing soured even further in September that year when a Chinese fishing trawler rammed two Japanese coast guard vessels in waters near the Senkaku Islands. Although the Japanese government continued to ask China to return to the discussions on this 2008 agreement, the hard-won negotiated compromise fell by the wayside as other sources of tension poisoned Japan-China relations.

Renting the Senkaku Islands

The Japanese government also took steps at the end of the 1990s to ensure its control over the privately owned Senkaku Islands. Over the years, the status of these islands had been largely hidden from the public. But as activists in Hong Kong and Taiwan began to focus their attention on them, concern grew over the Japanese government's deliberately low-key management of this issue. The JCG had long patrolled the waters around the Senkakus, but local officials from Okinawa were barred from making conspicuous trips there. Thus, the Seinensha's decision to construct a lighthouse there had considerable local support, and fishermen and others who wanted a more overt Japanese government presence on the Senkakus were happy to see this intervention on their behalf.

Physical control by the Japanese government over the privately owned islands, however, was a bigger challenge. One of the five islands already was in government hands. The Japanese government had leased another island, Kubajima, since Okinawa reversion because the United States had used it as a bombing range.[87] At the reversion, this island was treated like other U.S. facilities and bases, and a contract was drawn up for the owner to lease the land to the Japanese government. Under this agreement, the United States was ostensibly allowed to continue using the facility; it has not. Ownership of the islands has changed hands three times since then, and today the owner refuses to accept the terms of the lease in protest against the idea of using the land as a military facility. Nonetheless, the Ministry of Defense still maintains legal control over Kubajima and pays rent on the island.[88]

The status of the other three privately owned islands changed in 2002. The *Yomiuri* reported on the government's effort to strengthen its control over the disputed islands, claiming that the government's "light protection" approach was no longer effective in light of the growing Chinese pressure.[89] The Japanese government became increasingly concerned about Chinese pressures on the East China Sea, and the fear that these islands would be purchased by Taiwanese or Chinese interests led to discussions between the Japanese government and the family that owned the islands. The Kuriharas agreed to lease their three islands, Uotsurijima, Minamikojima, and Kitakojima, to the national government. The cabinet secretariat negotiated the terms of the lease, and the Ministry of Internal Affairs and Communications was given the budget for the lease. The contract began in April 2002 for ¥22.56 million in rent per year (approximately $180,000 at the time). In 2006, the Japanese government raised the amount by 10 percent, to ¥24.5 million. Thus, while the property rights still belonged to the Kurihara family, the Japanese government's lease of the islands ensured that the property could not be sold to any third party that might compromise Japan's control.[90] The lease also signaled to China the Japanese government's intent to maintain its control over the Senkakus. Interestingly, the negotiation with the Kuriharas took place at around the same time that the Japanese government was negotiating the salvage of a North Korean vessel sunk by Japan's coast guard in China's EEZ. The quiet discussions reflected the concern over the mounting number of maritime interactions in the East China Sea, as well as the concern that interests hostile to Japan might find a way to put pressure on the government by purchasing the Senkakus.

Japan and China have yet to resolve their differences over the East China Sea. Although Japan has the resource extraction technology and the ambition to shape these interactions, it has not been successful in pushing China toward a common vision of how to share resources there. Although the territorial dispute has affected both the Chinese and Japanese positions on their maritime boundary, it has not kept them from negotiating around their differences, despite the citizen activists that have made these compromises between diplomats unsustainable at home.

The impetus for negotiations on the East China Sea began with Deng Xiaoping's injunction to leave the sensitive territorial dispute to future generations. This idea today, however, seems to have little credibility in Japan. Increasingly, China's efforts to declare its sovereign rights in the East China Sea are making Japan less likely to compromise. Nonetheless, Japan's diplomats continue to argue for a negotiated compromise that in theory includes both the Shirakaba/Chunxiao gas field and the as yet untouched concession farther north.

As with many maritime regions across the globe, the two nations figure their EEZ boundaries in the East China Sea differently. The UNCLOS argues for bilateral negotiations when interpretations differ, but the Japanese and Chinese governments have not yet been able to find a compromise. The UNCLOS created new global rules for demarcating national and international waters, China and Japan have tried to justify their own maritime approaches in the broader context of this emerging body of international law. The JCG continues to perform the primary function of policing Japan's coastal waters, and Japan has increased its fishery and survey activities. China, in contrast, had multiple agencies engaged in maritime policing (including the Maritime Police of the Border Control Department, Maritime Safety Administration, Fisheries Law Enforcement Command, General Administration of Customs, and State Oceanographic Administration). In 2013, Beijing consolidated some of its maritime forces under the new Chinese Coast Guard.

As geographic proximity has created the potential for more frequent and unprecedented interactions between the two militaries, China's growing naval capabilities have brought to the fore a new dimension of this maritime rule making. China's increasing maritime presence in and around Japanese waters has also led to significant changes in Japan's policymaking. It took almost a decade for Japan's political and bureaucratic leaders to grasp the full impact of the UNCLOS on their own national interests and to develop a more coherent maritime strategy that would allow Tokyo to compete with China's claims on the East China Sea. Furthermore, strong political leadership in Tokyo was necessary to navigate the domestic politics of the sovereignty debate. While Prime Minister Koizumi sought to diminish the impact of Chinese activism surrounding the Senkakus by demonstrating Japan's legal right to punish those who ignored its maritime boundaries, he also quietly arranged for the return of those arrested. Within Japan, Koizumi had greater success in calming nationalist activists, but this proved difficult for the new party, the Democratic Party of Japan (DPJ), that took over the government in 2009. The very next year, it faced the most serious diplomatic crisis in Japan-China relations since normalization when tensions over a provocative Chinese fishing trawler captain made it even more difficult for Tokyo to seek a negotiated solution to its differences with Beijing.

The two countries' inability to conclude a bilateral understanding on their maritime boundaries in the East China Sea in 2008 came back to haunt their relationship in 2012. In 2010, the trawler incident spurred a reassertion by the United States of its intent to defend the Senkakus, thus raising the stakes for Beijing if it challenged Japan's administrative control.[91] The abandonment of the effort to build cooperation through joint energy development has had far-reaching consequences. The loss of trust, coupled with the lack of a track record on communicating on East China Sea maritime issues, contributed to the rapid deterioration of relations. This lack of communication raised the stakes and further escalated popular antagonisms in September 2012 when a far more dangerous clash between Tokyo and Beijing over their island dispute resulted in a maritime standoff around the Senkakus that threatened military action. By the end of that year, the Japan-China territorial dispute had blossomed into a full-blown diplomatic crisis and stimulated a rewriting of Japan's Basic Ocean Plan that included enhancing its ability to protect its maritime environment and also to strengthen its policing and defense capabilities. The new plan argued that Japan had to transform itself from "a country protected by the ocean [*umi ni mamorerareta kuni*] to one that defends the ocean [*umi wo mamoru kuni*]."[92]

5

FOOD SAFETY

On July 30, 2013, Lu Yueting, a thirty-nine-year-old temporary worker at a food plant in China, pleaded guilty to poisoning frozen dumplings. The plant was located in Shijiazhuang, in the northern province of Hebei, and owned by Tianyang Food. Both Lu and his wife worked there. A small number of foreign diplomats and journalists attended the court proceedings, a rare event for a Chinese district court.[1] After the three-hour trial ended, the English-language *China Daily* quoted an unidentified court official who stated that the sentence would likely be at least ten years, if not life, in prison.[2] Lu's crime was discovered in large part because his victims were Japanese. Early in 2008, just a month after Lu had injected the frozen dumplings with a toxic chemical at his plant in northern China, ten people in Japan's Chiba and Hyōgo Prefectures fell ill.

In court, Lu reportedly apologized to his victims, admitting that he had committed the crime because he was dissatisfied with his low wages and angry that his wife had not received her bonus when she went on maternity leave. The incident soured diplomatic relations between Tokyo and Beijing, and it had taken a couple of years and the discovery of three more victims of Lu's poisoning in Chengdu before the Chinese police made an arrest. Lu's testimony revealed, however, that it was not anti-Japanese sentiment but frustration with labor conditions in China that motivated his crime. On January 20, 2014, the Shijiazhuang Intermediate People's Court sentenced Lu to life imprisonment for his crime, reflecting the growing Chinese concern about their country's food safety.[3]

The food-poisoning scandal exposed the vulnerability that attended Japan's economic interdependence with China. As trade and investment figures show, Japan has become increasingly dependent on access to the Chinese market. Profits for Japanese corporations are tied to operations there, and Chinese middle-class consumers offer new opportunities for Japanese manufacturers. But Japan's consumers also have become deeply entwined with Chinese producers as more and more Japanese products are being made in joint ventures with Chinese firms. Overseeing the quality and safety of those products depends on both the vigilance of Japanese managers and the regulatory framework for product safety being developed by the Chinese government. This economic interdependence thus has created economic benefits as well as anxiety.

Nowhere is this tension more obvious than in the debate over food safety. While Japanese trading companies compete with Chinese firms on the global market for access to grain and other food imports, more striking is the extent to which Japan now depends on Chinese farmers and joint food-processing ventures to feed its people. Despite a dip in 2008 when the *gyōza* poisoning occurred, Japan's food dependency on China has steadily risen over the past twenty years. The value of food imports has tripled (figure 5.1), and the percentage of Japan's total food imports from China has more than doubled, to almost 14 percent (figure 5.2). A snapshot of Japan's global food sources in 1990 and again in 2007 shows that Japan's imports of agricultural produce from China have continued to outpace imports from other parts of the world (figure 5.3).[4] China's share of Japan's food imports has grown as the U.S. share has dropped. In addition, Japanese consumers' preferences have shifted to less expensive and processed foods, creating more incentive for Japanese food-processing companies to shift their operations to China. Consequently, China has become "Japan's kitchen" as both cost and convenience have changed the way Japanese eat, with Japan depending more heavily on, and competing more intensely with, China for access to food.[5]

THE CONTROVERSY: THE IMPORT OF POISONED *GYŌZA*

The downside to this dependence on China was abruptly demonstrated in 2008. On January 5, three members of a family in Takasago City,

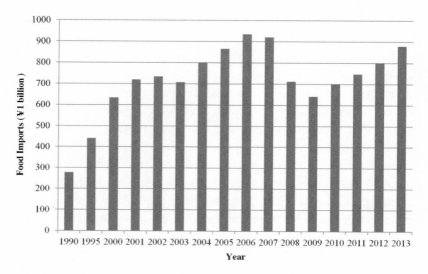

FIGURE 5.1 Imports of food and food products from China. The years 1990 and 1995 are included at the beginning of the chart for comparative purposes. (Ministry of Finance, Japan, "Trade Statistics of Japan," http://www.customs.go.jp/toukei/info/index_e.htm)

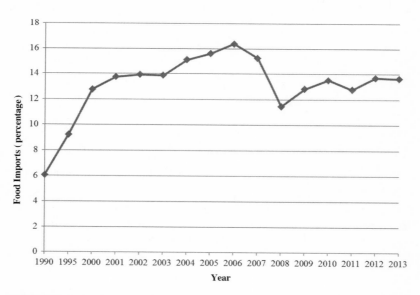

FIGURE 5.2 Food imports from China as a percentage of total food imports. The years 1990 and 1995 are included at the beginning of the chart for comparative purposes. (Ministry of Finance, Japan, "Trade Statistics of Japan," http://www.customs.go.jp/toukei/info/index_e.htm)

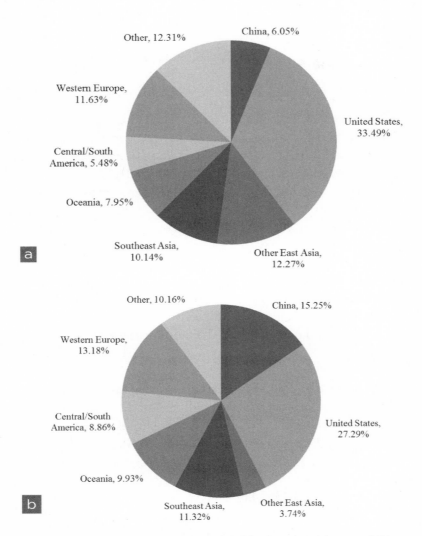

FIGURE 5.3 Diversification of Japanese global food imports: (*a*) 1990 and (*b*) 2007. (Ministry of Finance, Japan, "Trade Statistics of Japan," http://www.customs.go.jp /toukei/info/index_e.htm)

Hyōgo Prefecture, fell ill soon after eating frozen dumplings with the brand name CO-OP tezukuri gyōza. Three weeks later, five more cases of food poisoning, of a woman and her four children, were reported after they ate Chukade gochisō hitokuchi brand *gyōza* in Ichikawa City, Chiba Prefecture. Two more cases were subsequently reported in Chiba. In all, ten cases of severe food poisoning were attributed to frozen *gyōza* sold by JT Foods. Police in Chiba found methamidophos—a cheap but highly toxic insecticide used widely in China and many developing countries—in both the hospital test results and the packages containing the frozen *gyōza,* indicating that this was a case of criminal intent.

Methamidophos is classified by the World Health Organization (WHO) as a "Class 1b Highly Hazardous Chemical," which, if ingested by humans, can cause severe abdominal pain, vomiting, and diarrhea. Both brands were sold by JT Foods but made by Tianyang Food in Hebei Province, China. On January 30, JT Foods began a recall of its twenty-three frozen-food products produced at the same Tianyang Food factory, stating that methamidophos had been detected inside both the dumplings and the packages. Other Japanese food makers, Katokichi and Ajinomoto, initiated a recall of their products made in the same factory, and the Ministry of Health, Labor, and Welfare (MHLW) announced that Nikkyo Foods and One Trading Company, based in Osaka, also had been importing the same dumplings made by Tianyang Food.[6]

The Japanese and Chinese governments met at the Cabinet Office in Tokyo on February 3 to discuss the case.[7] Officials from China's General Administration of Quality Supervision, Inspection, and Quarantine (AQSIQ) were included in the group, as well as Japanese officials from the MHLW and the Ministry of Agriculture, Forestry, and Fisheries (MAFF). On February 5, a Japanese investigating commission traveled to Beijing and met with Wang Daning, director of the AQSIQ's Bureau of Import and Export Food Safety, and the two governments immediately agreed to cooperate to resolve this case.[8] The Japanese investigating team also visited the Tianyang Food factory. On February 6, the vice-minister of AQSIQ, Wei Chuanzhong, announced that someone, in either Japan or China, who wanted to derail the Sino-Japanese relationship might have deliberately poisoned the dumplings.[9]

But there was no doubt that Chinese officials were taking the question of food safety seriously. On February 15, the AQSIQ announced a large-scale inspection of companies exporting food from China. The focus of these inspections was to be the usage and management of pesticides and food additives. At the end of the month, the *Nikkei shinbun* reported that the Chinese enforcement of export quarantines was actually holding up food deliveries to Japan.[10] In early March, the Chinese government also cracked down on the individual purchase of poisonous and deleterious substances in an effort to prevent crimes involving poisons. At the National People's Congress in early March, the *gyōza*-poisoning incident was discussed, and press statements about the case were released. On March 6, local officials from Hebei publicly denied the possibility of poisoning at the factory in their province. On March 10, officials from China's Ministry of Agriculture emphasized the safety of Chinese agricultural products, including the vegetables and seafood products exported to Japan.[11]

Meanwhile, the Japanese government continued its high-level discussions on how to respond. Japan's finance minister, Nukaga Fukushirō, raised the issue with his Chinese counterpart, Xie Xuren, after the G-7 Conference, and both agreed to coordinate their efforts to solve it and to prevent future incidents. On February 21, Prime Minster Fukuda Yasuo met with State Councillor Tang Jiaxuan in Tokyo to propose establishing a medium- and long-term framework for Sino-Japanese cooperation on food security.[12] The leaders of both countries had been working hard to restore confidence in their bilateral ties, and Chinese President Hu Jintao was scheduled to visit in May 2008, the first visit to Tokyo of a Chinese president in ten years.[13] This summit meeting would be the culmination of two years of diplomatic effort, begun after Prime Minister Koizumi Jun'ichirō left office in September 2006, to redefine Japan's relations with China. The public outcry over the *gyōza* poisoning, though, threatened to ruin a carefully orchestrated effort at reconciliation.

In the end, the *gyōza* incident was only one of several issues on the agenda of an otherwise highly successful summit. In the joint statement released by the Chinese and Japanese governments on May 7, 2008, defining their "mutually beneficial relationship based on common strategic interests," food safety was mentioned only briefly: "To promote mutually beneficial cooperation and expand common benefits in a wide range of fields, including trade, investment, information and communication technology, finance, *food and product safety*, protection of intellectual property rights, business environment, agriculture, forestry and fisheries industries, transport and tourism, water, and healthcare" (italics added).[14] Public interest in the issue in Japan, however, ensured that it would be addressed at the separate press conference held by President Hu and Prime Minister Fukuda. In their statement on implementing this new vision, the two leaders released a set of seventy points. Point 49 stated, "Both sides will further strengthen their cooperation for the protection of the lives and health of the peoples of the two countries. Regarding the recent case of food poisoning caused by frozen processed foods, both sides will further strengthen their investigation and cooperation in both Japan and China in order to discover the truth as soon as possible."[15] During the question-and-answer session, President Hu observed,

> Concerning the issue of toxic substances being mixed in with frozen dumplings, the Chinese Government places a strong emphasis on food safety and on human health. The Chinese Government has conducted a serious probe into this incident. Concerning the state of the investigation, the department in charge has already communicated sufficiently with the Japanese side. As for the next step, the relevant departments of both countries will continue with the investigation, strengthening their cooperation so as to uncover the whole truth about the incident as soon as possible.

Prime Minister Fukuda replied at the end of the press conference: "Regarding the issue of toxic substances mixed in with frozen dumplings, given that the Chinese side is expanding the effort, I think both sides should further step up their investigations and cooperation."[16]

In early August, however, the *Yomiuri shinbun* broke the story that the same batch of frozen dumplings produced by Tianyang Food's processing plant in Hebei Province that had led to the Japanese cases had also poisoned four Chinese citizens.[17] Methamidophos had been discovered after these new cases were reported in June. The day after the *Yomiuri shinbun* ran the story in Tokyo, Japan's foreign minister, Kōmura Masahiko, acknowledged that a month earlier, the Ministry of Foreign Affairs had been informed by Chinese authorities about the case but had kept it quiet at the request of Chinese government so as to not hinder its domestic investigation of the crime.[18] An official from the Asia and Oceanic Affairs Bureau of the Ministry of Foreign Affairs told Democratic Party of Japan (DPJ) legislators that Chinese officials had told the Japanese government on July 7, the first day of the Hokkaido G-8 Summit meeting, and had requested that it not be publicized. The ministry had reported this to the prime minister's office with the recommendation that Japan comply with China's request, since the investigation was ongoing, and the prime minister's office seemed to agree.[19] The following week, Foreign Minister Kōmura visited Beijing and met with State Councillor Dai Bingguo and the Chinese minister for foreign affairs, Yang Jiechi, and the two governments agreed to wrap up the case as quickly as possible.

The Criminal Investigation

Diplomacy aside, the police agencies of Japan and China encountered several hurdles in their investigation of the case. Local police in Hyōgo and Chiba began their investigation immediately and then turned to the National Police Agency (NPA) for guidance on preventing any further harm. The NPA then convened a policy meeting at which the two prefectural police agencies coordinated their investigations.[20] The NPA became the primary agency working with its Chinese counterparts and met with officials of China's Ministry of Public Security (MPS) in Tokyo on February 21 and 22 to discuss the case. Several days later, a high-level conference between the two countries' police agencies was held in Beijing, at which they agreed to accelerate the investigation by exchanging evidence. Japan's NPA agreed to provide its test results related to the methamidophos and asked the MPS to share the written statements by the Tianyang Food factory workers.[21] On April 12, the NPA called an end to its investigation of the gyōza poisonings without having discovered when the imported dumplings had been poisoned.[22]

The Japanese police had investigated the full distribution route, from the Chinese subsidiary's factory that made the gyōza, to the shipment from the port in Tianjin, China, to Yokohama City, Japan. Two of the poisoning cases involved gyōza that took this route to Chiba. The gyōza that went to Hyōgo traveled from Yokohama to Osaka and from there to Hyōgo. The NPA pointed out that the methamidophos found in the dumplings and their packaging was pure and unlikely to have found its way into the food unless it was deliberately inserted. Moreover, according to the NPA, it is not possible to get methamidophos in Japan, as it is very strictly regulated.[23] Over the year following the poisonings, the Chinese police visited Tokyo twice, and the NPA delegation visited China twice, to consult on each other's investigation of the case. Chinese authorities disputed the allegation that the crime was committed in China, claiming that they had found no evidence of the crime.

The investigation was not resolved until 2010. Although the police in both countries seemed to have reached a stalemate, diplomacy continued in an effort to build confidence in bilateral cooperation on food safety. Japan's new ruling party, the DPJ, took office in September 2009 and agreed with the need to strengthen government protections for consumers. The party was just as anxious to hasten the resolution of the gyōza case as its predecessors were, although it had differed with the LDP on the design of the new consumer affairs agency. Thus, when Prime Minister Hatoyama Yukio visited Beijing for the trilateral summit meeting in October with China and South Korea, he met with Wen Jiabao and they concluded the Japan-China Food Safety Initiative, a high-level dialogue on food safety issues.[24] These issues also were on the agenda for the trilateral meeting of health ministers from China, Japan, and South Korea in November 2009. All three health ministers committed their countries to the timely notification of any health and/ or sanitation problems, a timely response to any incident, and simultaneous notification and cooperation with the WHO.[25]

Nonetheless, Japan's media began to raise concerns that the Chinese government had lost interest in the gyōza case. In March 2010, the Yomiuri shinbun reported a press statement by a provincial official from Hebei Province who would say only that there were no additional results and the investigation team should not be interfered with, which created concern in Japan that in fact the investigation had come to an end. Also, the local branch of Tianyang Food had new plans that included consolidating its factories elsewhere, effectively destroying the place where the crime was suspected to have been committed.[26]

Then on March 26, 2010, Xinhua reported the arrest of a Chinese suspect in the gyōza case.[27] The following month, the Japanese NPA and the Chinese MPS met in Tokyo for two days to consult on the case. Lu Yueting, a temporary worker at Tianyang Food, had been detained by the

Chinese police, and he had admitted to being disgruntled with his pay and benefits at the factory. The Chinese police had already confiscated the needle that Lu used to insert the poison into the dumplings and had corroborated the facts with eyewitnesses. The Chinese MPS reportedly agreed to formally accuse Lu for the cases in Hyōgo and Chiba Prefectures,[28] and on August 10, China's prosecutors indicted him for the crime.[29] After more than two years since the incident, Chinese authorities closed the case on the *gyōza* food-poisoning case in Japan.

In May 2010, the health ministers of Japan and China met in Tokyo to conclude a Memorandum of Understanding on Food Safety Promotion. Their agenda was broad, including coping with new strains of influenza and establishing disaster emergency responses and food safety policies. The memorandum created a vehicle for sharing information on relevant laws and standards, inspection procedures and technology, and control measures regarding harmful organisms, diseases, and toxic and harmful residues.[30]

China's Food Safety Challenges

Japan's food importers were deeply wounded by the incident. The market immediately responded to the heightened concerns over the safety of Japan's imported food from China, and Japan's food industry was confounded. While imports of vegetables from China declined, sales of domestically produced vegetables, such as garlic and ginger, increased. Domestic pork prices also soared. Other incidents of mishandled food from overseas were discovered, including rice containing residues of pesticides, eel labeled as domestically produced but found to be of Chinese origin, and products advertised as blowfish and clams falsely labeled. Rising global food prices also added to the public concern over Japan's food supply. Higher feed prices pushed up the price of milk, and the higher cost of oil resulted in surcharges to fisheries and agricultural businesses.

Japan's consumers were shocked to find how dependent they had become on food, both raw and processed, imported from China. In China, its own scandal involving the chemical melamine found in milk products had created a furor, and its coming on the heels of the *gyōza*-poisoning cases only further cemented the Japanese view of Chinese food products as being unsafe. Restoring consumer confidence was difficult when incident after incident revealed problems with the Japanese food industries' management of food safety. The industries then came under further suspicion when later that year yet another Chinese import, this time involving kidney beans, was discovered to contain unacceptable levels of the chemical fertilizer dichlorvos. The frozen kidney beans had been grown on a Chinese farm and sold by Nichirei Foods.

The kidney bean case had been discovered just as consumer confidence in China's efforts to improve its food safety measures was starting to recover. According to the MAFF's monthly statistics on imports, the volume of imports to Japan of Chinese vegetables dropped suddenly in February 2008 after the *gyōza* food-poisoning cases, to 28,000 tons, 33 percent less than the same month the year before, and by May, the monthly import volume had dropped 49 percent from the year before. Yet from June onward, there seemed to be an upward trend, and by September, the volume of vegetable imports was only 3 percent less than it had been in 2007. In large part, this confidence was attributed to the efforts by Japan's own food industry to enhance its oversight of local production sites and farms in China.[31]

The Policy Challenge

The *gyōza*-poisoning case raised several policy challenges for Japan. The first and most pressing was not directly related to food safety. Rather, it was the need for a legal framework of cooperation on criminal investigations with China's police. At the time of the *gyōza* incident, which, early on, was identified as a case of criminal intent, there were no formal mechanisms for Japanese and Chinese police agencies to collaborate in investigating crimes. For years, this had been a concern for the Japanese police, as incidents involving Chinese suspects and cross-border crime networks required a fuller understanding of and cooperation with China's police agency. Both the number of Chinese residents in Japan and the number of arrests by the Japanese police of Chinese suspects were growing. By 2008, Chinese nationals comprised 40 percent of the total number of foreign residents in Japan, the largest national group of non-Japanese residents. The Japanese police were investigating more and more crimes involving Chinese nationals. In 2002, 36.5 percent of criminal cases and 40 percent of the foreign nationals arrested in Japan were Chinese, a ratio that stayed almost the same through the decade (table 5.1).

TABLE 5.1 Arrests of Foreign Nationals Visiting Japan

	Year	2003	2004	2005	2006	2007	2008	2009	2010	2011	2012
Total	Cases	40,615	47,128	47,865	40,128	35,782	31,252	27,836	19,809	17,272	15,368
Clearances	Persons	20,007	21,842	21,178	18,872	15,914	13,885	13,257	11,858	10,048	9,149
China	Cases	16,708	16,950	17,006	14,170	12,611	12,430	12,572	7,231	7,839	6,483
		41.1%	36.0%	35.5%	35.3%	35.2%	39.8%	45.2%	36.5%	45.4%	42.2%
	Persons	8,996	9,259	8,691	6,978	5,353	4,864	4,812	4,657	4,010	3,719
		45.0%	42.4%	41.0%	37.0%	33.6%	35.0%	36.3%	39.3%	39.9%	40.6%
Brazil	Cases	4,819	7,281	7,183	4,518	7,696	4,750	4,013	2,819	1,572	1,205
		11.9%	15.4%	15.0%	11.3%	21.5%	15.2%	14.4%	14.2%	9.1%	7.8%
	Persons	1,224	1,322	1,298	1,348	1,256	1,091	988	730	593	599
		6.1%	6.1%	6.1%	7.1%	7.9%	7.9%	7.5%	6.2%	5.9%	6.5%
Turkey	Cases	5,496	7,478	6,914	4,504	940	77	121	53	58	49
		13.5%	15.9%	14.4%	11.2%	2.6%	0.2%	0.4%	0.3%	0.3%	0.3%
	Persons	170	128	139	129	90	62	62	47	55	51
		0.8%	0.6%	0.7%	0.7%	0.6%	0.4%	0.5%	0.4%	0.5%	0.6%
Korea	Cases	2,973	3,207	3,176	3,585	3,631	2,711	2,588	2,318	1,181	1,658
		7.3%	6.8%	6.6%	8.9%	10.1%	8.7%	9.3%	11.7%	6.8%	10.8%
	Persons	1,793	2,063	2,013	2,151	2,025	1,600	1,641	1,394	1,071	1,007
		9.0%	9.4%	9.5%	11.4%	12.7%	11.5%	12.4%	11.8%	10.7%	11.0%
Colombia	Cases	1,289	1,013	1,905	2,234	562	1,124	723	375	87	62
		3.2%	2.1%	4.0%	5.6%	1.6%	3.6%	2.6%	1.9%	0.5%	0.4%
	Persons	284	207	183	151	88	79	49	51	20	35
		1.4%	0.9%	0.9%	0.8%	0.6%	0.6%	0.4%	0.4%	0.2%	0.4%
Philippines	Cases	1,569	1,745	1,986	2,152	2,036	1,673	1,503	1,159	1,058	938
		3.9%	3.7%	4.1%	5.4%	5.7%	5.4%	5.4%	5.9%	6.1%	6.1%
	Persons	1,333	1,637	1,791	1,922	1,807	1,490	1,357	1,128	1,035	789
		6.7%	7.5%	8.5%	10.2%	11.4%	10.7%	10.2%	9.5%	10.3%	8.6%
Vietnam	Cases	936	954	1,073	1,342	1,473	1,789	1,714	1,764	1,749	1,430
		2.3%	2.0%	2.2%	3.3%	4.1%	5.7%	6.2%	8.9%	10.1%	9.3%
	Persons	718	713	778	842	806	789	876	799	716	661
		3.6%	3.3%	3.7%	4.5%	5.1%	5.7%	6.6%	6.7%	7.1%	7.2%
Peru	Cases	877	915	1,079	832	630	709	674	564	710	371
		2.2%	1.9%	2.3%	2.1%	1.8%	2.3%	2.4%	2.8%	4.1%	2.4%
	Persons	573	576	582	527	463	478	477	402	330	256
		2.9%	2.6%	2.7%	2.8%	2.9%	3.4%	3.6%	3.4%	3.3%	2.8%

(continued)

TABLE 5.1 (*continued*)

	Year	2003	2004	2005	2006	2007	2008	2009	2010	2011	201.
Thailand	Cases	831	864	982	778	600	521	484	422	270	251
		2.0%	1.8%	2.1%	1.9%	1.7%	1.7%	1.7%	2.1%	1.6%	1.6%
	Persons	699	761	790	702	570	490	431	363	256	232
		3.5%	3.5%	3.7%	3.7%	3.6%	3.5%	3.3%	3.1%	2.5%	2.5%

Source: National Police Agency, Japan, "Rainichi gaikokujin no omo na kokuseki betsu kenkyo jōkyō no su heisei 15 nen–24 nen" [Arrests of Foreign Nationals Visiting Japan by Nationality, 2003–2012], Keisatsu hakush heisei-25 [National Police Agency White Paper, 2013], http://www.npa.go.jp/hakusyo/h25/data.html.

Until 2003, the two police agencies interacted mainly through diplomatic channels, with regular consultations with the police attaché at the Chinese embassy in Tokyo. In 2004, however, officials from the NPA and China's MPS began to meet directly about five times a year. In 2005, the two police agencies agreed to work on drafting a mutual legal assistance treaty (MLAT) that would allow for closer cooperation on investigations and indictments. Japan had concluded a MLAT with the United States in 2006 and with South Korea in 2007, and the *gyōza* case in January 2008 accelerated the conclusion of the Japan-China MLAT. In May 2008, Japan approved the treaty, and on August 29, 2008, China ratified the Treaty Between Japan and the People's Republic of China on Mutual Legal Assistance in Criminal Matters.[32]

Beyond the Chinese *gyōza* poisonings, however, the NPA had to contend with the rising number of crimes pertaining to Japan's own food safety (table 5.2). In 2008 alone, the number of arrests for violations of the Sanitation Law and crimes such as falsifying labels and other violations of the fair trade law had risen to thirty-seven, involving ninety-one suspects. Of these, sixteen cases, resulting in fifty-seven arrests, had to do with the false labeling of food products, the highest number of food safety–related crimes in fourteen years. Some of the headline cases of false labeling involved imports from China. One was a marine seafood producer that mislabeled eels imported from China as being from Japan, and another was a fisheries merchant who, to import inspectors, identified shucked oysters imported from China as fishing bait but then sold them at retail as food. Both

TABLE 5.2 Food Safety-Related Crimes, 2006–2008

Time Period	Details	Response by National Police Agency
May 2006–October 2007	A meat-manufacturing and -processing company labels chicken from outside the prefecture as "local produce" and extracts nearly ¥63 million from its eleven retailers.	From May to June 2008, one company and six people are charged with fraud and violating the Unfair Competition Prevention Act.
November 2007	A seafood import sales company declares 82 lbs. (400 kg) of shucked oyster from China as bait to cut costs for poison inspection but sells them to retailers as edible produce.	In February 2008, one company and one individual are charged with violating the Food Sanitation Law by failing to properly declare imports.
October–December 2007	A seafood-processing company sells 1,036 lbs. (470 kg) of globefish the have not passed necessary tests to be legal to sell.	In April 2008, one company and one individual are charged with violating the Food Sanitation Law by illegally selling unsanitary foods.
December 2007–January 2008	Three cases of food poisoning occur from frozen *gyōza* containing methamidophos, an organophosphate insecticide.	To prevent further incidents from occurring, prefectural police from Chiba and Hyogo undertake a joint investigation and publicize these cases under their regulations. The National Police Agency exchanges information with the Chinese Ministry of Public Security for further fact-finding.
February–April 2008	A seafood import sales company purposely mislabels approximately 15 tons of grilled eel (*unagi*) from China as produced in Mikawa Isshiki, Aichi.	From November to December 2008, three companies and eight people were charged with violating the Prefecture Unfair Competition Prevention Act.

Source: National Police Agency, Japan, "Tokushu: nichijo seikatsu wo obiyakasu hanzaihe no torikumi" [Special Report on Policies on Crimes That Threaten the Daily Lives of Japanese Citizens]), Keisatsu hakusho heisei-21 [National Police Agency White Paper, 2009], http://www .npa.go.jp/hakusyo/h21/honbun/html/ld120000.html.

were Japanese companies, and the individuals charged with the crimes were Japanese nationals.[33] The increasing amount of imports and an insufficient regulatory system for the food trade with China had opened the door to this type of false labeling.

The second challenge posed by the Chinese *gyōza* case was ensuring that Japan's food imports were safe. The *gyōza*-poisoning cases were ample proof that Japan's regulatory framework for food safety was inadequate, and enhancing the oversight of imports and imposing stricter controls over Japanese companies importing food from abroad so that imported food passed domestic food safety requirements were paramount. But as the proportion of Japanese food products from overseas grew, the mechanisms for monitoring and identifying their origin became even more difficult. Two aspects of this process were particularly troubling. The first was that the *gyōza* dumplings were processed in China, and processed food coming into Japan was subjected to only random sampling for inspection purposes. The second was that although a number of agencies had a role in food safety, there was no overarching regulatory policy or mechanism for ensuring food safety.

Finally, Japan's consumers were shocked by this incident and by the revelation that there was so little oversight over food production and distribution in China. Neither Japan's consumers nor Japanese food-processing companies had fully understood the implications of the rapid expansion of Japanese investment in food production in China. In the mid-1980s, Japanese companies had begun to invest with Chinese partners in food production, with Suntory Beer announcing its joint venture in China in March 1984, the first major Japanese joint venture for food processing. This was soon followed by several new Japanese food-processing joint ventures. Mitsubishi Corporation and Yamada Food Trading Company announced their investment in a Chinese joint venture in June of the same year, including the construction of a food-processing center in Zhejiang Province.[34] In November, Marubeni Corporation and Marubeni Foods announced their investment in growing strawberries in China that would be frozen and imported to Japan.[35] Seafood production by Kyushu Trading Company in China was announced the following spring as a means of introducing Japan's seafood-processing technology to Chinese manufactures in return for reimporting products back to Japan.[36] By the 1990s, Japanese joint ventures with Chinese firms had taken off, and by 2008, more than two hundred Japanese food companies were producing food in China.[37]

A result of these Japanese food industry mergers was that more and more of the food consumed in Japan came from China. Yet especially for processed food, which was increasingly popular in both restaurant and household food consumption, there was little information about its source or the conditions under which it had been produced. The reaction of Japan's consumers, therefore, was to refuse to purchase Chinese food products, and as sales dropped, imports from China plummeted.

It was not only Japanese who worried about food safety in China. Chinese consumers, too, began to demand better food safety regulation in their country. Months after the *gyōza* food-poisoning in Japan, a catastrophic case exposing the ineffectual food monitoring in China was reported. On July 16, 2008, sixteen babies in Gansu Province were diagnosed with kidney stones after having consumed milk powder containing melamine that was produced by the Sanlu Group, also based in Hebei Province. Melamine is commonly used to manufacture plastics, but it can also be used to artificially increase the protein content in food products like milk. Digesting melamine can lead to renal and urinary problems, especially in infants. Although Sanlu was the main target of investigation and the primary abuser, twenty-one other companies in China also were found to have used melamine as a synthetic food additive.[38]

The scandal gained international attention in September 2008 after China's agriculture minister, Sun Zhengcai, revealed that contaminated milk had sickened more than 54,000 babies and killed four.[39] The WHO announced on September 18 the discovery of more than 6,240 cases of kidney stones in infants, including three deaths. Although the exact onset date of illness was unknown, according to the Chinese Ministry of Health, a Chinese manufacturer had received a complaint of illness in March 2008.[40] An update by the WHO four days later revised the totals to 40,000 people who had sought medical attention and 12,900 who had been hospitalized with contamination. By December 1 that year, Chinese Ministry of Health officials had readjusted this figure to nearly 300,000 affected by the contaminated milk.[41] This case led to a number of criminal prosecutions: two people were executed; one person was given a suspended death sentence; three were given life imprisonment; and two received fifteen-year jail terms. Several government officials, including Li Changjiang, director of the AQSIQ, were forced to resign. On September 20, the MHLW in Japan asked food producers and importers to ensure that their inventories of Chinese-made milk products were safe and to carry out melamine tests on any newly imported milk. Then on September 22, the MHLW extended this request by asking importers also to test milk imported before the crisis broke on September 20.[42] Equally important, however, was the overall policy context for protecting Japan's consumers. The melamine scandal reinforced yet again Japanese consumers' sense that food produced in China was not properly regulated—and was dangerous.

DOMESTIC INTERESTS AND ACTIVISTS

Opinion polls in Japan revealed the great impact of the *gyōza* poisoning on people's overall perceptions of China. In polls taken by the Genron NPO / *China Daily* series in 2008—the year of the incident—and 2009 and 2010, many Japanese indicated that the unresolved case of food poisoning factored largely into their concerns about whether or not they could trust China. Many of those who had a negative impression of China attributed it to "[continued] concerns about the Chinese government's handling of food safety issues."[43] Even in 2012, when asked directly about how they felt about the safety of food produced in China, 92.8 percent of the Japanese polled said that they still had anxiety.[44] Beyond this diffuse impact on public attitudes toward China, however, were a number of domestic interests affected by the *gyōza* case that were not normally associated with diplomacy.

Japan's Food Industry

About 10 percent of Japan's manufacturing is in the food business, including livestock and fisheries, as well as bakeries, drinks, and other processed foodstuffs. Like most other Japanese manufacturers, Japan's food industry expanded its production through joint ventures with

Chinese firms. During the 1990s as Japan's economic growth slowed, joint ventures with Chinese agricultural producers and food processors expanded as Japanese consumers' demand for low-cost food products grew.

According to Komori Masahiko, director of research for the Japan Development Bank (Nihon seisaku tōshi ginkō), changes in Japanese eating habits, as well as the growing Chinese demand for a more varied diet, led to more joint ventures between Japanese food companies and the newly modernizing food industry in China. Direct investment by Japanese food companies in China grew from ¥1.3 billion in 1990 to ¥24.9 billion in 2005. In 2008, according to Komori, when the Chinese *gyōza* poisoning occurred in Japan, 212 processed-food companies and 15 agricultural companies were located in China,[45] the bulk in the eastern provinces. Concentrations of Japanese joint ventures also could be found in Shanghai City (59 companies), as well as Shandong (47), Guangdong (21), and Jiangsu (19) Provinces (figure 5.4).

Japan's trading companies are significant players in the food trade as well and have expanded their involvement in food processing in China.[46] For example, Itōchū has long been invested in the food industry in China, but its investment in food safety management and traceability systems put it in a significantly advantageous position in the China market after the *gyōza* incidents.[47] In November 2008, Itōchū invested in the Ting Hsin Holding Corporation, a Taiwanese conglomerate that is the largest food and distribution business group in China and Taiwan. In 2010, together with Asahi Breweries, Itōchū significantly expanded its partnership with Ting Hsin. Itōchū brought its management and, particularly, its food safety management expertise to the deal and, in return, got access to Ting Hsin's operational platforms in China's and Taiwan's food and distribution markets. Based on the expectation that China's economic growth and consumer spending would continue to be strong, Itōchū reorganized its operations to make China the springboard for a global strategy that would include Asia and Australia. Itōchū bet not only on China as a location for its operations but also on Chinese consumers' rising demand and more sophisticated preferences as the driver of future corporate growth.

FIGURE 5.4 Japanese food joint ventures in China, 2007–2008. In addition to joint ventures, Japanese food companies also had 31 representative offices in China: Beijing (6), Guandong (2), Hong Kong (2), Liaoning (3), Shandong (5), and Shanghai (13). (Data from *Chuugoku shinshutsu kigyou ichiran hijyou jyougaisha hen 2007–2008* [*A Look at Expanding Chinese Businesses and Privately Held Companies, 2007–2008*]; and *21 seiki chuugoku souken* [*21st Century China Research*], Sososha, December 2007. A similar map also appears in Komori Masahiko, *Chugoku Shokuhin Douran* [*Chinese Food Incidents*] [Tokyo: Toyo Keizai Shinposha, 2008], 96, but Komori has aggregated the data differently. Original artwork courtesy of Martin Hinze)

Japanese food companies that imported processed food from China, not the major trading companies, were the hardest hit by the *gyōza*-poisoning scandal. Japan Tobacco, of which JT Foods is a subsidiary, is the largest food company in Japan and, of course, felt an immediate impact.[48] In early March after the poisoning, the CEO of JT, Kimura Hiroshi, held a press conference announcing that his company would reduce its outsourcing of food processing in China and would impose stricter management standards at its factories.

But Kimura also acknowledged that JT and other Japanese food-processing companies would be hard-pressed to completely cut off production in China. Production in China gave these companies easy access to raw food products, and labor costs were low. Furthermore, Japan's food companies already had invested heavily in the frozen-food infrastructure there.[49] By early May, JT and other food-manufacturing companies in Japan were announcing curtailed production of frozen-food products in China.[50] Other companies announced additional monitoring measures, including stricter quality controls and factory management procedures. Maruha Nichiro Foods, for example, introduced surveillance cameras, while Ajinomoto installed a new hygiene maintenance team.[51] JT Foods ultimately merged with Katokichi and completely renovated its food development center in Tokyo as a result of the loss of consumer confidence in its products after the *gyōza* incident. In an effort to focus on the growing demand for lower prices and greater food security, its executives described this initiative as a make-or-break effort for the company to regain consumer confidence in its brand.[52]

Food Imports and Japan's Aim of Food "Self-Sufficiency"

The outbreak of food poisoning from Chinese dumplings fed into the broader debate in Japan about the nation's self-sufficiency in food production. The MAFF had long articulated a policy of raising Japan's self-sufficiency levels, and in large part, Japan's postwar agricultural subsidies to farms were justified in view of the country's need to improve its ability to feed its own people. Imports of food-stuffs were increasing. Trade liberalization, especially since the Uruguay Round of the General Agreement on Tariffs and Trade (GATT) negotiations in the 1980s, had reduced protections for Japan's agriculture sector, and less costly imports were becoming widely available to Japanese consumers. In addition, as Japan's economy slowed in the 1990s, Japan's consumers were more willing to buy less expensive imported food, despite the widely held view that their preferences were for Japanese food products. After the MAFF documented the decline in Japan's food self-sufficiency in terms of caloric intake, an approach that was criticized, it shifted its calculation to include the

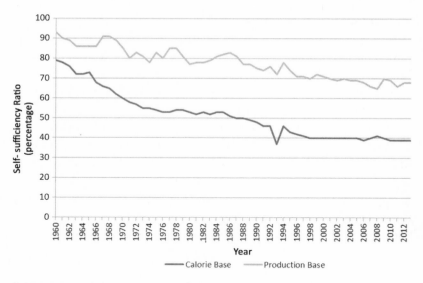

FIGURE 5.5 Japan's food self-sufficiency ratio. The information is presented in fiscal years. (Ministry of Agriculture, Forestry, and Fisheries [MAFF], Japan, *Shokuryō jikyūritsu heya* [*Food Self-Sufficiency Room*], http://www.maff.go.jp/j/zyukyu/. For more information on how each rate is calculated, see MAFF, *Yoku wakaru shokuryō jikyūritsu* [*Understanding the Food Self-Sufficiency Ratio*], November 2013, http://www .maff.go.jp/j/zyukyu/pdf/260219factbook.pdf)

production-based trend (figure 5.5). Whichever indicator is used, however, the trajectory of food self-sufficiency was downward.

As the primary regulator of agricultural products, the MAFF was responsible for ensuring the first line of defense for Japan's food imports. But it also was responsible for supporting and promoting Japan's domestic agriculture. Japan's Cabinet Office had long advocated a policy goal of ensuring food self-sufficiency of 50 percent.[53] The growing tensions between the policy debate over trade liberalization and agricultural reform produced a myopic defense of Japanese agriculture and a policy focus by the MAFF on enhancing domestic production rather than ensuring a stable and safe supply of food.[54]

The MAFF's calculations of the country's food self-sufficiency have been seen as problematic, however, and the overall goal of defending Japan's domestic agriculture has been called into question. The variables affecting self-sufficiency are, of course, beyond the control of the Japanese government. For example, factors affecting the share of caloric intake in 2011, which remained essentially unchanged from 2010, were the improvement in the wheat crop due to weather conditions, allowing for an increase in production. The Great East Japan Earthquake prompted a temporary increase in the demand for rice, though this soon stabilized. Then the nuclear meltdown at Fukushima Daiichi introduced a new variable: radiation poisoning. The domestic production of seafood fell because of the contamination of Japan's coastal waters, and the demand for beef and vegetables fell as well, leading to a drop in prices and lower production. The entire Tohoku region where the earthquake and tsunami struck is home to a large share of Japanese agriculture, thereby creating tremendous pressure on its food supply.[55]

As the country's food imports grew, the regulatory framework for monitoring Japan's imports relied increasingly on the cooperation of its food industry to oversee its partners abroad. Japan's food companies are subject to stringent food safety and hygiene regulations. Raising foreign-sourced food products to that level of oversight, however, was difficult, if not impossible, for the health officials in the MHLW to monitor by itself. In 1988, forty food companies created a voluntary study group to discuss improving the safety of food imports. Most of the companies that joined the Association for the Safety of Imported Food (Nihon yunyū shokuhin anzen suishin kyōkai) were trading companies, food manufacturers, and some distributing companies. The MHLW became interested in the association and in 1992 sponsored it as an incorporated body. By then, its membership had expanded to eighty companies. Staffed by former industry employees, this association became a critical link in regulating the industry, providing seminars and briefings on new regulatory requirements and facilitating the interaction between MHLW inspectors and food safety managers at the plant level.[56]

Consumer Advocates

Food safety has been a crucial postwar cause for Japan's consumer movement. As Patricia Maclachlan argues, food safety has played a leading role "in Japanese definitions of the consumer interest."[57] In her pathbreaking study of the postwar Japanese consumer movement, she describes the efforts of the Japanese consumer activists in the pursuit of food safety, such as setting labeling standards, restricting both synthetic food additives and pesticides, and banning imports that use postharvest chemicals. But in her study of the consumer movement's battle against food additives in the 1970s and 1980s, she concludes that the movement ran headlong into the neoliberal policy coalition formed under Prime Minister Nakasone Yasuhiro in support of government deregulation. The MHLW sided in the end with the Japanese food industry, which favored cost-effective production, rather than with Japan's consumer activists, who wanted strict controls over food safety.[58]

Ironically, it was the very organization, Japan's Consumer Cooperatives Union (JCCU), which was created to serve the interests of food safety for Japan's consumers, that became embroiled in the Chinese *gyōza* controversy. In 2007, the JCCU had 24,687 members, with 79.5 percent of its merchandise sold by 496 retail co-ops. Retail sales by product category were predominantly food and grocery sales, with fresh foods accounting for 53.7 percent of sales and grocery, 24.8 percent. These community-based retail co-ops sold through stores, home delivery, and catalog mail order and were organized in ten systems of distribution around Japan (Kobe, Sapporo, Tokyo, Kanagawa, Saitama, Miyagi, Chiba, Kyoto, Toyota, and Pal-system Tokyo).

The devastating discovery of poisoned *gyōza* distributed by the JCCU's CO-OP brand brought home the extent to which Japan's ability to provide food for its people was shaped by economic realities, and much of what Japanese consumers were now demanding was frozen or otherwise processed foods that were family friendly and easy to prepare. Frozen *gyōza* were a common treat for most households, and their production was concentrated in China. Even for the quality-conscientious JCCU, cost was trumping what had long been seen as a cultural preference for Japanese food products.

The JCCU responded rapidly and comprehensively to the *gyōza*-poisoning cases.[59] In contrast to JT Foods, it did not simply focus on slowing its outsourcing from China. Rather, it concentrated internally on its own management system and how it had failed.

The JCCU engaged outside experts to investigate the causes and remedies required to prevent any further incidents. The goal was to develop an effective crisis management system within the organization. The investigation team reexamined all six cases and determined that the JCCU had not responded appropriately. In three separate incidents in October and November 2007, consumers reported to their cooperatives in the Tohoku region the presence of bad smells emanating from frozen *gyōza* packages. Because there was no damage to the packaging, this was written off as a problem in distribution, but a more careful examination of the cases could have prevented the harm caused in later incidents. Furthermore, the JCCU did not issue a warning to consumers. Local cooperatives did not alert the head of the JCCU until after the police had visited the cooperative, and this delayed the notification to others in the JCCU network. Finally, drawing on international and U.S. efforts to ensure a safe food supply, the JCCU introduced the concept of food defense as it sought to develop future prescriptions. The intentional poisoning of the *gyōza* raised awareness of the need to guard against not only the misuse of chemical additives or fertilizers but also acts of terrorism or malign intent.

The JCCU's investigatory committee conducted a detailed analysis of the cases, including open hearings at local cooperatives. The JCCU's commission then recommended policies that were implemented across its national cooperatives and became part of the discussion at the national government level on improving Japan's food safety.[60] On July 28, 2008, the chairman of the JCCU, Yamashita Toshifumi, was invited to present his views to Prime Minister Fukuda, who was reforming Japan's consumer policy priorities.[61]

When the *gyōza* controversy erupted, well-established consumer advocates also played an important role in considering how to prevent a recurrence. One of the country's most active consumer advocacy groups is the Japan Housewives Association (Shufu rengōkai, or Shufuren). Shufuren works on all consumer issues, and on food safety issues it conducts seminars and study groups, with smaller, local citizen activist groups that focus solely on food issues. On the Chinese *gyōza* issue, Shufuren worked on shaping the Japanese government's response within its broader aim of enhancing consumer protections.

As Sano Mariko, the director-general of Shufuren, pointed out during an interview, even though food was the founding issue of Japan's consumer movement, as Japan's imports of food grew, consumer advocates found themselves less able to ensure that consumers had direct knowledge of where and how their food was produced.[62] She bemoaned Japan's declining ability to grow its own food and saw this as part of a bigger challenge resulting from the changing structure of the Japanese economy.

Cost and distribution factors were now given top priority in Japan's food supply choices. For example, cooperatives had long been one means for ensuring that consumers could have the best information possible about their sources of food, but because even the co-ops in Japan had become more and more like retail supermarkets, they were just as susceptible to food safety problems.[63] As Sano observed, even before the Chinese *gyōza* debate over food safety, a number of false labeling cases had been publicized in Japan,[64] a warning to the consumer movement that it had to change its focus as Japan's economy changed. Thus, Shufuren's immediate response to the *gyōza* case was an emphasis on product labeling and on persuading the government to require companies to declare the origin of food imported from abroad.

The large-scale, cost-effective production of food—more and more of which came from abroad—meant that labeling and advertising became the target of consumer activists' attention. Once the government began to move toward creating a consumer affairs agency, Sano Mariko took a more prominent role in the deliberations of its mandate and goals and served on the Consumer Affairs Commission established to advise the new agency. Along with Sano were other experts on consumer affairs, including several consumer advocates who had worked on consumer advisory boards or on product liability law issues, as well as a board member from Yukijirushi who had come from a consumer advocacy group. During the first few years, this commission produced a serious discussion, according to Sano, because of the consumer affairs movement's expertise and work experience.[65]

Local governments are the first public health interface between consumers and producers in Japan, and none was more influential in the response to the *gyōza*-poisoning case than the Tokyo Metropolitan Government (TMG). It was its first experience with managing a food safety crisis, and it became involved as soon as the food-poisoning case in Hyōgo Prefecture was discovered. Because the importer of the *gyōza* had its home offices in Shinagawa Ward in Tokyo, officials from the Tokyo government were included in the investigation of the supplier. Furthermore, when the China case broke out, the metropolitan government conducted an on-site investigation of JT Foods, and when it determined that all the poisoned *gyōza* had come from the same lot, it informed the MHLW and issued a warning to consumers not to eat this brand of *gyōza*. There were no victims from Tokyo, and while the Tokyo government did random sampling tests of *gyōza* being sold at retail shops, no evidence of methamidophos was found.[66]

Afterward, the MHLW drew up a list of contacts for all local officials responsible for food safety issues, which allowed the Tokyo government to have, for the first time, direct consultations with its counterparts in other localities in Japan. Nakajima Hideo, both the deputy director of the food safety control section in the Tokyo government's health and safety division and its food-poisoning investigator, began carrying a cell phone so that he could respond around the clock to any outbreak in Japan of a similar food-poisoning event. Japanese companies now are legally required to contact local authorities immediately in case of food-poisoning cases, and hospitals and doctors are required to contact the Japan Medical Association in case of incidents regarding the use of chemicals on vegetables. Now, as a result of the *gyōza* case, the manufacturing process of processed foods, too, is subject to local government inspection.

Since Tokyo residents had become very worried about foreign goods, the TMG recommended requiring labels showing the country of origin of imported processed foods. Then in February 2008, the metropolitan government began to consider requiring labels showing the origin of both the ingredients and the processing of food products. Considerable effort was made to solicit the opinions of Japan's large frozen-foods manufacturers as Tokyo considered whether to issue a local ordinance that would create a labeling law separate from the national government's labeling requirements in the Japan Agricultural Standard (JAS) law.[67] On March 27, 2008, the Tokyo government hosted a deliberation council on consumer policy, composed of experts and Tokyo residents, and it solicited public comments from residents. The conclusion of this policy review on April 30 produced the following decisions. First, frozen processed foods would be labeled with the country where the raw materials originated and the country where the top three raw ingredients (meat, vegetables, seafood, etc.) were produced. Second, when packaging made it difficult to show this information, the manufacturer could put it on its homepage or at its retail site or disclose it through its customer service telephone number. Although the national JAS law already required the labeling of fresh produce and foods, the TMG was the first to require labeling that included the origin of ingredients and the production site of processed frozen foods.

The significance of the Tokyo government's response to the *gyōza* poisonings cannot be understated. Tokyo is home to 13 million people and thus has the largest local government constituency in Japan. Moreover, the city is, in fact, a food importer, as it has few food production facilities within its administrative boundaries. Thus it has some experience with consumer safety issues regarding food products. Its testing system is relatively well developed, and it has had experience with residual pesticides and even with the radioactive testing in the aftermath of Chernobyl. According to Teramura Wataru, the Tokyo Metropolitan Government's supervisor for imported and harmful food, the Tokyo government can play an effective role in supplementing the efforts of the national government in ensuring the safety of imported food products. The national government's random sampling covers about 10 percent of Japan's food imports, but, he argues, there is no reason to be sanguine about the other 90 percent. The incentive for the Tokyo government is to be as assertive as possible in ensuring food safety.[68] Although the national government has the administrative responsibility for creating a legal framework for food safety, as Deputy Director Nakajima pointed out, "Tokyo is a locality composed almost exclusively of consumers, and thus the consumer voice in our policy is strong. Therefore, Tokyo Metropolitan Government, on its own, can develop a framework for policies that cannot be covered by national law."[69]

REGULATORY ADJUSTMENT

Frozen dumplings (*gyōza*) made in China—but distributed by two well-known and respected Japanese companies—poisoned several Japanese families, and by the end of the Chinese police's investigation, it was clear that this was not an accidental case of residual pesticide but an intentional act. The Japanese and Chinese police's lack of investigative protocols limited their cooperation and delayed the investigation. This in turn further enraged the public, and Japan's consumers stopped buying Chinese agricultural imports. Anti-Chinese sentiment simmered as months and then years passed with no apparent resolution of the case.

The *gyōza*-poisoning case revealed the lack of coordinated government policy and institutions to protect Japan's consumers. While bureaucrats in several ministries claimed a role in regulatory supervision, there was no overarching policy framework for regulating Japan's growing food imports. Moreover, private industry in Japan was virtually left to its own devices to decide how it would organize food safety in its purchases and production arrangements with Chinese factories. While the *gyōza* case flared into considerable bilateral tension between Japan and China, it also became the catalyst for pressure on the Japanese government to improve its own regulatory infrastructure for food safety.

The Fukuda cabinet responded to the food-poisoning incident in three ways. First, and most immediately, it sought China's cooperation in determining the cause of the incident, and it moved to centralize the management of food safety in the Japanese government. Second, the government expedited the regulation of imported agriculture and processed foods and drafted new guidelines for food importers. Finally, while not directly a consequence of the incident, the cabinet hastened deliberation of the legislation forming Japan's first Consumer Affairs Agency, in order to centralize its policy efforts to protect consumers' interests.

Japanese Food Safety Regulations and Chinese Manufacturers

The *gyōza*-poisoning case of 2008 exposed the continuing vulnerabilities in Japan's regulatory oversight of imported food. Food safety had become a pressing issue for the Japanese government long before Chinese food production became suspect, and the government already had significantly reformed its monitoring of Japan's food supply. Japan drew up its Food Safety Basic Law in 2003 in response to a rash of food safety problems, including the outbreak of bovine spongiform encephalopathy (BSE) in Japan and a series of cases of falsified food-labeling incidents. Japan's own domestic regulations for the handling of food and food products by Japan's food industry were established in the 1947 Food Sanitation Law, which was revised to ensure better risk management and to tighten even further the government's oversight of Japan's food supply.

The new 2003 Food Safety Basic Law defined the responsibilities of food business operators for ensuring that imported foods adhered to Japan's own sanitation and safety standards. Primary responsibility for compliance rested on the food companies, and they were monitored by the MHLW through visits to factory sites and random sampling of food products. The MHLW's food-monitoring plan was based on the strengthened Food Sanitation Law, and a new Food Safety Commission was established in the prime minister's office. The idea was to rationalize the task of overseeing food safety from the perspective of consumer interest. Past bureaucratic control had produced ineffectual oversight and conflicts of interest. The MAFF, for example, had a mandate for both inspecting livestock feed and encouraging Japanese livestock production, which contributed to the weak oversight found after the BSE outbreak.[70]

Ensuring adherence in overseas factories was a difficult task and depended on regular on-site inspections of Chinese factories. Local management was entrusted with implementing agreed-on standards, and for many Chinese companies, this meant retooling their factories to suit Japanese production methods. According to Watanabe Kōhei, the former president of Itōchū's food company, the best insurance was to have its Chinese partner, Longda Foodstuff Group, purchase Japanese production machinery and adopt the quality-control production techniques used in Japanese factories.[71]

After the *gyōza* case, the MHLW established even more rigorous safety and monitoring guidelines for both imported food and that processed abroad. Published in June 2008, these new Guidelines on

Hygiene Control of Import Processed Foods emphasized the need to "ensure and confirm the safety of imported processed foods in the exporting country to a level equivalent to that within Japan, *at all stages of the food supply process*, including raw materials, manufacturing and processing, storage and transportation" (italics added).[72] The stages were

- Supervision by the exporting country's government.
- Acceptance of raw materials.
- Product manufacturing and processing.
- Product storage, transportation, and distribution.

Also included were the acceptable procedures for recalling and disposing of products when a food hygiene problem was discovered. These new guidelines were designed for food manufacturers and importers under direct contract with overseas manufacturers and stipulated the need for written confirmation at the time of contract. The MHLW's guidelines also required Japanese importers to conduct field surveys, post local representatives, and test and inspect products to ensure compliance.

The criminal aspect of the *gyōza* food-poisoning case also had precedent for Japan's food safety reform. Also referenced in the drafting of these guidelines was the Special Measures Law Concerning the Prevention of Poisonous Substances from Contaminating Food in Distribution, which was created in 1987 in response to a food-poisoning case involving Ezaki Glico and Morinaga, Japanese confectioners. This case drew national attention in March 1984 when the president of Ezaki Glico was kidnapped from his home. Afterward, food products manufactured by Glico and Morinaga were randomly vandalized by a criminal group, which called itself the Kaijin 21 mensō (The 21-Face Monster), to blackmail the companies. The Japanese police registered twenty-eight cases of poisoning (attempted murder) in relation to this case, and they reported that between 1985 and 1987, they investigated 410 cases of copycat blackmail against Japanese companies that threatened product safety. Accordingly, new measures were adopted specifically for the criminal poisoning of food during the distribution process.[73]

The MHLW guidelines, of course, were intended for the industries' implementation and relied heavily on the assistance of the Association for the Safety of Imported Food (ASIF) for dissemination and explication. These guidelines became the focal point of briefings conducted by the ASIF to inform Japanese companies of the regulatory changes resulting from the *gyōza* cases.[74] In addition, the guidelines were expanded to include updates and alerts to events and policy changes in China. The ASIF, which became an independent nonprofit organization in 2011, now has ninety-three members, more than double the number when it began. Its managing director, Samejima Futoshi, came from a position at a major food manufacturer.[75] His assessment is that Japan's challenge really boils down to whether current laws are sufficient to regulate today's level of imports. Under current law, although the government must approve a Japanese company that manufactures food, many small importers today are not legally required to register with the government. They are inspected only if they submit an import request, and their facilities need not be inspected. Thus, Samejima argues, the biggest policy question is really how to impose self-regulation on all of Japanese industry.[76]

Beyond the new inspection guidelines of 2008 lies the deeper question of how to prevent intentional harm to Japan's food supply. Here industry has had a less unified approach. Because of the criminal intent in the Chinese *gyōza* case, those from industry involved in the policy debate have been considering various ways of improving the oversight of the food-manufacturing process. At the core of the MHLW guidelines are the Hazard Analysis and Critical Control Point (HACCP) procedures developed in the United States and now seen as the global standard for ensuring food safety in production.[77] According to Samejima, virtually all of Japan's major food makers employ HACCP practices. But the broader goal of "food defense," including surveillance of staff and other intrusive monitoring on the factory floor, has faced considerable resistance in Japan. "To prevent criminal behavior, we would have to suspect everyone, and that is just not consistent with Japanese management practices," Samejima pointed out.[78] Whether Japanese industry and government will move toward adopting a stringent food defense plan remains to be seen. For now, industry has consented to the new regulations put out by the MHLW, and those larger Japanese food companies that operate in China have ensured that their Chinese business partners fully subscribe to Japanese regulatory expectations. Small and medium-size businesses, however, do not have the resources to implement on-site inspections overseas.

Food Safety and the New Consumer Affairs Agency

The Japanese government's response to the *gyōza* cases was widely criticized for being slow and uncoordinated. Prime Minister Fukuda began to remedy this in February 2008 by creating food-danger information officers in the cabinet and three ministries that would be responsible for gathering and disseminating information on food safety. These officers met each month to consolidate information and centralize the follow-up on the *gyōza* case as well as other issues that arose. The meetings were staffed by the director-general of the Citizens' Quality of Life Bureau (Naikakufu kokuminseikatsu kyokuchō). At the time, this bureau in the Cabinet Office was responsible for consumer affairs, but it was not well positioned in the bureaucracy to serve as a control center when the *gyōza* case erupted, as it had little authority across bureaucratic lines and was insufficiently staffed.

The crisis management group established by the Fukuda cabinet brought together officials from the Cabinet Food Safety Commission staff, the MHLW's planning and information office, the MAFF's food safety bureau, and the director of the school health and education division of the Ministry of Education.[79] A month later, this new food safety staff had written an emergency response manual emphasizing the need to put consumer safety ahead of all other goals. The main goals were to speed up the government's response and to get information out as soon as possible to the Japanese public. It had taken far too long—almost a full month—for information on the frozen *gyōza* produced in China to be made available.[80]

A second response by the Japanese government to the *gyōza* food-poisoning cases was to develop a centralized government agency dedicated to consumer affairs, both food safety and other consumer-related issues. While the dumpling incident focused national attention on the idea of a consumer affairs agency, other consumer safety problems called for greater government attention to consumer protection. In November 2007, the LDP had begun a study group on consumer problems (*shōhisha mondai chōsakai*), headed by Noda Seiko, in response to the product liability cases that seemed to be proliferating in Japan.[81] On January 4, 2008, just weeks before the *gyōza* food poisonings, Prime Minister Fukuda announced his intention to centralize the policies managed by various bureaucracies related to consumer issues. When the *gyōza*-poisoning case was discovered, the Fukuda cabinet accelerated its discussions, and on February 6, 2008, just days after it had held a ministerial conference in response to the *gyōza* poisonings, Chief Cabinet Secretary Machimura Nobutaka announced that he was convening the Council for Promoting Consumer Policy (Shōhisha gyōsei suishin kaigi). The head of this council was Professor Sasaki Takeshi of Gakushuin University, along with ten other experts. From the beginning, this was an effort to centralize the government's management of consumer affairs. Prime Minister Fukuda himself had been shocked at the lack of a unified government response to the *gyōza* poisonings, and on the same day he appointed Kishida Fumio, then minister of state for Okinawa and the Northern Territories affairs, as the minister for consumer affairs.

The pressures of the *gyōza* case abbreviated the deliberative effort to design the new Consumer Affairs Agency. The council was tasked with coming up with recommendations quickly, and Chief Cabinet Secretary Machimura acknowledged that the dumpling issue expedited the discussion. Even the prime minister felt that the accelerated time frame was not to his liking and admitted to the press that he wished he had more time to work on consumer affairs.[82] Similarly, in his opening remarks to the council at its first meeting on February 12, Fukuda explained that the Chinese-made dumplings incident had made him realize how important it was to act to prevent such harm from occurring in the future.[83] Information sharing between the national and the local governments was necessary to improve their response. Not only were bureaucracies not communicating effectively among themselves, but the local governments also were not communicating effectively with the national government.[84] Furthermore, not all of Japan's local governments had consumer affairs centers. Although the prefectural governments are mandated by law to have them, the municipalities are not. Nominally, the centers are part of the local municipal and prefectural governments and therefore are funded by local government budgets. Although they are the primary window for direct government information on consumer grievances, local budgets have limited the staffing and support for their administration.

Beyond the *gyōza* incident, a host of other products had lowered confidence in the government's handling of consumer protection, and it became clear that China was not to blame for most of them. Indeed, most of these incidents involved the recall of Japanese products. For example, children and elderly people had died trying to swallow bite-sized *konnyaku* jellies, and gas appliances made by Paloma Industries were recalled for leaking carbon monoxide. Accidents involving faulty exhaust ports in pools had resulted in the death of children. On May 19, 2008, Prime Minister Fukuda met with the families of victims of the Paloma Industries' faulty gas water heaters and the choking incidents involving *konnyaku* jellies. Both these cases had gone to court, and the families had been actively lobbying for greater national government attention to consumer protections.[85]

Beyond the management of food safety with China, Prime Minister Fukuda tried to elevate the issue by streamlining the government's management of consumer affairs. The idea was to create a "control tower" for consumer affairs, a single centralized agency with direct authority over consumer affairs. By late March, the prime minister had drafted a concept paper on a new consumer affairs agency for discussion by the Council for Promoting Consumer Policy. In late May, the council revised its findings and, on June 13, issued its final report. The new Consumer Affairs Agency would be in place by 2009 and would be able to act without being hindered by other agencies.[86]

Nonetheless, the new Consumer Affairs Agency, based on the new Consumer Affairs Agency and Consumer Commission Establishment Act, would not have full responsibility for food safety.[87] During the Council for Promoting Consumer Policy's final deliberations, it decided to keep the Food Safety Commission as a separate entity. The argument was that because of the scientific nature of its mandate of overseeing the safety of food and medical products, the Food Safety Commission needed to maintain its independence. Thus it would remain in the Cabinet Office. In late September, the Diet agreed to deliberate on the new Consumer Affairs Agency bill and related legislation. Although the agency was not as fully independent of the cabinet as opposition legislators wanted, it was given primary responsibility for centralizing information on consumer-related policies. In deliberations over the bills in the spring of 2009, the LDP and the DPJ disagreed over the structure of the new agency, but they had few substantive differences over the need for rationalizing administration related to consumer affairs.

This new agency was not the Goliath that many in the consumer protection agency wanted.[88] In its first year, it had only 202 employees, and its first budget was only ¥8.92 billion ($90.4 million).[89] By 2012, the Consumer Affairs Agency still was small compared with Japan's other bureaucracies, and its ministers carried multiple portfolios, making it difficult for them to assert leadership on consumer affairs in the cabinet. The agency's staff numbered only 270, and its annual budget was ¥9.04 billion ($109 million). By contrast, in 2012 the bureaucracy charged with managing Japan's industrial policy, the Ministry of Economic, Trade, and Industry (METI), employed a staff of 8,582 and managed a budget of ¥4.83 trillion ($61.9 billion), and the MHLW, which oversees food safety and other safety issues, employed 32,485 and had a budget of ¥32.09 trillion ($411 billion).[90]

Nonetheless, Japan's experience with the Chinese *gyōza* shaped the new consumer agency. At the final meeting on January 29, 2009, of the Council for Promoting Consumer Policy, attended by Fukuda's successor as prime minister, Asō Tarō, the council summarized its activities: "The dumpling and melamine milk incident has added uncertainties to Chinese imports and increased demand for domestic production, but at the same time, food camouflage in Japan has made it clear that at this point, there is no public office that can think from the perspective of our consumers."[91] The controversy over the import of the frozen *gyōza* not only changed Japan's food safety policies, but it also stimulated the creation of a new government institution designed to protect consumer interests.

Food Safety and China's Consumers

The *gyōza* incident transformed Japanese and Chinese governments' cooperation on food safety. New policy mechanisms were created to handle the growing interdependence between Japanese food-processing companies and their Chinese joint-venture partners. The first initiative, though, was not about food safety but about how the two governments would manage cross-border criminal investigations. As noted earlier, the MLAT provided the crucial link for the Japanese and Chinese police to cooperate in investigations and to include each other's evidence as part of a formal indictment. This was a mutual interest and one that faced virtually no opposition from either government.

The cooperation on food safety took somewhat longer to establish. The Ministry of Foreign Affairs remained the primary bureaucratic contact on the food safety issue until the case was resolved in 2010. From the time the food poisonings occurred in January 2008 until the Chinese government notified Tokyo of the arrest of a suspect in China, the Japanese Ministry of Foreign Affairs brought up the issue of food safety in virtually every high-level meeting with China's leaders. On November 13, 2008, Vice-Minister Hashimoto Seiko announced a new webpage, entitled the Food Security Problem, under the foreign policy section for health and medical issues.[92] This was followed by the creation of an official position within the ministry that was dedicated to managing food safety issues.

On May 31, 2010, however, the Japanese and Chinese governments came up with a more practical and focused way of working together on food safety issues. This was the first cabinet-level meeting on the new Japan-China food safety initiative, and it was attended by Nagatsuma Akira, Japan's minister of MHLW, and Wang Yong, China's director of the AQSIQ. Both ministers signed the memorandum of understanding (MOU) on the new initiative and agreed on an action plan for the coming year.[93] The MOU cited four basic goals. First, in compliance with the WTO Agreement on the Application of Sanitary and Phytosanitary Measures and the domestic laws of each country, Japan and China would develop a framework for cooperation on ensuring food safety. Second, they agreed to hold ministerial-level meetings once a year and working-level meetings regularly to study and develop policy initiatives on food safety. Third, materials on the laws, regulations, and procedures used to regulate the food industry would be prepared in both the Japanese and Chinese languages. Finally, the two governments would prepare an action plan to set annual targets for cooperation.

The *gyōza* incident also shed much needed light on two other constituencies in the Japan-China relationship: Chinese workers and Chinese consumers. When his trial opened in the Shijiazhuang Intermediate People's Court, Lu Yueting, the cook who deliberately injected insecticide into Tianyang Food's frozen dumplings, confessed that his motivation was not to cause harm to consumers but to attract the attention of his managers.[94] As a temporary worker, Liu received far less than others in annual bonuses and salary, and he claimed he wanted a more stable job after fifteen years of working for the company. Liu said he had written three anonymous letters to his manager alerting him to the poisoned dumplings. What began as a management problem at a food-processing plant in northern China ended with a serious food safety crisis and yet another round of tensions in the Japan-China relationship. In the end, the Tianyang Food plant was closed, with a loss of 1,300 jobs and 5.5 million yuan ($897,000). Even with his conviction, however, Japan's confidence in its increasing dependence on China for its food supply was far from assured.

The Japan-China Food Safety Promotion Initiative fed into China's awareness of the need for stricter food safety regulations. Japanese companies became part of the solution by making the high quality of Japanese food production the standard for the emerging Chinese food industry. But in 2011, Japan suffered "triple disasters": a 9.0-magnitude earthquake followed by a disastrous tsunami and the meltdown of the Fukushima Daiichi nuclear plant situated on the coast of Tohoku. Now the two governments had a new problem: Chinese consumers' concern about the safety of food produced in Japan. The effort to build confidence in the provision of food from China now had to be redirected to tackle Chinese concerns about the safety of imported Japanese food products.

By 2010, Japan was exporting $593 million worth of agricultural products to China each year.[95] Japan's exports of food included high-value-added rice and saké as well as other quality products that were becoming favorite products for China's middle-class urban consumers. According to the Japan External Trade Organization, in 2001 Japan exported less than 6 percent of its total food exports to China, but by 2006, that had jumped to almost 14 percent. The share of food destined for China fluctuated thereafter, but in 2010 Japan's food exports to China comprised roughly 11 percent. But that share plummeted after March 11. Japan's reputation for maintaining one of the world's safest food safety regimes was shattered, and Chinese consumers, now highly sensitive to food safety issues, were deeply concerned about Japanese food products (figures 5.6 and 5.7).[96]

The Japanese government's March 19 announcement of radioactive contamination in food products originating from the region close to the Fukushima Daiichi nuclear plant alerted foreign governments and international agencies of the danger in food coming from Japan. On March 21, the WTO announced "serious" readings in spinach grown some distance away from the reactor, and China's

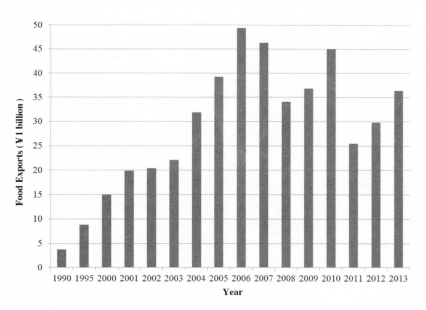

FIGURE 5.6 Exports of food and food products to China. The years 1990 and 1995 are included at the beginning of the chart for comparative purposes. (Ministry of Finance, Japan, "Trade Statistics of Japan," http://www.customs.go.jp/toukei/info /index_e.htm)

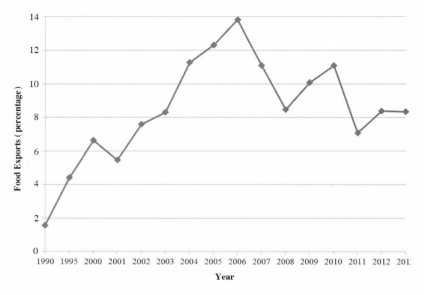

FIGURE 5.7   Food exports to China as a percentage of total food exports. The years 1990 and 1995 are included at the beginning of the chart for comparative purposes. (Ministry of Finance, Japan, "Trade Statistics of Japan," http://www.customs.go.jp /toukei/info/index_e.htm)

AQSIQ asked local authorities to monitor foods imported from Japan for signs of radiation. On March 23, the MHLW urged people not to eat eleven types of vegetables grown near the Fukushima plant, and two days later, China banned imports from five Japanese prefectures. Then on April 8, China expanded its ban on Japanese food products to include twelve prefectures.

The Japanese government urged foreign governments not to over-react. On April 8, the MAFF's Fisheries Agency assured consumers that it was safe to consume fish sold in Japan's markets, pointing out that none came from the sea near the Fukushima plant. Similarly, Chief Cabinet Secretary Edano Yukio announced that Japan was lifting restrictions on milk and spinach from regions other than Fukushima. Chinese authorities agreed to allow imports of Japanese goods produced before March 11, but media reports indicated that they still were not clearing customs. On May 5, former Prime Minister Hatoyama Ryūtarō met with Xi Jinping in Beijing, and Xi asked him for accurate information from Japan about the Fukushima accident. When Prime Minister Kan Naoto met with Chinese Premier Wen Jiabao in Tokyo on May 22, Wen agreed to lower the number of banned prefectures and to deem as unnecessary the radiation inspection of products other than dairy, vegetables, and marine products.

In practice, however, China did not relax its restrictions on the import of Japanese foods until November 2011. In the intervening months, Prime Minister Noda Yoshihiko and several of his cabinet ministers continued to appeal to the Chinese government to comply with Wen's promise. In October, Japan's minister of economy, trade, and industry, Edano Yukio, visited Beijing to meet with Wen and China's minister of commercial affairs, Chen Deming, to discuss imports from Japan. On November 13, Minister of Health, Labor and Welfare Komiyama Yōko met again with the head of China's AQSIQ in an effort to persuade China to lift import restrictions on Japanese foods and other products. Finally, on November 24, China notified Japan that it would lift most of its bans on Japanese products, including most processed foods, saké, and seasonings, if the Japanese government provided a place-of-origin certificate. Nonetheless, food products from ten prefectures continued to be banned.

The reason for China's reluctance to lift its ban was unclear, but the *China Daily* suggested that the Chinese government had become very sensitive to Chinese consumers' concerns about food safety. The melamine scandal in 2008 had prompted the formation of a food safety commission, and Vice-Premier Li Keqiang was appointed in February 2009 to lead the commission. The NPC Standing Committee also adopted a food safety law, and monitoring centers were set up in 31 provinces, 218 prefectures, and 312 counties. Continuing food safety scandals provoked even stricter controls in 2011. In early March, just before Japan's "triple disasters," Zhao Qicheng, the spokesman for the Fourth Session of the Eleventh National Committee of the Chinese Peoples' Political Consultative Conferences, warned that the criminal law extending to food safety had been revised to deter food contamination.[97] Punishment for food safety crimes and insufficient oversight of food production became increasingly harsh. Given this domestic climate, Chinese authorities reportedly worried about their capacity to independently test Japanese products.

It was not just Chinese who worried about the safety of Japanese food after March 11, however. Restrictions on Japanese food imports were announced in countries around the globe, including India, Russia, Singapore, the Republic of Korea, Brazil, Canada, Chile, and the European Union, just to name a few. For more than a year, Japanese officials argued for relaxing restrictions on their foods and other products after global fears of radioactivity tarnished the sale of Japanese products, appealing to the WTO for regulatory assistance to prevent trade discrimination against Japanese products.

The bilateral Japan-China Food Safety Initiative, created after the *gyōza*-poisoning case, emerged as the primary forum for considering Chinese concerns about Japanese food safety after March 11. In the action plan devised for the second year of the Japan-China consultations on food safety, the Chinese included in their list of concerns the need for greater information about Japan's radioactive contamination.[98] While Chinese authorities did not agree to lift their ban on Japanese food imports completely, the vehicle for conveying information and for consultations on Chinese concerns that had been established in the wake of the *gyōza*-poisoning case allowed for a more thorough exchange of views. Moreover, the bilateral food safety initiative ensured regular meetings between health and welfare officials and undoubtedly played a valuable role in informing Chinese food safety deliberations at home.

Perhaps the greatest irony, however, was Japanese consumers' growing interest in food produced abroad after March 11. Fears of tainted water, rice, and other food products in Japan after the Fukushima Daiichi accident clearly affected consumers' perceptions of the safety of their own food supply and production system. The briefings by the government and the Tokyo Electric Power Company (which owns the Fukushima Daiichi plant) on the impacts of the nuclear meltdown caused confidence to drop, which also extended to consumer behavior. Chinese rice became more and more popular among Japanese consumers, and large retail supermarkets increased their stocks. Although the Japanese media reported this as a consequence of the rising price of domestic rice in the wake of the Fukushima accident, it is likely that both food safety and price were affecting consumers' choices.[99] Whether motivated by price or safety, Japan's food companies accelerated their investment and expanded their production of food in China after Japan's disasters.

Rice production in China was a conspicuous area of interest, with a number of companies announcing their intention to buy and produce more rice there, with the aim of selling it to Chinese consumers and, ultimately, of exporting it to Japan.[100] A year after the disasters struck Japan, Japanese rice producers and retailers all were looking to China. For example, on April 8, 2012, Sumitomo announced a new initiative to produce more than 1 million tons "under Japanese safety standards" in China, with possible exports to Japan.[101] Japan's farmers also are considering growing their rice in China. The *Niigata nippō* reported that farmers were beginning to consider production overseas of their highly regarded rice brands. Seeds for the renowned *koshihikari, hitomebore*, and *Akita komachi* varieties of rice are being tested in Chinese soil with an eye to expanding the volume of Japanese rice grown by Chinese farming cooperatives and Japanese agricultural joint-venture firms in China.[102] Continued Chinese concerns about food safety, and even Japanese consumers' shaken confidence in their own rice, has reinforced Japan's dependence on China as a location for enhanced food production.

6

ISLAND DEFENSE

A harrowing confrontation at sea between a Chinese fishing trawler and two Japan Coast Guard (JCG) vessels in September 2010 prompted a serious diplomatic crisis between Japan and China and marked the beginning of a new contentious phase in their handling of the disputed Senkaku Islands. The captain, Zhan Qixiong, of the *Minjinyu 5179*, refused to allow the JCG to inspect his vessel, which was found fishing in Japan's twelve-nautical-mile territorial waters off the islands.[1] Instead, the trawler attempted to flee and, when confronted by JCG patrol ships, struck first the *Yonakuni* and then the *Mizuki*. Finally the *Minjinyu* was boarded, the captain and crew detained, and the ship confiscated. No one was injured, but the inherent danger was enough for the ship and its crew to be escorted to Ishigaki Island, where the captain was charged with obstructing the JCG in the execution of its duties.[2]

Japan's detention of, and clear intent to prosecute, the captain soon escalated into a major diplomatic incident. China condemned the captain's detention, claiming it was a departure from past practices of managing such incidents. As the days unfolded into weeks and the detention turned into the prospect that Japan's prosecutors would indict Zhan, Beijing turned up the diplomatic pressure. A particularly charged speech by Chinese Premier Wen Jiabao at the United Nations in New York suggested that China would continue to escalate tensions until the captain was released. This in turn prompted a reminder by U.S. Secretary of State Hillary Clinton that any incident deliberately aimed at challenging Japan's control over the Senkaku Islands would invoke the U.S.-Japan security alliance. For the first time in Japan's and China's postwar diplomacy, their differences over this remote group of islands moved from quiet bilateral discussions to public contention and an appeal to a global audience for support in confronting each other.

The rapid escalation of the crisis took the Japanese government by surprise. An even greater shock, however, was the public's understanding of what this meant for Japan. What came to be called the *Senkaku shokku* (Senkaku shock) made clear to the public just how far relations between Japan and China had deteriorated and what could happen if China became more unpredictable—or even hostile. Indeed, Japan's policy challenge was perceived as far more than an isolated incident between a Chinese fishing trawler captain and the Japan Coast Guard. After almost a decade of recurrent incidents and frictions, the incident revealed how quickly a small event could escalate into a serious confrontation. In the end, it forced the Japanese government to change its management of the disputed islands and, in 2012, led to an even bigger conflict between Tokyo and Beijing.

What had largely been perceived by Japan as a diplomatic challenge now seemed to have become a security challenge. The two countries had tried, but ultimately failed, to develop a common basis for managing their shared maritime boundary. China's maritime claims under the UN Convention on the Law of the Sea (UNCLOS) had changed the understanding between Tokyo and Beijing on the Senkaku Islands. China's 1992 law on the territorial sea and contiguous zone clearly identified the disputed islands as territory belonging to the People's Republic of China (PRC) and as part of the "land territory" that, the law claimed, defined China's territorial sea.[3]

The 2010 Chinese fishing trawler crisis also demonstrated that Japan and China could no longer solve their dispute bilaterally. Communication was impossible, and Japan had to turn to the United States to slow, and stop, China from threatening further action. Moreover, there was no prior indication that this sort of incident would devolve into a crisis. Chinese fishermen had had far more volatile interactions with South Korean coast guard vessels, yet had rarely tested Japan's policing of its territorial waters. In fact, the fishing trawler captain's behavior seemed to be an isolated case of bad judgment, and many suspected he was drunk at the time. This speculation aside, the incident also revealed that the East China Sea had become an increasingly populated maritime space.

The political management of this crisis drew worldwide attention. Policymakers in both Tokyo and Washington were surprised by the intensity of Beijing's response. But just as quickly as tempers had flared, the crisis ended. Tokyo released the captain, and he was flown home to a hero's welcome.

A much more difficult clash over the islands followed in 2012, driven largely by Japan's own politics. Activists, including the well-known critic of China, Tokyo Governor Ishihara Shintarō, began to mobilize around the cause of Senkaku sovereignty. In order to prevent their sale to those who would only cause even more problems with China, Prime Minister Noda Yoshihiko purchased the islands from their owners. But Noda's decision only sent Japan-China relations into a tailspin. Demonstrations broke out across China, and Beijing decided to challenge Japan's administrative control of the islands by sending paramilitary ships to patrol them. Until 2010, what had largely been perceived as a manageable difference between Tokyo and Beijing, of interest only to small groups of nationalist activists in both countries, had blown up into a major confrontation between the two states. In Japan, defending its sovereignty over the Senkakus became entwined with its larger security goal of defending its home islands.

THE CONTROVERSY: A PROVOCATION NEAR THE SENKAKUS

Two crises over the disputed islands drew global attention to the deteriorating Japan-China relationship. But within Japan, it was the 2010 incident that overturned Japanese thinking about its ability to deal with a rising China. Tokyo's confrontation with Beijing in 2010 was deeply shocking and prompted serious concern over Japanese security. China responded immediately and harshly to the arrest of the trawler captain. On September 8, Japan's ambassador was called to the Chinese Ministry of Foreign Affairs, and when the captain was turned over to prosecutors, Minister of Foreign Affairs Yang Jiechi again called in Ambassador Niwa Uichirō to demand the captain's release. The following day, the ministry announced the suspension of the East China Sea Agreement, citing the incident as the cause. On September 13, the Japanese government decided to release both the trawler and the crew. On September 16, Maehara Seiji, the minister of land, infrastructure, transport, and tourism (MLIT)—the ministry responsible for the JCG—flew to Ishigaki to inspect the damaged ships, and three days later, the Ishigaki court extended the detention of the Chinese captain until September 29 in order to complete its investigation.

It was at this point that tensions suddenly escalated. On September 20, China detained four Japanese citizens for entering a restricted military area in Hebei Province. The four were Fujita Corporation employees who had been sent to China as part of a Japanese project to reclaim World War II chemical weapons left behind by the Japanese Imperial Army. The following day, a Chinese Foreign Ministry spokesperson, Jiang Yu, stated in her news briefing that "the time is not proper for a meeting between Chinese Premier Wen Jiabao and Japanese leaders at the United Nations conferences in New York."[4] Already in New York, Wen Jiabao met with Chinese American leaders and delivered an emotionally charged appeal for the "immediate and unconditional" release of the Chinese captain.[5] Japan's foreign minister met with U.S. Secretary of State Hillary Clinton on the sidelines of the UN General Assembly. *Kyodo News* reported that the two allies consulted on the Chinese fishing trawler incident, but the State Department spokesman noted publicly only that the United States would not take a position on the sovereignty dispute.[6] More to the point, however, in a press conference at the U.S. Department of Defense in Washington, D.C., U.S. military leaders told reporters that the United States would "fulfill its alliance responsibilities."[7] For the first time in the postwar era, the governments of Tokyo and Beijing sought to resolve an incident involving the Senkaku Islands by appealing to outside actors.

Another dimension of the crisis was new as well. Beijing had put pressure on Tokyo by new means. As diplomats sought to manage the crisis, Minister of Economy, Trade, and Industry (METI) Ōhata

Akihiro announced at a press conference on September 24 in Tokyo that a number of trading companies had reported an embargo on the export of Chinese rare earths to Japan, although he also referred to the statement by the Chinese Department of Commerce that there was no evidence to support these reports.[8] Meanwhile, the *New York Times* reported from China that Beijing was preparing to cut its exports of rare earth minerals to Japan.[9] China produces about 97 percent of the global supply of rare earths, which are used in variety of goods, such as high-quality electronics, although it possesses only 30 to 40 percent of the world's reserves.[10] Japan accounts for 20 percent of the world demand (approximately 30,000 tons) and relies on China for 90 percent of its imports.[11]

This resort to economic sanctions eventually had far-reaching repercussions, but at the time, information on the extent of the embargo and how stringently the Chinese government was imposing it was unavailable. Then on October 19, the *China Daily* reported that the country would cut its total exports of rare earths by 30 percent in 2011 in order to "protect overexploitation."[12] The following week, China's vice-minister of commerce, Jiang Yaoping, visited Tokyo to meet with METI Minister Ōhata. Ōhata repeated Japan's request that China ease its restrictions on the export of rare earths. On November 13, Minister Ōhata met with Zhang Ping, China's director of the Development and Reform Commission, on the sidelines of the Yokohama APEC Summit. The METI had initiated this meeting, which lasted for two and a half hours. Afterward, Zhang noted that the rare earth issue would be "properly resolve[d] very soon." The next day, Minister Ōhata announced that twenty-six of the twenty-seven companies surveyed by the METI reported that for the first time since the trawler incident, they could see "signs of improvement."[13] By the end of the first week of December, Ōhata reported that twenty-one shipments were confirmed the week before and an additional ten more shipments were released that week. More shipments were still stuck in customs, but the Chinese government was working with the METI to clear them.[14] By late December, shipments had returned to normal levels.

In addition to the embargo on rare earths, the Chinese government used the detention of Japanese citizens to pressure Tokyo. The day after Chinese, Japanese, and American leaders met in New York, Suzuki

Tōru, the Naha district deputy chief prosecutor, publicly announced in Ishigaki the release of the captain, Zhan Qixiong. One day later, September 25, Japanese Ministry of Foreign Affairs officials were allowed access to the four Japanese detained by China. The Chinese Ministry of Foreign Affairs then called for an apology from Japan and compensation for the arrest of their trawler captain, but Prime Minister Kan Naoto rejected the request. On September 27, Chief Cabinet Secretary Sengoku Yoshito suggested that instead, China compensate Japan for the damage to the two coast guard patrol ships. Three days later, three of the four Japanese businessmen arrested in China were released.

Even though the diplomatic confrontation with Beijing had receded, the Japanese government came under intense criticism at home for its failure to manage the crisis. Opposition critics in the Diet called for release of the video taken on the scene by the coast guard. The Lower House Budget Committee on October 13 submitted a formal request to the Naha Special Prosecutor's Office to hand over the coast guard video. The political pressures on the Kan cabinet to release the video to the Diet grew, and the Lower House Budget Committee insisted on a secret viewing.[15] Five days later the cabinet complied with the Budget Committee's request, and on October 27 the Japanese government released a six-minute, edited copy of the incident to the committee. Once the video was seen, however, comments by members of the committee to the media only increased criticism of the government's decision to treat the video as evidence in a domestic legal procedure. Many members wanted the government to broadcast the egregious behavior of the Chinese captain to show the public—and the world—who was to blame. But when the video was later leaked on YouTube, it brought to the surface deeper domestic tensions over Japan's strategy of relying on negotiation with Beijing to defend its interests. By keeping the video secret, they charged, Prime Minister Kan had allowed Beijing to get the upper hand in the dispute.

Throughout this time, relations with China continued to be difficult, and diplomacy was complicated by the eruption of anti-Japanese protests related to the Senkaku Islands, which took place in Beijing, Shanghai, Chengdu, Xian, and Zhengzhou during the week of October 16. Although China had released the fourth Fujita Corporation employee, Takahashi Sadamu, on October 9, in the midst of these protests, Prime Minister Kan expressed his concern about Japanese citizens in China, and Ambassador Niwa in Beijing communicated this concern to Foreign Minister Yang on October 18, leading to another round of anti-Japanese protests from October 23 through 25.

Meanwhile, the Chinese government took issue with Japan's new foreign minister, Maehara Seiji. Maehara had been in charge of the Ministry of Land, Infrastructure, Transportation, and Tourism (MLIT) when the incident occurred and became minister of foreign affairs on September 17, 2010, when Prime Minister Kan reshuffled his cabinet.[16] Testifying in the Upper House on October 18, Foreign Minister Maehara publicly characterized the Chinese reaction to the incident as "hysterical" (*kiwamete hisuterikku na monoda*) and rejected the Chinese claim that Japan and China had agreed in 1978 to shelve the sovereignty debate over the Senkaku Islands.[17] In response, Chinese Vice-Minister for Foreign Affairs Hu Zhengyue described Maehara's attacks on China as "extreme words" used to "attack China," words "that should not come out of the mouth of a foreign diplomat."[18] On October 24, the JCG reported that Chinese fishing boats were again operating in Japan's territorial and exclusive economic zone (EEZ) waters, and the Japanese Ministry of Foreign Affairs lodged another protest with China.

At the end of October, with bilateral relations between Tokyo and Beijing deeply strained, Secretary of State Clinton met with Foreign Minister Maehara in Honolulu. In their joint statement on October 27, Secretary Clinton clearly reiterated Washington's commitment to assist Japan in the defense of the Senkakus and Japan's security: "The Senkakus fall within the scope of Article 5 of the 1960 U.S.-Japan Treaty of Mutual Cooperation and Security . . . [part of] the larger commitment that the United States has made to Japan's security. . . . [T]he U.S.-Japan alliance [is] one of the most important alliance partnerships we have anywhere in the world and we are committed to our obligations to protect the Japanese people."[19] The bilateral alliance was invoked to reassure those in Japan as well as to communicate to others in the region that the United States and Japan remained close allies. The alliance had had some difficulties during the first year of the DPJ's government under Prime Minister Hatoyama Yukio when disagreement over the U.S. air base at Futenma, Okinawa, created friction between Tokyo and Washington. Regional concerns over the political strains in the U.S.-Japan alliance were growing, and the Hatoyama government's effort to rebalance Japan's diplomacy away from Washington and toward more cooperation with Beijing had unsettled the Obama administration.[20] Thus, Secretary Clinton's reiteration of the U.S. alliance commitment to Japan ended a year-long period of frustration and doubt about the role of the alliance in managing Japan's security concerns.

China's behavior in its dispute with Tokyo did not go unnoticed around the globe. Both the use of economic sanctions and the arrests of Japanese nationals in China suggested that Beijing might be willing to use military power should a more serious confrontation in and around the islands arise. Around the region, Japan's distress in the face of China's pressure also was a surprise. If Beijing was willing to behave in this manner toward one of its largest economic partners, then it was likely to use similar tactics in disputes with smaller countries. In Tokyo, however, the media and politicians defined the problem as Japan's problem, and while many around Asia—and indeed around the globe—concentrated on China's missteps, in Japan it was Japan's leaders, institutions, and actions that were found wanting.

Although the Chinese trawler incident did not escalate to armed conflict, it did renew the antagonism between China and Japan over the Senkaku Islands. In the past, confrontations had been dealt with under Japanese law, but there had been no effort to prosecute offenders. In 2004, for instance, when Chinese activists landed on the Senkaku Islands, the JCG detained them, but they were returned to China rather than prosecuted in the Japanese courts. Moreover, Tokyo's final decision to release the captain and forgo prosecution reinforced the impression that Japan was operating from a position of weakness with China and had succumbed to its pressure.

Three aspects of the incident called into question Japan's policymaking. The first was the impact of the incident on Japan's maritime defenses. The second was the way the incident tested the premise that Japan's economic relations with China were impervious to political tensions. Finally, the perennial question of whether a serious crisis with China could be effectively managed by the Japanese government reemerged. All three of these aspects reflected concerns about how China's growing power would affect Japan's postwar security choices.

Japan's Maritime Defenses

As an island nation, Japan's national defense depends on both its ability to patrol and guard its maritime boundaries and its ability to ensure secure sea-lanes for the global trade that sustains its economy. Ninety-six percent of Japan's energy supply and 60 percent of its food supply come from overseas. The Japanese archipelago is made up of the four main islands of Hokkaido, Honshu, Shikoku, and Kyushu, as well as the southernmost Ryukyu and Bonin island chains. The government of Japan has more than 21,000 miles (roughly 35,000 km) of coastline and 6,847 offshore islands to defend, in addition to its maritime territory and EEZ, which covers almost 2.8 million square miles (4.47 million sq km), the sixth largest maritime area in the world.[21]

The task of defending Japan's maritime territory rests on the JCG and the Maritime Self-Defense Force (MSDF).[22] The JCG, which was called the Maritime Safety Agency (MSA) until April 1, 2000, polices Japan's territorial and EEZ waters.[23] It has more than four hundred ships, twenty-seven airplanes, and a light helicopter squadron for search-and-rescue missions of forty-six craft.[24] The JCG's annual budget has risen nearly every since the early 1990s, despite the ceiling imposed on Japan's military services, reflecting the political consensus that has emerged over the protection of Japan's maritime territory. As of 2013, the JCG had an annual budget of ¥173.9 billion and has been modernizing its fleet since 2005.[25] According to Richard Samuels, the JCG's "new fighting force" is both an adjunct to Japan's navy and a critical political asset to the Japanese government as it seeks cooperation throughout the Asian region.[26]

It is in its core mission of policing Japan's territorial waters that the coast guard has its principal challenge. Especially in and around Japan's southwestern waters, the JCG has improved its surveillance and patrol capabilities. Perhaps most important, the JCG has been on the front line of almost every major territorial dispute that Japan has had with its neighbors.[27] The area surrounding the Senkaku Islands is thus a prominent concern for the JCG, and after several incidents with

Taiwanese and Chinese activists, deployments there were increased. All five islands of the Senkakus (Uotsurijima, Kubajima, Taishōjima, Kitakojima, and Minamikojima) are uninhabited and are located far from the shores of mainland China (205 miles) and Taiwan (105 miles) (figure 6.1). The closest JCG station is 105 miles away from the islands in Ishigaki, and the JCG's eleventh regional fleet, which is based in Naha, is 255 miles away.[28] The largest challenge for the JCG, therefore, is sustaining patrols at a distance.

Japan's navy, the MSDF, carries out the armed defense of Japanese waters, and its investment in maritime defense capabilities has been growing, although not as quickly as that of its coast guard. Maritime missions have evolved as the strategic balance in Northeast Asia has changed and as new coalitions of maritime cooperation beyond the region have formed in the post–Cold War era. The MSDF continues to protect Japan's sea-lanes of communication and also operates alongside twenty-five other navies in the antipiracy mission in the Gulf of Aden.[29] In addition, Japan continues to contribute to the Proliferation Security Initiative (PSI) that monitors

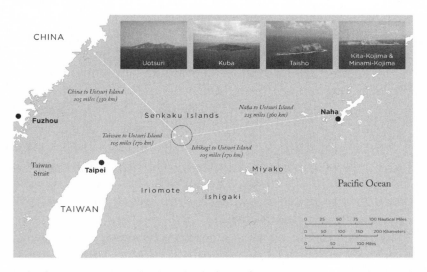

FIGURE 6.1 Senkaku Islands. (Island photos from Japan Coast Guard, Annual Report [2011], http://www.kaiho.mlit.go.jp/info/books/. Original artwork courtesy of Martin Hinze)

maritime transport in an effort to curb the proliferation of weapons of mass destruction.

Closer to home, Japan's territorial defense missions include capabilities, such as antisubmarine warfare (ASW), that complement U.S. maritime capabilities in the region. During the Cold War, the MSDF's ASW capability played a crucial role in the U.S.-Japan alliance's response to the former Soviet Union's military capabilities in the Western Pacific. That same capability is deployed to monitor and limit the options available to China's expanding maritime forces. In Japan's 2010 defense plan, the MSDF reorganized from five regional fleets to four (for a total of forty-eight destroyers) but has enhanced each fleet to include destroyers with a flexible, high-alert response capability. Japan also has strengthened its submarine fleet, with a particular emphasis on its southwestern waters (East China Sea), in addition to the Sea of Japan, and maintains a fleet of twenty-two submarines organized into six groups.[30]

China's maritime expansion also is changing the balance of its forces off Japan's coastal waters and has had a clear impact on Japan's thinking about its defense missions (figure 6.2). The emerging Chinese maritime doctrine has resulted in a naval presence beyond what Beijing describes as the first island chain, including Japan. This trajectory of Chinese military expansion is in part driven by the desire to control the waters surrounding the Taiwan Strait. Political tensions across the straits prompted a serious military crisis in 1995/1996 that resulted in the deployment of a U.S. carrier battle group. Since then, Japan has concentrated on developing its naval forces' ASW capabilities as well as its intelligence, surveillance, and reconnaissance (ISR) operations. In addition, Japan has enhanced its naval-based antiballistic missile capabilities, and in response to missile tests by the North Koreans, Tokyo successfully deployed and operated these capabilities with U.S. naval forces in the Sea of Japan (2009) and East China Sea (2012).

China's influence on Japan's defense missions extends beyond its navy. In Japan's 2004 and then 2010 National Defense Program Guidelines, China's expanding military reach influenced both the priorities of Japan's Self-Defense Forces (SDF) and its agenda of military cooperation with Washington. Japan reset the geographical

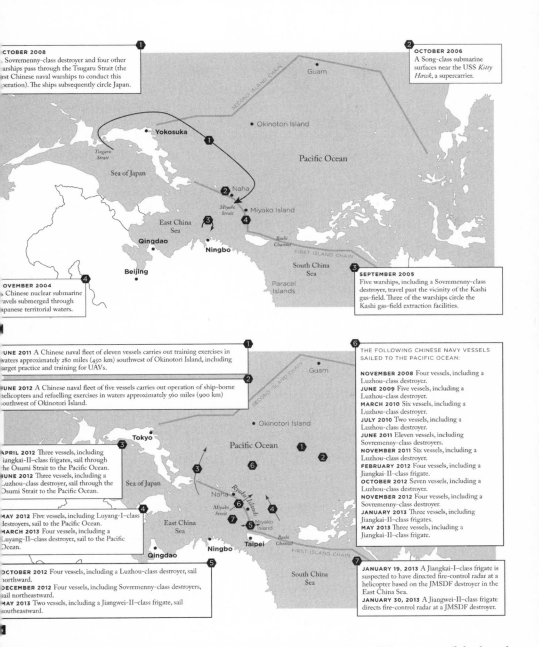

FIGURE 6.2 Chinese naval activities in waters near Japan (*a*) 2004–2008; (*b*) 2008–2013. ([*a*] adapted from National Institute for Defense Studies, Japan, *China Security Report* [2010], 15, http://www.nids.go.jp/english/publication/chinareport/pdf/china_report_EN_4C_A01.pdf; [*b*] adapted from National Institute for Defense Studies, Japan, *China Security Report* [2011], 11, http://www.nids.go.jp/english/publication/chinareport/pdf/china_report_EN_web_2011_A01.pdf;andMinistry of Defense, Japan, "Recent Activities in Waters Near Japan," *Defense of Japan 2013*. Original artwork courtesy of Martin Hinze)

priorities for its national defense, putting the southwestern region first, and elevated its island defense mission (*tōshō bōei*), which guards Japan's far-reaching airspace and its many offshore islands. The *Senkaku shokku* and subsequent concerns about protecting Japan's sovereignty over the many other islands in the southwestern region accelerated Japan's island defense training and led its Ground Self-Defense Forces (GSDF) to train with the U.S. Marines in amphibious-landing exercises.[31] In addition, Japan's Ministry of Defense (MOD) plans to redeploy an additional fighter squadron to Okinawa and has increased the number of submarines. Just as important, the MOD has moved quickly to strengthen its ISR capabilities, especially for maritime regions. All branches of the SDF now have a role in defending the islands.[32]

Defending territory that includes a broad swath of maritime interests is an increasingly difficult task for Japan, and as Chinese influence in this maritime domain spreads, Japan's ability to defend its boundaries is being tested in new ways. The Chinese trawler incident did not directly call into question Japan's military defenses. But it had a tremendous impact on the policy debate in Tokyo. The prospect of a similar incident escalating into an armed conflict worried policymakers in Tokyo. As Richard Bush points out, the possibility of an inadvertent clash between China's maritime forces and Japan's civilian and military forces has created new pressures on the crisis management capacities of both Tokyo and Beijing.[33]

The incident in September 2010 revealed the need for closer coordination between Japan's coast guard and its navy. The relationship between coastal policing and maritime defense is often defined geographically, with the coast guard charged with defending territorial waters up to twelve nautical miles, and the navy, with the waters beyond. But two factors complicate this understanding. The first is the close proximity of national maritime claims in the East China Sea. Japan, South Korea, North Korea, China, and Taiwan all border on the Yellow Sea, the Sea of Japan, and the East China Sea, and their geostrategic interests often conflict. The second complicating factor is their overlapping EEZs, regions that also include claims of fisheries stocks and seabed resources by these states.

The Costs of Interdependence

The diplomatic clash over the Chinese trawler incident alerted Japanese leaders not only to the possibility of a vertical escalation of tensions but also to horizontal escalatory dynamics. The incident created new sources of pressure on Japan's decision makers, who already were dealing with, first, the embargo of rare earth materials to Japan and, second, the arrest of four Japanese citizens in China. The Chinese government's effort to influence Japanese behavior suggested a willingness to use multiple points of pressure, introducing a new, and more difficult, challenge for Japanese policymakers.

Japanese and Chinese leaders had earlier sought to separate their economic relationship from their political disputes, and the use of an embargo came as a shock to many in Japan. Japan's dependence on the Chinese market notwithstanding, rare earth materials are an integral component for many of Japan's manufacturing industries and one area in which Chinese influence on Japan would be felt keenly and immediately. Whether the Chinese government used this as a threat during the crisis remains suspected but unconfirmed. The difficulty in assessing the exact role of Chinese officials in the embargo of rare earth materials lies partly in the lack of transparency over the export process. If an embargo was imposed, it was informally imposed, and the question remains whether the Beijing officials were aware of the actions being taken by customs officials at the point of export.

Even before the 2010 incident, the Japanese government struggled to gain Chinese acquiescence in maintaining access to these rare earth minerals. Then in 2006 China began to impose quotas on its exports to ensure environmentally sound practices of extraction but also to ensure that its domestic manufacturers had priority access to them.[34] Although Japanese government officials sought continued access to China's rare earths, Japan's quota has already been reduced, as have the quotas on exports to other nations, with China cutting its exports by half since 2005, from 65,580 tons to 31,130 tons in 2012.[35]

Beijing's willingness to extend spats like these to international trade was worrisome. Tokyo accelerated its efforts to diversify its sources of rare earths, and the private-sector companies that depended on these materials began to invest more heavily in recycling in order to recapture them. The Japanese government also found common cause with other countries that depended on access to the Chinese supply. In their Honolulu meeting, Foreign Minister Maehara and Secretary of State Clinton pledged to continue to discuss diversification strategies. Then, for the first time, Japan joined European and American governments in requesting consultations at the WTO with China concerning its restraints of rare earth exports.[36] On March 14, 2012, Chief Cabinet Secretary Fujimura Osamu stated,

> The Government of Japan has taken a variety of measures in response to the export restrictions on rare earth. This has included the development of alternative materials, the reduction of rare earth use, and the diversification of supply sources. The Government has also requested thorough dialogue with the Government of China that improvements are made to the export restrictions as well as to domestic and overseas price difference.[37]

The second difficulty for Japan was China's decision to arrest four Japanese citizens in Hebei. The Xinhua news agency reported that they were arrested on September 20, 2010, and taken into custody by the Hebei National Security Authority. The Fujita employees were charged with filming objects in an off-limits military-controlled area. In 1999 the Fujita Corporation had bid for and won the Japanese government's contract to build a mobile detoxification and disposal facility in China as part of Japan's bilateral assistance program to collect and dispose of weapons abandoned by the Imperial Japanese Army during World War II.[38]

Coming as it did on the heels of the arrest of the Chinese trawler captain, the arrest of the Fujita Corporation employees in China suggested a tit-for-tat response designed to raise the stakes for Tokyo. On September 25, the Japanese embassy asked that the Chinese authorities resolve the problem as quickly as possible, and Deputy Secretary Qiu Yuanping of the Chinese Foreign Ministry responded that he understood Japan's interest but that China would rule in accordance with its own law.[39] The DPJ sent Deputy Secretary-General Hosono Gōshi secretly to Beijing on September 29, resulting in the release of three of the four Fujita employees on the following day. They all later acknowledged that they did not know they were in a military-controlled area and signed apology letters before their release. When Takahashi, the final employee to be released, returned to Japan two weeks later, he held a press conference during which he explained that he was unaware he was filming in a military area and thought he was being detained longer because he was the one holding the camera. The Chinese National Security Authority declared one year later, on October 10, 2011, that the enforcement measures imposed on Takahashi had been officially terminated.[40] Nine months earlier, the Japanese prosecutors had dropped their indictment against the Chinese fishing trawler captain.

The Policy Challenge

In Japan, the Senkaku shock of September 2010 raised fundamental questions about the country's crisis management practices. This was only the second time that the prime minister's office had to manage Chinese citizens' challenge to Japan's control of the islands. In 2004, seven Chinese activists sailed from Shanghai with the explicit purpose of landing on the Senkaku Islands and planting the Chinese flag. They, too, were apprehended by the Japan Coast Guard and detained. Although Japan's prime minister at the time, Koizumi Jun'ichirō, approved the arrest of the activists, he had them sent back to China within five days without prosecution.

Japan's decision to subject the captain to domestic legal proceedings in 2010 was new. Ramming the two JCG ships not only caused considerable damage to the ships but also endangered both the trawler and the coast guard vessels on the high seas. The Japanese government thus decided that this posed sufficient danger to charge the Chinese captain with more than simply trespassing in Japan's territorial waters, so he was criminally charged with interfering with the official duties of the Japan Coast Guard, a charge similar to resisting arrest. On September 10, the JCG handed over the captain to local prosecutors for possible indictment. MLIT Minister Maehara concurred with the seriousness of the incident and approved the charges on September 19, and the Ishigaki court extended the detention of the Chinese captain to September 29 to allow a full investigation. It was this decision that incensed Beijing, as it indicated that a Chinese citizen would be subjected to Japanese law over behavior in a territory that China claimed as its own.

Beijing's intense—and very public—ratcheting up of diplomatic pressure was new as well. The two countries' inability to work through a solution introduced a new level of uncertainty in the relationship and heightened popular sensitivities in both countries. The citizen activism that had seemed manageable by the governments in the past now threatened diplomatic accommodation. The Senkaku Islands were now at the forefront of Japan's domestic politics.

This small incident was magnified by Japan's worry about China's growing maritime presence in and around Japanese territory, especially that this may not be simply an isolated case of bad behavior. The fishing trawler incident suggested the possibility of more difficulty in the future and foreshadowed the strategic implications of further maritime interactions between Japanese and Chinese vessels. More and more Chinese research and survey ships were now in Japan's territorial and EEZ waters. Their underwater mapping clearly had military implications, and surveys to collect data indicated that Beijing was preparing for a new approach to defining its maritime boundaries under the UNCLOS's terms. But it was the growing Chinese military presence in the East China Sea that worried Tokyo planners the most about their ability to police and defend Japan's extensive coastline and offshore islands.

With this in mind, the Japanese Ministry of Foreign Affairs argued for beginning maritime talks between Japan and China. In December 2011 when Prime Minister Noda Yoshihiko visited Beijing, the two countries agreed on a search-and-rescue agreement that would allow cooperation in responding to an accident at sea. In addition, the two nations began low-level, government-to-government maritime talks.[41] The participants on the Japanese side included representatives from the Asian and Oceanic Affairs Bureau; Cabinet Secretariat; Headquarters for Ocean Policy; Ministry of Foreign Affairs;

Ministry of Education; Agency for Natural Resources and Energy; Ministry of Land, Infrastructure, Transport, and Tourism; Ministry of Environment; Defense Ministry; and the Japan Coast Guard. On the Chinese side were the Department of Boundary and Ocean Affairs, Ministry of Foreign Affairs, Ministry of National Defense, Ministry of Public Security, Ministry of Transportation, Ministry of Agriculture, National Energy Administration, and State Oceanic Administration, in a nascent effort to identify whom to contact in case of an emergency.[42] In June 2012, the Japanese and Chinese defense ministries also agreed to establish a hotline to facilitate crisis communications. Despite all the diplomatic effort to restore confidence in the bilateral relationship, however, Japanese became far more skeptical of their government's ability to manage their nation's security and of Beijing's commitment to confidence building.

DOMESTIC INTERESTS AND ACTIVISTS

Japan's diplomatic confrontation with China over the trawler incident unleashed a firestorm of protest against the Japanese government, sparking a national debate over its policy choices in its relationship with China. Coming as it did after almost a decade of simmering anxiety over Chinese maritime activities in Japanese waters, the actions of a small fishing trawler in the waters near the Senkaku Islands took on a significance far beyond that of any previous incident. Activists took to the streets, and demonstrations in front of the Chinese embassy in Tokyo were frequent over the two-week crisis. Opposition parties clamored for information on the government's talks with China, and the pressure on the Kan cabinet intensified as Chinese authorities spoke out to international audiences, criticizing Japan's arrest of the Chinese captain. The DPJ government's decision to prosecute the Chinese fishing captain under domestic law was a new approach, an effort that at first seemed to satisfy many in Japan. But as the crisis intensified, government critics began to demand that they be allowed to see the JCG video of the incident. Then, the arrest of four Japanese in China compounded the sense that China was intensifying its pressure on Japan in an effort to force a compromise.

This was the DPJ's first diplomatic crisis with China. The party had come into power with a strong commitment to friendly relations with Japan's northeast Asian neighbors, plus a stated preference for building closer ties with the East Asian community. In addition, the DPJ was committed to reconciliation with Japan's neighbors over the country's wartime behavior, so many anticipated that the party would emphasize engagement over confrontation in its management of the Japan-China relationship. The cabinet's decision to handle the incident under Japanese domestic law drew fire early on when the country seemed unable or unwilling to respond to Chinese criticism. Chief Cabinet Secretary Sengoku Yoshito, who led the government's effort to manage the crisis, insisted that because the captain was being charged with obstructing the JCG while it was conducting its duties, the video had become evidence in a domestic legal prosecution and therefore could not be made public. As a result, the Japanese government could not show the world the Chinese fishing captain's provocative behavior. Individual members of the Japanese cabinet came under intense scrutiny in the Diet. Similarly, Mabuchi Sumio, who succeeded Maehara Seiji as MLIT minister just days after the incident occurred, also felt the wrath of opposition legislators. The DPJ's lack of experience in handling diplomacy, coupled with the perception that its leaders were far too forgiving of China, amplified public concerns.

China seemed intent on escalating the diplomatic pressure on Japan, and Wen Jiabao's speech in New York on the eve of the UN General Assembly meeting all but threatened Japan if it did not release the captain—saying that China would take "further actions" and that "all the consequences should be borne by the Japanese side."[43] Foreign Minister Maehara's meeting with the U.S. secretary of state the next day presented a calmer front, with a quiet statement by a State Department spokesperson to the effect that the U.S. government would not take a position on the sovereignty dispute.[44] But the U.S. chairman of the Joint Chiefs of Staff, Admiral Mike Mullen, expressed his support for Japan when questioned at a press conference, and U.S. Secretary of Defense Robert Gates noted that the United States would "fulfill its alliance responsibilities."[45] Clearly, what had begun as an incident between a Chinese fishing captain and the Japanese coast guard had, in just two short weeks, become a test of the U.S.-Japan alliance and Japan's national security.

The LDP in Opposition

The LDP was a formidable critic, with the advantage of having managed Japan-China relations over the decades since normalization. The DPJ government therefore could count on little support during the crisis from its main opposition party, and the long-standing differences between Japan's liberals and conservatives were on prominent display in the Diet. While these differences partly concerned how best to manage Beijing, the Diet debates quickly devolved into a split between the two over the principles that should guide Japan's security policy. As liberals and conservatives spelled out their differences regarding the Japanese military, the debate became very personal and heated.

A second, but related, point of contention was the exercise of civilian control. The DPJ came under scathing attack from the LDP for its position on the leak of the coast guard's video. The Kan government's attempt to punish the officer who had leaked the video as well as to sanction the senior bureaucrat in charge of the JCG drew particular fire, and Kan was accused of sidestepping his own responsibility for the leak. Critics claimed he was not exercising civilian control, a criticism regularly lobbed by liberal critics at the LDP while it was in power. Pushed to the limits of his patience at one debate, Chief Cabinet Secretary Sengoku blurted out the need to keep civilian control over the Self-Defense Forces (SDF), which he described as an "instrument of violence" (*bōryoku sōchi*).[46] This only heightened the acrimony. The national debate over how Japan ought to prepare for a rising China swirled for months in the Diet and the media, reflecting the heightened anxiety in Japan about its ability to manage a confrontational China.

The LDP focused on punishing those in the government who had handled the dispute. On November 26, 2010, the LDP introduced a censure motion in the Upper House against Sengoku Yoshito, the chief cabinet secretary, and, with some hesitation, a censure motion against the new minister of land, infrastructure, transportation, and tourism,

Mabuchi Sumio, for his role in overseeing the Japan Coast Guard. These censure motions forced a reshuffle of the cabinet on January 14, 2011, which was particularly damaging for the prime minister, as Sengoku had been Kan's strongest asset with great skill at organizing and sustaining policy dialogue across the party and the bureaucracy. Parliamentary tactics aside, this political struggle over who should bear ultimate responsibility for Japan's crisis management decision— politicians or bureaucrats, including those in uniform—during the Diet discussions revealed one of the country's greatest vulnerabilities.

Japan's weakness became the dominant theme. Decrying Prime Minister Kan's ending of the crisis as having no backbone (*yowa-goshi*), the LDP argued the need for a stronger Japanese position vis-à-vis Beijing. In response, Cabinet Secretary Sengoku pointed out that diplomacy required making decisions that took into consideration both long-term and short-term goals. He then described a strategic approach that allowed flexibility during times of stress, which he termed as having *yanagigoshi*, a "willowy" or more flexible backbone.[47] Terminology aside, it was clear that the *Senkaku shokku* had brought to the surface not only ideological differences over Japan's defense posture but also a new conversation about whether confrontation or flexible accommodation was Japan's best approach to dealing with China. Both sides recognized that Japan's skill and institutional capacity for handling crises had been sorely tested.

Previous Japanese leaders had chosen to accommodate rather than confront China in such cases. Koizumi's decision to detain the PRC activists in 2004 had similarly resulted in a negotiated release. In this sense, the DPJ had broken with precedent, but to others at home, a more egregious error had been the announcement by the deputy prosecutor in Naha that the Chinese captain would be sent home. To many, this sent a signal to Beijing that Japan's government was weak and confused. Here the contrast between Koizumi and Kan could not have been starker. China's call for an apology and compensation for the incident, however, provided the opportunity for Chief Cabinet Secretary Sengoku to have the last word. His refusal to pay compensation for the captain's arrest and his demand that China compensate Japan for the damaged coast guard ships seemed to restore some equilibrium in the eyes of the DPJ's domestic critics. Criticism of the government was certainly not new to Japan's domestic debate over China policy. Previous LDP prime ministers also had faced conservative critics skeptical of Japan's diplomacy toward China. These critics, however, were largely to be found within the LDP itself. But the predominant understanding in Japan was that their country had buckled under Chinese pressure, and it was this problem that had to be remedied as soon as possible.

The prosecutor's office and the local Okinawa branch charged with prosecuting the captain of the trawler were not formally investigated for their handling of the incident, but the lackluster way in which they handled the indictment was widely seen as an embarrassment. Long after the Chinese captain was allowed to return to China, the prosecutors in Naha dropped all charges against him.[48] Months later, with the public still chafing over the crisis, the case against Captain Zhan was reopened under the newly reformed prosecutorial review system, which allowed citizen-based committees to force the Japanese prosecutor's office to reopen dismissed cases. An indictment was issued, but with no ability to deliver the indictment to the captain, the court was powerless, and on May 17, 2012, the case was finally closed.[49]

Politicians and bureaucrats alike were found wanting in their deliberations with Beijing, but the Kan cabinet was the main target of domestic discontent. The DPJ-appointed ambassador to Beijing, the former chairman of Itōchū trading company, Niwa Uichirō, also was criticized for his lack of diplomatic experience. Tokyo's ability to work through back channels seemed compromised as well, which many in the LDP saw as a DPJ problem. Yet the DPJ did have contacts in the Chinese Communist Party. Hosono Gōshi, the former deputy secretary-general of the party who was close to the inveterate politician Ozawa Ichirō, went to China to reach out to Chinese leaders, as did former ambassador to China Anami Koreshige and many others who had personal relationships with Chinese leaders. But all this was not enough to restore trust in the two countries' relationship.

Japan's Coast Guard

Japan's own institutions also were reexamined, including the Japan Coast Guard and its role in defending Japanese waters. There was no criticism of the JCG's response to the trawler and its detention of its captain and crew. Footage of the incident taken by the Japan Coast Guard clearly showed the captain's intent to ram both JCG vessels, and thus there were few questions about the circumstances of its confrontation with him. Rather, it was the politicians who led the MLIT at the time, Maehara Seiji, and his successor, Mabuchi Sumio, who bore the brunt of the Diet's discontent. Maehara was criticized for the decision to arrest the captain, and Mabuchi was accused of a lack of oversight during the investigation of the YouTube video.

The oversight responsibility for the video leak also resided with the senior bureaucrat, the commandant of the JCG, Suzuki Hiroyasu. A dispute erupted in the Diet over how to respond as the investigation into his conduct went forward, and a testy exchange ensued between Chief Cabinet Secretary Sengoku and his critics in the Diet over whether it was the political leadership or the bureaucratic leadership that was ultimately responsible. In the end, however, the commandant was not asked to resign. Nonetheless, new procedures for classifying material (video and written) relating to incidents at sea were adopted.

The Japan Coast Guard jealously defended its role as a civilian policy agency. Organized before the U.S. Occupation of Japan ended, and called the Maritime Safety Agency until 2000, the Japan Coast Guard had a longer history than Japan's postwar navy, the Maritime Self-Defense Force (MSDF). Japan's ability to cope with China's civilian and military presence in and around its waters thus raised new questions about bridging the distinctly different missions of the JCG and the MSDF. Since the early 1950s, the JCG and the MSDF have had distinct areas of operating responsibility, and until the late 1990s, when foreign ships began to intrude into Japan's territorial waters, there was little dialogue between the two on how to operate in a contingency.

In 1999, the two forces began discussing operational coordination and information sharing. The rules of engagement for dispatching the JCG and the MSDF differed, depending on the nature of the intrusion. In the late 1990s, North Korean vessels operating suspiciously off Japan's western coastline signaled a new phase of thinking about the need to defend its coastal waters. Consequently, the MSDF publicly clarified the rules of engagement for maritime mobilization in response to North Korea's activities. During the several incidents in which MSDF destroyers gave chase to North Korean vessels, however, no ship was fired on.

That line was crossed in December 2001 when a North Korean vessel pursued by the JCG refused to stop for boarding within Japan's EEZ in the East China Sea, northwest of the Japanese island of Amami ōshima. The JCG patrol ship *Inasa* then gave chase out of Japan's territorial waters and into the EEZ claimed by China, where it fired on and ultimately sank the North Korean vessel.[50] On December 23, 2001, the JCG recovered from the East China Sea the bodies of three of the fifteen North Koreans killed in the incident.[51] Although the ship had sunk in 295 feet (90 m) of water, Japan was able to bring it to the surface after months of negotiation with Beijing.[52] Intelligence reports revealed that the North Korean vessel had visited Chinese ports before arriving in Japanese waters, and the Japanese media widely speculated on the relationship between North Korean criminal activities and Chinese interests. Once it was brought to the surface, the North Korean vessel—later described by Japanese authorities as a spy ship—found its way into a public exhibit at the Japan Coast Guard Museum in Yokohama.

The second maritime security order was issued in 2004 when a Chinese Han-class submarine entered Japanese territorial waters. Here the intruder in Japanese waters was clearly a foreign military, and therefore this was an MSDF mission. As noted in chapter 3, the MSDF tracked the Chinese sub for more than a day and, once it entered Japanese territorial waters, forced it to surface. More recently, in 2010 and again in 2011, an MSDF destroyer was tracking a Chinese naval vessel when it was approached by a Chinese helicopter dispatched to warn off the destroyer.

China's People's Liberation Army Navy (PLAN) and other maritime ships regularly transit Japan's territorial and contiguous waters, blurring the lines between the operations of the JCG and the MSDF. Joint exercises and a joint response manual drafted by the Ministry of Defense and the Maritime Safety Agency (MSA) provide a framework delineating the boundaries of defending and policing Japan's maritime territory.[53] Information sharing increased and local coordination of regional commands increased. The dilemma for Japan is coping with the many Chinese paramilitary forces, including the Maritime Police, the Maritime Safety Administration, the Fisheries Law Enforcement Command, the General Administration of Customs, and the State Oceanographic Administration. Many of these agencies operate in and around Senkaku waters, and most, if not all, are armed. China consolidated some of these forces, and streamlined national command, in 2013. Although the JCG remains a strong force in Northeast Asia, these Chinese maritime patrols are testing the JCG's ability to police Japan's waters and EEZ.[54]

Ishigaki City and Conservative Activists

Those Japanese who lived closest to the Senkakus seemed less enraged by the incident, despite their proximity. Nonetheless, local leaders in Okinawa noted their concerns about the Ishigaki fishermen and others in the island region that might be affected by Chinese activities in their waters.[55] The detention and arrest of the Chinese captain and his crew on September 7, 2010, put the spotlight on Ishigaki City, the administrative home of the Senkaku Islands. By the following year, 2011, Ishigaki had become the home of various activists, most of them from the main Japanese islands, who wanted to make Senkaku a national cause. The Ishigaki City assembly thus found it expedient to declare January 14 as Senkaku Day to mark the anniversary of the Japanese government's incorporation of the Senkaku Islands on January 14, 1895.[56]

Japanese activism regarding Senkaku sovereignty dates back to the late 1970s and intensified in the 1980s when Taiwanese and Hong Kong activists began attempting to land on the islands (table 6.1). Initially, a right-wing group, the Seinensha, built a lighthouse on Uotsurijma (table 6.2). Later the Seinensha's leaders were found criminally liable for tax evasion and other criminal activities, which weakened their organizational capacity. A decade later, a less controversial but well-organized conservative group, the Nippon kaigi, began to confront Hong Kong and Taiwanese activism over the Senkakus.[57] Police records of all attempted landings is not publicly available, but it wasn't until September 18, 2012, that the first arrest of Japanese citizens for landing on one of the islands was made.

TABLE 6.1 Incidents of Non-Japanese Activism near the Senkaku Islands

Date	Origin of Activists	Number of Ships	Number Entering Territorial Waters	Outcome
September 26, 1996	Hong Kong	1	1	Four protesters jump overboard (and one drowns) after their ship is blocked by the Japan Coast Guard.
October 7, 1996	Hong Kong; Taiwan	49	41	Protesters land on Uotsurijima and depart after planting Chinese and Taiwanese flags.
May 26, 1997	Hong Kong; Taiwan	30	3	Three protesters leap from their boats onto Japanese vessels. They are detained briefly and then are returned to their boats.
July 1, 1997	Taiwan	1	1	The ship is warned and then departs.
June 24, 1998	Hong Kong; Taiwan	6	1	One of the Hong Kong protest boats transmits a distress signal. Its crew is transferred to one of the Taiwanese ships, and the Hong Kong boat sinks in Japanese waters.
June 23, 2003	China	1	1	The ship is warned and then departs.
October 9, 2003	China	1	1	The ship is warned and then departs.
January 15, 2004	China	2	2	The ship is warned and then departs.
March 24, 2004	China	1	1	Seven protesters land on Uotsurijima and are arrested by Japanese police for illegally entering Japanese territory. They are later released and sent back to China.

(continued)

TABLE 6.1 (*continued*)

Date	Origin of Activists	Number of Ships	Number Entering Territorial Waters	Outcome
August 17, 2006	Taiwan	1	1	The ship is warned and then departs.
October 27, 2006	China; Hong Kong	1	1	The ship is warned and then departs.
October 28, 2007	China	1	1	The ship is warned and then departs.
June 16, 2008	Taiwan	1	1	The ship is warned and then departs, accompanied by a Taiwanese patrol boat.
September 14, 2010	Taiwan	1	0	The ship enters Japan's contiguous zone but does not enter territorial waters. It is warned and then departs, accompanied by a Taiwanese patrol boat.
June 29, 2011	Taiwan	1	0	The ship enters Japan's contiguous zone but does not enter territorial waters. It is warned and then departs, accompanied by a Taiwanese patrol boat.
August 15, 2012	Hong Kong	1	1	Fourteen protesters travel to the disputed islands. Five of them swim ashore and are arrested by Japanese police. The Japan Coast Guard later arrest the nine others who stayed on the fishing boat. On August 17, Japan deports all fourteen activists.
September 25, 2012	Taiwan	40–50	40	Fishing and maritime ships enter the contiguous zone. Afterward, forty Taiwanese fishing ships enter Japanese territorial waters. They are warned and depart four hours after entering.

Date	Origin of Activists	Number of Ships	Number Entering Territorial Waters	Outcome
January 25, 2013	Taiwan	1	0	A ship enters Japan's contiguous zone but does not enter its territorial waters. The Japan Coast Guard fires water cannons and warns the ship, which departs after the confrontation.
August 4, 2013	China	1	1	A ship is blocked by the Japan Coast Guard and then leaves Japan's territorial waters.
August 14, 2013	Taiwan	0	0	Hong Kong's Action Committee for Defending the Diaoyu Islands calls offits its plan to sail to the Senkaku Islands from Taiwan. The captain of the Taiwanese ship said he was reluctant to go because of "pressure from authorities."
November 13, 2013	Hong Kong	1	0	A ship with fifteen crew members, including Hong Kong activists, sailors, and Taiwanese reporters, sets off for the Senaku Islands but is stopped and brought back by the Hong Kong police thirty minutes after departing.
January 1, 2014	China	1 (balloon)	0	A Chinese man attempting to land a hot-air balloon on the Senkaku Islands crashes into the sea about 14 miles (22 km) south of the islands. He is rescued by the Japan Coast Guard and handed off to a Chinese patrol ship.

Source: Data from 1996 to 2010 from Japan Coast Guard, "Annual Report, 2010," and data from 2011 to 2013 were compiled from media reporting from the *Asahi shinbun*, *Nikkei shinbun*, and *Yomiuri shinbun*.

TABLE 6.2 Incidents of Japanese Activism near the Senkaku Islands

Date	Incident
August 11, 1978	Activists from the right-wing group Nihon seinensha land on Uotsurijima and erect a lighthouse.
September 30, 1990	Activists from the Seinensha rebuild a lighthouse on Uotsurijima with the permission of the owners and register it in Ishigaki City. The Seinensha then asks the Maritime Safety Agency for permission to register the lighthouse internationally.
July 26, 1996	Seven members from the Seinensha land on Kitakojima and spend the night there to build another lighthouse. The Seinensha asks Ishigaki City to register the lighthouse as an official aid to navigation.
May 6, 1997	One Diet member from the Shinshintō Party lands and conducts a survey of the Senkaku Islands.
May 10, 2001	One member from the Seinensha lands on the islands.
April 8, 2004	In response to the Chinese activists' landings on Senkaku, Seinensha members head out to Uotsurijima. The JCG does not stop the group from embarking on their trip, given their promise that they will not land on the island.
January 3, 2012	Four people from Ishigaki City approach and land on Uotsurijima.
June 9, 2012	Six members from the Lower House, together with members of Ishigaki City and Tokyo and activists from Ganbare nippon, approach the Senkaku Islands but do not land.
July 5, 2012	Nakama Hitoshi and two other members of the Ishigaki City assembly land on Kitakojima.
August 19, 2012	Ten Japanese activists, including members from Gambare nippon and the local assembly, land on Uotsurijima and erect a Japanese flag. Five of the activists are assembly members from Tokyo, Hyōgo, and Ibaraki. The other five are private citizens. On August 18, 150 activists had set out on twenty-one ships to participate in a memorial service for Japan's war dead in waters near the islands.

TABLE 6.2 (*continued*)

Date	Incident
September 18, 2012	Two members of the Kagoshima-based political party Satsuma shishi no kai land on Uotsurijima. The members stay on the island for about an hour, place flowers by a memorial erected for the victims of a shipwreck during World War II, and plant a Japanese flag. The two are prosecuted by the Naha District Public Prosecutors Office on September 29. This is the first time that charges are pressed against Japanese for landing on the islands.
April 22, 2013	Approximately eighty members from Ganbare nippon set out for the Senkaku Islands in ten ships. The group says they intend to survey fishing in the area and have no plans to land.
June 30, 2013	Thirty participants of a "Senkaku Islands fishing tour" approach the islands and begin to fish. A patrol vessel of the Japan Coast Guard sails along to protect them and prevent them from landing on the islands. The act also attracts eight Chinese surveillance ships, which trail the fishing boats.
August 18, 2013	Five ships of Ganbare nippon come within about two-thirds of a mile (1 km) of the Senkaku Islands. They are then surrounded by Japan Coast Guard patrol vessels and driven out of the area.

Source: A Japanese government compilation of activist incidents involving Japanese citizens is not publicly available. Data compiled from media reporting from *Asahi shinbun*, *Nikkei shinbun*, and *Yomiuri shinbun*.

The 2010 Chinese trawler incident whetted the national appetite for a debate over how to manage Chinese claims against the islands. At the time of the incident, demonstrations were held in front of the Chinese embassy in Tokyo, which continued for weeks and at times numbered up to 2,800 demonstrators.[58] Those who regularly beat the anti-China drum also targeted Japan's Ministry of Foreign Affairs, but in 2010, it was the political leadership of the ministry rather than the bureaucrats themselves who were under the microscope. The Japanese nationalist media and blogosphere also erupted, from the conservative television channel, Channel Sakura,[59] to other websites of groups known to harbor anti-Chinese sentiments, such as Nihon seinensha, Ganbare nippon, Takenoma, and the sites of conservative commentators Sakurai Yoshiko and Takeda Tsuneyasu.

Tokyo's governor, Ishihara Shintarō, also has been an outspoken advocate for firmer Japanese government action in defense of Japan's sovereignty claims over the Senkakus. He has long criticized China's claims to these islands and often ignored similar claims by Taiwan. The leak of the JCG video of the incident, however, openly challenged the Japanese government's decision making during the crisis and opened for public debate the question of whether the Kan cabinet had chosen wisely when deciding not to allow the video to be seen by the public. Ishihara expressed his sympathy for the JCG officer, Isshiki Masaharu, who leaked the videos on YouTube, openly praising him for his decision and defending him against those who wanted to have him legally prosecuted for the leak. When Isshiki appeared at the Foreign Press Club of Japan to speak about the incident and his book, Ishihara stood by his side. Despite the questionable legality of his decision to put the video on the web, many in Japan celebrated this "whistle-blower" for doing what they thought their government ought to have done.[60]

It was the governor's plan to have the Tokyo Metropolitan Government purchase the Senkaku Islands. In a somewhat rambling address at the Heritage Foundation in Washington, D.C., on April 16, 2012, Ishihara claimed that as governor of Tokyo, he was involved in negotiations with the Kurihara family, who owned the islands, to buy them.[61] He maintained that if the national government of Japan was unwilling or unable to defend Japan's sovereignty adequately, he would be happy for the Tokyo Metropolitan Government to step in and do it.[62] He advocated developing the islands and making the conservation of their natural resources a focal point of his plan.

The national government was placed in a difficult position. Chief Cabinet Secretary Fujimura Osamu stated the next day that the government was satisfied with the current arrangement with the owners of the Senkaku Islands, but if it became necessary, the Japanese government would consider buying them.[63] Ishihara's proposal consumed the Japanese media for days afterward. Initial media surveys of Tokyo residents revealed a deep ambivalence about Ishihara's plans, and many wondered aloud in front of TV cameras why their taxes should go to such a plan. The governor's office, however, began a national appeal for donations to buy the islands, and in the following months, a steady flow of cash poured in.

Other politicians flirted with joining Governor Ishihara. Osaka Mayor Hashimoto Tōru publicly announced that he, too, would explore the possibility of Osaka's helping with the purchase. His city assembly, however, was less than enthusiastic, and Hashimoto later dropped the issue. The mayor of Ishigaki City, Nakayama Yoshitaka, was taken by surprise by Ishihara's initiative. While he initially seemed in favor of having the Tokyo Metropolitan Government purchase the islands, after a visit to Tokyo and deliberations within his own constituency, he launched his own plan to raise money to help buy the Senkakus. As the municipality with direct administrative duties over these islands, Nakayama ultimately wanted Ishigaki to have its own share in the ownership of the islands.

The Senkaku Fund (Senkaku kifukin), organized by the Tokyo Metropolitan Government, quickly grew, and as of September 13, 2012, it had a total of ¥1.47 billion ($14.8 million).[64] The question was whether the Kurihara family would be willing to sell. The governor's long-term interest in asserting Japanese sovereignty over the Senkakus and his personal effort to work through the Kurihara family to accomplish this aim seemed to have finally have paid off. National sentiment was far more sympathetic to Ishihara's brand of activism on the Senkakus, and defending Japan's sovereignty there became the focus of mainstream politics. Whereas previous episodes of tension over Taiwanese or Chinese activists claiming their rights to the islands led to isolated incidents of reaction, mostly from small, fringe nationalist groups, in 2012 the call to rally around Japan's sovereign claims over the islands attracted a wide variety of Japanese citizens in the effort to demand a more assertive defense of the islands.

STRATEGIC ADJUSTMENT

The *Senkaku shokku* changed the domestic debate on Japan's security. For many, this was the wake-up call for much needed reform of Japan's crisis management practices and even its military objectives. Tokyo's past practice of relying on Beijing's cooperation no longer seemed fitting. The defense of Japan's southernmost islands, identified in 2004 as a priority for Japan's SDF, and the diversification of Japan's supply of rare earth minerals, a goal since the Chinese imposed restrictions on exports in 2006, were given greater attention after the diplomatic run-in with Beijing in 2010. At a different level, Japan's new ruling party also sought to develop a better set of mechanisms for working through its problems with the Communist Party of China (CCP), and the DPJ and the CCP created a new agreement to expand personnel exchanges and to build better relations among their party members. But the lack of communication channels was not really the problem.

Three factors continued to shape Japan's policymaking after 2010, which limited its strategic adjustment to this new, more contentious China. The first was the acrimony between the ruling and opposition parties at the time. The DPJ had little experience in crisis management and even in its management of foreign policy. Moreover, unlike the LDP leaders of the past, the DPJ had few personal networks that they could use to communicate with China's party leaders. The LDP, now in opposition, relentlessly criticized the DPJ's handling of the crisis. In the Diet, Prime Minister Kan and his cabinet secretary, Sengoku, were attacked for not dealing with China strongly enough. Opposition party criticism was not a new phenomenon in Japan, of course. In 2008 when Prime Minister Fukuda Yasuo's summit with Chinese President Hu Jintao produced cooperative solutions to their differences, including the East China Sea agreement, groups outside the Diet, particularly the media and nationalist activists were critical. In opposition at the time, the DPJ did not accuse the more conciliatory Fukuda cabinet of being weak, because in many ways reconciliation with China was exactly what the DPJ itself advocated. Now, however, LDP conservatives had little reason to hold back since the DPJ was in power, and so the Diet as well as the media became a source of intense political pressure.

Second, Japan's policy coordination mechanisms were demonstrably ill prepared to cope with escalating crises with China. The conclusion of the two-week crisis may have infuriated government critics, but never before had the government had to coordinate an array of instruments in support of a diplomatic crisis. With an embargo on rare earths, the arrests of Japanese businessmen, an impending showdown at the United Nations, and the prosecutor's need for investigating a crime, the prime minister's office was overwhelmed. China seemed to be calling the shots, and Japan was having trouble keeping up. The day after the New York meetings at the UN General Assembly, a beleaguered deputy prosecutor in Ishigaki announced the release of the Chinese trawler captain. His statement that the investigation was being suspended for the time being, out of concern for the Japanese public and Sino-Japanese relations, only raised more questions than it answered about how the prime minister's office was handling the issue.[65] The linkage between the captain's detention and the detention of the four Fujita Corporation employees in China could not be revealed because of the need to gain their release. Only after the Chinese captain's release was announced could Japanese diplomats in China gain access to the detained Japanese citizens in China.

Finally, the Senkaku shock enraged nationalist activists and energized their effort to mobilize public support for Japanese sovereignty over the disputed islands. Yet again, standing up to China became a rallying cry for those who wanted to see a more militarized Japan. Notable conservative politicians, including anti-China nationalists like the governor of Tokyo, Ishihara Shintarō, were joined by General Tamogami Toshio, the Air Self-Defense Force general dismissed from active service by former Prime Minister Asō Tarō for his essay denying Japan's responsibility for its prewar aggression.[66] Tamogami led demonstrations and was joined at rallies by the LDP's executive council chairman, Koike Yuriko, a former LDP minister of defense.

The leak of the Japan Coast Guard video by a disgruntled officer only added fuel to the fire. For one day, the JCG video of the incident appeared on YouTube and then was removed at the request of the Japanese government. The JCG officer who leaked the material—which later was found to have been made widely available via the Coast Guard Academy in Kure[67]—was heralded by conservatives in the Diet as a hero and a whistle-blower. A government investigation into the incident revealed that the JCG video, as well as the ambiguous treatment of information regarding incidents in and around

Japanese territorial waters, had not been treated as classified information and thus was widely available within the coast guard.

Diplomacy with Beijing, Defense with Washington

Japan's diplomats reached out to Beijing to encourage a bilateral effort at confidence building and dispute resolution in the East China Sea, as well as to return to a more positive relationship based on strategic reciprocity. The foreign policy reforms also included actively seeking out partners and friends across Asia and using multilateral institutions to articulate shared interests with other advanced industrial democracies. Most conspicuous was the Japanese government's decision to use the WTO's dispute settlement mechanism to engage China in discussion about access to rare earths. Across the board, the idea that Japan could work its problems out with Beijing only through bilateral channels had been severely undermined.

Bilateral diplomacy took time to recover, however. When Prime Minister Kan Naoto met with President Hu Jintao on the sidelines of the November 2010 Asia-Pacific Economic Cooperation (APEC) meeting, the two leaders had little to talk about. China's premier, Wen Jiabao, visited Japan repeatedly in 2011 in the aftermath of Japan's "triple disasters" and spoke publicly of the friendship between the peoples of China and Japan.[68] Disaster diplomacy had also been a valuable opportunity in 2008 when China suffered tremendous losses in the Sichuan earthquake.[69]

Prime Minister Noda Yoshihiko repaid Wen's visits in 2011 with a visit in December of that year. Although originally scheduled for December 13, the visit was postponed because of sensitivity over the anniversary of the rape of Nanjing. While in Beijing on December 25, Noda emphasized the positive, and the two countries focused mostly on their shared interest in stability on the Korean Peninsula and the economic importance of their relationship.[70] They agreed to push forward with an agreement to trade in their own currencies, which became effective on June 1, 2012, and to pursue discussions on a free-trade agreement. Less attention was paid to the maritime initiative, which included working on a search-and-rescue agreement and maritime confidence-building talks for the East China Sea.

The incident also drew attention to Japan's own maritime defenses. Japan's National Defense Program Guidelines were scheduled for release by the end of 2010, and although the incident did not change the overall focus of the national defense plan, it did reinforce the notion that Japan's southwestern waters were a concern. New deployments to that region—including the shift of one F-15 squadron, the deployment of a signals intelligence unit of the GSDF to Yonaguni Island, and the added presence of six submarines for patrol around Japanese waters—all signaled the country's new sensitivity to incursions into its waters by Chinese vessels.

The JCG reviewed its coverage of the waters in and around the Senkakus and upgraded its patrols there.[71] It also developed a system to protect video and other materials and reviewed its ability to manage activism in and around the Senkaku Islands. Several revisions were included in new legislation for the JCG. First, the revised coast guard law would give the JCG policing authority on Japan's remote islands, thereby filling in a gap in the postwar division of labor between the coast guard and Japan's police. Many of Japan's remote islands have few or no people living on them, and therefore no police. Second, the new law would expand the range of individuals who could be questioned by the JCG regarding maritime behavior: not only the crew or passengers of vessels suspected of illegal activity but also those individuals or companies who owned the ship as well as those who might have knowledge about issues related to maritime safety and transit of Japanese waters. Finally, the revised law gave the JCG the authority to order any ship out of Japanese waters, with a fine if necessary, without first having to issue a warning, if the foreign vessel stopped without apparent reason, or without boarding for inspection, if the foreign vessel refused to obey warnings. These revisions were designed to give the JCG greater authority to deal with individuals who landed illegally on Japan's remote islands or with ships that behaved suspiciously in Japanese territorial waters. Despite the tensions between the ruling and opposition parties, Japan's Lower House and Upper House both unanimously passed the revised law—on August 10 and August 29, respectively—allowing the JCG to undertake criminal investigations and make arrests on remote islands such as the Senkakus. The revised law went into effect on September 25, 2012.[72]

Japan's new maritime emphasis also was discernible in bilateral talks with the United States on defense cooperation. Enhanced consultations with the MSDF were held, and Tokyo also moved forward with revising the Common Strategic Objectives with Washington, including an emphasis on maritime security in the Asia Pacific. In addition, the Japanese GSDF stepped up its amphibious landing capabilities, including exercises with the U.S. Marine Corps at Camp Pendleton, California, on January 26, 2012,[73] and an agreement in February 2012 for joint training and exercises with the SDF and U.S. forces in the Mariana Islands in the Western Pacific. By August, U.S. and Japanese forces were preparing for sustained amphibious landing training, and Japan had decided to purchase several amphibious landing ships for its GSDF.[74]

Nationalism and the Government's Purchase of the Senkakus

Perhaps the most profound legacy of the incident was its impact on Japan's domestic politics. As noted earlier, activism against China was intense in the weeks of the crisis, but it continued long after the Chinese captain was sent home. Senkaku nationalism became a new mantra for a variety of politicians and activists. The mayor of Ishigaki City, Nakayama Yoshitaka, and even the governor of Okinawa Prefecture, Nakaima Hirokazu, lobbied for greater attention to Japan's defenses in their waters. Governor Ishihara's announcement that he would purchase the islands began a new surge of Senkaku nationalism, and on May 31, 2012, the LDP announced a resolution to nationalize the Senkaku Islands as part of its updated party manifesto.[75]

The political salience of the Senkaku issue only grew larger. By early July 2012, the national government was convinced of the need to take action, and Prime Minister Noda announced his intention to have the government purchase the islands. Discussions with Tokyo Governor Ishihara began, and unlike the Tokyo Metropolitan Government, the national government had no legal limitations on the purchase. Direct discussions with the family were initiated in the summer of 2012 with the aim of completing the purchase by the end of 2012, but this time frame had to be accelerated as activism surrounding the sovereignty dispute intensified. On August 14, 2012, Japanese faced further protests when they commemorated the anniversary of the end of World War II. Chinese activists landed on the Senkaku Islands, inflaming the public in both countries. Earlier, on August 10, South Korean President Lee Myung-bak had added to Tokyo's consternation by visiting the disputed Takeshima/Dokdo Islands, the first Korean president ever to do so.

The impact of China's rise on Japan's sense of security was reflected in the two episodes of confrontation over the Senkakus. Quite literally, many in Japan were shocked at the intensity of the escalating crisis with China. Across the world, China's behavior during this crisis was witnessed with deep concern. But in Tokyo, it was the vulnerabilities of Japan's own crisis management capacity that monopolized attention. The lack of an agreement with Beijing on the East China Sea also was a cause for lingering resentment, and the inability of the two neighbors to discuss calmly the behavior and treatment of Captain Zhan revealed just how fragile the trust between Tokyo and Beijing had become.

The crisis that erupted in 2010 caught the DPJ off guard. Beijing's effort to discredit Japan's foreign minister, Maehara Seiji, by trying to work around him created another difficulty for the Japanese government. The greater challenge for the Japanese government came later and from inside the government. The leak to YouTube of JCG material that ought to have been classified dealt another blow to the struggling Kan cabinet, and even though it was removed from circulation within a day, it produced a serious dilemma for the ruling party. The more pragmatic question of whether Japan should prosecute the JCG official who had leaked the video while allowing the Chinese trawler captain to go free framed the political management of the leaked video. But the more compelling question of whether Japan's civil servants should obey their political leaders remained just below the surface of this controversy.

Protest demonstrations against China also were a new factor in the Japanese response to the trawler incident. Demonstrations continued for weeks after the Senkaku clash but gained steam after the JCG video was released to the public. Ganbare nippon (Japan, Be Strong!), a non-profit advocacy group headed by General Tamogami, organized most of the protests.[76] In the first few weeks following the crisis, protesters gathered in front of the Chinese embassy in Tokyo, with the largest crowd, 2,800 people, on October 16.[77] But on November 6, right after the video was leaked, Ganbare nippon organized a protest that drew a crowd of 4,500 people at the Hibiya outdoor concert hall. Tamogami was joined by LDP Diet member and former Defense Minister Koike Yuriko. Both angrily criticized the Kan cabinet and decried the DPJ's management of the crisis with China. Media accounts of this rally noted that after the JCG video leak, the demonstrations drew a more varied group of Japanese. For the first time, younger participants and families joined in, and in interviews with reporters, many referred to the leak of the JCG video as the deciding factor in their decision to participate.[78] On November 13, around 4,000 protesters gathered outside the APEC meeting in Yokohama to further protest against China, and a week later, 3,300 people gathered outside the Chinese consulate in Osaka at a Senkaku protest.[79]

Activists who had once been on the margins of Japanese politics were shaping the public's understanding of the Senkaku dispute with China, and Governor Ishihara directly confronted the national government on its management of the issue in the wake of the 2010 Chinese fishing trawler incident. The incident also revealed deep misgivings in Japan about the DPJ's ability to conduct foreign policy. Governor Ishihara took advantage of this domestic criticism of the DPJ and in 2012 surprised the country by his an appeal for a national purchase. His long-standing interest in the Senkakus made him a frequent commentator on the issue, but the fact that the LDP was out of power gave him a political opportunity he had not had in the past. The Japanese media sat up and took notice, more notice perhaps than they would have if he had said the same thing in Tokyo. The Heritage Foundation gave him the platform he had long hoped for to signal that this was an issue he was willing to push, even if it upset Washington. Yet it was the surprising success of Ishihara's Senkaku Fund that energized the governor's subsequent challenge of the central government. Millions of dollars (billions of yen) poured into the new Tokyo Metropolitan Government's Senkaku Fund, and by the end of the summer, more than 100,000 Japanese had donated in support of his plan to purchase the islands.

The pressure on the Noda government therefore intensified. By late August, the Noda government was visibly weakened by its run-in with opposition parties in the Diet. An agreement to cooperate over tax and social security reform dissolved into a testy standoff, including an unsuccessful no-confidence vote in the Lower House on August 9. Then on August 29, in the final days of the parliamentary session, the Upper House passed a censure motion against the prime minister in an effort to force him to dissolve the Diet. Conservatives in the LDP were focusing their attention on a September 26 leadership race as the fate of their president Tanigaki Sadakazu, who had worked with Noda, became increasingly dim. Preparation for the next Lower House election began and undermined the LDP's commitment to working with the Noda government.

Just as party frictions were heating up in Tokyo, a fishing boat full of Hong Kong–based activists landed on the Senkaku Islands on August 15, the anniversary of Japan's surrender in World War II. The Japanese government was prepared for them and had stationed a group of thirty police and immigration officials on Uotsurijima. Seven of the fourteen protesters evaded the JCG and jumped overboard. Two returned to the boat, but five managed to swim ashore. The Japanese police arrested them on suspicion of illegal entry into Japan, and a few hours later, the nine activists onboard the fishing boat also were arrested for violating immigration law. Except for that of Captain Zhan Qixiong, these were the first arrests since March 2004 when seven Chinese landed on the Senkaku Islands. It is noteworthy that Taiwan refused the fishing boat permission to refuel and also warned any Taiwan-based activists against joining in the protest.[80]

On August 17, Japan's Chief Cabinet Secretary Fujimura announced that the fourteen activists would be deported. When they returned to Hong Kong, a crowd of about one hundred, including the media, were on hand to greet them. Several activists spoke to the press, with one insisting that they would return again and again to assert Chinese sovereignty and another denying that they had help from the Chinese government.[81] Their point had been made: Chinese activism on the Senkaku Islands was alive and well, and Japan could expect further visits to the islands. Unlike the 2010 incident, however, the Noda cabinet approved the immediate release of the JCG's video of its effort to stop the landing. The director of the JCG's Territorial Waters Guard, Okushima Takahiro, told reporters, "We decided to release the video to show that the Coast Guard took appropriate measures against the protestors."[82]

Renewed Chinese activism accelerated the national government's plans to purchase the Senkaku Islands from the Kurihara family.[83] Ishihara's public announcement of his plans to construct a port and send Tokyo government officials to live on the islands led the Tokyo Metropolitan Government to organize a survey of the islands. Emboldened by his success with the Senkaku Fund, Ishihara requested the national government's permission to land on the islands and conduct a survey on August 22, 2012, days after the China-based activists had landed there. Several days later, the governor upped the ante by stating that he would land on the Senkakus, regardless of whether the Noda cabinet gave him permission.[84] Quiet discussions between the prime minister's staff and the governor ensued.[85] On August 27, the Japanese government refused to give the governor permission to land. On September 2, a twenty-five-member Tokyo Metropolitan Government survey team carried out their survey of the Senkakus, but from onboard their ship.[86] Japanese television crews captured the event live and broadcast it on the evening news.

On September 10, Chief Cabinet Secretary Fujimura announced that the Noda government would move forward with purchasing the islands "in order to continue to appropriately implement maritime navigation safety operations in the Senkaku Islands and ensure their peaceful and stable maintenance and management in the long term."[87] The next day, the Japanese government reportedly paid the Kurihara family ¥2.05 billion ($26 million) for three of the five Senkaku islands.[88]

China's Challenge of Administrative Control

In the summer of 2012, the Japanese government's decision to purchase the three islands that the Kurihara family owned set off a second major diplomatic confrontation between Beijing and Tokyo.

Multiple factors contributed to this new crisis with China. Domestic Japanese activism surrounding the islands had prompted Prime Minister Noda to act. The LDP, in opposition, had taken up the territorial dispute with China in its electoral manifesto, and the Chinese activists yet again landed on the islands in commemoration of Japan's surrender on August 15. The outcome this time, however, was much different. The Chinese government announced that it would send its own patrol ships to the disputed islands. No longer would JCG vessels be the only ships policing Senkaku waters.

The first Chinese ships arrived on September 14, and over the fall, the Marine Oceanic Administration established regular patrols of the disputed islands. Month by month, the Chinese patrols increased. In September, the Marine Oceanic Administration sent 81 ships into the contiguous waters around the disputed islands, and 13 ships into Japan's twelve-nautical-mile territorial waters. In October, 122 ships visited the contiguous zone; 19 entered territorial waters; and a similar number of patrols continued in November.[89] China's patrols of the Senkaku waters would become a regular part of Japan-China maritime interaction (figure 6.3).

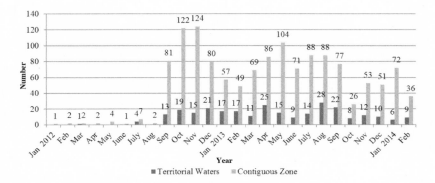

FIGURE 6.3 Intrusions by Chinese ships into Japanese waters near the Senkaku Islands. (Japan Coast Guard, "Chūgoku kōsen nado ni yoru senkaku shotō shūhen no setsuzoku suiikinai nyūiki oyobi ryōkai shinnyū sekisū" [Intrusions by Chinese Ships in the Territorial and Contiguous Waters Surrounding the Senkaku Islands], http://www.kaiho.mlit.go.jp/senkaku/index.html [accessed March 6, 2014])

In December 2012, the standoff between Japanese and Chinese coast guard ships took an ugly turn. A small Chinese surveillance plane entered Japanese airspace over the islands for the first time and was spotted by a JCG crew. Japan's Air Self-Defense Force had not picked up the small propeller craft, but once alerted by the JCG, F-15 fighter jets were scrambled in response.[90] Over the following weeks, China again dispatched small surveillance aircraft to the Senkaku Islands, but now they were accompanied by China's own fighter jets and other aircraft.[91] No direct contact between Japanese and Chinese fighter jets was reported, but the intensification of military alerts raised the danger of interaction between Chinese and Japanese forces. Moreover, by April 2013, the Japanese Ministry of Defense noted that the number of scrambles by ASDF fighters against the Chinese had overtaken the number annually reported against the Russian air force, the only air force in East Asia that had alerted Japan's air defenses since World War II. The decision to purchase the islands had caused a jump in interaction between the Japanese and Chinese air forces as China intensified its surveillance activities around the Senkakus.[92]

Another troubling interaction between militaries occurred in January 2013 when Japan's Maritime Self-Defense Force (MSDF) announced that a Chinese naval vessel had locked onto its radar one of the MSDF's frigates, the *Yūdachi*, located about 112 miles (180 km) north of the disputed islands. A similar radar-lock incident was also reported for a MSDF helicopter on January 19. This was not the first time that the Chinese and Japanese navies had had these kinds of incidents, but in the midst of the tense standoff over the territorial dispute, it was particularly worrisome. The new Japanese minister of defense, Onodera Itsunori, made a public announcement of the incident and urged China to take steps to prevent miscalculation by local commanders.[93] The Chinese government initially seemed unaware of the incident, and the Chinese Ministry of Defense began an investigation.[94] Two days later, the ministry reported that no such radar-lock incident had occurred but did acknowledge the seriousness of an incident of that sort.[95]

Unlike the 2010 crisis, the Japanese government took steps publicly to respond to China's behavior. The Chinese reconnaissance flight into

Japanese airspace, in fact, coincided with Japan's Lower House elections. With a leadership transition under way in Tokyo, the incident offered an opportunity to change the government's approach to crisis management. During his bid for party leadership, Japan's new prime minister, Abe Shinzō, had advocated strongly for government personnel to be stationed on the islands. Moreover, he was well known to be an ardent supporter of a strong Japanese defense posture and the revision of Japan's constitution to allow the SDF a freer hand in operations designed for Japanese defense, including operations with U.S. forces. In response to the Chinese airplane's intrusion, Abe ordered Defense Minister Onodera to review the rules of engagement (ROEs) for air defense.

The new Abe cabinet also immediately reviewed Japan's security policy priorities. Onodera initiated a review of Japan's National Defense Program Guidelines, the five-year national defense plan, and argued for a review of U.S.-Japan defense cooperation guidelines. Japan's new foreign minister, Kishida Fumio, visited Washington, D.C., to meet with U.S. Secretary of State Hillary Clinton, and in their joint statement on January 18, Secretary Clinton clearly reiterated that the islands would be protected under the U.S.-Japan security treaty, stating that the United States "would oppose any unilateral actions that would seek to undermine Japanese administration."[96] On April 14 in Tokyo, newly appointed U.S. Secretary of State John Kerry went even further, saying that the United States would "oppose any unilateral or coercive action that would somehow aim at changing the status quo."[97] The U.S. security guarantee had also been clearly confirmed in response to the 2010 crisis and again by Secretary Clinton and Secretary of Defense Leon Panetta in their meetings with Chinese leaders in the fall of 2012.

The Abe cabinet treated the crisis with China far differently than the Kan cabinet had. When the radar lock occurred, for example, the Japanese government immediately publicized the incident, putting the Chinese government on the defensive. In his statements to the Diet, Prime Minister Abe urged China to "strictly refrain from dangerous acts that would escalate the situation,"[98] but he also contended that Japan must remain calm. U.S. officials were briefed on the incident, and the electronic data revealing the interaction with the

Chinese ship were shared with U.S. military officials. Consultations between U.S. and Japanese governments on the incident also led to a discussion on how to de-escalate the rising tensions with China. During his visit to Washington, D.C., on February 22, 2013, Prime Minister Abe openly stated that Japan had "absolutely no intention to climb up the escalation ladder" and assured Washington policymakers that the Japanese Self-Defense Forces would continue to exercise restraint in the face of Chinese actions.[99]

Finally, the new Japanese government tried to lay the groundwork for a meeting between the new prime minister and China's new leader, Xi Jinping. The protracted Chinese leadership transition, a process of nomination and selection that began in November at the Eighteenth National Congress of the Communist Party of China and concluded in March with the Twelfth National People's Congress, undoubtedly influenced decision making in Beijing. Abe sent Yamaguchi Natsuo, the head of his coalition partner the Kōmeitō, to Beijing on January 25 to deliver a letter to Xi on his behalf. Before his departure from Tokyo, Yamaguchi stated publicly that perhaps the two countries should return to the quiet management of the island dispute, setting aside their differences in the interest of the broader relationship.[100] In Beijing, Yamaguchi met with Xi for one hour and returned to Tokyo with Xi's greetings to Abe. Although the radar-lock incident interrupted diplomatic overtures, former prime minister Fukuda Yasuo, a longtime LDP China hand now retired from politics, also sought to communicate Japan's desire for diplomacy.[101] But Xi's government was not ready to respond formally and asked Seoul to postpone the annual PRC-Japan-ROK summit meeting because of the Senkaku Island dispute.[102]

This standstill in high-level diplomacy lasted through the year. In late November 2013, Beijing abruptly announced the creation of a new Air Defense Identification Zone (ADIZ) in the East China Sea. Japan and South Korea had long maintained similar zones within which entering foreign aircraft were requested to identify themselves and their destinations. China's ADIZ, however, overlapped with those of both countries and aligned largely with the airspace above its continental shelf. Thus, China's ADIZ challenged Japan's in roughly the same way as its continental shelf claim did. Moreover,

China's ADIZ included the disputed Senkaku Islands, establishing a clear contest between Chinese and Japanese air patrols over the islands. Interestingly, the new ADIZ also included an island whose sovereignty Seoul and Beijing disputed. When the South Korean government asked China to redraw its ADIZ line, Beijing refused, forcing Seoul to take a far more rigid position than it otherwise might have. Both the timing and the way in which Beijing declared it would enforce its ADIZ bothered its neighbors. China's Ministry of Defense made this announcement on November 23, 2013,[103] just a week before U.S. Vice President Joe Biden was due to make a visit to Tokyo, Beijing, and Seoul to discuss how to alleviate regional tensions. Chinese Ministry of Defense officials also stated bluntly that all aircraft must comply with its new notification requirements, or the Chinese military would take all necessary "defensive measures." Needless to say, the Japanese government refused to acknowledge China's new ADIZ, as did the South Korean government.[104] For its part, the U.S. Department of Defense announced that China's new ADIZ would in no way affect U.S. military operations in and around the East China Sea and reiterated the U.S. security commitment to Japan.[105]

The stalemate in Japan-China relations continues, as does the escalation of their military tensions in the East China Sea. The prospect of an accident or miscalculation haunts security planners in both Tokyo and Washington, but China seems to have little interest in discussing how to reduce the risk of such close interaction between the militaries operating in the East China Sea. A decade of adjustment to China's rising economic and military power has not served Tokyo well. Antagonism at home has been steadily growing, and concern about Japan's own security has been added as the maritime interactions between Chinese and Japanese forces became more unpredictble. While neither country seems to want an armed clash, the dynamics of their interaction seem ever more likely to take them there. An absence of serious, high-level diplomatic attention to their shared interests, as well as a decidedly more competitive military dynamic, makes political compromise more difficult. The new climate in Japan, in which nationalists now have a political opportunity that did not seem to exist in the past, may temper the argument that the benefits of trade with and investment in China should be enough to keep the peace.

Leadership transitions in Japan have helped determine its diplomatic relationship with China. Over the last decade, the domestic politics surrounding the island dispute and Japan's broader security changed rapidly as compromise with China seemed to become more and more elusive. Politicians with nationalist ambitions took advantage of the two episodes of contention over the Senkaku Islands, first in 2010 and again in 2012, to carve out tougher positions for a Japanese demonstration of sovereignty. Popular sentiment regarding the Japan's need to defend its sovereignty over these islands was far different in 2013 than it was in 2009. The coincidence of tensions with China over the Senkakus, first with the LDP's leadership race in September 2012 and then with the Lower House election that December, could not have been unintentional. During the LDP race, only one contender (ironically, Ishihara Shintarō's son, Nobuteru) did not mention the need to bolster Japan's "effective control" of the Senkaku Islands. Abe Shinzō, the candidate who ultimately won the race, pushed the hardest, advocating for Japanese government officials to inhabit the islands. In the Lower House election called by Prime Noda Yoshihiko two months later, a strong defense of Japan's sovereignty over the Senkakus was part of the LDP's manifesto. Then on December 16, 2012, the LDP won a clear majority, and Abe Shinzō became Japan's next prime minister.

Undoubtedly, the defeat of Noda's DPJ in that election can be attributed partly to doubts about the Japanese government's longstanding policy of cooperation with China. Equally important to that Lower House election was the victory of Ishihara Shintarō, who joined Osaka's mayor, Hashimoto Tōru, to lead the new Japan Restoration Party, which won 54 seats in its first Lower House election. Noda's embattled DPJ barely survived, dropping from 230 seats to only 57. Although it is a stretch to argue that the Senkaku confrontation with China determined this electoral outcome, the sense of crisis in Japan resulting from the clash with China clearly created a political opportunity for Ishihara and his followers.

The ability of the Japanese and Chinese governments to sustain their bilateral, low-key management of citizen activism was ultimately undermined as concern over the Chinese government's power and intentions grew. The 2010 Chinese fishing trawler incident revived popular interest in the islands and created sympathy for the plight of the JCG patrolling the waters. By 2012, Tokyo Governor Ishihara's campaign to push the national government into a more assertive stance drew even more popular support. Unable to stop the sale of the islands, the Noda cabinet faced two alternatives: to allow the Tokyo Metropolitan Government to buy and develop the islands or to have the national government buy them.[106] In the end, Noda chose to buy the islands as a last-ditch effort to try to dissuade Ishihara and dampen Japanese popular sentiment. The subsequent outrage in China, however, simply gave credence to Ishihara's belief that the Chinese—and especially their leaders in the Chinese Communist Party—are hostile to Japan. The long-standing policy of compromising with Beijing came to an end as Japan's conservatives came back to the idea that their country should demonstrate its control of the islands in the face of Chinese pressure, thereby coming full circle back to the debate in their party in the 1970s when Tokyo and Beijing were first negotiating their postwar peace.

Forty years after Japan and China decided to set aside their territorial dispute in order to normalize their relations, sovereignty over five small, uninhabited islands has reemerged as a potent nationalist cause that seems destined to define Tokyo's and Beijing's future. More and more of China's state-owned ships patrol the Senkaku Islands, and the Japanese government's repeated protests of the presence of these ships seem to have fallen on deaf ears.[107] Each nation's unresolved claims continue to offer an incentive to establish its sovereignty over the Senkakus. International law notwithstanding, Tokyo's priority became deterring Chinese preemptive action to establish control over the islands. The politicization of the dispute will undoubtedly continue, and the potential for heightened tension—and perhaps even conflict—over these small uninhabited islands will make it increasingly difficult for the two governments to go back to Deng Xiaoping's approach of leaving the problem to future generations to resolve.

CONCLUSION

Japan's relationship with China over the past decade was characterized by repeated incidents of contention and seemingly irreconcilable
differences over policy. Despite the tremendous economic interests at
stake for both countries, the two governments were unable to manage and resolve their disputes. Diplomatically, China's regional and
global influence seemed to eclipse Japan's international standing, and
in Japan, China was viewed more and more as an antagonistic rival.
Popular sentiment in Japan grew skeptical of Beijing, making government compromise more difficult and creating more opportunities for
political opportunism. China had become fair game in Japan's electoral campaigns.

Most Japanese citizens did not see China's rise as a distant phenomenon but as a recurring stream of incidents and crises that could
affect their daily lives. Prescriptions for Japanese policymaking,
however, differed. In some cases Japanese citizens called for greater
regulatory protections, whereas in others they wanted Tokyo to
negotiate more forcefully with Beijing. Over the decade, an intan-
gible fear of China created anxiety, so when the territorial dispute
over the Senkakus erupted, nationalist activists were able to use it
as a broader contest between Beijing and Tokyo over sovereignty
and power.

THE NEW BALANCE OF ADVOCACY ON CHINA

The wide variety of Japanese interests in some aspect of China policy both complicated the government's problem-solving efforts with China and made it more difficult for government leaders to sustain their logic of reconciliation and cooperation. Starting in 2006, Chinese and Japanese leaders sought to redefine their diplomatic relationship to reflect a new "reciprocity" and "mutual benefit." But the idea that Japan and China could find a "win-win" formula for building future cooperation seemed hollow in view of domestic grievances. Japan's leaders found it harder and harder to justify cooperation with Beijing as public opinion at home became more sensitive to Chinese behavior and more skeptical of Chinese motives.

China's growing impact on Japanese life, therefore, has had several implications for Japan's domestic policymaking. First, the voices in the debate have diversified. For decades, Japanese businesses with direct trading or investment interests in China were the dominant voice advocating for good relations with Beijing, and the relationships between Japan's economic leaders and China's elite were an asset. Japan's well-known business associations, the Keidanren (Japan Business Federation) and the Keizai dōyūkai (Japan Association of Corporate Executives), continued to push the economic benefits to Japan of a positive Japan-China relationship, although other voices had a stake in the discussion as well. As this book has demonstrated, interest groups as disparate as the Izokukai veterans' family association and the leading consumer advocate, Shufuren, chafed at the extent to which their government appeared to defer to Chinese interests.

Second, the debate over China policy became an integral part of Japan's debate over its own need for governance reform. Interest groups wanting regulatory changes found their positions strengthened as the influence of China's economic growth created a new source of concern in Japan. Japan's consumer advocates, for example, found a willing partner in the Tokyo Metropolitan Government in changing food safety regulation, which in turn added weight to the argument for a national consumer protection agency. In addition, policy differences with China provided the opportunity for cross-party cooperation on domestic policy reform, examples being the new oceans law for implementing a comprehensive maritime strategy and the consumer protection agency for ensuring food safety.

Despite these policy responses, though, the Japanese public became more concerned about negotiated solutions with Beijing and looked more carefully at their government's compromises with China. Accusations of "kowtowing" to Beijing were lobbed at nearly every Japanese prime minister, regardless of political party, and Japanese leaders found it harder to justify negotiated solutions with Beijing, as those who did, such as Fukuda Yasuo, could not demonstrate that these agreements provided results. Finally, this gradual loss of confidence in Japan's ability to negotiate successfully with Beijing encouraged those with a history of anti-China advocacy. Those who had occupied only a marginal place in Japanese politics now found a broader audience for their views.

In this way, politics at home created the opportunity for using the Senkaku issue against a sitting government. For example, in 2012, the Noda cabinet's decision to purchase the Senkaku Islands erupted into an issue of deep contention between the Democratic Party of Japan (DPJ) and the Liberal Democratic Party (LDP). Both parties agreed that the national government needed to assert its control over the islands, but the approach of the Lower House election gave the issue far greater political salience than it otherwise might have had.

Economics could no longer be separated from politics in Japan's relationship with China. Japan's strategy of enhancing economic interdependence with China as a means to improve political relations had run its course. Several factors made Japan's economic relationship with China more entangled with its politics. First, the idea that close economic relations were immune from Japan's political spats with China underestimated the possibility that economic sanctions could be used in the context of political disputes. A case in point is China's use of an informal, albeit temporary, embargo of rare earths against Japan in the 2010 Chinese fishing trawler incident, as well as fears that the Chinese might slow trade or use other informal economic pressures in a future political dispute. In the past, Tokyo was able to use its economic leverage on Beijing through the size and use of its yen loans. But they ended in 2008, whereas Chinese influence over Japanese commercial interests continued to grow. Indeed, Japan's own economic performance now depends heavily on the China market, thereby enabling China's leaders to use economic leverage to harm Japanese interests.

Second, the Japanese economy was now more extensively intertwined with China's domestic market. Japan's consumers had become more vulnerable to the standards and regulation of the Chinese economy, leading to the need for consumer protections, as shown in the food safety case. Equally important, the dependence of Japanese industry on Chinese consumer preferences was increasing as a consequence of China's economic rise. Nonetheless, this did not lead to greater compromise by the Japanese government on political issues such as the Yasukuni Shrine visits or the Senkaku Islands dispute. Instead, it raised the political risk for Japanese companies and investors and prompted some companies to diversify their investments. Chinese consumers' behavior, too, played a new role in Japanese investment in China, with political tensions, like the 2012 clash over the islands, resulting in a decline in Chinese purchases of Japanese products. Whether these incidents have produced a temporary dip or a longer-term decline in trade and investment between Japan and China still is unclear.

The domestic politics of the China policy debate became as diffuse and complex as the relationship itself. Nationalist advocates on the periphery of Japan's foreign policy making assumed a more influential role, focusing on specific issues as a way of mobilizing popular support and limiting government action. As Japanese interests in the relationship with China grew, so too did the impact of more ideologically driven advocates in the policymaking process. Yet those in Japan with a nationalist agenda did not move across issue areas; indeed, even in the two cases in which an ideological agenda was most conspicuous, the Yasukuni Shrine visits and the Senkaku sovereignty dispute, citizen-based advocacy was based largely on the issues.

Each case revealed distinct interest groups, with some of the voices in the debate seeming to speak louder than others. That of Tokyo Governor Ishihara Shintarō, for example, continued to be heard over several decades in the Senkaku Island dispute. In the 1980s, Ishihara had been active as an LDP Diet member supporting the cause, and it was his assertion that the Tokyo government would purchase the islands that in 2012 killed the policy of quietly managing the dispute. Likewise, some of the right-wing groups that supported Senkaku nationalism sounded similar themes, such as the need to defend Japanese sovereignty by ensuring "effective control" (*jikkō shihai*) over the islands. The position of those LDP members in 1978 who were unsuccessful in persuading the government to confront China over its sovereignty claim was vindicated four decades later. Abe Shinzō's argument in 2012 that Japan ought to put government personnel on the island was in fact much the same argument that his father, Abe Shintarō, had made in the conservative party during the peace treaty negotiations with Beijing. Moreover, "effective control" was not a wildly provocative slogan; it was the language used in international law as one means of proving the basis of sovereignty claims. That is, even though the members of these groups may have seemed "right wing" in Japan's postwar political context, their policy advocacy position drew on international legal norms.

Thus a new generation of politicians and activists rallied around the cause of Senkaku nationalism. Activists for a stronger defense of Japanese sovereignty over the disputed islands used social media as well as other venues for mobilizing support. Politicians still rented fishing boats to go out in the choppy waters to wave the Japanese flag and assert their right to land on Japanese land, but now they met not only the Japan Coast Guard but also the newly reorganized China Coast Guard, sent to defend Chinese sovereignty. Their government after 2012 was also willing to arrest them for landing on what was now government property.

What also was different was the stage on which these groups and their ambitions for the Senkakus were heard. Whereas the activists' actions had been a thorn in the side of previous governments, they were better able to mobilize popular support for their cause after the 2010 Chinese fishing trawler incident. Perhaps as a result, their cause claimed center stage in the LDP party's platform when it was voted into power with a majority, first in the Lower House in 2012 and then in the Upper House in 2013. The convergence of political opportunism and Senkaku nationalism also informed Ishihara's decision to leave the Tokyo governor's office and join the mayor of Osaka,

Hashimoto Tōru, to form a new parliamentary party, showing that the Senkaku issue had sufficient salience to the Japanese public to attract more than one political party.

Although the Senkaku nationalists found a more advantageous role in national politics, they had little interest in or influence on the other three cases of controversy with China. Indeed, even the case of the Yasukuni Shrine, in which these groups might be expected to join forces, attracted quite different interests and advocates. Conservative politicians were most likely to find common cause in both the Senkaku dispute and the state visits to the Yasukuni Shrine. The LDP continued to be the biggest advocate for the shrine, and the party advocated the strongest defense of Japanese sovereignty over the islands. But not all LDP members embraced the shrine or the idea that it should be a national memorial to Japan's imperial veterans. Likewise, politicians from the DPJ and other opposition parties visited the shrine, though in a private capacity. To Beijing, however, Japan's conservatives were all the same.

Beyond the politicians, the citizen activist groups supporting the Yasukuni Shrine visits were not the same as those most active on the Senkaku sovereignty dispute. Not, that is, until popular sentiment toward China soured and the political opportunity for identifying as a Japanese nationalist in the face of challenges by China became too advantageous to ignore. In many instances, although the conservative interest groups that focused on Yasukuni—such as the Izokukai—may have shared many of the sentiments and goals expressed by the nationalist activist group Nippon kaigi, they did not always line up together on the same causes, nor were they politically active across issue areas. Accordingly, popular sentiment could not be rallied around the Yasukuni Shrine under Koizumi's leadership in the same way that it could in 2012 with the Senkaku Islands.

The agenda of Japan's nationalists was not uniform across issue areas, nor was it cohesive or organized under a collective banner of anti-China nationalism. Prime Minster Koizumi Jun'ichirō of the LDP, for example, handled the Senkaku issue in much the same way that Prime Minister Noda Yoshihiko of the DPJ did. Koizumi negotiated national government control over the islands through leases with the private owner. But his administration was able to do this quietly, whereas Noda's government in 2012 faced a conspicuously public challenge by the Tokyo governor. Likewise, even though the LDP and DPJ had differing positions on the issue of the Yasukuni Shrine visits, their members did not always agree with their party's stance. Although as the ruling party, the DPJ did not support state visits to Yasukuni, party members not in the cabinet did go to the shrine. Similarly, the LDP took a variety of positions on the question of whether cabinet members should visit, with only some, like Nakasone Yasuhiro and Koizumi, pushing for state visits. Even Abe, a strong supporter of the shrine visits, did not go during his first term in office and sent his deputy, Asō Tarō, in his place during the early phase of his second term. The Diet group that supported the Yasukuni Shrine as the nation's memorial was populated with members from across Japan's political parties, demonstrating that on the question of Japan's history and defeat, their sentiments were less affiliated with political preference in Japan than was widely assumed.

The LDP leaders also differed on both the desirability of prime ministers' visits to the Yasukuni Shrine and the management of the territorial dispute with Beijing over the Senkaku Islands. In 2012, even though Abe did not need to demonstrate his conservative credentials, his electoral campaigns were replete with language that had been entirely absent in his bid for prime minister in 2006. At the end of 2013, however, Abe took a different approach and visited the Yasukuni Shrine. His willingness to flaunt his conservative credentials, even in the face of U.S. concerns about the impact of such a visit on regional tensions, revealed the new political appetite in Japan for embracing Yasukuni as a nationalist icon.

The economic interests in Japan's policymaking toward China also were more varied and did not speak with one voice in the policy debate. Although it still was a conspicuous presence in the domestic debate over China policy, the Japanese business community became only one of many interests advocating positions on China policy, even those affecting their commercial decisions. In the deliberations with China over the maritime boundary in the East China Sea, for example, the private sector's interest in the Japanese petroleum industry was closely aligned with the government's position on joint development.

While Minister of Economy, Trade, and Industry Nakagawa Shōichi argued for allowing Japan to drill on its side of the median line, no steps were taken to counter China's own gas field development on the other side. Japanese government officials may have been frustrated by the lack of follow-through by Beijing on the 2008 joint development agreement, but they did not push private companies to advertise Japan's willingness to claim its own gas.

Consumers as well as producers joined the China debate. On the food safety issue, only a few domestic interest groups openly opposed Beijing. Instead, government officials—from the police to the Ministry of Health, Labor, and Welfare to the Ministry of Foreign Affairs— sought to develop new mechanisms for cooperating with the Chinese government. Although regulatory oversight of the food industry intensified, the first line of defense for Japanese consumers was the Japanese food companies doing business in China. Even Japan's consumer advocates responded relatively mildly to food imports from China. For its part, China's own attention to food safety and then its efforts to regulate food from Japan after March 11, 2011, revealed the growing influence of Chinese consumers on bilateral trade. Consumers in both societies thus demonstrated their power over companies that were irresponsible in their production of food, a welcome sign that citizens in Japan and China were demanding greater accountability from their governments.

While the trend lines in public opinion polling showed a trajectory of suspicion and concern about China's influence on Japan's choices, the Japanese people continued to support established policymaking frameworks. A reform of existing policy rather than a revision of national strategy continued to be the Japanese reaction to China's rise. Negotiated solutions remained the desired approach to problem solving. The widespread Japanese interest in trade, investment, and other forms of economic cooperation with Beijing continued. There were no calls for an embargo of Chinese foodstuffs or a boycott of Chinese goods. Those Japanese accustomed to take to the streets at moments of crisis with China did so in far smaller numbers than those who shouted anti-Japan slogans in Chinese cities. The territorial dispute may have evoked strong sentiment, but even this popular mood did not translate into a broad social movement. That is, although these contentious incidents have plagued Sino-Japanese relations over the past decade, they have not created a broad coalition of anti-China activism in Japan.

Political change in Japan altered the way that political parties lined up on China policy. The organization of political parties in Japan ended the bifurcation of voices on China policy into "right/conservative" and "left/liberal" agendas. While Chinese leaders claimed that the source of political tensions with Japan was to be found in "right-wing" or "militaristic" forces, those who took a critical stance on China were often not those typically associated with right-wing nationalism or a conservative ideology. In times of difficulty, the Chinese media simply dubbed those it deemed uncooperative as "conservative" or "militaristic," and not all of them were in the LDP. For example, Japan's liberal party, the DPJ, had its share of those who challenged Chinese political leaders and confronted Beijing on its failure to live up to its promises. When the DPJ's Maehara Seiji became foreign minister in the midst of the 2010 Chinese fishing trawler incident, Chinese leaders initially sought to avoid working with him, but Japan's cabinet secretary refused to allow that to happen. Earlier, when Maehara had stated publicly his concern about China's military buildup, Chinese leaders then tried to ostracize him for his "hawkish" views. This tactic by Beijing undoubtedly complicated the management of the crisis and contributed to the escalation of tensions.

Another by-product of Japan's political change was the revelation of the impact of generational change on the Sino-Japanese relationship. New politicians were coming to the fore, and with the shift to alternating parties in power, there was less systematic effort by political parties to develop networks with the new generation of Chinese leaders. The effort to build long-standing relationships—such as those developed in the past between Japan's conservatives in the LDP and the Chinese Communist Party (CCP), which formed an important channel for bilateral communication—was no longer adequate to ensure that the two governments could manage tensions. The 2010 trawler crisis therefore moved the DPJ to build a new mechanism for developing contacts with the up-and-coming next generation of leaders in the CCP. But this party-to-party agreement is a long-term initiative that may or may not pay off in future crisis management, as the party may not return to power in Japan.

Finally, like Japan's politicians, other leaders involved in the relationship with China have many perspectives, most of which pertain to their policy interests rather than ideology. Japan's political spectrum has a variety of prescriptions on how to cope with a rising China, many of which are rooted in the specific issue and policy aim of the advocacy group, political leader, or business. In fact, the different impacts of Chinese interests and decisions on Japanese interests has led to the diversification of policy advocacy on the issues that can now be identified as China policy. Ironically, these issue-specific complaints have fed into a broad dissatisfaction with Japan's policy approach to China. However, they are as much about Japan's own choices—to regulate or deregulate, to arm or not arm, to sanction or not sanction—as they are about what to do about Japan-China relations.

INCREMENTAL PROBLEM SOLVING

All four cases of contention with China that were so controversial over the past decade highlighted policy challenges that were considered, but not implemented, in Japan. For the most part, these episodes brought to light unresolved or underappreciated deficiencies in the Japanese government's ability to recognize and devise adequate policy responses. One reason for controversy in its relationship with China was Japan's inability to centralize decision making. All the cases examined here involved challenges to Japan's existing policies and its institutional capacity to advocate the country's interests. But there was no strategic shift—no discernible moment of transition— in Japan's policy toward China. Whether solving a particular problem with China or adjusting the premises of the Japan-China relationship, Tokyo's approach has consistently been incremental.

One of the most striking outcomes of the comparison of these four cases is the degree to which bureaucratic barriers to change got in the way of a strategic policy response. For example, the bureaucracies that managed various aspects of maritime-related policy proved to be inadequate to the challenge that emerged from the ratification of the UNCLOS, and Japan was conspicuously ill prepared to formulate a national maritime strategy. Similarly, the food safety issue also revealed the inadequacy of Japanese government institutions to protect consumer interests. Long an issue in postwar Japan, the government resisted the full development of institutions designed to protect consumers. Centralizing information sharing in a "control tower" seemed only a small step in the direction of protecting consumer interests and regulating industry in an increasingly globalizing market. Although it certainly did not satisfy Japan's consumer advocates, regulatory improvements were made as a result of the *gyōza* food-poisoning case. Ironically, it was Japan's conservatives—who in previous governments had resisted consumer protection in their effort to support market deregulation—who ultimately championed the cause. China's rise, in turns out, was a positive in that it brought long overdue policy attention to both Japan's consumers and its maritime interests.

All these cases reveal the tensions between popular support for Japan's own policies and a more cosmopolitan "best practices"–based approach to problem solving. Here the food safety case stands out as the most relevant, given the demand for mass-produced food at a lower cost. Japan's debate over the *gyōza*-poisoning case ultimately was focused on ensuring protection in a global food market, but at the same time, for interest groups such as the Ministry of Agriculture, Forestry, and Fisheries (MAFF), the case offered an opportunity to bring back the debate over self-reliance in agricultural production. Surprisingly, Japan's consumer advocate groups fell in line with the MAFF's self-reliance mantra, despite their desire for a consumer protection movement that was clearly informed by the American and European examples. The Tokyo Metropolitan Government was the leading advocate of moving Japan forward into more progressive policies of consumer regulation, and it tried to set standards by looking at the global policy innovations on food defense by the Food and Agriculture Organization of the United Nations (FAO) and the U.S. Department of Agriculture. Japan's own companies, however, seemed most concerned by the comfort level of Japanese worker-management relations, even though it was their profitability and reliability that were called into question by the food-poisoning scandal.

When the bilateral approach to managing differences between Beijing and Tokyo no longer offered an effective means for problem solving, Tokyo began to press its interests in global institutions and settings. The most obvious examples are the boundary dispute in the East China Sea and the territorial dispute over the Senkaku Islands. The UNCLOS forced Japan to defend its EEZ claims. Likewise, disputes over economic issues were referred for international adjudication. Once China joined the World Trade Organization (WTO) in 2001, new dispute resolution avenues were available for trade disputes, and Japan joined with other countries to confront trade practices that violated international norms. China's quotas (and temporary embargo) on rare earths is one powerful example.

Finally, Japan advocated its interests more forcefully against China in the United Nations, a body venerated in postwar Japan as the most appropriate multilateral setting for resolving disputes, and Prime Minister Noda articulated the Japanese position on the Senkakus there. The International Court of Justice (ICJ) may yet offer Japan and China an opportunity to submit their territorial dispute to third-party mediation. Whether these will be effective remedies to the various policy challenges Japan faces with Beijing remains to be seen; however, Tokyo's resort to third-party mediation and the adjudication of disputes in international institutions demonstrates the end of Japan's preference for relying on bilateral negotiation with Beijing.

The frustration in Japan over the country's inability to solve these problems also reignited the debate over governance. Those who had long advocated for a stronger Japan found ample ground for using the rise of China to question Japan's postwar foreign policy practices. China's maritime power, in particular, invigorated the debate over Japan's constitution and military self-restraint. Yet there was no groundswell of popular demand for a strategic reorientation for Japan, a bigger defense budget, or another means of bolstering Japanese defenses. Despite all the public discussion and concern about Chinese military activities in and around Japan, there was little immediate evidence of change in public support for Japanese restraint and calm, even during the island dispute.

Instead, in each of these cases, Japan's fragmented and bureau-cratically driven government struggled to cope with the complexity of a rising China. The first priority for Japan's maritime policy was centralizing its policymaking and coordinating the various aspects of its scientific, commercial, and policing tasks. Consolidating the country's capability to advocate and articulate maritime strategy is an example. Likewise, the dispute over the Senkaku Islands required Tokyo policymakers to think beyond the division of labor between the Japan Coast Guard (JCG) and the Maritime Self-Defense Forces (MSDF), but it also motivated a larger frame of reference for mari-time cooperation within the U.S.-Japan alliance. China's rise was seen as the rationale for reorganizing the Self-Defense Forces, the first reorganization since the end of the Cold War, to empha-size its southwestern islands. Reform in the JCG—and ultimately the decision to enhance its capabilities and overcome the post-war resistance to collaboration between the JCG and the MSDF—also was a product of the growing tensions with China in the East China Sea.

Similarly, the Japanese government's failure to address the dan-gers to consumers was dramatically demonstrated with the *gyōza*-poisoning case. But the fact was that food safety had been inadequately regulated in Japan even before it became dependent on processed foods from China. Economic realities already were causing fraudu-lent labeling and other types of crimes associated with food safety in Japan. Indeed, the bulk of the criminal cases were domestic. In addition, after the *gyōza*-poisoning incident, the reaction was not to impose greater regulatory limitations on imports of food from China but to urge greater corporate oversight of the joint ventures that pro-duced food in China. The Japanese state did not see an opportunity for greater involvement in bilateral food trade; it continued to leave the oversight of food safety to the private sector. Although the *gyōza* case reflected the complexity of Japan's growing dependence on China as a source of food, it also revealed a surprisingly weak government regulatory effort on behalf of Japan's consumers. The reforms adopted, moreover, were not sufficient to protect consumers from future inci-dents of criminal behavior or from other types of threats to Japan's food supply.

China's economic power challenged Japanese governance precisely when many Japanese already were questioning their government's effectiveness. Throughout the 1990s, the Japanese government was riddled by corruption scandals, and politicians, too, were found complacent in a system of government that no longer satisfied its citizens' needs. New demands on Japanese institutions arose as more and more Chinese traveled to and from Japan, as more and more Chinese products entered the Japanese market, and as more and more Japanese companies relocated their manufacturing to take advantage of lower wages in the emerging Chinese market. Across the region, Chinese and Japanese diplomats found themselves competing in a region where Japan had been the largest economic player. Militarily, too, China began to push forward a new maritime strategy, and by the early 2000s, more and more Chinese vessels were operating in and around Japanese waters. For all the debate about political reform over the past decade in Japan, nothing focused its leaders and its citizens on the country's national policy priorities more than the questions generated by China's rise.

ADAPTING TO A CHANGING CHINA

Japan's debate over the rise in China's power, therefore, was not simply a debate over which would be the better partner, Beijing or Washington. Instead, it was a broader and more self-reflective debate over Japan's ability to compete in a global economy increasingly shaped by China. In large part, Japan's postwar strategy depended on the very institutions that China is challenging. Domestic advocates call for neither a policy of accommodation nor a policy of confrontation with China. Rather, China's influence is testing Japan's ability to reform itself and to continue to rely on the norms and principles that have formed its own postwar ascension to global power.

Japan's capacity for adjustment was tempered by its domestic politics. The first decade of the twenty-first century revealed dissension and contest over its China policy and a decline in its success in negotiating its interests with Beijing. Support at home for a more cooperative relationship with China diminished as the two governments struggled to resolve their disputes. Japanese politicians and the public

urged their government to resist Chinese government calls for compromise. Why? What are the interests at stake, and how is domestic
advocacy in Japan influencing its policy toward China? In these four
cases of contention, although Chinese decision making complicated
Japan's choices, it did not produce a coherent strategy or even a unified stance on how to cope with this new and complex relationship
with China. The variety of interests in the policymaking process created a variety of solutions, but it did not result in a coalition of interests or a social movement capable of pressing government into a unified position toward China.

The policy dilemmas confronted by the Japanese government did
not result in either accommodation or confrontation. Rather, the four
cases examined in this book suggest that adaptation may be a better
description of Japan's response. In almost every case of contention
with China, ineffectual policies were reconsidered and new initiatives
were undertaken. Rather than being a cause for reaction and intran-
sigence, China's rise was, in some instances, the catalyst for long overdue internal reforms. Improving Japan's ability to craft and implement
its existing policy goals and to seek partners to help resolve disputes
with Beijing have been consistent responses thus far.

The focus of much of the debate in Japan was the country's capability and efficacy in meeting the challenges created by China's rise.
In two of the four cases, policy reform in Japan was the outcome of
a contentious quarrel with China. Japan crafted a new oceans law
for coping with the UNCLOS, and it created a new consumer protection agency and better regulations to include production abroad
as well as in Japan. In the third case, the Yasukuni Shrine controversy, a new approach that would create a secular national memorial has not been implemented. But the most difficult discussion of
managing the interactions of both the JCG and the MSDF resulted
in strengthening the JCG's policing functions and capability, as well
as improving military cooperation with the United States. Japan's
defense capabilities have not been drastically changed. Rather,
Tokyo has adjusted to Chinese military expansion by maintaining
its long-standing policy goals.

In each case, Japan's preference was to negotiate an incremental
adjustment in policy rather than to institute wholesale reforms. But

negotiating incremental change with Beijing rarely satisfied domestic interests. While Japanese negotiating preferences remain centered on cooperation and adjustment, the government's ability to gain Beijing's cooperation seemed inconsequential to the Japanese people. Moreover, in each case, domestic interests and their sensitivity to Chinese influence made compromise difficult. Setting aside the issues or downplaying their role in the overall relationship, therefore, was not a viable option.

The inability to agree on a solution with Beijing affected perceptions of both Chinese intentions and the Japanese government's inefficacy. In almost every case, even negotiated solutions became hard to implement. In three, and perhaps all four, of the cases, the Japanese and Chinese governments reached some sort of agreement, but in only one instance was the agreement actually implemented, and that was the food safety agreement concluded in 2009. Agreement on the joint development of resources in the East China Sea was heralded as a great achievement at the Hu-Fukuda summit in May 2008, but subsequent efforts to draft an implementing agreement failed.

Even the difficult issues of the Yasukuni Shrine visits and incursions into the waters of the Senkaku Islands brought proposals for some sort of compromise. In the effort at reconciliation after the difficult Koizumi years, Prime Minister Abe Shinzō and President Hu Jintao agreed to set aside the question of whether Abe would visit the controversial shrine. The formula that allowed resolution, at least for the purpose of rebuilding diplomatic relations, was that Japan's prime minister would not publicly declare his intentions to visit and China's leaders would not ask. Similarly, the Senkaku dispute that arose as a result of the Chinese fishing trawler's provocative behavior toward the JCG produced the governments' effort to overcome their territorial dispute by focusing on maritime cooperation in the East China Sea. The initiative for building confidence—which included the goal of a search-and-rescue agreement as well as maritime talks—bore fruit in early 2012 but did not relieve the domestic political pressures on either of the two governments.

For diplomats, the ability to negotiate a mutually acceptable resolution with Beijing was, of course, the ideal. Two of these cases, the East China Sea maritime boundary and the *gyōza* food-poisoning incident, produced mutually beneficial agreements. Implementation proved elusive, however. One of the cases, the Yasukuni Shrine visits, was not subject to formal negotiation, but still the leaders of Japan and China managed to find a formula for compromise. The reemergence of Yasukuni Shrine visits by members of the second Abe cabinet in 2013, however, showed that these compromises are very fragile indeed. The final case, the Chinese fishing trawler incident, prompted a very preliminary effort at maritime cooperation, but there was no overall resolution of the issue or a negotiated approach to the island dispute at the heart of the East China Sea controversy. Rather, negotiation by the diplomats on both sides seem to have been undercut by the political leaders on both sides. Despite efforts at negotiation, diplomacy was unable to produce sustainable solutions. Thus when compromise between Tokyo and Beijing proved unattainable, or too difficult to implement, support in Japan for a diplomatic solution weakened.

Tokyo's inability to implement negotiated agreements with Beijing has also had a discernible impact at home. The failure of the East China Sea agreement and Beijing's willingness to test Japan's resolve in the defense of the Senkaku Islands have encouraged activism in Japan for a more assertive and unilateral effort to defend Japanese sovereignty. The option of setting aside differences has disappeared. Interestingly, after Koizumi left office, the Yasukuni Shrine visits no longer seemed to attract attention. The DPJ made a commitment to avoid the shrine, thus taking this issue out of the spotlight during its time in power. Then, Abe's return to power and his personal support for Yasukuni, coupled with the LDP's electoral mandate in both houses, brought the question of prime ministerial visits back into the political spotlight. In contrast to Koizumi, Abe did not need to court the Izokukai or other groups to win his election to the LDP's leadership or to ensure his party's victory at the polls. Abe represented a new wave of Yasukuni nationalism, and his social media supporters trumpeted their historical revisionism alongside their Yasukuni sympathies. The prime minister's willingness to associate himself with this revisionist nationalism drew global attention.

The Japanese government's frustration in trying to find common ground with China created more opportunities for advocates of greater nationalist politics to influence the government's choices. Beyond the broad right-left divide between Japan's political parties in the postwar era were activist groups that were marginal to mainstream Japanese politics and policymaking and were associated with the conservative brand of anti-China sentiment. These groups—in many cases, small and disparate—were to be found mobilizing on behalf of specific causes, most notably the sovereignty claim to the Senkakus. In 2012, however, mainstream politicians started pushing the cause of nationalism more openly. Although Tokyo Governor Ishihara had long publicly championed the Senkaku sovereignty issue, by September 2012 it was echoed by nearly all the LDP leadership contenders. More interesting was the resonance of this conservative nationalistic rendering with the public's perception of how to respond to China. In the Yasukuni Shrine case, for example, despite the deep division in Japan, once it became an issue against which China spoke out strongly, Koizumi's pledge to visit took on a new—and more attractive—significance.

Conservatives differed significantly on how to pursue Japan's interests with China. Few wanted to alter Japan's economic relations, and no one wanted to abandon the formula of working toward "mutually beneficial relations based on common strategic interests." Frustration with China's lack of interest in Japan was pervasive, however. But even though China's view of the Yasukuni debate drew heated criticism, it did not encourage a broad nationalist social movement. Nor was there unanimity in the interests that were vocal in the national debate over Yasukuni. In the summer of 2006, Japanese debated one another and looked back at the choices of previous generations. In the end, though, they did not rally around the Yasukuni Shrine as a symbol of national pride or identity. Likewise in 2013, the media's response to Abe's visit was fairly predictable, despite concern about the U.S. expression of "disappointment" at the visit. Social media, however, provided a venue for more heated commentary, not only from the right but also from the left.

Nationalist activists found their most successful rallying point in the Senkaku Islands, enabling Tokyo Governor Ishihara Shintarō and others, such as the Nippon kaigi, Ganbare nippon, and Channel Sakura, to claim a bigger stage for their agenda. The Tokyo Metropolitan Government's public declaration that it would buy the islands pushed the national government to move beyond its existing status quo policy, and the rapid accumulation of donations to the Senkaku

Fund demonstrated that Ishihara was not alone in thinking that Japan ought to take a more fulsome stand on the issue. Territorial defense is an issue that defines the future terms of Japan's relationship to China, and therefore it carries a significantly different weight in the domestic political debate than do differences over the interpretation of past events.

Other disputes with China did not produce any links with nationalist advocates. The *gyōza* issue resonated broadly with the Japanese public but not with organized advocates. The food and consumer safety incidents may have prevented this case from being identified as specific to China or the Chinese. Or consumer protections may simply have been an issue that did not fit the conservative or nationalist agenda. In the past, advocacy for consumer protections came from women activists and/or those with a more progressive liberal agenda, so Japan's food supply may not have been an issue that engaged the groups in the territorial dispute. Even nationalist politics did not prevent policy change and adaptation. Creative problem solving and negotiation, plus reform of its own policymaking, resolved some of Tokyo's policy dilemmas. Finally, Japanese leaders began to refuse to accommodate Chinese demands and criticism. Even for the most contentious issues, those presented in depth here, it was the desire to resolve policy challenges, not the ideological impulses, that guided both government and citizen behavior in Japan. Persuading Beijing to be receptive to Tokyo's solutions, however, was not always possible.

IMPLICATIONS FOR POLICY

This study of Japan's responses to China's rise offers several insights into the future of the two countries' relationship. First, these four cases of contention reveal the complexity of shared problem solving. In all four cases, the Japanese government had only a limited capability to demonstrate to its people that working with Beijing would solve the problem. Although agreements were reached, the lack of implementation and concrete results only frustrated Japanese interest groups. Second, Japan's ability to make choices—about its economy and its foreign policy—is increasingly being affected by Beijing. This is a result not just of its growing material power but also of the greater integration of the two economies and societies. Interdependence is uncomfortable, and the effort to alleviate this discomfort will require more—not less—shared problem-solving effort. Moreover, it will require from both sides much more nongovernmental capability of understanding and analyzing policy and policy challenges. The two foreign ministries cannot manage the Japan-China relationship by themselves, and the carefully crafted compromises by political leaders seem fragile at best.

Third, Japan's policymaking institutions have largely managed problems rather than devised alternative policy options. Incremental adjustments to China's rise have not kept pace with the domestic demand for dispute resolution mechanisms. Although Japan's government does not necessarily need to be completely overhauled, the various effects of a rising China indicate that much stronger policy mechanisms for defending consumer interests, maritime interests, and regional dispute resolution efforts will be necessary. Japan's policy advocates will need to consider more fully the institutional requirements of a more competitive Japan-China relationship.

Fourth, Japan's response to China's rise is not one-dimensional, nor is it understood as simply a government exercise. Strategic choice may still be within the purview of a small group of elite political and policy leaders. But increasingly, Japan's choices seem to be decided by societal pressures. Activists, domestic interest groups, and opposition politicians are narrowing the scope of the Japanese government's response to China and its capability to find compromise and accommodation. The voice of the Japanese business community, long one of Japan's strongest supporters of the Japan-China relationship, seems more and more muted. Those companies with long experience in China continue to call for improving bilateral ties. But even some of them are wary of the politics in Beijing and the anti-Japanese demonstrators targeting their businesses during times of political tension. Nor are they convinced that their investments in China are sustainable over the long run. Business profitability rather than political risk seems to be the most frequently cited reason for diversifying Japan's choices of foreign direct investment.

This analysis of how China's rise has affected Japanese domestic politics has implications for policymakers in Tokyo and Beijing as well as Washington, D.C. The center of global economic power in Asia already has changed perceptions of China and its role in world affairs. Beijing's greater military reach also has prompted a rethinking of what the future might hold for regional security. Japan's domestic debate over the implications of China's transformation for its own foreign policy interests began more than a decade ago. In Japan, the focus of this debate has been the two governments' competence and reliability in negotiating its citizens' interests. Contention has come to characterize diplomatic relations as Tokyo has tried to adjust to the complex ways that Chinese decisions, both inside and outside government, affect Japanese society.

Japan's experience has demonstrated to other nations adjusting to China's new global power the importance of popular opinion about China. Elites are faced with a loss of confidence in their ability to solve problems with China. Worry about Japan's security has led political leaders to demand closer strategic cooperation with the United States, with anxiety about Washington's position on China also seeping into the public debate. Anxiety about China's intentions toward Japan—including the confrontation over the disputed Senkaku Islands—is raising new questions about Japan's postwar commitment to a limited military capability.

The balance of domestic interests that coalesced around China policy has changed. There now is far greater latitude in Japanese politics for those who argue that the nation should stand up to China, and a larger political opportunity for those who question Japan's postwar commitments to a limited military and a liberal trading order. The postwar global order was reassuring to Japan. But China's new role in global economic and security affairs, insofar as it threatens that order, has raised questions about whether Japan can rely on international institutions and its cooperation with the United States to protect its interests.

Policymakers should be aware of how popular skepticism of Beijing's intentions has weakened support for compromise with China. Not only is public opinion in Japan affording a political opportunity for those who worry about China's influence, but new criticism of

Japan's own government also is far more pervasive. Japan's inability to demonstrate the effectiveness of agreements with Beijing has become a cause for domestic concern, and it was the political transformation in Japan that diminished public confidence in governance overall. Japan's own policy woes suggest a country less equipped to compete globally. Advocates of a tougher stance toward China are getting a broader hearing, in large part because there is less confidence in Japan's ability to successfully negotiate its interests in this less predictable world.

This loss of confidence has several implications for future Japan-China relations. First, an effort by China to find shared solutions to issues that affect both countries would go a long way to changing elite perceptions of Beijing's intentions. Popular sentiments also could be changed by a track record of accomplishments. Second, because the causes of policy differences run deeper, it will be difficult to find areas of potential compromise and to agree to disagree when interests diverge. In regard to security, there clearly is a need for a dialogue on maritime stability, and in regard to the disputed islands, political leaders need to return to their effort either to manage the dispute themselves or to move forward with third-party mediation for resolution.

Finally, for decades, policymakers in Tokyo and Beijing have relied on their close economic ties to shield them from political differences. This investment in each other's economies still means that shared interests could prevail; even after a decade of growing bilateral tensions, Japanese businesses continue to invest in China. Indeed, after the 2010 Chinese fishing trawler incident, Japanese foreign direct investment (FDI) in China grew by almost 60 percent, to an annual ¥1 trillion ($10.3 billion). New investments in 2011 amounted to $6.3 billion, 5.5 percent of China's total new FDI. In 2012, this jumped to $7.4 billion, 6.6 percent of all new FDI in China, making Japan the second highest source of FDI (behind only Hong Kong) for China.[1] Nonetheless, as the events of 2012 show, this economic interdependence will not protect the two nations from intense political strain. Japanese manufacturers located in China could yet again become targets of violence, and the use of economic instruments of leverage during political crises may be repeated. The longer-term domestic consequence of political strain also is evident in the relatively diminished role of business leaders in the balance of interests in Japan's China policy.

Diplomatic success could change this. The opportunity for nationalist advocacy by politicians in Japan limits the government's ability to reach cooperative solutions with Beijing. China's ability to persuade Japanese that the future holds the promise of cooperation rather than conflict could reduce the political space for nationalist activism in Japan. But continuing to ignore problems or failing to implement agreed-on compromises would give greater credence to those in Japan who caution against working closely with China. As Japan's ally, the U.S. government has watched with great concern the growing tensions over the Senkaku Islands. The United States' clarification of its role in defending of Japan has somewhat eased the Japanese government's concerns about its defenses, and high-level discussions between the U.S. and Chinese governments have urged a de-escalation of the standoff of government vessels in the waters near the islands.

Japan's tensions with China pose a new dilemma for the United States. For the first time in the alliance's history, a conflict that begins between Japan and another power seems possible. Throughout the past half century of security cooperation, Tokyo and Washington have seen Japan's role as supporting a broader U.S. strategy in the Asia Pacific region. Japan considered the use of force only for defensive purposes, and even then, the most likely scenario was a conflict elsewhere—perhaps the Korean Peninsula or the Taiwan Straits. The alliance spent very little time on the possibility that Japan might become engaged in a direct conflict with China. This new scenario, however, raises questions about the U.S. ability to dissuade Tokyo as well as Beijing from escalating their military engagement over the island dispute. Political calculations in either capital could change the incentives for military action, and Washington would be forced to react.

Beyond the narrow issue of the island dispute, however, the United States has an interest in avoiding sustained tensions between Japan and China. The economic consequences of protracted tensions, including the loss of economic investment and trade between the two Asian economies, would have disastrous effects on the Asia Pacific region as well as the global economy. The United States relies heavily on

Japanese foreign direct investment and its purchase of U.S. Treasury bonds. China, too, is playing a more important role in the United States' economic performance, and a destructive economic relationship between Japan and China could directly affect U.S. economic growth.

Finally, the United States would find its regional diplomacy hindered should Japan and China compete for influence in the Asia Pacific. On a host of issues—from maritime stability to humanitarian disaster management to economic growth—the Asia Pacific region has expanded the institutional networks of cooperation. Protracted tensions between Japan and China could undermine these institutions' capability for regional confidence building and governance capacity. Indeed, a competitive relationship between Beijing and Tokyo in the region would severely compromise the effectiveness of ASEAN-based multilateral forums, such as the ASEAN Regional Forum, the ASEAN Defense ministerial meetings, and the East Asia Summit. Given the paucity of regional security consultative mechanisms, this would be a considerable loss at a time of significant geostrategic change in Asia.

The biggest challenge for U.S. policymakers will be developing a cooperative relationship with Beijing while not undermining the United States' close alliance with Tokyo. Beyond the policy debates, the popular debate in Japan over the U.S. commitment to Japanese defenses and U.S. leaders' attraction to a rising China continues. Reassuring allies in the context of a power transition of the magnitude currently under way in Asia will be a daunting task.

Without an opportunity to negotiate its interests with China, the Japanese government will be under great pressure to change some of its most basic postwar policy commitments. As the cases of policy contention between Japan and China described in this book show, three policy areas in particular would be of serious concern to the Japanese government should its relationship with Beijing worsen. The first is Japan's long-standing postwar commitment to limited military power of its own and its strategic dependence on the United States. Chinese military growth already has led to Japan's revaluation of its defense goals, and its identification of its southwestern islands as its top priority reflects concerns about the increasing capabilities of China's military and its interactions with Japan's Self-Defense Forces.

In the absence of a serious effort by Beijing and Tokyo to build confidence and understand each other's military goals and force postures, the likelihood is that Japan will need to significantly augment its military power to offset China's pressure on its defenses. Furthermore, China's intention to deny the United States access to the waters in the first island chain off its coastline means that the U.S. ability to defend Japan could be compromised. If Washington were unwilling or unable to expand its own military capability in and around Japan, Tokyo could reconsider its reliance on the United States for defense assistance, which, in turn, would lead to a reconsideration of its own offensive capabilities in order to deter Chinese aggression.

A second policy commitment by Japan that could be sorely tested by China is Tokyo's commitment to an open and liberal global trading order. Throughout the postwar era, Japan has sought to rebuild its national economy and expand its industrial base through the Bretton Woods commitment to open and free trade. While Tokyo was considering how to stimulate greater competitiveness, it began a new round of trade talks in 2013. Japan has agreed to join the Trans-Pacific Partnership with the United States and eight other Pacific nations. Equally important, Tokyo remains committed to a free-trade agreement with both South Korea and China. If China were to abandon this effort and turn instead to a more protectionist path in its economic relations with Japan, it would signal a challenge to the principles of free trade as well as restrict market access for Japanese companies in China. Likewise, if the Chinese government decided to discriminate against Japanese goods, companies, and/or capital, it would have a serious impact on Japan's own economic performance. Any tit-for-tat trade dispute or other kind of economic tension between Japan and China could alter Japanese attitudes toward free trade and an open Japanese economy. Japan's and China's economic interdependence will become an even greater source of anxiety when Japan's need to service its national debt forces it to sell its bonds on the global market. Already, China is beginning to buy Japanese government bonds, though not yet on a scale comparable to that of other advanced industrial economies. The more Chinese that purchase Japanese debt, the greater Japan's vulnerability to China will become, and this, too, could exacerbate domestic anxiety in Japan about the Chinese government's long-term ambitions.

Finally, if Chinese leaders continue to see Japan as an adversary rather than a neighbor, it will transform Japanese thinking about their postwar experience. The rise of China already has called into question Japan's postwar acceptance of the institutional reforms that were imposed under occupation after World War II. Conservative nationalists in Japan, who have long objected to the foreign origins of Japan's constitution, are now arguing more strenuously for its revision. External criticism has narrowed the Japanese debate over its wartime history and reframed the lessons that Japan learned from its war experience. Over time, the steady Chinese pressure on Japan could undermine Japanese confidence in their postwar accomplishments and produce a national mood that is reactive and defensive rather than focused on the country's options for the future.

As political tension creates repeated diplomatic chills in the Japan-China relationship, it is likely that the debate in Japan on whether to take more assertive steps to defend its interests will continue. The territorial dispute, especially, has touched a deep nerve, despite Japan's well-known postwar pacifism. A China that appears unwilling or unable to negotiate shared solutions with Japan seems increasingly hostile to its neighbor. After all, because Japan and China are close rivals, their national choices remain intertwined even when they keep their diplomatic distance. Centuries of shared culture, history, and geography created this intimacy, and the future of the Japan-China relationship will depend less on old formulas and more on new and creative solutions to current problems that the two countries cannot resolve alone.

Not all the cases of contention examined here have escalated into national causes. Tokyo and Beijing have found some space for compromise, even on sensitive issues. Although this book does not address Beijing's interests, its examination of how Japan and the Japanese perceive their ability to work with Beijing in the future should indicate where the opportunities for cooperative solutions may lie. This study also explored those issues most susceptible to politicization and opportunistic politics. In other words, not all controversial issues in Japan-China relations follow the same fault lines in Japan's domestic politics, and mutual interests have been found even in some particularly sensitive areas.

The more difficult task for policymakers will be determining how contention over policy choices with Beijing will be perceived at home. In each of the cases discussed here, there was a high degree of domestic sensitivity to the policy concerns raised in Japan's controversial interactions with Beijing. How each case is resolved also should indicate the potential for easing (or exacerbating) these sensitivities in the future. Can the two countries find instances of effective problem solving, and if so, what are the indicators of success? Does success in one issue area affect the two governments' ability to achieve success in other issue areas? What do these controversies tell us about Japan's ability to work with China? What are the pressures on Japanese policy institutions, and what are the likely reforms?

Japan's response to China's rise has not been just a government policy response, nor has it been defined solely in terms of Japan's strategic interests. Despite the diplomats' best efforts, a series of unpredictable run-ins with China have altered the way Japanese perceive their largest neighbor. Popular feelings about China are gradually changing how Japan's government negotiates with Beijing.

Increasing nationalist activism in Japan and reactive popular responses from China portend a very difficult future for the two countries. Anxiety about China reflects the broader Japanese anxiety about its government's ability to protect domestic interests both abroad and at home. Some issues of contention will be about Japan's relationship with China and their history. But it is today's China that is eroding Japan's confidence in the way it has pursued its interests during the postwar period. All the premises of Tokyo's choices are being challenged by Beijing: its reliance on international economic and political institutions to resolve disputes, its commitment to an open and liberal global economic order, and its alliance with the United States. From defense to food security to maritime policy, more and more Japanese see China challenging not only Japan but also the global order that Japanese see as the foundation of their postwar success.

NOTES

1. CONTENDING WITH CHINA

1. *Nikkei shinbun*, July 18, 2013.
2. The Chinese refer to these islands as the Diaoyu, and in Taiwan they are referred to as the Diaoyutai.
3. A journalistic account of Ishihara's bid to buy the islands includes negotiations with Prime Minister Noda's staff in which Ishihara claimed he would be quite happy to have a war with China if need be. Sunohara Tsuyoshi, *Antō senkaku kokuyūka* [*Secret Feud: The National Purchase of the Senkakus*] (Tokyo: Shinchōsha, 2013).
4. When Noda communicated this to China's president, Hu Jintao, on the sidelines of the Asia-Pacific Economic Cooperation summit in Vladivostok, Russia, Hu responded with a warning that "Japan must fully recognize the gravity of the situation and should not make wrong decisions." The next day, Japan's chief cabinet secretary, Fujimura Osamu, announced the purchase, setting off a storm of protest in China ("Hu: Diaoyu Islands Purchase Illegal, Invalid," *China Daily*, September 9, 2012).
5. Ministry of Foreign Affairs, China, "Announcement of the Air Defense Identification Rules for the East China Sea Air Defense Identification Zone of the P.R.C.," November 23, 2013, http://eng.mod.gov.cn/Press/2013-11/23/content_4476143.htm.
6. Ibid.

7.   Cabinet Office of Japan, "Address by H.E. Mr. Yoshihiko Noda, Prime Minister of Japan at the Sixty-Seventh Session of the United Nations General Assembly—Responsibility for Tomorrow and Three Pearls of Wisdom," September 26, 2012, http://www.kantei.go.jp/foreign/noda /statement/201209/26un_e.html.

8.   Ministry of Foreign Affairs, People's Republic of China, "Statement by H.E. Yang Jiechi, Minister of Foreign Affairs of the People's Republic of China at the Sixty-Seventh Session of the United Nations General Assembly—Work Together to Achieve Common Security and Development," September 27, 2012, http://www.fmprc.gov.cn/eng/zxxx/t975077.htm.

9.   On January 1, 2014, China's ambassador to Britain Liu Xiaoming published an opinion piece in the *Daily Telegraph* comparing Japanese militarism to Lord Voldemort, the villain from the Harry Potter series. Japan's ambassador to Britain, Hayashi Keiichi, responded on January 6 in an op-ed in the same paper asserting that China was the one who was at risk of becoming the Voldemort of Asia. See Liu Xiaoming, "China and Britain Won the War Together," *Telegraph*, January 1, 2014, http://www.telegraph.co.uk/comment/10546442/Liu-Xiaoming-China-and-Britain-won-the-war-together.html, and Keiichi Hayashi, "China Risks Becoming Asia's Voldemort," January 6, 2014, http://www .telegraph.co.uk/news/worldnews/asia/japan/10552351/China-risks -becoming-Asias-Voldemort.html.) On January 9, 2014, the Chinese ambassador to the United States, Cui Tiankai, published an opinion article in the *Washington Post* in which he criticized Prime Minister Abe's visit to the Yasukuni Shrine, Japan's military buildup, and Abe's denial of the Japanese military's use of sex slaves during World War II, known as "comfort women." On January 16, the Japanese ambassador to the United States, Sasae Kenichirō, responded in the same paper and accused China of launching a "global propaganda campaign against Japan." See Ciu Tiankai, "Shinzo Abe Risks Ties with China in Tribute to War Criminals," *Washington Post*, January 9, 2014, http://www .washingtonpost.com/opinions/shinzo-abe-risks-ties-with-china -in-tribute-to-war-criminals/2014/01/09/dbd86e52-7887-11e3 -af7f-13bf0e9965f6_story.html; and Kenichirō Sasae, "China's Propaganda Campaign Against Japan," *Washington Post*, January 16, http://www .washingtonpost.com/opinions/chinas-propaganda-campaign-against -japan/2014/01/16/925ed924-7caa-11e3-93c1-0e888170b723_story.html.

10.   U.S. Department of State, "Joint Press Availability with Japanese Foreign Minister Seiji Maehara," October 27, 2010, http://www.state.gov/secretary

/rm/2010/10/150110.htm. After the 2012 crisis, when Clinton met with Japan's new foreign minister, Kishida Fumio, in Washington on January 18, 2013, she reiterated that the islands are protected by the U.S.-Japan security treaty and that the United States "would oppose any unilateral actions that would seek to undermine Japanese administration" (U.S. Department of State, "Remarks with Japanese Foreign Minister Fumio Kishida After Their Meeting," January 18, 2013, http://www.state .gov/secretary/rm/2013/01/203050.htm). On April 14, 2013, the newly appointed U.S. secretary of state, John Kerry, went even further during a press conference in Tokyo, stating that the United States would "oppose any unilateral or coercive action that would somehow aim at changing the status quo" (U.S. Department of State, "Joint Press Availability with Japanese Foreign Minister Kishida After Their Meeting," April 14, 2013, http://www.state.gov/secretary/remarks/2013/04/207483.htm).

11. U.S. Department of Defense, "Joint Press Conference with Secretary Panetta and Japanese Minister of Defense Morimoto from Tokyo, Japan," September 17, 2012, http://www.defense.gov/transcripts/transcript.aspx ?transcriptid=5114; and "Secretary Panetta and Chinese Defense Minister Liang Guanglie Hold a Joint News Conference, China," September 18, 2012, http://www.defense.gov/transcripts/transcript. aspx?transcriptid=5116. The newly appointed secretary of defense, Chuck Hagel, reiterated that the Senkakus fall under U.S. treaty obligations, during a meeting with Japanese defense minister Onodera Itsunori in Washington in April 2013 (U.S. Department of Defense, "Press Conference with Secretary Hagel and Defense Minister Onodera from the Pentagon," April 29, 2013, http://www.defense.gov/transcripts /transcript.aspx?transcriptid=5230).

12. The resolution, "Sense of the Senate on the Situation in the Senkaku Islands," was added as an amendment to the FY2013 National Defense Authorization Act and signaled congressional support for the Obama administration's response to the East China Sea tensions and reiterated the United States' interest in a peaceful resolution of the island dispute and a de-escalation of the growing crisis (U.S. Senate, "Sense of the Senate on the Situation in the Senkaku Islands," FY2013 National Defense Authorization Act, Section 1251, adopted unanimously on November 29, 2012). On July 30, 2013, the U.S. Senate again reaffirmed this support for Japan by unanimously passing a resolution condemning the "use of coercion, threats, or force" and referring to recent Chinese provocations near the Senkaku Islands (U.S. Senate, "Reaffirming the Strong

Support of the United States for the Peaceful Resolution of Territorial, Sovereignty, and Jurisdictional Disputes in the Asia-Pacific Maritime Domains," Resolution 167, July 30, 2013).

13. White House, "Remarks to the Press by Vice President Joe Biden and Prime Minister Shinzo Abe of Japan," December 3, 2013, http://www .whitehouse.gov/the-press-office/2013/12/03/remarks-press-vice-president -joe-biden-and-prime-minister-shinzo-abe-jap.

14. Japan and the Republic of China in Taibei (Taiwan) signed the Treaty of Taibei on April 28, 1952. The United States pressured Japan to conclude this separate treaty, which was needed because Taiwan was not a signatory to the San Francisco Peace Treaty. For the text of the treaty, see "Treaty of Peace Between Japan and the Republic of China," April 28, 1952, available on the Database of Japanese Politics and International Relations, Institute of Oriental Culture, University of Tokyo, http://www .ioc.u-tokyo.ac.jp/~worldjpn/documents/texts/docs/19520428.T1E .html.

15. Cabinet Office of Japan, "Remarks by Prime Minister Shinzo Abe on the Occasion of Accepting Hudson Institute's 2013 Herman Kahn Award," September 25, 2013, New York, http://www.kantei.go.jp/foreign/96_abe /statement/201309/25hudson_e.html.

16. Some scholars see the seeds of conflict much earlier in the postwar relationship. Ming Wan, *Sino-Japanese Relations: Interaction, Logic and Transformation* (Stanford, Calif.: Stanford University Press, 2006).

17. The Japanese and Chinese governments used the metaphor of a "freeze" to describe the state of their relations by the end of 2006 when Prime Minister Koizumi Jun'ichirō left office. This metaphor was then applied by subsequent Chinese leaders to the process of reconciliation that was designed to restore confidence in the relationship. When Premier Wen Jiabao visited Tokyo in April 2007, he spoke of the "warming" of the relationship (Ministry of Foreign Affairs, People's Republic of China, "Speech by Premier Wen Jiabao of the State of the People's Republic of China at the Japanese Diet," April 13, 2007, http://www.fmprc.gov .cn/eng/wjdt/zyjh/t311544.htm). When Prime Minister Fukuda Yasuo visited Beijing later that year in December, he compared his visit to the "coming of spring" (Ministry of Foreign Affairs, Japan, "Forging the Future Together: Speech by H.E. Mr. Yasuo Fukuda, Prime Minister of Japan at Peking University, Beijing, People's Republic of China," December 28, 2007, http://www.mofa.go.jp/region/asia-paci/china /speech0712.html).

18. The beginning of the reconciliation blueprint was the visit to Beijing on October 8, 2006, by Koizumi's successor, Abe Shinzō, who despite his conservative leanings, managed to implement the design of mutual visits and summitry that led to a new vision for the bilateral relationship. Abe's visit was following by Chinese Premier Wen Jiabao's visit to Tokyo on April 11 to 13, 2007, and ultimately the visit by President Hu Jintao to Tokyo from May 6 to 10, 2008. For more information on the summits, see Ministry of Foreign Affairs, Japan, "Prime Minister Visits China (Japan-China Summit Meeting)," October 8, 2006, http://www.kantei .go.jp/foreign/abephoto/2006/10/08china_e.html; Ministry of Foreign Affairs, Japan, "Visit to Japan of His Excellency Mr. Wen Jiabao Premier of the State Council of the People's Republic of China," April 2007, http://www.mofa.go.jp/region/asia-paci/China/pv0704/index.html ; and Ministry of Foreign Affairs, Japan, "Visit to Japan of His Excellency Mr. Hu Jintao, President of the People's Republic of China," May 2008, http://www.mofa.go.jp/region/asia-paci/china/pv0805/index.html.

19. President Hu Jintao came to Tokyo in May 2008 to meet with Prime Minister Fukuda Yasuo. In their joint statement, the two leaders referred to the outcome of this two-year process of diplomatic revamping as the "strategic and mutually beneficial relationship" between Japan and China. For a full rendering of what this meant, see Ministry of Foreign Affairs, Japan, "Joint Statement Between the Government of Japan and the Government of the People's Republic of China on Comprehensive Promotion of a 'Mutually Beneficial Relationship Based on Common Strategic Interests," May 7, 2008, http://www.mofa.go.jp/region/asia-paci /china/joint0805.html.

20. *Yomiuri shinbun*, December 11, 2009.

21. *Asahi shinbun*, September 30, 2010. See also "Japan Urges Resolution on Nationals Held in China," Reuters, September 29, 2010.

22. Genron NPO and *China Daily*, "Nitchū kyōdō yoron chōsa—kekka" [Eighth Annual Japan-China Bilateral Survey—Results], August 2013, http://www.genron-npo.net/world/genre/tokyobeijing/post-240.html.

23. According to the Japan National Tourism Organization (JNTO), 3,658,300 Japanese people visited China in 2011, a 2 percent decrease from 2010 (3,731,100). This 2010 number represents a 70 percent increase over the decade since 2000 (2,201,528). This information is available from the Japan Tourism Marketing Co., "Tourism Statistics," http://www.tourism.jp/english/statistics/outbound.php (accessed June 2012).

24. As of 2009, according to the Ministry of Internal Affairs and Communications, there were 127,282 Japanese living abroad in China (Ministry of Internal Affairs and Communications, "Japanese Nationals Living Abroad," *Japan Statistical Yearbook 2013*, chap. 2, "Population and Households," http://www.stat.go.jp/english/data/nenkan/1431–02.htm [accessed September 2013]).

25. According to JNTO, 1,412,875 Chinese visited Japan in 2010. In 2011, this number dropped 35 percent to 1,043,245 (preliminary) because of safety concerns after Japan's disasters struck on March 11. Chinese sensitivities to the radiation risk after meltdowns at the Fukushima Daiichi Nuclear Plant affected not only travel to Japan but also trade with Japan.

2. DIPLOMACY AND DOMESTIC INTERESTS

1. For a sophisticated account of how China's rise is affecting national identity formation across East Asia, see David C. Kang, *China Rising: Peace, Power and Order in East Asia* (New York: Columbia University Press, 2007).

2. Academic theorizing on the systemic consequences of rising powers has long been central to international relations theory. Theorists have focused on the systemic consequences, especially the rise of Germany in the late nineteenth century, to develop a theory of power transitions suggesting that a new and rising power in the world can cause instability and perhaps even war. A. F. K. Organski introduced the theory of power transitions in *World Politics* (New York: Knopf, 1958) and developed it further with Jack Kugler in *The War Ledger* (Chicago: University of Chicago Press, 1980). Power transition theory is widely seen to contend with the more mainstream international relations theory of balance of power. Refinements of this theory focus mainly on the European experience at the turn of the nineteenth century and on the rise of Germany as a new power, in order to explore further the causes of war and the role of alliances in great power relations. See, for example, Edward Mansfield and Jack L. Snyder, "Democratization and the Danger of War," *International Security* 20, no. 1 (1995): 5–38; and Thomas J. Christensen, "Perceptions and Alliance in Europe, 1865–1940," *International Organization* 51 (1997): 65–97.

3. China's rise has prompted substantial theorizing about the transition in the balance of power among states. See, for example, Aaron L. Friedberg,

"Ripe for Rivalry: Prospects for Peace in a Multipolar Asia," *International Security* 18, no. 3 (1993–1994): 5–33; Victor Cha, *Alignment Despite Antagonism: The U.S.-Korea-Japan Triangle* (Stanford, Calif.: Stanford University Press, 1999); Robert S. Ross, "Balance of Power Politics and the Rise of China: Accommodation and Balancing in East Asia," *Security Studies* 15, no. 3 (2007): 355–95; Evelyn Goh, "Great Powers and Hierarchical Order in Southeast Asia: Analyzing Regional Security Strategies," 32, no. 3 (2007–2008): 113–57; and Charles Glaser, "Will China's Rise Lead to War?" *Foreign Affairs* 90, no. 2 (2011): 80–91.

4. Richard K. Betts and Thomas J. Christensen, "China: Getting the Questions Right," *National Interest*, no. 62 (2000–2001): 17–26; Thomas J. Christensen, "Fostering Stability or Creating a Monster? The Rise of China and U.S. Policy Toward East Asia," *International Security* 1, no. 31 (2006): 81–126.

5. Andrew J. Nathan and Andrew Scobell, "How China Sees America: The Sum of Beijing's Fears," *Foreign Affairs* 91, no. 5 (2012): 32–47.

6. Robert B. Zoellick, "Whither China: From Membership to Responsibility?" *NBR Analysis* 16, no. 4 (2005): 5–14; Elizabeth C. Economy and Adam Segal, "The G-2 Mirage: Why the United States and China Are Not Ready to Upgrade Ties," *Foreign Affairs* 88, no. 3 (2009): 14–23; Aaron L. Friedberg, "Bucking Beijing: An Alternative U.S. China Policy," *Foreign Affairs* 91, no. 5 (2012): 48–58.

7. For more details, see http://www.nytimes.com/2014/01/24/world/asia /japans-leader-compares-strain-with-china-to-germany-and-britain -in-1914.html?_r=0.

8. Obama's national security adviser, Susan Rice, worried Japanese when she remarked, "When it comes to China, we seek to operationalize a new model of major power relations." The White House, "Remarks as Prepared for Delivery by National Security Advisor Susan E. Rice," Georgetown University, November 20, 2013, http://www.whitehouse .gov/the-press-office/2013/11/21/remarks-prepared-delivery-national -security-advisor-susan-e-rice.

9. Richard Bush explores the ways in which crisis management is affected by Japan's geography in *The Perils of Proximity: China-Japan Security Relations* (Washington, D.C.: Brookings Institution Press, 2010).

10. Japan's coastline is approximately 21,000 miles (35,000 km); its territorial waters are approximately 166,000 square miles (430,000 sq km); and its exclusive economic zone (EEZ) is approximately 1.5 million square miles (4.05 million sq km). Japan's territorial waters and EEZ are

twelve times as large as its land area (approximately 235,000 sq. mi., or 380,000 sq km) and, taken together, are the sixth largest in the world (Japan Coast Guard, Policy Evaluation and Public Relations Office, *Japan Coast Guard* [pamphlet, March 2012], 1, http://www.kaiho.mlit .go.jp/e/pamphlet.pdf).

11. In 2003, China's GDP per capita (in current U.S. dollars) was $1,273.60, compared with $33,690.90 for Japan. In 2012, China's GDP per capita was $6,188.20, compared with $46,720.40 for Japan. Even though China's GDP per capita has quadrupled over the past decade, it still is only 13 percent that of Japan (World Bank, "GDP per Capita [Current US$]," October 2013, http://data.worldbank.org/indicator/N.Y.GDP.PCAP.CD).

12. October 2013, the International Monetary Fund cut the forecast for Chinese growth from 7.8 percent in 2013 to 7.6 percent, and from 7.7 percent in 2014 to 7.3 percent (International Monetary Fund, *World Economic Outlook: Transitions and Tensions*, October 2013, http://www.imf.org /external/pubs/ft/weo/2013/02/).

13. The structural shifts and Japan's policy response in retrospective are summarized in the *Nikkei shinbun*, August 16 and 17, 2010. A more skeptical stance toward China can be found in the coverage by the conservative *Sankei shinbun*, August 16 and 17, 2010.

14. "China Passes U.S. in Trade with Japan," *Washington Post*, January 27, 2005.

15. The Japanese economic dream was encouraged by the best-selling book by Harvard sociologist Ezra F. Vogel, *Japan as Number One: Lessons for America* (Cambridge, Mass.: Harvard University Press, 1979), and Japan's status as the only economic "superpower" seemed irrevocable until China's economic achievement in the 1990s.

16. See, for example, Chalmers Johnson, *Japan: Who Governs? The Rise of the Developmental State* (New York: Norton, 1995).

17. For more on the origins of the "flying geese" model, see Akamatsu Kaname, "A Historical Pattern of Economic Growth in Developing Countries," *Journal of Developing Economies* 1, no. 1 (1962): 3–25.

18. The most fully developed theorizing on how states respond to a rising power focuses on the notion of strategic hedging. Two kinds of hedging have been suggested, military or "hard" hedging, plus "soft" hedging relying on a variety of diplomatic and economic means. Those states whose security is affected by the power transition often "hedge"; that is, they attempt to manage relations between both the rising power and the status quo power so as to ensure a positive outcome for their national

interests, no matter which power becomes dominant. This dynamic is derived from the balance-of-power theory that explains the dynamic of state behavior toward a rising power as a choice between balancing against the rising power or joining with it. But the ways in which balancing and joining are conducted also matter. "Offensive realists" such as John Mearsheimer, in *Tragedy of Great Power Politics* (New York: Norton, 2001), contends that this choice must be based solely on material power, while "defensive realists" argue that the intentions as well as the capabilities of the rising power matter, and thus efforts to shape the intentions— through diplomacy, economic cooperation, and other means—are equally as important in responding as the acquisition of military power. See, for example, Stephen M. Walt, *The Origins of Alliances* (Ithaca, N.Y.: Cornell University Press, 1987). The literature on "hedging" is part of the "defensive realism" perspective developed largely after the Cold War to consider how other states responded to the United States' position as the sole superpower. See, for example, William C. Wohlforth, "U.S. Strategy in a Unipolar World"; Stephen M. Walt, "Keeping the World 'Off Balance': Self Restraint and U.S. Foreign Policy"; and Josef Joffe, "Defying History and Theory: The United States as the 'Last Remaining Superpower,'" all in *America Unrivaled: The Future of the Balance of Power*, ed. G. John Ikenberry (Ithaca, N.Y.: Cornell University Press, 2002).

19. Evelyn Goh, "Great Powers and Hierarchical Order in Southeast Asia: Analyzing Regional Security Strategies," *International Security* 32, no. 3 (2007–2008): 113–57; Cheng-Chwee Kuik, "The Essence of Hedging: Malaysia and Singapore's Response to a Rising China," *Contemporary Southeast Asia* 30, no. 2 (2008): 159–85; Yuen Foong Khong, "Coping with Strategic Uncertainty: The Role of Institutions and Soft Balancing in Southeast Asia's Post-Cold War Strategy," in *Rethinking Security in East Asia: Identity, Power, and Efficiency*, ed. J. J. Suh, Peter J. Katzenstein, and Allen Carlson (Stanford, Calif.: Stanford University Press, 2004).

20. Eric Heginbotham and Richard J. Samuels, "Japan's Dual Hedge," *Foreign Affairs* 81, no. 5 (2002): 110–21; Richard J. Samuels, *Securing Japan: Tokyo's Grand Strategy and the Future of East Asia* (Ithaca, N.Y.: Cornell University Press, 2008)

21. Mike M. Mochizuki, "Japan: Between Alliance and Autonomy," in *Strategic Asia 2004–05: Confronting Terrorism in the Pursuit of Power*, ed. Ashley Tellis (Seattle: National Bureau of Asian Research, 2004), 103–38; Mike M. Mochizuki, "Japan's Shifting Strategy Toward the Rise of China," *Journal of Strategic Studies* 30, nos. 4–5 (2007): 739–76.

22. For an excellent comparative analysis of Japan's views of history and the impact on regional relations, see Thomas U. Berger, *War, Guilt and World Politics After World War II* (Cambridge: Cambridge University Press, 2012), esp. chaps. 4 and 5. Yet another scholarly comparative tour de force on the topic of Japan's "apology diplomacy" is Jennifer Lind, *Sorry States: Apologies in International Relations* (Ithaca, N.Y.: Cornell University Press, 2010), although Lind focuses less on the Japan-China relationship and more on the Japan-South Korea relationship. Finally, historian Alexis Dudden, *Troubled Apologies Among Japan, Korea, and the United States* (New York: Columbia University Press, 2008), focuses on the difference between political apology and what she calls "apologetic history" in her comparative work on Japan, South Korea, and the United States.

23. Ozawa Ichiro, *Blueprint for a New Japan: The Rethinking of a Nation* (Tokyo: Kodansha International, 1994). Ozawa's book was first published in Japanese as *Nippon kaizō keikaku* [*Blueprint for a New Japan*] (Tokyo: Kodansha, 1993). Ozawa led a group of forty-three lawmakers out of the ruling LDP in 1993, effectively ending the conservatives' single-party dominance since 1955. A new electoral system was instituted, introducing single-member districts, and new constraints on political financing were adopted.

24. Ming Wan, *Sino-Japanese Relations: Interaction, Logic and Transformation* (Stanford, Calif.: Stanford University Press, 2006), 22.

25. Ibid., 331–46.

26. Tanaka Akihiko, *Ajia no naka no nihon* [*Japan in Asia*] (Tokyo: NTT shuppan, 2007).

27. Nihon no gaikō [Japan's Diplomacy] is a six-part series published by Iwanami shoten and ed. Inoue Toshikazu, Hatano Sunao, Sakai Tetsuya, Kokubun Ryōsei, and Oshiba Ryō. For Kokubun's analysis of Sino-Japanese relations, see Kokubun Ryōsei, "'1972-nen taisei' kara 'senryakuteki goei' he—taichū gaikō [From the "1972 System" to "Mutually Beneficial and Strategic"—Diplomacy Toward China], in *Taigai seisaku chiiki hen* [*Volume on Regional Foreign Policy*], ed. Kokubun Ryōsei et al., Nihon no gaikō [Japan's Diplomacy] (Tokyo: Iwanami shoten, 2013), 4:111–43.

28. See, for example, Mori Kazuko and Zhang Yun-ling, eds., *Nitchū kankei wo tō kōchiku suruka: ajia no kyosei to kyōryoku wo mezashite* [*How Can We Rebuild Japan-China Relations? Aiming for Coexistence and Cooperation in Asia*] (Tokyo: Iwanami shoten, 2004); and the collection of articles by the new generation of Japan scholars in Iechika

Ryōko, Dan Zuizō, and Matsuda Yasuhiro, eds., *Kiro ni tatsu nitchū kankei* [*Japan-China Relations at a Crossroads*] (Tokyo: Kōyō shobō, 2007). Authors include many Keio University Contemporary China Studies scholars, including Ichitani Kazuo, Nakaoka Mari, Kinoshita Keiji, Masuda Masayuki, Anami Yusuke, Kamo Tomoki, Tō Sei, and Itō Tsuyoshi.

29. Ezra F. Vogel, Yuan Ming, and Akihiko Tanaka, *The Golden Age of the U.S.-China-Japan Triangle: 1972–1989* (Cambridge, Mass.: Harvard University Asia Center, 2002), 87.

30. For a detailed analysis of the difficulties this issue created for Sino-Japanese negotiations, see Yung H. Park, "The 'Anti-Hegemony' Controversy in Sino-Japanese Relations," *Pacific Affairs* 49, no. 3 (1976): 476–90. In addition, see Hong N. Kim, Sino-Japanese Relations Since the Rapprochement," *Asian Survey* 15, no. 7 (1975): 559–73; Chae-jin Lee, "The Making of the Sino-Japanese Peace and Friendship Treaty," *Pacific Affairs* 52, no. 3 (1979): 420–45; Chalmers Johnson, "The Patterns of Japanese Relations with China, 1952–1982," *Pacific Affairs* 59, no. 3 (1986): 402–28; and Saburo Okita, "Japan, China and the United States: Economic Relations and Prospects," *Foreign Affairs* 57, no. 5 (1979): 1090–1110.

31. Tanaka Akihiko, *Nitchū kankei 1945–1990* [*Japan-China Relations, 1945–1990*] (Tokyo: Tokyo University Press, 1991); Soeya Yoshihide, *Nihon gaikō to chūgoku* [*Japanese Diplomacy and China*] (Tokyo: Keio tsūshin, 1995); and Soeya Yoshihide, "1970 nendai no beichūkankei to nihon gaikō" [U.S.-China Relations in the 1970s and Japanese Diplomacy], originally published in *Nihon seijigaku 1997* (*Annual Political Science Report 1997*), ed. Japanese Political Science Association and then published as part of *Kiki no nihon gaikō 70 nendai* [*Japanese Crisis Diplomacy of the 1970s*] (Tokyo: Iwanami shoten, 1998).

32. "Agreement Between Japan and the United States of America Concerning the Ryukyu Islands and the Daito Islands" [Okinawa Reversion Agreement], June 17, 1971, available from the Institute of Oriental Culture, University of Tokyo, "The World and Japan Database Project," http://www.ioc.u-tokyo.ac.jp/~worldjpn/documents/texts/docs/19710617.T1E.html (accessed September 2013).

33. "Joint Statement Between President Richard Nixon and Prime Minster Eisaku Sato," November 21, 1969, in Washington, D.C., available from the Institute of Oriental Culture, University of Tokyo, "The World and Japan Database Project," http://www.ioc.u-tokyo.ac.jp/~worldjpn/documents/texts/docs/19691121.D1E.html.

34. Paul J. Smith, "The Senkaku/Diaoyu Island Controversy: A Crisis Postponed," *Naval War College Review* 66, no. 2 (2013): 27–44.

35. Foreign Relations of the United States, "Document 115: Memorandum from John H. Holdridge of the National Security Council Staff to the President's Assistant for National Security Affairs (Kissinger)," Office of the Historian, U.S. Department of State 17 (1969–1971): 296. A handwritten comment by Kissinger in the margin reads, "But that is nonsense since it gives islands to Japan. How can we get a more neutral position?" The diplomatic record on the negotiations with Beijing that relates specifically to Kissinger's discussions with Chinese leaders on the Senkaku dispute remains classified. But there is no doubt that the territorial dispute was part of the bilateral discussions.

36. Jean-Marc F. Blanchard, "The U.S. Role in the Sino-Japanese Dispute over the Diaoyu (Senkaku) Islands, 1945–1971," *China Quarterly* 161 (2000): 102–15; Mark E. Manyin, "Senkaku (Diaoyu/Diaoyutai) Islands Dispute: U.S. Treaty Obligations," *Congressional Research Service Report*, January 2013; Alan D. Romberg, "American Interests in the Senkaku/Diaoyu Issue: Policy Considerations," *Center for Naval Analyses Maritime Asia Project,* April 2013.

37. Fifteenth G7 Arch Summit, "Political Declaration on China," July 15, 1989, available from the Ministry of Foreign Affairs, Japan, "Documents of G7/G8 Summit Meetings in the Past," http://www.mofa.go.jp/policy/economy/summit/2000/past_summit/15/e15_e.html.

38. For a discussion of this moment in Japanese foreign policy, see Tanaka, *Nitchū kankei 1945–1990.*

39. *Mainichi shinbun*, June 20, 1989.

40. *Asahi shinbun*, June 28, 1989.

41. *Mainichi shinbun,* September 20, 1989.

42. *Asahi shinbun*, November 16, 1989.

43. *Mainichi shinbun*, December 27, 1989.

44. The third yen loan was officially resumed on November 2, 1990, when Japan agreed to provide more than ¥36 billion to fund dams, factories, and other infrastructure in China (*Mainichi shinbun*, November 3, 1990). A second loan was made on December 21, 1990, when Japan provided ¥42 billion for the construction of ports and other facilities (*Yomiuri shinbun*, December 21, 1990).

45. For a detailed analysis of this group and of Japan's relationship with China before diplomatic normalization, see Yoshihide Soeya, *Japan's Economic Diplomacy with China, 1945–1978* (Oxford: Clarendon Press, 1998).

46. Mori Kazuko and Zhang Yun-ling, *Nitchū kankei wo tō kōchiku suruka*, 108–9.
47. Over time, the policy of giving yen loans to China became increasingly uncomfortable for the Japanese government. For example, during negotiations with China on the fourth yen loan, Japan initially tried to shift to a single-year commitment, but after China objected, the two countries eventually settled on a two-stage disbursement: ¥580 billion was given for the first three years, and ¥390 billion for the last two (totaling ¥970 billion). For an in-depth look at Japan-China negotiations over yen loans, see Ming Wan, *Sino-Japanese Relations*, 263–72.
48. Ministry of Foreign Affairs, Japan, "Japan's ODA Disbursements to China," http://www.mofa.go.jp/policy/oda/data/pdfs/china.pdf (accessed June 3, 2013).
49. Ministry of Foreign Affairs, Japan, *Diplomatic Blue Book* (1978–2011); *Japan's ODA Annual Report* (1994–1999); and *Japan's ODA White Paper* (2001–2011).
50. Machimura made the announcement during a joint meeting of the Liberal Democratic Party's divisions in charge of diplomatic affairs. He said that the Chinese foreign minister, Li Zhaoxing, had basically agreed to this policy during a telephone conversation earlier that week (*Yomiuri shinbun*, March 17, 2005).
51. Ministry of Foreign Affairs, Japan, "Japan-China Joint Press Statement," April 11, 2007, http://www.mofa.go.jp/region/asia-paci/china/pv0704/joint.html.
52. Ministry of Foreign Affairs, Japan, *ODA White Paper 2008*, http://www.mofa.go.jp/policy/oda/white/2008/html/ODA2008/html/honpen/index.htm.
53. The task force, Nōrin suisanbutsu bōeki chōsakai (Special Committee on Agriculture, Marine Products, and Trade), was headed by Nakagawa Shōichi, a former minister of agriculture (*Mainichi shinbun*, December 13, 2001).
54. *Yomiuri shinbun*, December 21, 2001.
55. *Mainichi shinbun*, April 6, 2004, and *NHK News*, July 9, 2004.
56. *Sankei shinbun*, October 29, 2006.
57. *Sankei shinbun*, September 25, 2010, July 15, 2011, and March 14, 2012.
58. Shikō Ryū, "Baoshan seitetsusho no gijutsu dōnyū wo meguru seisaku kettei" [Policy Decisions Regarding Technology Imports to the Baoshan Steel Plant], *Aziya kenkyū* 49, no. 2 (2003): 3–25.

59. Dong Dong Zhang, "Negotiating for a Liberal Economic Regime: The Case of Japanese FDI in China," *Pacific Review* 11, no. 1 (1998): 51–78.

60. For analysis of the various influences on Japanese FDI to China, see Shirō Armstrong, "Japanese FDI in China: Determinants and Performance," Asia-Pacific Economic Papers, no. 378 (2009): 1–34; John Hemmings and Maiko Kuroki, "Tokyo Trade-Offs," *RUSI Journal* 158, no. 2 (2013): 58–66; Khondaker Mizanur Rahman, "Theorizing Japanese FDI to China," *Journal of Comparative International Management* 9, no. 2 (2006): 16–29; Xiaoming Rong, "Explaining the Patterns of Japanese Foreign Direct Investment n China," *Journal of Contemporary China* 8, no. 20 (1999): 123–246; and Yuqing Xing, "Japanese FDI in China: Trend, Structure, and the Role of Exchange Rates," in *China as a World Factory*, ed. K. H. Zhang (London: Routledge, Taylor & Francis, 2006), 110–25.

61. For excellent analysis in Japanese, see the work of Seguchi Kiyoyuki, research director at the Cannon Institute for Global Studies, http://www .canon-igs.org/fellows/kiyoyuki_seguchi.html, esp. the two-part report "Dai yoji taichū boom no torai to chūgoku bijinesu no aratana kadai" [Arrival of the Fourth-Stage Investment Boom and New Challenges for Business in China], Canon Institute for Global Studies, May 12, 2010, http://www.canon-igs.org/column/network/20100512_110.html and http://www.canon-igs.org/column/network/20100512_111.html.

62. For a full analysis of the Sino-Japanese redress movement, see Ming Wan, *Sino-Japanese Relations*, chap. 12.

63. A decade later, the Japanese Society for Historical Textbook Reform was founded in December 1996, which sought to create revisionist textbooks that rationalized Japanese imperial ambitions, including the invasion of China. The group submitted its textbook to the Ministry of Education in late 2000. It was approved for use in 2001 and became yet another cause for Chinese (and South Korean) disquiet about Japanese conservatives and their views of their history. Despite its commercial success, the textbook was used by only a small handful of schools in Japan (Japanese Society for Historical Textbook Reform, *Atarashii rekishi kyōkasho* [*New History Textbook*] [Tokyo: Fusōsha, 2001]).

64. Japan's Ministry of Foreign Affairs announced on June 20, 1989, that it would freeze yen loans to China (*Yomiuri shinbun*, June 21, 1989).

65. *Nikkei shinbun*, July 7, 1990.

66. *Nikkei shinbun*, May 21, 1990.

67. *Nikkei shinbun*, July 7, 1990.

68. The Japanese government announced two official reasons behind the decision to resume yen loans: First, it felt that Japan needed to keep Prime Minister Takeshita Noboru's promise of a third loan of ¥810 billion, made during his visit to China in 1988; and second, it was worried about the country's stability and the huge effect that an isolated or underdeveloped China could have on the Asian region. Media reporting also cited the potentially negative security consequences that Japan could face should it continue to deny aid to China, as well as the strong belief of the Japanese business/industrial community that aid to China would open up the Chinese market and lead to further Japanese economic growth (*Yomiuri shinbun*, July 20, 1990).

69. *Yomiuri shinbun*, February 22, 1992.

70. *Mainichi shinbun*, March 21, 1992.

71. *Nikkei shinbun*, July 2, 1992. Interestingly, support varied by age group, with younger Japanese much more enthusiastic (more than 80 percent) than older Japanese (only 45 percent of those older than seventy supported the visit). In terms of political party affiliation, the most skeptical about the visit was the Japan Communist Party, with only 45 percent in support.

72. The full text of the emperor's speech is available from the Imperial Household Agency, Kokka shuseki shusai bansankai [jinmin taikai dō] ni okeru tennō heika no okotoba [Remarks by His Majesty the Emperor of Japan at a State-Sponsored Banquet], People's Republic of China, October 23, 1992, http://www.kunaicho.go.jp/okotoba/01/speech/speech -h04e-china.html#china.

73. In a joint poll of Japanese and Chinese opinion conducted by the *Mainichi shinbun* and the Ajia chōsakai (led by the well-known economist Ōkita Saburō) 88 percent of Japanese and 77 percent of Chinese polled had a favorable view of the emperor and empress's visit (*Mainichi shinbun*, December 23, 1992).

74. The full text of President Jiang Zemin's speech was printed in *Mainichi shinbun*, November 27, 1998.

75. President Jiang Zemin arrived in Japan on November 25 and attended a state banquet at the Imperial Palace on November 26. After the dinner, he stayed in Japan for three more days and left in the morning on November 30. Ministry of Foreign Affairs, Japan, "President Jiang Zemin and Mrs. Wang's State Visit to Japan," November 1998, http://www .mofa.go.jp/region/asia-paci/china/visit98/index.html.

76. Ministry of Foreign Affairs, Japan, "Visit to Japan of His Excellency the President of the Republic of Korea and Mrs. Kim Dae-jung," October

7–10, 1998, http://www.mofa.go.jp/region/asia-paci/korea/visit9810 .html. The full text of President Kim's speech was printed in the *Mainichi shinbun*, October 9, 1998.

77. Lee Teng-hui won reelection on March 23, 1996. He then stepped down, observing constitutional limits, and Chen Shui-bian won on March 18, 2000.

78. *Nikkei shinbun*, August 17, 1995. Further nuclear testing was done by Beijing in 1996. After its last nuclear test in July 1996, China declared a moratorium on nuclear testing and signed the Comprehensive Test Ban Treaty. Japan resumed grant aid to China in March 1997 (Ministry of Foreign Affairs, *Japan's ODA Annual Report* [Summary] 1996, "Japan's ODA Charter: Concrete Cases," 1996, http://www.mofa.go.jp/policy/oda /summary/1996/c_8.html).

79. Japanese Defense Agency, Heisei 8 nen bōei hakusho [Defense White Paper, 1996], chap. 1, sec. 3: "Wagakuni shūhen no gunji jōsei" [Military Affairs in the Areas Surrounding Japan], http://www.clearing.mod .go.jp/hakusho_data/1996/103.htm.

80. "Report by the Subcommittee for Defense Cooperation, Submitted to and Approved by the Japan-U.S. Security Consultative Committee" (Guidelines for Japan-U.S. Defense Cooperation), November 27, 1978, available from Institute of Oriental Culture, University of Tokyo, "The World and Japan Database Project," http://www.ioc.u-tokyo .ac.jp/~worldjpn/documents/texts/docs/19781127.O1E.html.

81. Ministry of Foreign Affairs, Japan, "The Guidelines for Japan-U.S. Defense Cooperation," September 23, 1997, http://www.mofa.go.jp /region/n-america/us/security/guideline2.html.

82. Katō described the growing concerns in Japan over North Korea's Nodong missiles and reportedly told the defense minister that although China had far greater military capability, Japanese were not worried about its intentions (*Sankei shinbun*, July 17, 1997).

83. *Asahi shinbun*, August 18 and 20, 1997.

84. The three pieces of legislation related to the 1997 U.S.-Japan Defense Guidelines revision are the Law for SDF in Areas Surrounding Japan [Shūhen jitai anzen kakuho ho] passed on May 28, 1999; the U.S.-Japan ACSA revision [Nichibei buppin yakumu sōgo teikyō kaisei kyōtei] passed on April 28, 1999; and an amendment of article 100 of the Self-Defense Force Law (May 28, 1999) allowing the SDF to evacuate Japanese citizens from a conflict area in case of war.

85. Prime Minister Murayama made his statement on April 15, 1995, at the fiftieth anniversary of the end of World War II. Ever since, conservatives

and liberals alike have supported this statement of Japan's responsibility and remorse. For the full text, see "Statement by Prime Minister Tomiichi Murayama—On the Occasion of the 50th Anniversary of the War's End," Ministry of Foreign Affairs, Japan, August 15, 1995, http://www .mofa.go.jp/announce/press/pm/murayama/9508.html.

86. Even Abe Shinzō, arguably the most conservative on issues of war memory since Jun'ichirō Koizumi, endorsed this statement of Japanese national policy on Japan's past. As Koizumi's immediate successor and a self-identified nationalist, Abe's views on this were of particular interest to China. Ironically, Abe's efforts to improve relations after Koizumi were widely supported in Beijing. See "Abe Endorses Murayama's War Apology," *China Daily*, October 7, 2006, http://www.chindaily.com.cn /china/2006–10/07/contnet_702556.htm.

87. *Asahi shinbun*, October 19, 2003.

88. The final report of the Twenty-First Century Japan-China Friendship Committee was jointly published in Japanese and Chinese on December 6, 2008. See Ministry of Foreign Affairs, Japan, "Nitchū 'senryaku gokei kantei' no kyōka he mukete" [Toward the Strengthening of the Japan-China "Mutually Beneficial Strategic Partnership"], December 6, 2008, http://www.mofa.go.jp/mofaj/area/china/jc_yuko21/pdfs/hokoku.pdf.

89. *Yomiuri shinbun*, December 20, 2001.

90. *Asahi shinbun*, June 14, 2005.

91. *Sankei shinbun*, June 2, 2006.

92. *Nikkei shinbun*, November 25, 2004.

93. Keizai dōyukai, "Kongo no nitchū kankei he no teigen—nitchū ryōkoku seifu he no message" [A Proposal for Future Japan-China Relations: A Message to the Governments of Japan and China], April 2006, http://www .doyukai.or.jp/policyproposals/articles/2006/pdf/060509.pdf.

94. *Nikkei shinbun*, May 10, 2006.

95. *Nikkei shinbun*, September 21, 2004, and *Mainichi shinbun*, January 12, 2005.

96. *Yomiuri shinbun*, January 20, 2005.

97. *Yomiuri shinbun*, January 12, 2005.

98. *Asahi shinbun*, January 21, 2005.

99. *Financial Times*, June 7, 2012.

100. *Nikkei shinbun*, June 7, 2012.

101. *Asahi shinbun*, December 21, 2012.

102. *Asahi shinbun*, August 30, 2006; for a slightly different assessment, see the editorial in *Yomiuri shinbun*, September 3, 2006.

103. *Asahi shinbun*, August 28, 2006.

104. Channel Sakura is a conservative Japanese broadcasting station "dedicated to the renaissance and preservation of Japanese traditional culture and the genuine Japanese spirit." It was established on April 6, 2004, by Takeo Tagata (a former fighter jet pilot in the Imperial Japanese Army) Shigeo Umezawa (president of the Japan Aviation Academy), Shiro Takahashi (professor at Meisei University), Yoshiko Matsuura (Suginami Ward council member), and Satoru Mizushima (film director and current president and chief executive officer of Channel Sakura). The channel broadcasts news reports and debate programs, and covers various topics—including Japan's Self-Defense Forces, the Senkaku Islands, comfort women, North Korea abductees, and history issues—but has had very limited airtime since 2009 owing to financial troubles. For more information, see "Channel sakura ni tsuite" (About Channel Sakura) last updated June 2009, http://www.ch-sakura.jp/about.html.
105. Genron NPO and the China Daily, "Nitchū kyōdō yoron chōsa—kekka" [Eighth Annual Japan-China Bilateral Survey—Results], August 2013, http://www.genron-npo.net/world/genre/tokyobeijing/post-240.html.
106. Ibid. Results from other years of the Genron NPO and *China Daily* polls can be found online at http://www.genron-npo.net/world/genre/tokyobeijing/.
107. Ibid. When asked to list reasons why they held negative opinions of China, 53.2 percent of the Japanese respondents pointed to China's position on the Senkaku Islands; 48.9 percent disliked China's criticism of Japan's historical issues; 48.1 percent mentioned concerns about food security; and 47.9 percent noted China's disregard for international rules.

3. JAPAN'S IMPERIAL VETERANS

1.   Sheila A. Smith, "Why Resurrect the Divisive Politics of Yasukuni?" *Asia Unbound*, Council on Foreign Relations, April 26, 2013, http://blogs.cfr.org/asia/2013/04/26/why-resurrect-the-divisive-politics-of-yasukuni/.
2.   *Nikkei shinbun*, April 22, 2013.
3.   Japan National Press Club, "Press Conference by Kurt M. Campbell [former assistant secretary of state for East Asian and Pacific Affairs] and Michael J. Green [former National Security Council senior director for Asian Affairs])," July 16, 2013; videos available online at http://www.jnpc.or.jp/activities/news/report/2013/07/r00025991/.
4.   "Abe Proxy, Cabinet Trio Visit Yasukuni," *Japan Times*, August 15, 2013.

5. Abe sent an offering to the shrine in his capacity as president of the LDP. The three cabinet ministers were Furuya Keiji, state minister for North Korean abductions of Japanese; Shindō Yoshitaka, state minister for internal affairs; and Inada Tomomi, state minister of administrative reform. Furuya told reporters afterward, "How to commemorate the war dead is purely a domestic issue. It isn't something to be criticized or interfered with by foreign countries" (Yuka Hayashi and Alexander Martin, "Three Japanese Cabinet Ministers Visit Controversial Shrine," *Wall Street Journal*, August 15, 2013, http://online.wsj.com/article/SB100 014241278873241394045790136041002020642.html).

6. In November 2012 when she was running for office, President Park put forward this view in an op-ed in the *Wall Street Journal* but went on to be more vocal in her criticism of historical revisionism in the region. See, for example, her speech to the U.S. Congress: Republic of Korea Blue House, "Address by President Park Geun-Hye of the Republic of Korea to the Joint Session of the United States Congress," May 9, 2013, http://english1.president.go.kr/activity/speeches.php?srh%5bpage%5d=2&srh%5bview_mode%5d=detail&srh%5bseq%5d=2623&srh%5bdetail_no%5d=7#sidebar-foot.

7. Chinese Foreign Ministry spokesperson Qin Gang said Abe's visit was "an attempt to whitewash the history of aggression and colonialism by militarist Japan, overturn the just trial of Japanese militarism by the international community, and challenge the outcome of WWII and the post-war international order." Chinese Ministry of Foreign Affairs, "The Statement by the Foreign Ministry Spokesperson Qin Gang on Japanese Prime Minister Shinzo Abe's Visit to the Yasukuni Shrine," December 26, 2013, http://www.fmprc.gov.cn/eng/xwfw/s2510/t1112096.shtml. Xinhua quoted Chinese Foreign Minister Wang Yi as saying that Japan's prime minister was taking the country in "a very dangerous direction" (December 27, 2013). Korean Foreign Ministry spokesperson Choi Tai-young responded that Abe's visit "clearly shows his wrong perception of history. It is an anachronistic act that fundamentally undermines not only the ROK-Japan relations but also stability and cooperation in Northeast Asia. South Korean Ministry of Foreign Affairs, "Statement by the Spokesperson of the ROK Government on Japanese Prime Minister Abe's Visit to the Yasukuni Shrine," December 27, 2013, http://www.mofa.go.kr/ENG/press/pressreleases/index.jsp?menu=m_10_20&sp=/webmodule/htsboard/template/read/engreadboard.jsp%3Fboardid=302%26typeID=12%26tableName=TYPE_ENGLISH%26seqno=313204.

8. U.S. Embassy in Tokyo, "Statement on Prime Minister Abe's December 26 Visit to the Yasukuni Shrine," December 26, 2013, http://japan.usembassy .gov/e/p/tp-20131226-01.html. The exact quotation: "Japan is a valued ally and friend. Nevertheless, the United States is disappointed that Japan's leadership has taken an action that will exacerbate tensions with Japan's neighbors."

9. Kokkai kaigiroku kensaku shisutemu [National Diet Minutes Search System] "Remarks by Koizumi Jun'ichirō, Plenary Session, House of Representatives," May 10, 2001, http://kokkai.ndl.go.jp/.

10. Xinhua, May 12, 2001.

11. Xinhua, July 10, 2001.

12. In his courtesy call to the prime minister, China's new ambassador to Japan, Wu Dawei, reportedly told Koizumi that all eyes in China were on him to see if he would actually go to Yasukuni (Xinhua, August 3, 2001).

13. Cui Tankai, at the time the director of the Asia Bureau of the Chinese Foreign Ministry, spoke in November 2005 at the ASEAN plus three (China, Japan, and South Korea) meeting in Kuala Lumpur. This also was the first East Asia Summit, a new regional multilateral initiative designed to build regional confidence and to discuss issues of common concern. Cui's remarks were reported in Xinhua, November 30, 2005.

14. See, for example, "Thousands Rally in Shanghai, Attacking Japanese Consulate," *New York Times*, April 16, 2005.

15. Koizumi visited the Marco Polo Bridge on October 8, 2001, during his visit to Beijing. The English translation of what Koizumi said is in "Japanese Leader, Visiting China, Is Mildly Rebuked on Army Role," *New York Times*, October 9, 2001, http://www.nytimes.com/2001/10/09/world /japanese-leader-visiting-china-is-mildly-rebuked-on-army-role.html. For more on his visit, see Ministry of Foreign Affairs, Japan, "Visit to the People's Republic of China by Prime Minister Junichiro Koizumi, October 8, 2001," http://www.mofa.go.jp/region/asia-paci/china /pmv0110/overview.html.

16. The first was Prime Minister Murayama Tomiichi, leader of the Japan Socialist Party and author of the Murayama apology to China, who visited on May 3, 1995.

17. Itō Tomonaga, *Ki wo terawazu: rikugunshō kōkyū fukukan Miyama Yōzō no shōwa* [*Without Attracting Attention: The Shōwa Era of High-Level Military Aide Miyama Yōzō*] (Tokyo: Kodansha, 2007), 151.

18. The terms of Japan's occupation were already being deliberated at the Potsdam Conference, and the details of how a U.S.-led Allied Occu-

pation Force would be organized began shortly thereafter in the U.S. Department of State. For a history of the U.S. planning process, see Hugh Borton, *American Presurrender Planning for Postwar Japan* (New York: East Asian Studies, Columbia University, 1967); and Hugh Borton, "Preparation for the Occupation of Japan," *Journal of Asian Studies* 25, no. 2 (1996): 203–12.

19. For a fascinating account of the repatriation of the Japanese who populated Japan's overseas empire, see Lori Watt, *When Empire Comes Home: Repatriation and Reintegration in Postwar Japan* (Cambridge, Mass.: Harvard University Asia Center, 2009).

20. In addition, 1.2 million non-Japanese living in Japan had to be repatriated to their home countries. Repatriation and Relief Bureau, Ministry of Health and Welfare, *Hikiage to engo sanjū-nen no ayumi* [*Repatriation and Relief: Thirty Years of Progress*] (Tokyo: Ministry of Health and Welfare, 1977), 25.

21. The debate over the emperor's war responsibility was the backdrop to this negotiated approach to demonstrating MacArthur's absolute authority during the Occupation. Negotiations between Japanese and U.S. authorities before the surrender had produced an agreement that the emperor himself would not be put on trial for war crimes. Instead, this effort to communicate to the Japanese people how the Occupation would proceed firmly established the fact that the Japanese emperor was no longer the ruler of Japan. The diaries of those who negotiated and attended this historic meeting between General Douglas MacArthur and Emperor Hirohito are included in the *Asahi shinbun*'s commemoration of the Shōwa emperor's life after he died in January 1989 (*Asahi shinbun*, January 26, 1989).

22. The service was called the Rinji daishokonsai (Extraordinary Rite to Summon the Great Soul), and Japan's war dead were included in the effort. By Yasukuni's standards, this was not a full enshrinement ceremony. Rather, it was a provisional acceptance of the souls of Japan's war dead until the full details of their name, place of birth, and unit assignment at the time of death could be fully compiled. This final enshrinement process became the focus of attention after the Occupation ended and Japan's postwar government could turn its attention to identifying for Yasukuni those who had died in uniform (Itō Tomonaga, *Ki wo terawazu*).

23. Itō Tomonaga, *Ki wo terawazu*, 162–67.

24. A complex process of reorganization followed as the effort to repatriate overseas Japanese got under way. By October it was clear that the scale

of the repatriation required a centralized agency to oversee the effort and to work with local authorities to absorb the large inflow of Japanese. The GHQ ordered the creation of such an agency (Kōseishō), which was attached to the Ministry of Health and Welfare. The Kōseishō also had responsibility for the war victims, the war wounded, and the families of war veterans. In August, created the Relief Division (Engoka) to consider the needs of the veterans and their families. In November, the Repatriation and Relief Commission was established, and offices were set up at major ports to meet those returning to Japan. In January 1946, with new ships provided by the U.S. Occupation authorities to transport the Japanese home, the pace of the repatriation effort soon overwhelmed this new set of organizations, so an agency for repatriation relief had to be created. Once the Imperial Army and Navy were disbanded in November 1945, their work was organized in the Demobilization Agency, with the first and second divisions dealing with army and navy personnel, respectively (Repatriation and Relief Bureau, Ministry of Health and Welfare, *Hikiage to engo sanjū-nen no ayumi*, 26–27).

25. When the Demobilization Agency was disbanded in 1947, the first bureau (army) became part of the Kōseishō, and the second bureau (navy) went to the prime minister's office. On May 31, 1948, they were combined into the Repatriation Relief Agency, created as an agency of the Kōseishō but with separate administrative responsibilities.

26. Article 20 of Japan's constitution reads: "Freedom of religion is guaranteed to all. No religious organization shall receive any privileges from the State, nor exercise any political authority. No person shall be compelled to take part in any religious act, celebration, rite or practice. The State and its organs shall refrain from religious education or any other religious activity" (Cabinet Office of Japan, "The Constitution of Japan," May 3, 1947, http://www.kantei.go.jp/foreign/constitution_and_government _of_japan/constitution_e.html).

27. Religious groups in Japan, including other Shinto shrines, emerged as a major force of opposition to the LDP government's effort to pass legislation that made Yasukuni a national memorial. I am grateful to Ashizu Yasukuni, former editor in chief, and Maeda Takakazu, of *Jinja shinpō*, for their insights into the postwar evolution of Shinto religious organzations (interview with author, June 23, 2009).

28. *Nikkei shinbun*, July 20, 2006.

29. The special status of interring (*gōshi*) Japan's war dead at Yasukuni came from the fact that the emperor himself paid tribute there until 1945.

During the enshrinement rites, Yasukuni's head priest would add the names of the war dead to a book of souls, thereby symbolically changing the soul's status to that of a national deity (rather than being attached to a particular household). The emperor would receive a sprig of the *sakaki* plant (considered sacred in Shinto) from the head priest, which he would hold for some time before the priest would place the plant on the altar. For more information, see Helen Hardacre, *Shinto and the State, 1868–1988* (Princeton, N.J.: Princeton University Press, 1989); and Mike M. Mochizuki, "The Yasukuni Shrine Conundrum: Japan's Contested Identity and Memory," in *Northeast Asia's Difficult Past: Essays in Collective Memory*, ed. Mikyoung Kim and Barry Schwartz (New York: Palgrave Macmillan, 2010).

30. This division of labor between former Imperial Army and Navy officers in the postwar management of veterans' affairs continued until April 1, 1956, when only one deputy was deemed necessary. In 1974, the deputy system was abolished (Repatriation and Relief Bureau, Ministry of Health and Welfare, *Hikiage to engo sanjū-nen no ayumi*, 30).

31. Hatsumi also played a critical role in rebuilding Japan's navy after it was disbanded in the early Occupation years. He was a founding member of the "Y Committee" of former Imperial Navy officers who quietly worked during the Occupation to design what became the postwar Maritime Self-Defense Force. See Atsushi Koketsu, *Nihon kaigun no shusen kosaku—ajia taiheiyō sensō no saikensho* [*Japanese Navy's Work at the End of the War—Inspecting the Asia Pacific War Again*] (Tokyo: Chūko shinsho, 1996).

32. The limitations of Japan's military under the postwar constitution are described in the annual white paper *Defense of Japan*, and the exclusive self-defense mission was included in the SDF Establishment Law of 1954. For the official explanation of this relationship between the constitution and Japan's self-defense right today, as well as a record of government interpretation of how this affects decisions regarding the SDF's military capability and Japan's use of force, see Ministry of Defense, Japan, *Nihon no bōei, heisei 23-nen* [*Defense of Japan 2011*] (Tokyo: Ministry of Defense, 2011), 145–46.

33. Umezawa Jirō, Personnel Affairs and Pension Bureau, Ministry of Internal Affairs and Communications, interview with author, June 17, 2011.

34. I am grateful to the staff of the Izokukai for their assistance with my research. In particular, I would like to thank Morita Tsuguo, vice president of Nihon izokukai, for his time (interview with author, June 30, 2009).

35. *Nihon izokukai no 40-nen* [*40 Years of the Bereaved Families of Japan's War Veterans*] (Tokyo: Nihon izokukai, 1987).
36. In 1952, the Law for the Relief of Wounded and Deceased Soldiers and Their Families was adopted. Japan's Law for State Pensions, which has been in place since 1923, was revised that same year to take into account the needs of the military personnel who had fought in World War II.
37. *Nihon izokukai no 40-nen*, 187.
38. Ibid., 188.
39. In the following pages, the supporters of the Izokukai are on display—the minister of Internal Affairs, the Ministry of Health and Welfare, the senior adviser of the LDP and Upper House legislator, the head priest of the Yasukuni Shrine, and the well-known son of the prewar army minister, Upper House member Itagaki Tadashi.
40. For the past leadership of the Izokukai since its creation in 1948 to 1985, see *Nihon izokukai no 40-nen*, 185.
41. *Mainichi shinbun*, July 20, 2005.
42. "Rensai—owaranai meiro 'yasukuni' to ha nanika, 2/senbotsusha no tsumatachi/katsudo no chukaku" [Serial—The Never-Ending Maze: What Is Yasukuni? Part 2 / The Wives of Those Who Have Fallen in Battle / The Core of Their Activities], *Tōoku nippō*, August 8, 2006, 2.
43. *Asahi shinbun*, September 4, 1999.
44. *Asahi shinbun*, June 25, 2001. Chief Cabinet Secretary Abe Shintarō explained this position to the Upper House Cabinet Standing Committee on August 17, 1978, and again on October 17 that year. See Kokkai kaigiroku kensaku shisutemu [National Diet Minutes Search System], "Remarks from Abe Shintarō, Cabinet Standing Committee, House of Councillors," August 17, 1978, and October 17, 1978, http://kokkai.ndl .go.jp/.
45. Translated and paraphrased from Matsudaira Nagayoshi, "Dare ga mitama wo yogoshita no ka—yasukuni hōshi jūyonen no munen" [Who Dishonored the Spirit of the Dead: Regrets from Fourteen Years of Yasukuni Service], *Shokun, Bungei shunjū*, December 5, 1992.
46. Prime Minister Ōhira Masayoshi, Fukuda's successor, did not visit the Yasukuni Shrine on August 15. Instead, Ōhira visited during the shrine's spring rites.
47. Cabinet Office of Japan, "Naikaku sōri daijin sono hokano kokumu daijin ni yoru yasukuni jinja no kōshiki sanpai ni tsuite no seifu toitsu kenkai, shugiin giin uneiiinkai rijikai ni okeru Miyazawa naikaku kanbō chōkan no setsumei" [Prime Minister of Japan's Opinion on Other State

Ministers Making an Official Visit to Yasukuni Shrine—Explanation from the Chief Cabinet Secretary in the Lower House], November 17, 1980, http://www.kantei.go.jp/jp/singi/tuitou/dai2/siryo1_5.html.

48. Hu Yaobang, "Create a New Situation in All Fields of Socialist Modernization," Report to the Twelfth National Congress of the Communist Party of China, September 1, 1982, Chinese Communist Party archives, http://cpc.people.com.cn/GB/64162/64168/64565/65448/4526432.html. In the speech, Hu says: "Xiànzài rìběn yǒuxiē shìlì hái zài měihuà guòqù qīnlüè zhōngguó hé dōng yǎ qítā guójiā de shǐshí, bìngqiě jìnxíng zhǒngzhǒng huódòng, wàngtú fùhuó rìběn jūnguó zhǔyì" (These days, Japan is beautifying its past aggression against China and other East Asian countries. It is carrying out activities that show the revival of Japanese militarism.)

49. *Nikkei shinbun*, August 15, 1983.

50. This study group led by Chief Cabinet Secretary Fujinami Takao was clearly aiming at gaining a consensus on the idea of making the Yasukuni Shrine visits official. In his visit to the shrine on August 15 the following year, Fujinami reportedly told a group of more than 150 Izokukai members gathered at Yasukuni that he would make every effort to guide the Cabinet Study Group—formed as a result of a strong desire by the Japanese people to have official state visits to Yasukuni—toward the correct conclusion (*Nikkei shinbun*, August 15, 1986).

51. Nakasone Yasuhiro, "50-nen no sengo seiji wo kataru" [Talking About Politics 50 Years After the End of the War] (Tokyo: Bungei shunjū, 1996), 489–97; and interview with author, June 30, 2012.

52. On August 14, a Chinese Foreign Ministry spokesperson said that any visit by the Japanese prime minister would "seriously hurt the feelings" of people in the Asia Pacific who were the victims of Japanese militarism (*Nikkei shinbun*, August 15, 1985).

53. *NHK News*, August 27 and 29, 1985.

54. Ministry of Foreign Affairs of Japan, "Statement by Chief Cabinet Secretary Masaharu Gotoda on Official Visits to Yasukuni Shrine by the Prime Minister and Other State Ministers on August 15 of This Year," August 14, 1986, http://www.mofa.go.jp/policy/postwar/state8608.html.

55. *Nikkei shinbun*, August 16, 1986.

56. The distinction made between visits of Japanese government officials in their "private capacity" and visits made as representatives of the Japanese state dates back to the Occupation. Japanese leaders argued strenuously for the right to pay homage to the country's war dead at the

Yasukuni Shrine, and eventually the Occupation authorities recognized only those visits that would not challenge the new constitution's separation of church and state. The idea was that as a private citizen, an individual Japanese person could visit any religious site.

57. During a meeting with President Bush on November 16, 2005, Prime Minister Koizumi was quoted as saying in regard to the Yasukuni Shrine visits, "I will never stop, even if asked by the United States not to" (Kyodo News, January 22, 2006).

58. The widespread belief that this was the first encounter by Koizumi with the kamikaze experience is mistaken. By his own admission, Koizumi was deeply moved by the book *Ah, dōki no sakura*, an account by those from the Imperial Navy's fourteenth class of reserve air cadets who survived the war. This reference was found in a 1983 campaign pamphlet put out by Koizumi's campaign office (*Mainichi shinbun*, August 9, 2001).

59. This was reportedly the first time a Japan leader had used the word *owabi*, "apology," and Koizumi also had no problem with describing the Marco Polo Bridge incident as Japan's invasion of China. Other Japanese conservatives—most notably, Abe Shinzō—continued to challenge this characterization of Japanese military activities in China. Appearing before the Upper House in April 2013, Abe responded to a question from a conservative member of his own party, Maruyama Kazuya, about whether he would consider revising the Murayama statement by saying, "The definition of what constitutes aggression has yet to be established in academia or the international community. Things that happened between nations will look different depending on which side you view them from" (Kokkai kaigiroku kensaku shisutemu [National Diet Minutes Search System], "Remarks by Abe Shinzō, Budget Committee, House of Councillors, Japan," April 23, 2013, http://kokkai.ndl.go.jp/). English translation is courtesy of "Shinzo Abe's Inability to Face History," *Washington Post*, April 26, 2013.

60. *Nikkei shinbun*, October 9, 2001.

61. *Asahi shinbun*, October 9, 2001.

62. *Tōkyō shinbun*, August 16, 2001.

63. *Tōkyō shinbun*, April 20, 2002.

64. When Koizumi made subsequent visits, he couched them in cultural terms rather than as commemoration for Japan's war dead. In 2003 and 2004, he visited in January, a time when most Japanese visit Shinto shrines. He stated in 2003 that he wanted to visit Yasukuni in a "refresh-

ing New Year" mood; likewise, in 2004, he noted that he would not criticize other countries' cultural practices. Both times he reiterated his desire to improve relations with China and South Korea (*Asahi shinbun*, January 14, 2003; NHK News, January 14, 2003; *Nikkei shinbun*, January 15, 2003). For the 2004 visit, see *Asahi shinbun*, January 3, including a long Q&A session with the prime minister.

65. "China Ready to Push Forward Ties with Japan: Hu," *People's Daily*, October 21, 2003, http://english.peopledaily.com.cn/200310/21/eng20031021 _126478.shtml; Ministry of Foreign Affairs, Japan, "Outline of New Japan-China Friendship Committee for the 21st Century," July 2005, http://www.mofa.go.jp/region/asia-paci/china/committee050.html.

66. Ministry of Foreign Affairs, People's Republic of China, "President Hu Jintao Meets with Japanese Prime Minister Koizumi," November 23, 2004, http://www.fmprc.gov.cn/eng/topics/huvisit/t171653.htm.

67. By April 2005, when Koizumi and Hu met next in Jakarta for the Asia-Africa Summit, Hu was far more pessimistic about the relationship (Ministry of Foreign Affairs, People's Republic of China, "Hu Jintao Meets with Japanese Prime Minister Junichiro Koizumi," April 24, 2005, http://www.fmprc.gov.cn/eng/topics/hjtfw/t193911.shtml).

68. Koizumi was backtracking significantly in 2005, shedding all pretense of an "official" visit and retreating to the idea that he was visiting only in his "private capacity." He was being increasingly criticized by his own party and reportedly told the LDP's Diet Affairs Committee chairman, Nakagawa Hidenao, that he would visit only during the autumn festival. See the media coverage of the 2005 visit in *Nikkei shinbun*, October 17, 2005; *Asahi shinbun*, October 17, 2005; and the critical *Asahi shinbun* editorial on October 17, 2005.

69. Iwai Ichirō, Planning Section, Relief Bureau, Ministry of Health, Labor, and Welfare, June 17, 2011. See also Ministry of Health, Labor, and Welfare, "Engo gyōsei no gaiyō ni tsuite" [Outline of the Relief Administration], interview with author, June 2011.

70. Cabinet Office of Japan, "Hōkokusho—tsuitō heiwakinen no tame no kinenhi nado shisetsu no arikata wo kangaeru kondankai" [A Panel Discussion Regarding the Establishment of a Monument for Memorial Prayer], December 24, 2002, http://www.kantei.go.jp/jp/singi/tuitou /kettei/021224houkoku.html (accessed April 29, 2011).

71. Interview with author, June 30, 2011.

72. Kyodo News, January 4, 2004.

73. *Asahi shinbun*, January 7, 2004.

74. Interview with author, June 30, 2011.

75. *Asahi shinbun*, August 9, 2002.

76. Koga was clear on his personal view of Yasukuni's role, however. The shrine was the only place where Japan's war dead should be memorialized. He saw no need for an alternative site and opposed Fukuda Yasuo's private study group to find a new memorial. His father fought in World War II, and for Koga, the way forward was to find a way for Japan's emperor to visit Yasukuni and to sustain annual prime ministerial visits to honor those who died fighting for their country (interview with author, June 25, 2009).

77. Interview with author, June 25, 2009.

78. Fukuda later acknowledged that his decision not to run was based on his desire to avoid having the Yasukuni issue be at the forefront of the national political debate (interview with author, June 30, 2011).

79. *Nikkei shinbun*, July 20, 2006.

80. Yasuoka Takashi, senior staff writer and editorial writer, and Inoue Makoto, senior staff writer, City News Department, Editorial Bureau, *Nikkei shinbun*, interview with author, June 23, 2009.

81. Indeed, Emperor Akihito has been seen as a more outspoken voice on Japan's prewar excesses, and his visits to China, Saipan, and Hawaii to demonstrate Japan's remorse have been widely seen as symbolizing Japan's new commitment to refuting the military adventures of the past. See Ministry of Foreign Affairs, Japan, "Remarks by H.M. the Emperor at His Departure for Saipan," June 27, 2005, http://www.mofa.go.jp/announce/announce/2005/6/0627.html.

82. Hosaka Masayasu, one of the three experts that examined the Tomita memo, interview with author, June 25, 2009. For more information, see works by Hosaka such as *Shōwashi nanatsu no nazo* [*History of the Shōwa Period: Seven Puzzles*] (Tokyo: Kodansha, 2003), and *Shōwashi no taiga wo iku 1—yasukuni to iu nayami* [*History of the Shōwa Period, the River Flows no. 1—The Trouble Called "Yasukuni"*] (Tokyo: Chūō kōron shinsha, 2013).

83. See, for example, *Nikkei shinbun*, August 15, 2006.

84. Miyazawa Yoshihiro, head of Public Relations Division, and Ogata Takatsugu, head of General Affairs Department, Yasukuni Shrine, interview with author, June 23, 2009.

85. See, for example, *Asahi shinbun*, August 10, 2001; and *Yomiuri shinbun*, August 6, 2005.

86. Interest in the Yūshūkan, the newly revamped war museum on the Yasukuni premises, rose as the narrative it presented received worldwide

attention. The museum, funded by private donations, proudly displays a revisionist account of responsibility for World War II. Translated into several languages, the accessibility of this narrative to foreign visitors makes this a site of interest to overseas media and other interested observers of postwar Japan. Criticism is intense, and it comes not only from Chinese and Korean visitors but also from Americans who challenge the version of the facts presented at the Yasukuni site. "Yūshūkan," http://www.yasukuni.jp/~yusyukan/ (accessed March 2014).

87. Another group related to veterans' affairs also was on the list—the Onseiren (Gunon renmei zenkoku rengōkai), an organization focusing exclusively on veterans' compensation. This group claimed 167,000 LDP party members, and thus the combined the LDP party membership organized around veterans' interests (304,000 LDP party members) remained at the top of the party's list of supporters.

88. *Asahi shinbun*, September 4, 1999.

89. According to article 11 of the San Francisco Peace Treaty,

> The power to grant clemency, to reduce sentences, and to parole with respect to such prisoners may not be exercised except on the decision of the Government or Governments which imposed the sentence in each instance, and on recommendation of Japan. In the case of persons sentenced by the International Military Tribunal for the Far East, such power may not be exercised except on the decision of a majority of the Governments represented on the Tribunal, and on the recommendation of Japan. (Treaty of Peace with Japan, signed in San Francisco, September 8, 1951, and entered into force on April 28, 1952, http://www.taiwandocuments.org/sanfrancisco01.htm)

> The Japanese Diet formally implemented these provisions under domestic law on the same day the San Francisco Peace Treaty went into effect. See House of Representatives, Japan, Heiwa jōyaku dai jūichi jō ni yoru kei no shikkō oyobi shamen tō ni kansuru hōritsu [Law Concerning the Execution of Sentences and Pardons Under Article 11 of the San Francisco Peace Treaty], Law no. 103, April 28, 1952, http://www.shugiin.go.jp/itdb_housei.nsf/html/houritsu/01319520428103.htm.

90. The Japanese government had to consult with foreign governments, most notably the United States, in order to change the legal status of the "war criminals." On September 4, 1952, President Harry Truman took the first step in absolving some of those citizens by issuing Executive Order 10393, which established the Clemency and Parole Board for War Criminals to advise the president on "recommendation by the Government of Japan for clemency, reduction of sentence, or parole, with respect to sentences imposed on Japanese war criminals" (White House,

Executive Order 10393: Establishment of the Clemency and Parole Board for War Criminals, September 4, 1952, available online at http://www .presidency.ucsb.edu/ws/index.php?pid=78495).

91. In 1952, the Japanese government began to address the legal status of those Japanese found guilty under the War Crimes Tribunal, and it passed two resolutions: House of Councillors, Japan, Senpan zaishosha no shakuhō tō ni kansuru ketsugian (Resolution Concerning the Release of War Criminals), June 9, 1952, http://kokkai.ndl.go.jp/SENTAKU/sangiin /013/0512/01306090512049c.html; and House of Representatives, Sensō hanzai ni yoru jūkeisha no shakuhō tō ni kansuru ketsugian [Resolution Concerning the Release of Prisoners Convicted of War Crimes], December 9, 1952, http://kokkai.ndl.go.jp/SENTAKU/syugiin/015/0512 /01512090512011c.html. The discussion continued throughout the 1950s, and two more resolutions were passed by the House of Representatives in 1953 and 1955: Sensō hanzai ni yoru jūkeisha no shamen ni kansuru ketsugian [Resolution Concerning the Parole of Prisoners Convicted of War Crimes], August 3, 1953, http://kokkai.ndl.go.jp/SENTAKU/syugiin /016/0512/01608030512035c.html; and Sensō jūkeisha no sokuji shakuhō yōsei ni kansuru ketsugian [Resolution Calling for the Prompt Release of All War Prisoners], July 19, 1955, http://kokkai.ndl.go.jp/SENTAKU /syugiin/022/0512/02207190512043c.html.

The last class-A war criminal was paroled on March 31, 1956, and pardoned on April 7, 1958. The final eighty-three class-B/C war criminals were released on December 29, 1958, alongside an official pardon for all class-B/C war criminals (*Yomiuri shinbun*, June 14, 1998). In 1962 the Japanese Diet abolished the 1952 domestic law pertaining to article 11 of the San Francisco Peace Treaty. See House of Representatives, Heiwa jōyaku dai jūichi jō ni yoru kei no shikkō oyobi shamen tō ni kansuru hōritsu wo haishisuru hōritsu [Law Abolishing the Law Concerning the Execution of Sentences and Pardons Under Article 11 of the San Francisco Peace Treaty], March 29, 1962.

92. "Yasukuni" to Koizumi Shusho: Watanabe Tsuneo, *Yomiuri shinbun* Shuhitsu vs. Wakamiya Yoshibumi, *Asahi shinbun* ronsetsu shukan ("Yasukuni" and Prime Minister Koizumi: Watanabe Tsuneo, *Yomiuri shinbun* Editor in Chief vs. Wakamiya Yoshibumi, *Asahi shinbun* Chief Editorial Editor) (Tokyo: *Asahi shinbun*, 2006).

93. Watanabe Tsuneo, foreword to *From Marco Polo Bridge to Pearl Harbor: Who Was Responsible?* ed. James E. Auer (Tokyo: Yomiuri shinbun, 2006).

94. The three parliamentary secretaries were Morita Takashi of General Affairs, Hamada Kazuyuki of the Internal Affairs Ministry, and Sasa Katsushi of the Ministry of Culture and Education (*Mainichi shinbun*, August 16, 2011).

95. Noda's questions can be found at the official website of the House of Representatives, Japan, "Senpan ni taisuru ninshiki to naikaku sōri daijin no yasukuni jinja sanpai ni kansuru shitsumon shuisho" [Questions on the Recognition of War Criminals and the Prime Minister's Visits to Yasukuni Shrine], October 17, 2005, http://www.shugiin.go.jp/itdb _shitsumon.nsf/html/shitsumon/a163021.htm. The Koizumi cabinet's response can be found on the same website at "Senpan ni taisuru ninshiki to naikaku sōri daijin no yasukuni jinja sanpai ni kansuru shitsumon ni taishi, besshi tōbensho wo sōfusuru" [A Written Response to the Questions on the Recognition of War Criminals and the Prime Minister's Visits to Yasukuni Shrine], October 25, 2005, http://www.shugiin .go.jp/itdb_shitsumon.nsf/html/shitsumon/a163021.htm.

96. *Nikkei shinbun*, September 2, 2011.

97. *Asahi shinbun*, April 23, 2013.

4. A SHARED MARITIME BOUNDARY

1. *NHK News,* August 1, 2013. Prime Minister Abe stated that this report urged an obvious course of action for Japan and that his government was taking appropriate actions. But he also encouraged Yamamoto and the LDP to continue to address the problem "with loud voices" to draw attention to Japan's problem.

2. Cabinet Office of Japan, "Press Conference by the Chief Cabinet Secretary," July 3, 2013, http://www.kantei.go.jp/foreign/tyoukanpress/201307/03_a .html.

3. "Exclusive: China in $5 Billion Drive to Develop Disputed East China Sea Gas," Reuters, July 17, 2013, http://www.reuters.com/article/2013/07/17 /us-cnooc-eastchinasea-idUSBRE96G0BA20130717.

4. CNOOC Chairman Wang Yilin spoke on August 20, 2013, at a press conference in Hong Kong, where he announced that the oil company had grown 7.9 percent, outperforming expectations (*South China Morning Post*, August 21, 2013). After the press conference, a Japanese reporter from the *Nikkei shinbun* asked Wang about the CNOOC's plans to develop seven new gas fields in the East China Sea. Wang stated that he had no knowledge of the plans but that if the Reuters report were true, then it would certainly be of interest (*Nikkei shinbun*, August 21, 2013).

5. For his analysis of the UNCLOS deliberations and the Japan-China maritime boundary dispute in the East China Sea, I am indebted to Mark E. Rosen of the Center for Naval Analyses (CNA) and his "Conflicting Claims in the East China Sea," presented at the Yellow and East China Seas Workshop, CNA Maritime Asia Project, May 2, 2012.

6. Vice-Premier Deng Xiaoping met with a broad range of Japanese on his visit to Japan in October 1978, including many individuals and groups that had sustained the Japan-China relationship before normalization. At the Japan National Press Center, in front of more than four hundred Japanese and foreign journalists on October 25, Deng answered a question from a Japanese journalist on the Senkaku/Diaoyu Islands, saying that it was wise to put this question aside:

> Our two sides agreed not to touch upon this question when diplomatic relations were normalized between Chain and Japan. This time when we were negotiating the Treaty of Peace and Friendship, the two sides again agreed not to touch on it. Some people seek to pick faults on this kind of question in an attempt to hinder the development of Sino-Japanese relations. (*Peking Review*, November 3, 1978, 16)

7. For a full discussion of the complexities of East China Sea legal battles over maritime energy resources, see Clive Schofield, ed., *Maritime Energy Resources in Asia: Legal Regimes and Cooperation*, National Bureau of Asian Research (NBR) Special Report no. 37 (Seattle: NBR, February 2012).

8. The MEXT is home to the Japan Agency for Marine-Earth Science and Technology (JAMSTEC), and the METI is home to the Japan Oil, Gas, and Metals National Corporation (JOGMEC). Both agencies conduct maritime research and have their own vessels as well as commissioned vessels that they use to conduct research and surveys. The MEXT has several research centers and is responsible for a wide variety of maritime research related to marine biology and marine technology development. The METI focuses on energy resource develop and the development of technology for seabed exploration and drilling. For more information, see "Japan Agency for Marine-Earth Science and Technology," http://www.jamstec.go.jp/e/index.html; and "Japan Oil, Gas, and Metals National Corporation," http://www.jogmec.go.jp/english/index.html (accessed October 7, 2013).

9. The Japan Fisheries Agency was the main bureaucracy associated with fisheries research, but not the only one. Nine separate government agencies were conducting fisheries research until 2000, when a government-

wide consolidation effort brought them all under one roof and the Fisheries Research Agency was created. For more information, see "Fisheries Research Agency," http://www.fra.affrc.go.jp/english/eindex .html (accessed October 7, 2013).

10. Kokubun Ryōsei et al., eds., *Nichū kankeishi* [*Modern History of Japan-China Relations*] (Tokyo: Yuhikaku, 2013).

11. *Mainichi shinbun*, May 27, 1978.

12. *Peking Review*, November 3, 1978, 16.

13. Ministry of Foreign Affairs, Japan, "Joint Communiqué of the Government of Japan and the Government of the People's Republic of China," September 29, 1972, http://www.mofa.go.jp/region/asia-paci/china /joint72.html.

14. "Statement of the Ministry of Foreign Affairs of the People's Republic of China," December 30, 1971; English translation in *Peking Review*, January 7, 1972, 12. On June 17, 1971, the U.S.-Japan Okinawa Reversion Agreement was concluded, which included the Senkakus, and thus their administration was transferred back to Japan.

15. The full text of the Japanese statement can be found at Ministry of Foreign Affairs, Japan, "The Basic View of the Sovereignty over the Senkaku Islands," http://www.mofa.go.jp/region/asia-paci/senkaku/senkaku.html (accessed October 2013).

16. Traditionally, coastal nations could claim three miles of coastal waters as their sovereign territory. In the twentieth century, concerns about fish stocks and mineral resources led to an extension of claims beyond three miles. In 1945, President Harry Truman claimed control over all the natural resources on the U.S. continental shelf, and other nations followed suit. Others in Latin America extended their rights to two hundred nautical miles because of the fisheries stocks in the Humboldt Current fishing grounds. But until the UNCLOS was concluded in 1982, the majority of nations used either the traditional three-mile limit or the twelve-mile limit.

17. Although *Yomiuri* reported that the Japanese government asked China to obtain consent before conducting any further surveillance activities inside Japan's EEZ, *Sankei* reported another Chinese vessel off the coast of Nagasaki Prefecture passing through the Osumi Strait between Tanegashima Island and Kagoshima City yet again in July (*Asahi shinbun*, May 31, 2000; *Sankei shinbun*, July 15, 2000).

18. Ministry of Foreign Affairs, Japan, "Japan-China Foreign Ministers Meeting," August 28, 2000, http://www.mofa.go.jp/region/asia-paci/china /fmv0008/meet_4.html.

19. Ministry of Foreign Affairs, Japan, "Japan-China Relations," *Diplomatic Bluebook 2001*, chap. 1, General Overview, 2001, http://www.mofa.go.jp /policy/other/bluebook/2001/chap1-d.html.

20. A 3,536-ton Chinese research ship was identified sailing north of the Okinotori Islands inside Japan's EEZ on October 17, and then two days later, it was found echo-sounding in Japanese territorial waters off the coast of the Tokara Islands. *Sankei* reported that the Japanese Maritime Self-Defense Force relayed this information to the Ministry of Foreign Affairs and the Japan Coast Guard. According to this report, the Japan Coast Guard sent an aircraft to warn the Chinese ship but got no response (*Sankei shinbun*, October 20, 2003).

21. Foreign Press Center, Japan, "China Gas Field Development in the East China Sea Emerges as a New Sore in Bilateral Relations," November 1, 2004, http://fpcj.jp/old/e/mres/japanbrief/jb_90.html (accessed April 15, 2012).

22. *Nikkei shinbun*, June 29, 2004.

23. Teikoku Oil Co., "Higashi shinakai ni okeru shikutsuken no settei ni tsuite" [Regarding Establishing a Claim on Mining Rights in the East China Sea], press statement, July 14, 2005.

24. *Asahi shinbun*, May 8, 2008.

25. On June 20, 1996, Japan became the ninety-fourth country to ratify the 1982 United Nations Convention on the Law of the Sea (UNCLOS). China had ratified it just a few weeks earlier.

26. Ministry of Foreign Affairs, Japan, *Diplomatic Bluebook 2006*, 43.

27. The Commission on the Limits of the Continental Shelf (CLCS) reviews scientific data for those states claiming a continental shelf as the basis of their EEZ demarcation, rather than the standard two hundred nautical miles from their coastline. This is permitted under article 76 of the UNCLOS. Japan submitted its report to the CLCS on November 12, 2008 ("Japan's Submission to the Commission on the Limits of the Continental Shelf," Commission on the Limits of the Continental Shelf, United Nations, November 12, 2008, http://www.un.org/depts/los/clcs _new/submissions_files/submission_jpn.htm).

28. "Preliminary Information Indicative of the Outer Limits of the Continental Shelf Beyond 200 Nautical Miles of the People's Republic of China," Commission on the Limits of the Continental Shelf, United Nations, May 11, 2009, http://www.un.org/depts/los/clcs_new/submissions_files /preliminary/chn2009preliminaryinformation_english.pdf. In the midst of the 2012 diplomatic crisis, China submitted further information on its claim ("Partial Submission by the People's Republic of China

Concerning the Outer Limits of the Continental Shelf Beyond 200 Nautical Miles in Part of the East China Sea," Commission on the Limits of the Continental Shelf, United Nations, December 14, 2012, http://www.un.org/depts/los/clcs_new/submissions_files/submission _chn_63_2012.htm).

29. Japan Fisheries Agency, *Suisanchō 50-nen shi* [*Japan Fisheries Agency: 50 Years*] (Tokyo: Dai Nihon suisankai, 1999).

30. The Japan-China Private Sector Trade Agreement was concluded by Diet members Takara Tomi, Hoashi Kei, and Miyakoshi Kisuke during a visit to Beijing on their return from the International Economic Conference convened in Moscow in June 1952 (Dai ichiji nitchū minkan bōeki kyōtei [First Japan-China Private-Sector Trade Agreement], June 1, 1952, available from the archives of Tokyo University Institute of Oriental Culture's World and Japan Database, http://www.ioc.u-tokyo .ac.jp/~worldjpn/documents/texts/JPCH/19520601.T1J.html).

31. This group included some of the representatives from the seven groups that had made the initial overture to China in late 1952. The groups are Dai Nihon suisankai, Nihon enjōkai gyogyōkai, Zenkoku gyogyō kyōdō kumiai rengōkai, Zen Nihon kaiin kumiai, Suisan seitō ryōdō kumian kyōgikai, Suisan kenkyūkai, and Nitchū gyogyō kondankai (*Suisancho 50-nen shi*, 111).

32. China had designated the entry to the Yellow Sea as a military zone and the coastal region around the Shanghai open sea as a maritime region where trawlers would be prohibited. As a result, Japanese fishing boats would not be allowed to fish in these areas (Ministry of Foreign Affairs, Japan, "Nihonkoku to chūka jinmin kyōwakoku to no aida no gyogyō ni kansuru kyōtei" [Fisheries Agreement Between Japan and the People's Republic of China], August 15, 1975, http://www3.mofa .go.jp/mofaj/gaiko/treaty/pdf/A-S50–119.pdf. An amendment to this agreement was signed on January 16, 1979, and came into force on February 20, 1979 (Ministry of Foreign Affairs, Japan, "Nihonkoku to chūka jinmin kyōwakoku to no aida no gyogyō ni kansuru kyōtei no fuzokusho no shūsei kankoku no jūtaku ni kansuru kōkan kōbun" [Accepted Supplementary Notes to the Fisheries Agreement Between Japan and the People's Republic of China], August 15, 1975, http://www3 .mofa.go.jp/mofaj/gaiko/treaty/pdf/A-S54–251.pdf).

33. *Suisancho 50-nen shi*, 250–51.

34. The new agreement was initially signed on November 11, 1997, and entered into force on June 1, 2000 (Ministry of Foreign Affairs, Japan,

"Gyogyō ni kansuru nihonkoku to chūka jinmin kyōwakoku to no aida no kyōtei" [Fisheries Agreement Between Japan and the People's Republic of China], June 1, 2000, http://www3.mofa.go.jp/mofaj/gaiko/treaty /pdf/A-H12–343.pdf).

35. Statistics provided by the Shige Yoshiyuki, Senior Executive Managing Director, Japan Fisheries Association, interview with author, Tokyo, June 2011.

36. According to Shige Yoshiyuki, Japan's total proceeds from fisheries in 2008 were ¥16,274,670,000, of which ¥1,674,040,000 came from East China Sea catch (interview with author, June 21, 2011).

37. See, for example, *China Daily*, July 4, 2011.

38. Uehara Kameichi, head of the Yaeyama Fisheries Cooperative, interview with author, June 27, 2011.

39. Japan's economic growth in the 1960s translated into a huge demand for oil and other energy sources. By the end of the decade, with no oil resources of its own, Japan became the world's largest importer of oil. In 1971, it was consuming 4.4 million barrels a day, 85 percent of which was imported. In contrast, the United States was consuming 15.5 million barrels a day, and West Germany, 3.1 million. Thus Japan's push for expanding access to oil around the globe in this era was viewed much as China's global search for energy resources is today. In the early 1970s, however, China was consuming roughly 525,000 barrels a day—one-eighth of Japan's consumption at the time ("Oil for Japan: A Global Project," *New York Times*, April 9, 1972).

40. The participants were K. O. Emery (Woods Hole Oceanographic Institution, United States), Yoshikazu Hayashi (Japan Petroleum Development Corporation, Japan), Thomas W. C. Hilde (Pacific Support Group, U.S. Naval Oceanographic Office, San Diego, United States), Kazuo Kobayashi (Japan Petroleum Development Corporation, Japan), Ja Hak Koo (Geological Survey of Korea, Republic of Korea), C. Y. Meng (Chinese Petroleum Corporation, Taibei, Taiwan), Hiroshi Niino (Tokyo University of Fisheries, Japan), J. H. Osterhagen (Pacific Support Group, U.S. Naval Oceanographic Office, San Diego, United States), L. M. Reynolds (Pacific Support Group, U.S. Naval Oceanographic Office, San Diego, United States), John M. Wageman (Pacific Support Group, U.S. Naval Oceanographic Office, San Diego, United States), C. S. Wang (National Taiwan University, Taibei, Taiwan), and Sung Jin Yang (Geological Survey of Korea, Republic of Korea) ("Geological Structure and Some Water Characteristics of the East China Sea and the Yellow Sea," *CCOP Technical Bulletin*, May 1969).

41. *CCOP Technical Bulletin*, May 1969, 41.

42. A December 5, 1970, report out of Hong Kong carried by the *New York Times* notes that Taiwan's government awarded contracts in the continental shelf area around the Senkakus to the American Gulf Oil Company and rights elsewhere along China's continental shelf to the Clinton and Amoco Oil companies. South Korea gave concessions to Wendell Phillips, Gulf, Imperial, and Royal Dutch Shell along the continental shelf off Korea, and Japan Oil Development Corporation was moving forward with exploration along the same areas ("Peking Claims Disputed Oil-Rich Isles," *New York Times*, December 6, 1970).

43. An Okinawan, Koju Omija, had already filed survey data and applied to the Japanese government for exploration rights. Following suit, the Japan Petroleum Corporation also filed thousands of applications for drilling rights. The Japanese government began to survey the area in June 1969 and reportedly began its study of the waters within a three-mile radius of the Senkakus. At the time it was thought that drilling would begin four or five years later ("Deposit Is Sought in East China Sea," *New York Times*, May 17, 1969).

44. "Oil Under East China Sea Is the Crux of 3-Nation Issues," *New York Times*, January 30, 1971.

45. *Peking Review*, January 7, 1972, 12.

46. To this day, with the Japanese government's permission, the U.S. military uses the bombing ranges on Kubajima.

47. Transcripts of the U.S.-PRC negotiations are not available to the public, so it is difficult to know if, and how, the Senkaku sovereignty dispute may have emerged in that conversation. Nonetheless, the conversation between the Nixon administration and the government of Chiang Kai-shek in Taibei is available, and the Office of the Historian in the U.S. Department of State has published several detailed discussions among President Nixon, Assistant for National Security Affairs Henry Kissinger, and other senior government officials that clearly show Taiwan's influence on their thinking (Foreign Relations of the United States, *China, 1969–1972*, Office of the Historian, U.S. Department of State 17, nos. 106, 109, 114, 115, 133, 134, 180, 327, 427, and 431, 1969–1972, http://history .state.gov/historicaldocuments/frus1969–76v17).

48. State Department press officer Charles Bray said that in March 1971 the State Department advised the Gulf Oil Company, Caltex, Amoco, the Clinton Oil Company of New York, and the Oceanic Exploration Company of Denver that they could be in a vulnerable position. Bray said that the State Department has

advised the oil companies to the danger of operating in those areas and of our desire to avoid any incident that would put American lives in jeopardy or create tension in the area. We have informed the American companies we consider it undesirable to undertake operations in these disputed areas. (Murrey Marder, "U.S. Cautions Oil Seekers near China," *Washington Post*, April 10, 1971, and "U.S. Warns Oil Firms Against Explorations Near Taiwan," Associated Press, April 10, 1971)

49. "Oil Hunt off China Stirs U.S. Warning," *New York Times*, April 10, 1971.
50. The demonstrations were held in Washington, San Francisco, Los Angeles, Seattle, Chicago and Houston, the largest-ever Chinese demonstrations in the United States at the time. Students from U.S. college campuses across the country participated, and the media estimated around two thousand participants ("U.S. Chinese Ask Backing on Isles," *New York Times*, April 12, 1971).
51. The demonstrations prompted the government in Taibei to raise the Senkaku sovereignty dispute with President Nixon and National Security Adviser Kissinger. The ambassador to the United States, Chow Shu-kai, told the president that President Chiang Kai-shek was worried about the impact the Senkaku Island dispute would have on the Chinese people. According to the State Department's transcript of the meeting, Ambassador Chow stated,

    even when the Japanese had occupied Taiwan and the Ryukyus, legal matters involving the Senkakus had been handled by courts on Taiwan, and the fishing boats which went to the Senkakus had been from Taiwan. From the Japanese point of view, they didn't care how the Senkakus were administered. For the Chinese though, the issue of nationalism was deeply involved. (Foreign Relations of the United States, "Memorandum of Conversation," *China, 1969–1972*, Office of the Historian, U.S. Department of State 17, no. 114, April 12, 1971)

52. The leaders of the LDP had to call an emergency meeting in the midst of the crisis to craft a unified stance on the issue. The three-pronged position that emerged was that (1) the Senkakus were Japanese territory and the illegal activities of the Chinese fishing vessels were deeply troubling; (2) the Japanese government would convey to China that these activities must stop immediately and the ships must be withdrawn; and (3) the Japanese government would continue to work with Beijing along the lines of the Joint Statement to negotiate a treaty (*Asahi shinbun*, April 15, 1978).
53. *Asahi shinbun*, April 19, 1978.
54. *Nikkei shinbun*, April 14, 1978.

55. *Asahi shinbun*, April 20, 1978.

56. *Asahi shinbun*, April 26, 1978.

57. The budget was approved for the 1979 fiscal year, and the construction project proceeded with survey and construction planning. Contention erupted again as Japan and China approached the conclusion of the 1978 Treaty of Peace and Friendship, and in an effort to avoid conflict over building on the Senkaku Islands, the Japanese government decided to abandon the plan. For the budget decision, see *Asahi shinbun*, October 31, 1978, and for the decision to abandon the plan, see *Asahi shinbun*, April 22, 1979.

58. Moriyama Kinji, Japan's minister of transport, whose ministry oversaw the Maritime Safety Agency, announced at a press conference on January 16, 1979, that he had a green light from Foreign Minister Sonoda to proceed with his plan to construct a provisional heliport on the Senkakus (*Asahi shinbun*, January 16, 1979).

59. This survey project began in the summer of 1978 and included smaller islands in the Senkaku group as well (*Asahi shinbun*, March 31, 1979).

60. The MSA announcement was on May 28, 1979, and the Chinese protested on May 29 (*Nikkei shinbun*, May 30, 1979).

61. *Asahi shinbun*, October 14, 1990.

62. In parliament on October 12, 1990, Taiwan's president, Lee Teng-hui, warned that he would defend the Diaoyutai. On October 18, China's foreign ministry spokesman denounced the Seinensha's construction of a lighthouse and demanded that the Japanese government prevent this type of activity (*Nikkei shinbun*, October 22, 1990).

63. According to the Japan Coast Guard, Aids to Navigation Law (1949, amended in 1993),

> The term "aid to navigation" . . . shall mean a lighthouse, lighted beacon, beacon, buoy, fog signal station, radio direction finding station or any other facility which provides a guiding mark for vessels navigating in the ports, harbors, straits, and other coastal waters of Japan by means of light, shape, color, sound, electric wave, etc.

   For an English translation, see Aids to Navigation Law (Law no. 99 of 1949 as amended through Law no. 89 of 1993), Nippon Foundation Library, http://nippon.zaidan.info/seikabutsu/2001/00500/contents/00023.htm.

64. *Sankei shinbun*, September 10, 1996.

65. Okinawa had only recently come under Japan's formal jurisdiction. Okinawa was formally incorporated into Japan as a prefecture in 1879 when

the Meiji state issued the Ryukyu Dispensation (Ryūkyū shobun). This formal colonization of the Ryukyus transformed the islands into Japan's southernmost prefecture of Okinawa and opened the way for increased settlement by Japanese from the main islands of Japan. According to his son, Koga Tatsushiro, was one of these early entrepreneurs who settled in Okinawa in the early Meiji era. He moved out from Naha to establish a shop on Ishigaki Island, and it was there that he became intrigued by the stories of young fishermen and local residents about the flocks of seabirds who gathered on the Senkaku Islands. According to his son, in 1884 Tatsushiro explored these uninhabited islands, which led to Koga's appeal to the Meiji government to recognize his claim on them. See Koga Zenji, "The Senkaku Islands Are My Property," *Gendai* 6, no. 6 (1972): 142–47.

66. *Mainichi shinbun*, August 4, 1990.

67. Interview with Kunioka Kurihara's younger brother, Hiroyuki, in the weekly *Asahi geinō*, a weekly magazine known for its reporting on *yakuza* (gangsters) and other illicit activities in Japan. Under the banner headline, "We Will Never Give the Islands to China!" the two-hour-long interview with the younger brother focused on the family's relationship to the islands and the Koga family, as well as their reasons for holding on to the Senkakus.

68. *Yomiuri shinbun*, October 6, 1996.

69. For full text of the LDP announcement, see Liberal Democratic Party of Japan, "Tairikutana chōsa ni zennendohi 7-bai wo keijo, kaiyō taisaku tokubetsu iinkai—kaiyō giinrenmei godō kaigi" [Continental Shelf Survey, Special Committee on Maritime Policy, Joint Diet Members Conference on Maritime Issues], February 4, 2004, http://origin.jimin.jp/jimin/daily/04_02/04/160202e.shtml (accessed July 18, 2011).

70. For more information on China's position that its EEZ should be based on its continental shelf, see Peter Dutton, "Carving Up the East China Sea," in *China's Strategy: The Impact on Beijing's Maritime Policies*, ed. Gabriel B. Collins, Andrew S. Erickson, Lyle J. Goldstein, and William S. Murray (Annapolis, Md.: Naval Institute Press, 2008): 252–78.

71. Cabinet Office of Japan, "Press Conference by Prime Minister Junichiro Koizumi on the Passage of the FY 2004 Budget," March 26, 2004, http://www.kantei.go.jp/foreign/koizumi/speech/2004/03/26yosan_e.html.

72. Nakashima Eiichi, retired rear admiral, Japan Maritime Self-Defense Force, and commander of maritime security operation against the Han-class submarine intrusion, interviews with author, July 1, 2010, and June 26, 2011. On its website, the Japanese Maritime Self-Defense Force

(MSDF) describes its response to the Han-class submarine in explaining its mission of precautionary surveillance of Japan's surrounding waters. The website erroneously dates the event as November 10, 2005, but otherwise provides a detailed time line of Japanese MSDF activities (Ministry of Defense, Japan, "Precautionary Surveillance," http://www.mod.go.jp/msdf/formal/english/surveillance/ (accessed April 15, 2012).

73. The first time a maritime security order was issued was in the early hours of March 24, 1999, in response to incursions into Japanese waters by North Korean vessels. A North Korean (Democratic People's Republic of Korea, DPRK) ship was spotted early in the morning of March 23 by P-3C surveillance aircraft off the Noto peninsula in the Sea of Japan. After this ship was joined by another suspicious vessel, the Japan Coast Guard pursued the DPRK ships and ordered them to stop. The DPRK vessels refused to comply, and a little after midnight the Japan Coast Guard informed the MSDF that it did not have the capability to catch the ships. The cabinet then decided to mobilize the MSDF to respond. For a detailed outline of the incident, see Ministry of Defense, Japan, *Bōei handobukku, heisei 23-nen* [*Defense Handbook 2011*] (Tokyo: Asagumo shinbunsha, 2011), 227.

74. Peter Dutton, "Scouting, Signaling, and Gatekeeping: Chinese Naval Operations in Japanese Waters and the International Law Implications," U.S. Naval War College, *China Maritime Studies*, no. 2 (2009): 6.

75. See Takemi Keizō, "Kaiyō seisaku no hitsuyōsei to kinkyūsei ni tsuite" [The Necessity and Urgency of Maritime Policies], Kaiyō gijutsu fōramu [Maritime Technology Forum], "Heisei 17-nendo katsudō hōkokukai" [2006 Activities Report], July 26, 2006, 1–5.

76. Takemi Keizō, interview with author, June 29, 2011.

77. The Ministry of Economy, Trade, and Industry; the Ministry of Agriculture, Forestry, and Fisheries; the Construction and Transportation Ministries (which became the Ministry of Land, Infrastructure, Transport, and Tourism [MLIT]); the Science and Technology Agency of the Ministry of Education; and the Ministry of Defense (MOD) all had administrative responsibilities associated with Japan's maritime management.

78. Takemi, "Kaiyō seikaku," 2. As an example of this lack of awareness, Takemi gave the following example:

> When I was in the Upper House Foreign Affairs Committee, I asked about the Japanese government response to the exploratory drilling in the East China Sea by the Chinese ship, *Tankan no. 3*. The Ministry of Foreign Affairs

response to my question was simply that MoFA lodges a protest about once a
year (at the level of the Asia Pacific Bureau's Counselor). They had no greater
sense of urgency than that.

79. The bill was discussed in the Lower House Budget Committee (February 9, 2007), the Lower House Land, Infrastructure, Transport and
Tourism Committee (April 3, 2007), the Lower House Agriculture,
Forestry, and Fisheries Committee (April 10–11, 2007), and the Lower
House Foreign Affairs Committee (April 25 and June 8, 2007). It also
was discussed in the Upper House Land, Infrastructure, Transport, and
Tourism Committee on March 20 and again on April 19, 2007.

80. *Yomiuri shinbun*, April 4, 2007.

81. Basic Act on Ocean Policy (Kaiyō kihon ho) of July 20, 2007 (Cabinet Office, Japan, Basic Plan on Ocean Policy, March 2008, http://www
.kantei.go.jp/jp/singi/kaiyou/kihonkeikaku/080318kihonkeikaku_E.pdf).

82. The government outlined a comprehensive plan for implementing the
new law, which was adopted by cabinet decision on March 18, 2008.
Various bureaucracies were included, but primarily the MLIT and
the MOD were involved in the planning for protecting and defending
Japan's maritime borders and EEZ as well as developing plans for the
security of Japan's offshore islands.

83. Akiba Takeo, Ministry of Foreign Affairs, interview with author, December 12, 2008.

84. The foundation for this discussion had been laid in the fall of 2005 in
the third Japan-China Consultations on the East China Sea and Other
Matters. Two sets of talks in 2005 led by Sasae Ken'ichirō, the director-
general of the Asian and Oceania Affairs Bureau of the Japanese Minister of Foreign Affairs; and Cui Tian Kai, the director-general of the
Department of Asian Affairs of the Chinese Ministry of Foreign Affairs,
succeeded in defining the parameters of a joint development approach
to ending the tensions over divergent legal claims. The identification
of where and under what terms joint development would proceed,
was announced at the joint press conference by Minister for Foreign
Affairs Kōmura Masahiko and Minister of Economy, Trade, and Industry Akira Amari (Ministry of Foreign Affairs, Japan, "Joint Press Conference Regarding Cooperation Between Japan and China in the East
China Sea," June 18, 2008, http://www.mofa.go/jp?announce?fm_press
/2008/6/0618.html).

85. Richard J. Samuels, *3.11: Disaster and Change in Japan* (Ithaca, N.Y.: Cornell University Press, 2013), chap. 3.

86. Ministry of Foreign Affairs, Japan, "Summary of Japan-China Ministerial Meeting," January 17, 2010, http://www.mofa.go.jp/region/asia-paci/china/meet1001.html.

87. This did not come to light until recently because of the secrecy involved in identifying the properties leased to the U.S. military in Okinawa after its reversion to Japan. In the bilateral discussions on this island, the U.S.-Japan Joint Military Committee agenda had the island listed as Kopyō rather than Kubajima. The contract ran for twenty years and in 1992 was renewed again for another twenty years. The new owners, however, did not agree to the lease, and so the Defense Facilities Administration Agency pays rent.

88. *Yomiuri shinbun*, January 8, 2003.

89. *Yomiuri shinbun,* January 1, 2003.

90. *Mainichi shinbun*, January 3, 2003; Tsuyoshi Sunohara, *Antō senkaku kokuyūka* [*Secret Feud: The National Purchase of the Senkakus*] (Tokyo: Shinchōsha, 2013).

91. U.S. Department of State, "Joint Press Availability with Japanese Foreign Minister Seiji Maehara," October 27, 2010, http://www.state.gov/secretary/rm/2010/10/150110.htm. Article 5 of the Treaty of Mutual Cooperation and Security Between Japan and the United States of America reads,

> Each Party recognizes that an armed attack against either Party in the territories under the administration of Japan would be dangerous to its own peace and safety and declares that it would act to meet the common danger in accordance with its constitutional provisions and processes. Any such armed attack and all measures taken as a result thereof shall be immediately reported to the Security Council of the United Nations in accordance with the provisions of Article 51 of the Charter. Such measures shall be terminated when the Security Council has taken the measures necessary to restore and maintain international peace and security. (Ministry of Foreign Affairs, Japan, "Japan-U.S. Security Treaty," January 19, 1960, http://www.mofa.go.jp/region/n-america/us/q&a/ref/1.html)

92. Cabinet Office of Japan, Kaiyō kihon keikaku [Basic Ocean Plan], April 26, 2013, http://www.kantei.go.jp/jp/singi/kaiyou/kihonkeikaku/.

5. FOOD SAFETY

1. *Japan Times*, July 30, 2013.

2. *China Daily*, July 30, 2013.

3. Xinhua, January 20, 2014.

4. According to figures released by the Ministry of Agriculture, Forestry, and Fisheries (MAFF), Japan's imports from China jumped conspicuously in 2001 at a rate nearly double that of total agricultural imports. Total annual food imports increased 8.3 percent over the previous year, but despite provisional safeguards imposed on many agricultural imports from China, such as onions, the amount of imports jumped 15.5 percent. (Both of these figures are based on value rather than volume.) See *Nikkei shinbun*, April 6, 2002.

5. For a comprehensive analysis of the growing interdependence of Japanese and Chinese food industries, see Komori Masahiko, *Chūgoku shokuhin dōran* [*Chinese Food Incidents*] (Tokyo: Tōyō keizai shinpōsha, 2008); *NHK News*, January 30, 2008. Japan Tobacco Foods had received a call from CO-OP Chiba in December 28, 2007, about a woman and her daughter who had reported toxic food-poisoning symptoms from the CO-OP tezukuri gyōza product. *NHK* reported the following day that in fact the Japan Consumers Cooperation Union (CO-OP) had found a trace of organophosphate insecticide in the same brand of frozen dumplings when it conducted a random sample test in August 2002. Yet the CO-OP continued to sell the product because the amount of chemicals was below the standard identified for concern.

6. *Mainichi shinbun*, January 31, 2008.

7. On January 31, 2008, the Ministry of Foreign Affairs announced that Foreign Minister Kōmura Masahiko spoke initially about the *gyōza* incident with the director-general of protocol for the Chinese Ministry of Foreign Affairs, who was visiting to prepare for President Hu Jintao's spring visit to Tokyo. For the details of that conversation, see the press release of January 31, 2008: Ministry of Foreign Affairs, Japan, "Chūgokusan reitō gyōza ga genin to utagawareru kenkō higai jirei ni kansuru yaritori" [Press Conference on the Source of the Chinese Frozen Gyōza and the Case on the Suspected Damages to the Public Health], January 31, 2008, http://www.mofa.go.jp/mofaj/press/release/h20/1/1177494_900.html.

8. *Nikkei shinbun*, February 4, 2008; *Asahi shinbun*, February 5, 2008.

9. *Mainichi shinbun*, February 7, 2008.

10. *Nikkei shinbun*, February 28, 2008.

11. *Nikkei shinbun*, March 7 and 11, 2008.

12. *Nikkei shinbun*, February 22, 2008.

13. The visit by Hu's predecessor, Zhiang Zemin, in 1998, included a publicly delivered rebuke of Japan's approach to history at the dinner held with

the Japanese emperor, which ushered in a long period of difficult relations between the two countries.

14. The full statement can be found at Ministry of Foreign Affairs, Japan, "Joint Statement Between the Government of Japan and the Government of the People's Republic of China," May 7, 2008, http://www.mofa.go.jp/region/asia-paci/china/joint0805.html.

15. Ministry of Foreign Affairs, Japan, "Joint Press Statement Between the Government of Japan and the Government of the People's Republic of China," May 7, 2008, http://www.mofa.go.jp/region/asia-paci/china/pvo805/press.html.

16. The transcript of the press conference can be found at Cabinet Office of Japan, "Joint Japan-China Leaders' Press Conference," May 7, 2008, http://www.kantei.go.jp/foreign/hukudaspeech/2008/05/07kaiken_e.html.

17. *Yomiuri shinbun*, August 6, 2008.

18. *Yomiuri shinbun*, August 8, 2008.

19. *Yomiuri shinbun*, August 12, 2008. According to the *Nikkei shinbun*, August 13, 2008, the DPJ then sent a written request to Prime Minister Fukuda for closed hearings on this incident.

20. National Police Agency, Japan, "Tokushu: nichijo seikatsu wo obiyakasu hanzaihe no torikumi" [Special Report on Policies on Crimes That Threaten the Daily Lives of Japanese Citizens]), Keisatsu hakusho heisei-21 [National Police Agency White Paper, 2009], 18, http://www.npa.go.jp/hakusyo/h21/honbun/html/ld120000.html.

21. *Nikkei shinbun*, February 22 and 26, 2008.

22. Prefectural police in Hyōgo and Chiba, however, were continuing to collect information on the cases (*Asahi shinbun*, April 12, 2008). On April 29, the Hyōgo prefectural police announced another discovery of methamidophos inside a package of frozen dumplings (*Nikkei shinbun*, April 29, 2008). Then at the end of May, the Hyōgo police revealed that the Chinese chives in the dumplings involved in the poisoning case in their prefecture in January contained a level of methamidophos that was 44,000 times the acceptable standard (*Nikkei shinbun*, May 30, 2008).

23. Tsuruya Akinori, chief superintendent and director of International Investigative Operations and Yoshida Naomasa, chief superintendent and director, First Investigation Division, National Police Agency, interview with author, June 24, 2009.

24. Ministry of Foreign Affairs, Japan, "Joint Press Conference by Prime Minister Yukio Hatoyama of Japan, Premier Wen Jiabao of the People's

Republic of China, and President Lee Myung-bak of the Republic of Korea Following the Second Japan-China-ROK Trilateral Summit Meeting," October 10, 2009, http://www.kantei.go.jp/foreign/hatoyama /statement/200910/10JCKkyoudou_e.html.

25. For the text of the Memorandum of Cooperation, as well as the Joint Statement of the Third Tripartite Health Ministers Meeting (THMM) of the People's Republic of China, the Republic of South Korea, and Japan, see Ministry of Health, Labor, and Welfare, Japan, "Daisankai nitchūkan sangoku hoken daijin kaigō ni tsuite" [About the Third Tripartite Health Ministers Meeting], November 23, 2009, http://www.mhlw.go.jp/stf /houdou/2r98520000002mwp.html. Chinese Health Minister Chen Zhu, Japanese Minister of Health, Labor, and Welfare Nagatsuma Akira, and South Korean Minister of Health, Welfare, and Family Affairs Jeon Jae Hee all attended the meeting.

26. *Yomiuri shinbun*, March 8, 2010.

27. Xinhua, March 26, 2010.

28. *Sankei shinbun,* April 23, 2010.

29. According to Article 115 of the Chinese criminal code, the statutory penalty for the crime is imprisonment for at least ten years, indefinite imprisonment, or capital punishment (*Mainichi shinbun*, August 11, 2010).

30. For the text of the Memorandum of Cooperation as well as more information on the meeting, see Ministry of Health, Labor, and Welfare, Japan, "Nitchū shokuhin anzen suishin inishachibu dai ikkai kakuryōkyū kaigō no kekka nado ni tsuite" [Results of the First Cabinet Ministers Meeting of the Japan-China Food Safety Promotion Initiative], May 31, 2010, http://www.mhlw.go.jp/stf/houdou/2r98520000006r22.html.

31. MAFF officials concluded that in addition to measures taken by Japanese food-importing companies, Chinese officials and export companies had significantly improved their food inspection policies (*Mainichi shinbun*, October 16, 2008).

32. Although the Diet approved this treaty on May 16, 2008, it was actually signed by both foreign ministers on December 1, 2007. See Ministry of Foreign Affairs of Japan (MOFA), "Treaty Between Japan and the People's Republic of China on Mutual Legal Assistance in Criminal Matters," December 1, 2007, http://www.mofa.go.jp/policy/treaty/submit /session169/agree-13-1.pdf.

33. National Police Agency, Japan, "Tokushu: nichijo seikatsu wo obiyakasu hanzaihe no torikumi," 18–20.

34. *Nikkei shinbun*, June 25, 1984.
35. *Nikkei shinbun*, November 14, 1984.
36. *Nikkei shinbun*, April 4, 1985.
37. Komori Masahiko, *Chūgoku shokuhin dōran*, chap. 8.
38. Xinhua, September 25, 2008.
39. Associated Press, September 23, 2008.
40. World Health Organization, "Melamine-Contaminated Powdered Infant Formula in China," September 18, 2008, http://who.int/csr /don/2008_09_19/en/print.html; and "Melamine-Contaminated Powdered Infant Formula in China—Update," September 22, 2008, http://www .who.int/csr/don/2008_09_22/en/print.html.
41. *New York Times*, December 2, 2008.
42. *Nikkei shinbun*, September 21 and 23, 2008. NPR also carried the story of Japan's government asking food companies to make sure that their milk products were safe (Anthony Kuhn, "Japan Loses Confidence in Chinese Dairy Products," NPR, September 24, 2008).
43. First they ask respondents if they have a positive or negative impression of China, and then they ask why. In 2011, the second-most cited negative reason after the Chinese fishing trawler incident in Senkaku waters (64.6 percent) was "shokuhin anzen mondai de no chūgoku seifu no taiō ni gimon ga aru kara" (because you have concerns about how the Chinese government has handled food security) (61.8 percent). This was the most often cited negative response in 2008, 2009, and 2010. The response was not offered in the 2012 poll. Genron NPO, "Nitchū kyōdō yoron chōsa" [Japan-China Joint Public Opinion Poll], 2008–2012, http://www.genron-npo.net/world/genre/cat119/2012-a.html.
44. Genron NPO, "Nitchū kyōdō yoron chōsa." In a separate question in the survey, Genron asks how people feel about the safety of food produced in China [Chūgoku shokuhin no anzensei]. In 2012, 92.8 percent responded that they felt anxious (50.8 percent very anxious, 42 percent somewhat anxious). This was up from 2011 (90.5 percent) and marked the fifth straight year that more than 90 percent of Japanese felt anxious about Chinese-produced food since the question had first been asked in 2008. Interestingly, after Japan's March 11, 2011, nuclear plant disaster at Fukushima Daiichi, the safety of food products from Japan became a major concern of Chinese consumers. According to a poll by the *China Daily* (Genron's partner in China) in 2012, 80.7 percent of Chinese felt anxious about Japanese food (up from 78.9 percent in 2011).

45. For a detailed breakdown of the operations of Japanese companies by locale, see ibid., chaps. 9–13.

46. In the food trade, most of the trading companies' exposure is to the global food market. The bulk of Japanese grain and soy imports come from North and South America, where trading companies like Marubeni Corporation and Itōchū have invested heavily in the grain trade. But the growing demand from China is raising the stakes for Japan's trading companies in the global food market. For an update on these pressures, new global activities, and the impact of China's growing food needs on Japan's trading houses, see "Hinomaru shōsha kokumotsu he ugoku" [Japan's Major Trading Companies Move to Grains], *Shukan Tōyō keizai*, October 17, 2009.

47. According to Itōchū, the company strategy is a "strategic integrated system (SIS)," "which is a supply and demand system based on customer needs that seamlessly links upstream food resource development and processing, midstream distribution and downstream retail and sales" ("Strengthening Our Partnership with the Ting Hsin Group," www .Itōchū.co.jp/en/business/food/project/01/[accessed October 2013]).

48. On the basis of profits in 2006, the top-ranking Japanese food companies are Japan Tobacco, Asahi Breweries, Kirin Brewery, Suntory Holdings, Ajinomoto Co., Yamazaki Baking Company, Suntory Foods Limited, Meiji Dairies Corporation, Morinaga Milk Industry, Itoham Foods, Nichirei Corporation, Kirin Beverages, Nestle Japan Group, Meiji seika kaisha (Bakery) Ito en, Nisei Food Products, Katokichi (now TableMark Co.) Kewpie Corporation, LOTTE Co., and Kinki Coca-Cola Bottling Co. (Komori Masahiko, *Chūgoku shokuhin dōran*, 45).

49. *Nikkei shinbun,* March 5, 2008.

50. JT explicitly stated it would reduce frozen food products by 50 percent, while Nichirei and Ajinomoto were less specific in their target figures (*Nikkei shinbun*, May 2, 2008).

51. *Nikkei shinbun*, June 18, 2008.

52. *Nikkei shinbun*, December 17, 2009.

53. The MAFF uses two different rates: the percentage of the food supply based on caloric intake and the percentage of the domestic supply based on production value. For example, in Japanese fiscal year 2011, the MAFF announced that Japan's self-sufficiency in food production was 39 percent on a caloric intake basis and 66 percent on a production value basis. See Ministry of Agriculture, Forestry and Fisheries, Japan, "Nōrin suisan shō, heisei-23 nendo shokuryō jikyūritsu nado ni

tsuite" [Regarding the Food Self-Sufficiency Rate for 2011], August 10, 2012, http://www.maff.gp.jp/j/press/kanbo/anpo/120810.html (accessed August 23, 2012).

54. See, for example, the editorial "Push Agricultural Reforms Without Fretting About Target," *Yomiuri shinbun*, August 23, 2012.

55. According to data from the MAFF, the damage done by the triple disasters to agriculture, forestry, and fisheries totaled ¥2.38 trillion ($23.4 billion). Between March 11 and April 20, 2011, the MAFF responded to requests for emergency food by providing 25.842 million packs of food, 7.62 million drink bottles, and 53,000 cans of formula milk for infants (Ministry of Agriculture, Forestry, and Fisheries, Japan, "The Damage Caused by the Great East Japan Earthquake and Actions Taken by the Ministry of Agriculture, Forestry, and Fisheries," last updated March 12, 2013, http://www.maff.go.jp/e/quake/press_since_120605.html).

56. Samejima Futoshi, managing director, Association for the Safety of Imported Food, interview with author, July 25, 2012.

57. Patricia Maclachlan, *Consumer Politics in Postwar Japan: The Institutional Boundaries of Citizen Activism* (New York: Columbia University Press, 2002).

58. Ibid., chap. 7, "The Right to Safety: The Movement to Oppose the Deregulation of Food Additives."

59. The discussion of the JCCU and its internal investigation is based on my interviews with JCCU managers Uchibori Nobutake, general manager of the Quality Assurance Department, and Aotake Yutaka of the Public Relations Office, June 24, 2009, and June 14, 2011. Itō Jirō, government/political liaison of the Public Relations Office, joined the interview on June 14, 2011.

60. The final report of this third-party investigatory committee was published on May 30, 2008, and included a detailed account of each case and the individual cooperatives response. Nihon seikyoren—reitō gyōza mondai kenshō iinkai [Investigation Committee into the Deaths Caused by Frozen Gyōza] met nine times, and its members included Yoshikawa Yasuhiro (chair), Ishigawa Yūji, Imamura Tomoaki, Irumada Noriko, Ouse Hiroki, Ōwada Takashi, Kaji Yoshifumi, and Tobe Yoriko. The final report is available online at Japan's Consumer Cooperatives Union (JCCU), "Nihon seikyoren—reitō gyōza mondai kenshō iinkai saishū hōkoku" [Final Report of the Investigation Committee into the Deaths Caused by Frozen Gyōza], May 30, 2008, http://jccu.coop/info /announcement/pdf/announce_080530_01_01.pdf.

61. "'Shohisha gyōsei ichigenka' ni tsuite no nihon seikyōren no iken," July 28, 2008, prepared for Prime Minister Fukuda Takeo by Nihon seikatsu ryōdō kumiai rengokai kaichō, Yamashita Toshifumi. Provided to author by the JCCU, June 24, 2009.

62. Sano Mariko, secretary-general, Shufuren, interview with author, July 25, 2012.

63. Sano referred to the scandal involving the meat wholesaler Meat Hope that broke in June 2007 when it was discovered that the company had falsely labeled ground chicken and pork as beef. For a concise account of that scandal, see *Asahi shinbun*, December 19, 2007.

64. Four major cases of false labeling hit the press in the mid-2000s, all of which involved food products. Well-known brands, such as Yukijirushi milk and Fujiya baked goods, were found guilty, as were lesser-known companies. For a synopsis of the four main controversies over the false labeling of food products, see *Chūnichi shinbun*, October 20, 2007.

65. Sano Mariko, interview with author, July 25, 2012.

66. The Tokyo Metropolitan Government's involvement in the *gyōza* food-poisoning cases in January 2008, as well as the policies followed afterward to enhance consumer awareness of food safety, was discussed in an interview on July 24, 2012, with officials of the Tokyo Metropolitan Government's Food Supervision Division who have direct responsibility for consumer food safety. The following TMG officials took part in the interview: Nakajima Hideo, deputy director for Food-Poisoning Investigations; Nakamura Shigenobu, director, and Nakamura Hideo, deputy director, Food Supervision Division; Sakuma Yuki and Okada Junya, supervisors for Quality Labeling; Teramura Wataru, supervisor for Imported Food products and Harmful Food Products; and Taira Kimitaka, supervisor for Food Safety.

67. According to Sakuma Yuki, at the time of the *gyōza* food-poisoning cases, the JAS law required labeling twenty foods and four food products (*katsuobushi*, processed eel, pickled vegetables, frozen vegetables), and today it has added two more foods: rolled *konbu* and black sugar products (interview with author, July 24, 2008).

68. Teramura Wataru, interview with author, July 24, 2012.

69. Nakajima Hideo, interview with author, July 24, 2012.

70. Concerns about framework of Japan's food safety monitoring continued, however, and skepticism of the new 2003 Food Safety Law continued to be reflected in the media. See, for example, *Mainichi shinbun*, April 12 and May 17, 2003.

71. Watanabe Kōhei served as president of the Food Company, Itōchū Corporation, from April 2002 to March 2006 (interview with author, July 19, 2012).

72. For an English translation, see Ministry of Health, Labor, and Welfare, Japan, *Guidelines on Hygiene Control of Imported Processed Foods* (Annex to Notice Shoku-an no. 0605001 of June 5, 2008), http://www.mhlw.go.jp/english/topics/importedfoods/guideline/01.html.

73. Following the Glico Morinaga food-poisoning incidents, another scandal involving insider trading at another food company, Lotte, raised even further the number of blackmail crimes against Japanese food industries and other companies and led to the drafting of a new law by the LDP. For a retrospective on these dramatic blackmail cases, see *Asahi shinbun*, September 16, 1987.

74. The Association for the Safety of Imported Food had been briefing food companies since 1992. In 2012, it organized its twenty-first annual course on food safety for importers, to which it reported the number of participants at around 150 to 160 per year. To date, more than 2,700 industry personnel have been briefed on regulatory requirements.

75. The staff of the Association for the Safety of Imported Food (ASIF), Japan, is composed of eight personnel, some of whom work on a part-time basis, who come from Japanese industry. Although the association does have some adjunct advisers who are former MHLW bureaucrats, it is a private-sector initiative. The ASIF also publishes a handbook for Japanese food importers: *Shokuhin yunyū handobukku: shokuhin wo anzen ni yunyū suru tami ni* [*The Handbook for Food Imports: Complying with the Law to Import Food Safely*] (Tokyo: ASIF, 2010).

76. Samejima Futoshi, interview with author, July 25, 2012.

77. According to the U.S. Food and Drug Administration, the HAACP is "a management system in which food safety is addressed through the analysis and control of biological, chemical, and physical hazards from raw material production, procurement and handling, to manufacturing, distribution, and consumption of the finished product." For more information, see U.S. Food and Drug Administration, "Hazard Analysis and Critical Control Points (HAACP)," last updated April 27, 2011, http://www.fda.gov/food/foodsafety/hazardanalysiscriticalcontrolpointshaccp/default.htm

78. Samejima Futoshi, interview with author, July 25, 2012.

79. Consumer Affairs Agency, "Shokuhin kigai jōhō sōkatsukan kaigi unei kitei" [Food Danger General Information Meeting on Manage-

ment and Regulation], March 5, 2008, http://www.caa.go.jp/seikatsu /kenkouhigai/080305kigaiunnei.pdf.

80. Food Safety Commission of Japan, "Shokuhin ni yoru kigai ni kansuru kinkyūji taiō jisshi kihon yōkō [Outline of Emergency Response and Implementation of Measures Related to Food Danger], April 23, 2008.

81. *Nikkei shinbun*, November 25, 2007.

82. *Mainichi shinbun,* February 7, 2008.

83. *NHK News*, February 12, 2012.

84. *NHK News*, March 13, 2008, included a synopsis of the third meeting of the Council for Promoting Consumer Policy attended by Prime Minister Fukuda.

85. Unlike the *gyōza* food-poisoning case, these cases involved multiple deaths. The *Sankei shinbun* carried a very dramatic account of the meeting on May 20, 20008, describing the mothers of the victims in both cases making a tearful appeal to Prime Minister Fukuda. Other accounts of the meeting ran in the *Asahi shinbun*, May 20 and 21, 2008. The *"konnyaku* jellies" case was settled out of court on September 6, 2008. A total of thirteen children and elderly died choking on the jellies. The president of Paloma was found guilty for the deaths in the case brought against him by the Kobayashi family on May 11, 2011, in the Tokyo District Court. In all, twenty-eight deaths or injuries since 1985 were attributed to Paloma gas heaters (*Yomiuri shinbun*, May 12, 2012).

86. *Asahi shinbun*, June 17, 2008. For more information, see Cabinet Office of Japan, "Shōhisha gyōsei suishin kaigi torimatome" [The Final Report of the Council for Promotion Consumer Policy], June 13, 2008, http://www .kantei.go.jp/singi/shouhisha/dai8/siryou1.pdf.

87. The Consumer Affairs Law was passed on May 29, 2009. For the full text of the law, see House of Councillors, National Diet of Japan, Shōhishachō sechi hōan [Consumer Affairs Law], updated June 5, 2009, http://www .sangiin.go.jp/japanese/joho1/kousei/gian/171/meisai/m17103170001 .htm.

88. Media criticism of the new agency continued even after it was up and running. See, for example, the editorial "Consumer Affairs Agency," *Asahi shinbun*, March 16, 2010, which decried the agency's inability to exercise autonomy and execute its mandate to work on behalf of Japan's consumers. The editorial focused on the Toyota recall in the United States and the Japanese government's lack of effort to demand more information from Toyota.

89. For the initial FY2010 budget, see Consumer Affairs Agency, Japan, "Shōhishachō no heisei 22-nendo yosan oyobi kikō—teiin yōkyū" [About the Consumer Affairs Agency FY2010 Budget and Organization Appropriations Request], September 2009, 4, http://www.caa .go.jp/info/yosan/pdf/090902h22yosan_honbun.pdf. For the number of employees, see Consumer Affairs Agency, Japan, "Heisei 22-nendo shōhishachō kankei yosan oyobi kikō teiin yōkyū no gaiyō" [Outline of the Consumer Affairs FY2010 Budget and Organization Appropriations Request], September 2009, http://www.caa.go.jp/info/yosan /pdf/090902h22yosan_gaiyou.pdf.

90. Budget and staff numbers for the Consumer Affairs Agency can be found at Consumer Affairs Agency, Japan, "Shōhishachō heisei 24-nendo yosanan no gaiyō—kikō teiin yōkyū no kekka ni tsuite" [Consumer Affairs Agency FY2012 Draft Budget Outline: Outcome of Appropriations Request], December 24, 2011, http://www.caa.go.jp/info/yosan /pdf/h24gaisankettei.pdf. Budget figures for the Ministry of Economy, Trade, and Industry (METI) are available at METI, "Yosan, zeisei, zaitō" [Budget, Tax System, and Fiscal Investment and Loan Program], http:// www.meti.go.jp/main/31.html; and staff numbers were provided by the General Affairs Division on August 27, 2012. Budget figures for the Ministry of Health, Labor, and Welfare (MHLW) can be found at MHLW, "Yosan" [Budget], http://www.mhlw.go.jp/wp/yosan/yosan/; and the staff numbers were provided by the Personnel and Planning Office on August 27, 2012.

91. Translated by Cabinet Office of Japan, "Dai jūichikai shōhisha gyōsei suishin kaigi giji yōshi" [Summary of the Eleventh Session of the Council for Promoting Consumer Policy], January 29, 2009, http://www .kantei.go.jp/jp/singi/shouhisha/dai11/11gijiyousi.pdf.

92. Ministry of Foreign Affairs, Japan, "Shoku no anzen mondai" [Food Security Issues], last updated August, 2012, www.mofa.go.jp/mofaj /gaiko/shoku_anzen/index.html.

93. The MOU and the action plan can be found at Ministry of Health, Labor, and Welfare, Japan, "Nitchū shokuhin anzen suishin inishachibu dai ikkai kakuryō kyū kaigō no kekka nado ni tsuite" [Results of the First Cabinet Ministers' Meeting of the Japan-China Food Security Initiative], May 31, 2010, http://www.mhlw.go.jp/stf/houdou/2r9852000000006r22 .html.

94. *China Daily*, July 30, 2013.

95. Xinhua, May 21, 2011.

96. According to the Genron NPO / *China Daily* poll, 80.7 percent of Chinese felt anxious about Japanese food, up from 78.9 percent in 2011. For years, it had been Japanese consumers' concern about China's food safety that had dominated the survey data. In 2012, 92.8 percent stated that they felt anxious (50.8 percent very anxious, 42 percent somewhat anxious). This was up from 2011 (90.5 percent) and marked the fifth straight year that more than 90 percent of Japanese felt anxious about Chinese-produced food since the question was first asked in 2008.

97. *China Daily*, March 3, 2011.

98. See the agenda for the second working-level consultations between Japan and China and the action plan for fiscal year 2011 (April 2011–March 2012) at Ministry of Health, Labor, and Welfare, Japan, "Nitchū shokuhin anzen suishin inishachibu dai nikai kakuryō kyū kaigō no kekka nado ni tsuite" [Results of the Second Cabinet Ministers' Meeting of the Japan-China Food Security Initiative], November 12, 2011, http://www.mhlw.go.jp/stf/houdou/2r9852000001ukt5.html.

99. *Asahi shinbun*, May 22, 2012.

100. Of the retail restaurants and bars surveyed by the *Nikkei shinbun*, March 8, 2012, 70 percent reported that they were interested in foreign rice because of the higher cost of domestic Japanese rice. The Seiyu supermarkets, Japan's largest supermarket chain, announced that starting on March 10, 2012, they would begin selling Chinese-grown rice and that they would also use imported rice in their "revolving sushi" and "beef bowl" restaurants. The rice would retail for ¥1,299 for 11 pounds (5 kg) and ¥449 for 3-pound bags (1.5 kg), a 30 percent savings over even the cheapest domestically produced rice (*Asahi shinbun*, March 9, 2012).

101. *Nikkei shinbun*, April 8, 2012.

102. *Niigata nippō*, May 12, 2012.

6. ISLAND DEFENSE

1. *NHK News*, September 8, 2010.

2. Agence France-Presse, September 7, 2010. On September 7, 2010, a Chinese fishing trawler collided with two JCG patrol boats near the Senkaku Islands. At about 10:15 A.M. (JST), the JCG's *Yonakuni, Mizuki*, and *Hateruma* encountered the Chinese trawler *Minjinyu 5179* about 7.5 miles (12 km) northwest of the Senkaku Islands and ordered it to stop for inspection. The *Minjinyu* refused and attempted to flee. During the ensuing chase, the Chinese trawler rammed first the *Yonakuni* and then, forty minutes later, the *Mizuki*. The JCG subsequently boarded the ves-

sel and escorted it to Ishigaki Island, where the captain, Zhan Qixiong, and his crew were detained. Three days later, the JCG released the crew and ship but turned over the Chinese captain to Japanese prosecutors for possible indictment.

3. "Law of the People's Republic of China on the Territorial Sea and the Contiguous Zone," translated by the Legislative Affairs Commission of the Standing Committee of the National People's Congress of the People's Republic of China, and attached as appendix 2 in Bureau of Oceans and International Environmental and Scientific Affairs, U.S. Department of State, "Straight Baseline Claim: China," *Limits in the Sea*, no. 117, July 9, 1996, http://www.state.gov/documents/organization/57692.pdf.

4. Xinhua, September 21, 2010.

5. Ibid.

6. U.S. Department of State, "Remarks to the Press," Philip J. Crowley, assistant secretary, Bureau of Public Affairs, September 23, 2010, http://www.state.gov/r/pa/prs/ps/2010/09/147726.htm.

7. At a press conference, Chairman of the Joint Chiefs of Staff Admiral Mike Mullen expressed his support for Japan in response to a question on the Senkaku tensions with China. Secretary of Defense Robert M. Gates also stated that the United States would "fulfill its alliance responsibilities" (U.S. Department of Defense, "DOD News Briefing with Secretary Gates and Adm. Mullen from the Pentagon," September 23, 2010, http://www.defense.gov/transcripts/transcript.aspx?transcriptid=4690).

8. *Nikkei shinbun,* September 24, 2010.

9. *New York Times*, September 23, 2010. Given the time difference with Asia, Minister Ōhata's report and the *New York Times* article were virtually simultaneous.

10. *Nikkei shinbun*, September 19, 2010.

11. *Nikkei shinbun,* July 24, 2010; *Yomiuri shinbun*, January 5, 2011.

12. *China Daily*, October 19, 2010.

13. *Asahi shinbun*, November 19, 2010.

14. Ministry of Economy, Trade, and Industry, Japan, "Press Conference by Minister Ōhata Akihiro," December 7, 2010, http://www.meti.go.jp/speeches/data_ed/ed101207j.html. At the end of December, Ōhata stated that "Chinese exports of rare earths have now, for the most part, returned to normal amounts" (*Nikkei shinbun*, December 24, 2010).

15. *Nikkei shinbun*, October 13 and 19, 2010.

16. Ministry of Foreign Affairs, Japan, "Press Conference by Minister for Foreign Affairs Seiji Maehara," September 17, 2010, http://www.mofa.go.jp/announce/fm_press/2010/9/0917_01.html.

17. *Nikkei shinbun*, October 18, 2010. The comment also was reported in the global press. See, for example, "Maehara Calls China's Response to the Incident 'Hysterical,'" Agence France-Presse, October 18, 2010, http://www.france24.com/en/20101018-japan-foreign-minister-calls-china-reaction-island-dispute-hysterical.

18. *Japan Times*, October 22, 2010.

19. For a full account of Secretary Clinton's remarks, see U.S. Department of State, "Joint Press Availability with Japanese Foreign Minister Seiji Maehara," October 27, 2010, http://www.state.gov/secretary/rm/2010/10/150110.htm.

20. Jeffrey A. Bader, "Japan: From LDP to DPJ Rule," in *Obama and China's Rise: An Insider's Account of America's Asia Strategy* (Washington, D.C.: Brookings Institution Press, 2012), 40–47.

21. Ministry of Land, Infrastructure, Transport, and Tourism, Kokudo kōtsu hakusho, 2010 [Annual White Paper of the Ministry of Land, Infrastructure, Transport, and Tourism, 2010] (Tokyo: Nikkei insatsu KK, 2010), 83.

22. In addition to the JCG and the MSDF, the Japan Fisheries Agency in the Ministry of Agriculture, Forestry, and Fisheries (MAFF) has a total of forty-one vessels (thirty-nine enforcement vessels and two fisheries research vessels), of which four enforcement vessels are currently deployed near the Senkaku, Miyako, and Yaeyama Islands (Japan Fisheries Agency, *Suisanchō* [*Japan Fisheries Agency*] [pamphlet, 2012], 10, http://www.jfa.maff.go.jp/j/koho/pr/pamph/pdf/pamph_2012.pdf). The fourth vessel was added after Suematsu Yoshinori, deputy minister in the Cabinet Office, announced on November 5, 2010, that an additional vessel would be needed in response to the Chinese fishing trawler incident (*Yomiuri shinbun*, November 6, 2010). A statement from the MAFF about the additional vessel can be found online at MAFF, "Suisanchō jimuhi no uchi shidō kankaku oyobi torishimarihi" [Japan Fisheries Agency Cost of Business, Guidance, Supervision, and Management], 2012, http://www.maff.go.jp/j/aid/hozyo/2012/suisan/pdf/32.pdf. Finally, apart from the Japan Fisheries Agency, the Japan Fisheries Research Agency, an incorporated administrative agency affiliated with the MAFF, also has ten research vessels, of which one, the *Shin yoko maru*, operates in the East China Sea out of Nagasaki (Japan Fisheries Research Agency, "Higashi shina kai sunadori jōhō" [Information on East China Sea Fishing], http://snf.fra.affrc.go.jp/gyokaikyou/index.html [accessed October 2013]).

23. Sam Bateman, "Coast Guards: New Forces for Regional Order and Security," *Asia Pacific Issues, East-West Center*, no. 65 (2003): 1–8.

24. Japan Coast Guard, Policy Evaluation and Public Relations Office, *Japan Coast Guard* (pamphlet, March 2012), http://www.kaiho.mlit.go.jp/e/pamphlet.pdf.

25. Japan Coast Guard, "Budget," August 27, 2013, http://www.kaiho.mlit.go.jp/info/kouhou/h25/k20130827/24yosan.pdf.

26. Richard J. Samuels, "New Fighting Power! Japan's Growing Maritime Capabilities and East Asian Security," *International Security* 32, no. 3 (2007–2008): 84–112.

27. In addition to the suspicious ships from North Korea operating in Japanese waters, the Japan Coast Guard (JCG) also has tried to limit the activities of South Korea and Chinese ships in waters surrounding disputed islands. In 2006, Japan dispatched two 550-ton survey ships to the disputed Takeshima/Dokdo Islands, but Seoul responded with much larger coast guard patrol ships. The JCG withdrew to Japan's coast, but despite the cooperation between South Korean and Japanese coast guards, the incident revealed how sensitive these disputes continue to be. Likewise, the JCG regularly tracks Chinese activities in and around the Senkaku/Diaoyu islands, but Beijing has been hesitant to engage Japan in joint coast guard drills.

28. The Japan Coast Guard does not publish fleet details, but a report in December 2012 estimated that "as many as 40 to 50 of the Coast Guard's 120 larger ships from around the nation are deployed in the area's waters at any time, having been redeployed there in September [2012]" (Yuka Hayashi, "Island Spat Tests Japan's Coast Guard," *Wall Street Journal*, December 12, 2012, http://online.wsj.com/article/SB10001424127887324339204578170733637585700.html).

29. BBC, February 21, 2012.

30. For the details on Japan's new southwestern defense enhancements, see Ministry of Defense, Japan, *Nihon no bōei, heisei 23-nen* [*Defense of Japan 2011*] (Tokyo: Ministry of Defense, 2011), 168–75.

31. Ibid., 230–31. For a full rendition of Japan's response to an invasion, see pp. 253–60.

32. In 2010, the National Institute for Defense Studies (NIDS) of Japan published the inaugural issue of its *China Security Report*. The preface clearly lays out Japan's concerns:

> China, now the second largest economy in the world, has become an essential economic partner to Japan and other East Asian countries. At the same

time, however, China has used its economic growth as leverage to increase military spending and move forward the modernization of the PLA. China's military expansion without sufficient transparency, in tandem with the more assertive nature of the PLA, has raised concerns among neighboring and other countries. (National Institute for Defense Studies, *NIDS China Security Report* [Tokyo: NIDS, March 2011], i)

33. Richard Bush, *The Perils of Proximity: China-Japan Security Relations* (Washington, D.C.: Brookings Institution Press, 2009).

34. At its peak in 2009, China produced 129,000 tons of the 132,000 tons produced worldwide (97%) but exported just 40 to 50 percent. In August 2009, China's Ministry of Industry and Information Technology unveiled a rare earths development plan through 2015 that capped export volume at 35,000 tons (production at 120,000 to 150,000 tons) (Damien Ma, "China Digs It: How Beijing Cornered the Rare Earths Market," April 25, 2012, ForeignAffairs.com, http://www.foreignaffairs .com/articles/137602/damien-ma/china-digs-it).

35. Wayne M. Morrison and Rachel Tang, *China's Rare Earth Industry and Export Regime: Economic and Trade Implications for the United States*, Congressional Research Service Report, April 30, 2012, http://www.fas .org/sgp/crs/row/R42510.pdf (for monthly exports to Japan in 2010, see p. 32).

36. This request for consultations was the first step in the dispute settlement process at the WTO. The request (Dispute Settlement 431, DS431) by the European Union, the United States, and Japan for consultations with China at the WTO on rare earth export restraints was made on March 13, 2012, and came on the heels of a prior dispute settlement panel finding against China on "measures related to the exportation of various raw materials" (DS394). Although Japan did not participate in this dispute settlement case, the WTO panel found that "China's export duties were inconsistent with the commitments China had agreed to in its Protocol of Accession. The Panel also found that export quotas imposed by China on some of the raw materials were inconsistent with WTO rules" ("DS394 Summary of Key Findings," released on July 5, 2011). China appealed this decision the following month, but in January 2012 it lost its appeal on export restrictions on raw materials. Thus, the case on rare earths followed immediately on the heels of the WTO finding against China.

37. Cabinet Office of Japan, "Press Conference by the Chief Cabinet Secretary," March 14, 2012, http://www.kantei.go.jp/foreign/tyoukanpress /201203/14_a.html.

38. Ministry of Foreign Affairs, Japan, "Nihon koku seifu oyobi chūka jinmin kyōwakoku ni yoru chūgoku ni okeru nihon no iki kagaku heiki no haiki ni kansuru oboegaki" [Japan and People's Republic of China Agreement to Remove Abandoned Chemical Weapons in China], July 30, 1999, http://www.mofa.go.jp/mofaj/area/china/cw/oboegaki .html.

39. *Nikkei shinbun*, September 29, 2010.

40. *Nikkei shinbun*, October 9, 2011.

41. A summary of the May 16, 2012, Japan-China maritime discussions in Huangzhou can be found at Ministry of Foreign Affairs, Japan, "The First Round Meeting of Japan-China High Level Consultation on Maritime Affairs (Outline)," May 16, 2012, http://www.mofa.go.jp/policy /maritime/jchlc_maritime01.html.

42. *Asahi shinbun*, May 17, 2012.

43. *China Daily*, September 22, 2010.

44. U.S. Department of State, "Remarks to the Press," Philip J. Crowley, September 23, 2010.

45. U.S. Department of Defense, "DOD News Briefing with Secretary Gates and Adm. Mullen from the Pentagon," September 23, 2010.

46. "Kokkai kaigiroku kensaku shisutemu" [National Diet Minutes Search System], Remarks by Sengoku Yoshito, Upper House Budget Committee, National Diet Library of Japan, November 18, 2010, http://kokkai .ndl.go.jp.

47. Sengoku used the term *yanagigoshi* in two separate sets of Diet deliberations to explain his view of Japan's foreign policy challenge in working with Beijing. He explained the Cabinet's thinking best on October 12 in the Lower House Budget Committee, when he responded to LDP Secretary-General Ishihara Nobuteru's use of the word *yowagoshi* (spineless) to describe the Kan cabinet's handling of the crisis. He stated,

> We don't see this as a case of being spineless. Rather, in response to your charge of spineless, we would like to consider a more flexible and well considered strategy for dealing with China—this is *yanagigoshi*. There are many visions of the future, but China is rising to become a major power, and we are trying to build a strategic mutually beneficial relationship with China. We have no choice but to work with Beijing to build this relationship, and we must consider when to compromise and when to insist that China accept responsibility as a major power, to join the international consensus. This is our challenge, and to accomplish this we must be both flexible and assertive in our approach to China. This is our approach.

This discussion is paraphrased in English and can be found at Kokkai kaigiroku kensaku shisutemu [National Diet Minutes Search System], Remarks by Sengoku Yoshito, Lower House Budget Committee, October 12, 2010, http://kokkai.ndl.go.jp.

48. Charges were dropped on January 21, 2011, the same day that the Tokyo District Public Prosecutors Office announced that it was dropping all charges against Isshiki Masaharu for the leak of the JCG video (*Yomiuri shinbun*, January 22, 2011).

49. On March 15, 2012, the Chinese captain was indicted by court-appointed lawyers acting as prosecutors. Following the indictment, on March 28 the Japanese Ministry of Justice asked its Chinese counterpart under a mutual legal assistance treaty to deliver the indictment to Zhan Qixiong on its behalf. The Chinese Ministry turned down the request on May 15. With no ability to deliver the indictment within two months as required by law, the case was closed on May 17 (*Mainichi shinbun*, May 18, 2012).

50. Although the *Inasa* eventually sank the North Korean vessel, it was the patrol ship *Amami* that first encountered it. In total, three Japanese patrol ships (*Inasa*, *Amami*, and *Kirishima*) were damaged in the incident (*Nikkei shinbun*, December 23, 2001).

51. *Telegraph*, December 24, 2001.

52. *Mainichi shinbun*, September 11, 2002.

53. Interview with author, July 27, 2012. This manual outlines information-sharing protocols as well as the ways in which each service fulfills its own mission of policing (JCG) and defending (MSDF) Japanese waters.

54. For an analysis of China's maritime enforcement capabilities, see Lyle J. Goldstein, *Five Dragons Stirring Up the Sea: Challenge and Opportunity in China's Improving Maritime Enforcement Capabilities*, China Maritime Studies Institute, no. 5 (Newport, R.I.: Naval War College, 2010).

55. Interview with author, June 27, 2011. See Ishigaki Mayor Nakayama Yoshitaka's statement after visiting the prime minister's residence and the DPJ headquarters, in *Nikkei shinbun*, October 4, 2010, and Okinawa Governor Nakaima Hirokazu's press conference, available on the website of the Okinawa Prefectural Government, "Happyō jigō" [Announcement Items], October 15, 2010, http://www.pref.okinawa.jp/chiji/announce/teirei/201010/1015.html#yousei. On June 10, 2011, Mayor Nakayama submitted a request to Prime Minister Kan Naoto asking for permission to land on the Senkaku Islands in order to pay tribute to the lives lost during an incident in 1945 in which a ship evacuating to Taiwan

from Ishigaki carrying 180 civilians was attacked by the United States. The ship drifted to Uotsuri Island, and the survivors died from starvation. Nakayama's request also is available online at the Ishigaki City government website, June 10, 2011, http://www.city.ishigaki.okinawa .jp/110000/110100/pdf/senkaku-yosei.pdf.

56. *Asahi shinbun*, December 18, 2010.

57. "Nippon kaigi," http://www.nipponkaigi.org (accessed October 2013). The Nippon kaigi has branches in every Japanese prefecture, and according to its website, its conservative agenda includes promoting constitutional revision, the abduction issue, educational reform and "correct" history textbooks, visits to the Yasukuni Shrine (including opposition to the creation of an alternative memorial), and protection of Imperial Household traditions, such as not allowing women to become emperor. In 2011, to demonstrate Japan's control over the Senkakus, it held a major rally on June 18, one day after the anniversary of the return of Okinawa to Japanese sovereignty. Even though local residents had been less than enthusiastic about Senkaku nationalism in the past, after the Chinese fishing trawler incident and the debate it spawned, this meeting attracted around five hundred participants, a significant turnout for a small island with a population of roughly 48,000.

58. *Sankei shinbun*, October 17, 2010.

59. Japanese Culture Channel Sakura (Nihon bunka channeru sakura), also known as "Channel Sakura," is a Japanese television production company whose agenda is a stronger Japanese defense and a revisionist interpretation of Japanese history. Founded by Satoru Mizushima in 2004, the channel has a YouTube presence of 30,000 subscribers and more than 50 million views (as of August 2012). The channel is well known for hosting a variety of Japanese nationalist academics and commentators who have portrayed Japanese imperialism in a positive light, denied past war crimes, and espoused anti-Korean and anti-Chinese sentiments in an attempt to create a "pure" Japanese cultural image. Channel Sakura's founder, Mizushima, directed the film *The Truth About Nanjing* (2008), which portrayed the 1937 Nanjing massacre as a myth. The film was backed by the Tokyo governor Ishihara Shintarō, and Mizushima himself has said that this film was meant to counter the film *Nanking* (1997), an American documentary that portrayed the brutality of the Japanese army during the massacre. For more information, see "Channel Sakura," http://www.ch-sakura.jp/about.html (accessed October 2013).

60. Isshiki Masaharu's account of his actions after he left the Japan Coast Guard details his doubts about the Japanese government's stance on the Senkakus and what he considered to be token criminal charges against the Chinese trawler captain. His complex feelings regarding his sense of his responsibility as a government civil servant and his personal feelings regarding those who were making decisions on behalf of the Kan cabinet are obvious in the chapter explaining why he chose the name Sengoku38 as his YouTube user name. The chief cabinet secretary at the time, Sengoku Yoshito, was clearly a target of his contempt (*Nanika no tame ni sengoku38 no kokuhaku* [Tokyo: Asahi shinbun shuppan, 2011]).

61. Ishihara Shintarō, "The U.S.-Japan Alliance and the Debate over Japan's Role in Asia" (speech presented at the Heritage Foundation, Washington, D.C., April 16, 2012), http://www.heritage.org/events/2012/04 /shintaro-ishihara#watch.

62. Governor Ishihara outlined his rationale in Ishihara Shintarō, "Senkaku shotō to iu kokunan" [A National Crisis over the Senkaku Islands], *Bungei shunjū*, July 2012, 148–56.

63. Cabinet Office of Japan, "Press Conference by Chief Cabinet Secretary Fujimura Osamu," April 17, 2012, http://www.kantei.go.jp/foreign /tyoukanpress/201204/17_p.html.

64. Tokyo Metropolitan Government, "Current State of Donations for the Senkaku Islands," September 13, 2012, http://www.chijihon.metro.tokyo. jp/senkaku/en/kifu-jyokyo.html. Procedurally, the governor did not have full authority over the use of Tokyo's municipal revenues. Both the use of Tokyo Metropolitan government funds of more than ¥200 million, as well as the purchase of more than five acres (20,000 sq m) of land require the approval of the Tokyo Metropolitan Assembly, thus its recourse to donations from those in Japan who approved of the governor's plans (*Japan Times*, May 3, 2012).

65. In a statement following the release of the captain without indictment, Ishigaki Deputy Prosecutor Suzuki Toru said, "Wagakuni kokumin he no eikyō to kongo no nichibei kankei wo kōryo suru to, sore ijō, migara wo kōsokushite sōse wo keizokusuru koto wa sōtō de nai to handanshita" (Considering the influence on our country's people and on the future of Sino-Japanese relations, we judged that the restraint and continued prosecution of one individual was not a proportionate response) (NHK, September 24, 2010).

66. Tamogami Toshio, "Was Japan an Aggressor Nation?" Apa Group, October 31, 2008, http://www.apa.co.jp/book_report/images/2008jyusyou_saiyuusyu_english.pdf.

67. *Yomiuri shinbun*, November 14, 2010, http://www.Yomiuri.co.jp/dy/national/T101113002944.htm.

68. For a full account of China's assistance to Japan after the March 11, 2011, Great East Japan Earthquake, see Ministry of Foreign Affairs of Japan, "Overview of the Japan-China Summit Meeting," May 22, 2011, http://www.mofa.go.jp/region/asia-paci/china/mm1105.html.

69. Ministry of Foreign Affairs, Japan, "Dispatch of Japan Disaster Relief Teams in Response to the Earthquake Disaster in Sichuan Province," May 16, 2008, http://www.mofa.go.jp/announce/announce/2008/5/1180016_1010.html. See also "In Departure, China Invites Outside Help," *New York Times*, May 16, 2008.

70. Ministry of Foreign Affairs, Japan, "Japan-People's Republic of China Summit Meeting (Summary)" December 25, 2011, http://www.mofa.go.jp/region/asia-paci/china/meeting1112.html.

71. Captain Iwanami Shūichi, director, Security Division, Guard and Rescue Department; and Ikegami Hiroyuki, assistant director, Guard and Rescue Department, Japan Coast Guard, Tokyo, interviews with author, July 27, 2012.

72. House of Councillors, National Diet of Japan, "Kaijō hoanchohō oyobi ryōkai nado ni okeru gaikoku senpaku no koko ni kansuru hōritsu no ichibu wo kaisei suru hōritsuan" [Revised Bill of the Japan Coast Guard Law Concerning Navigation of Foreign Vessels in Territorial Waters], updated September 5, 2012, http://www.sangiin.go.jp/japanese/joho1/kousei/gian/180/meisai/m18003180045.htm.

73. The local community at Camp Pendleton welcomed Japan's GSDF's Western Army Infantry Regiment, which came to train with the Fifteenth Marine Expeditionary United during Iron Fist 2012. This was the seventh Iron Fist exercise between the U.S. Marines and the GSDF ("Marines to Train with Japanese Ground Self-Defense Force at Camp Pendleton," *Village News*, January 3, 2012, http://www.thevillagenews.com/story/60840/). The U.S. Marines and U.S. Navy regularly exercise, including the Thirty-First Marine Expeditionary Unit (MEU) stationed in Okinawa and the *Bonhomme Richard* amphibious assault ship, which is part of the Bonhomme Richard Amphibious Ready Group, which operates in the Seventh Fleet's area of operation and reports to the

commander of the Amphibious Force Seventh Fleet headquartered in Okinawa, Japan. For a description of the recent Okinawa-based Marine-Navy exercise on August 22, 2012, see U.S. Navy, "*Bonhomme Richard* ARG Embarks 31st Marine Expeditionary Unit," August 22, 2012, http://www.navy.mil/submit/display.asp?story_id=69145.

74. The *Asahi shinbun* reported on September 20, 2012, that the exercises on Guam had been planned since April of that year.

75. Liberal Democratic Party of Japan, "Nihon no saiki no tame no seisaku" [Policies for the Revival of Japan], May 31, 2012, http://www.jimin.jp /policy/policy_topics/pdf/seisaku-117.pdf.

76. A full list of their protest and other activities in late 2010 can be found at Ganbare nippon, "Katsudō heisei 22-nen" [2010 Activities], http://www.ganbare-nippon.net/22_2.html (accessed October 2013).

77. *Sankei shinbun*, October 17, 2010.

78. *Asahi shinbun*, November 7, 2010.

79. *Nikkei shinbun*, November 14 and 21, 2010. According to Ganbare Nippon, the protests persisted into December, with two thousand people gathering on December 1 in front of the Diet and the prime minister's residence and four thousand people gathering on December 18 in Shibuya. But these were not covered in the media and could not be confirmed.

80. *Japan Times*, August 16, 2012, http://japantimes.co.jp/text/nn20120816a1 .html.

81. *Japan Times*, August 18, 2012, http://www.japantimes.co.jp/text/nn20120 818a2.html.

82. *Japan Times*, August 28, 2012, http://wwww.japantimes.co.jp/text /nn20120828a2.html.

83. Negotiations already were under way over the summer, and the price and timing were all that needed to be set. Despite several unpublicized incidents of Japanese activists swimming to shore, once the Chinese activists landed, another effort was made by two Japanese who successfully planted a Japanese flag on the top of the cliff before being arrested (Kose Tatsuyuki, counselor, Cabinet Secretariat, Office of the Assistant Chief Cabinet Secretary, interview with author, July 27, 2012).

84. *Asahi shinbun*, August 25, 2012.

85. Tsuyoshi Sunohara, *Antō senkaku kokuyūka* [*Secret Feud: The National Purchase of the Senkakus*] (Tokyo: Shinchōsha, 2013).

86. Tokyo Metropolitan Government, "Tōkyōto senkaku shotō genchi chōsa hōkokusho" [Written Report on the Tokyo Metropolitan Government's Field Investigation of the Senkaku Islands], October 2012, http://www.chijihon.metro.tokyo.jp/senkaku/en/tyosa-report.html.

87. Cabinet Office of Japan, "Press Conference by Chief Cabinet Secretary Fujimura Osamu," September 10, 2012, http://www.kantei.go.jp/foreign/tyoukanpress/201209/10_p.html.

88. Cabinet Office of Japan, "Press Conference by Chief Cabinet Secretary Fujimura Osamu," September 11, 2012, http://www.kantei.go.jp/foreign/tyoukanpress/201209/11_a.html. The Kurihara family owned only three of the five islands. The other two islands are Kubajima and Taishōjima. Although unused, the former was under lease by the Ministry of Defense for possible use by U.S. military forces, and the latter had been owned by the national government since the islands were claimed in the name of Emperor Meiji in 1895.

89. This information is based on compiling media reports from the *Asahi*, *Nikkei*, and *Yomiuri* newspapers from September to November 2012.

90. *Asahi shinbun*, December 14, 2013.

91. For example, on January 10, ten aircraft, including a number of planes from China's Air Force, flew north around the Senkaku Islands in Japan's Air Defense Identification Zone, and the Air Self-Defense Force scrambled F-15 fighter jets in response. The Chinese military aircraft came within 105.6 miles (170 km) of the Senkakus but did not enter Japanese airspace (*Asahi shinbun*, January 11, 2013).

92. The jump in number of scrambles coincided with the decision to nationalize the islands: ASDF jets were scrambled 91 times from October to December 2012 and 146 times from January to March (or 237 times overall) (*Asahi shinbun*, April 18, 2013).

93. Ministry of Defense, Japan, "Extra Press Conference by the Defense Minister," February 5, 2013, http://www.mod.go.jp/e/pressconf/2013/02/130205a.html.

94. *NHK News*, February 6, 2013.

95. *China Daily*, February 8, 2013.

96. U.S. Department of State, "Remarks with Japanese Foreign Minister Fumio Kishida After Their Meeting," January 18, 2013, http://www.state.gov/secretary/rm/2013/01/203050.htm.

97. U.S. Department of State, "Joint Press Availability with Japanese Foreign Minister Kishida After Their Meeting," April 14, 2013, http://www.state.gov/secretary/remarks/2013/04/207483.htm.

98. Cabinet Office of Japan, "Policy Speech by Prime Minister Shinzo Abe to the 183rd Session of the Diet," February 28, 2013, http://www.kantei.go.jp/foreign/96_abe/statement/201302/28siseuhousin_e.html.

99. Cabinet Office of Japan, "'Japan Is Back,' Policy Speech by Prime Minister Shinzo Abe at the Center for Strategic and International

Studies," February 22, 2013, http://www.kantei.go.jp/foreign/96_abe/state
ment/201302/22speech_e.html.

100. "Xi Seriously Considers First Summit Meeting with Abe," *Asahi shinbun*, January 25, 2013, http://ajw.*Asahi*.com/article/behind_news /politics/AJ201301250086; "Japan Envoy Meets Chinese Leader Amid Islands Dispute," BBC, January 25, 2013, http://www.bbc.co.uk/news /world-asia-21191780; "Japan Gives Letter to China's Xi in Island Dispute," Associated Press, January 25, 2013, http://bigstory.ap.org/article /japan-gives-letter-chinas-xi-island-dispute.

101. *Asahi shinbun*, April 8, 2013.

102. *Yomiuri shinbun*, April 18, 2013.

103. Chinese Ministry of Defense, "Announcement of the Aircraft Identification Rules of the East China Sea Air Defense Identification Zone of the P.R.C.," November 23, 2013, http://eng.mod.gov.cn/Press/2013-11/23 /content_4476143.htm.

104. Ministry of Foreign Affairs, Japan, "Statement by the Ministry of Foreign Affairs on the Announcement of the 'East China Sea Air Defense Identification Zone' by the Ministry of National Defense of the People's Republic of China," November 24, 2013, http://www.mofa.go.jp/press /release/press4e_000098.html.

105. U.S. Department of Defense, "Hagel Issues Statement on East China Sea Air Defense Identification Zone," November 23, 2013, http://www .defense.gov/news/newsarticle.aspx?id=121223.

106. Even after Noda purchased the islands, the Senkaku Fund established by the Tokyo Metropolitan Government continued to attract some donations. The fund was officially closed on January 31, 2013. In all, 103,000 donations were received, totaling ¥1.485 billion ($14.93 million) (Tokyo Metropolitan Government, "Current State of Donations for the Senkaku Islands," January 31, 2013, http://www.chijihon.metro.tokyo.jp /senkaku/en/kifu-jyokyo.html).

107. On July 12, 2012, three Chinese patrol ships repeatedly entered the waters near the Senkakus, despite repeated protests by Japan's foreign minister, Genba Kōichirō, and vice-minister Sasae Ken'ichirō to the Chinese ambassador to Japan, Cheng Yonghua.

CONCLUSION

1. For aggregate Japanese FDI to China, see the Ministry of Finance, Japan, "Outward/Inward Direct Investment, 2008–2012," https://www.mof

.go.jp/english/international_policy/reference/balance_of_payments /ebpfdi.htm. For new investment in China, see Ministry of Commerce, People's Republic of China, "Foreign Investment, 2009–2012," http: //english.mofcom.gov.cn/article/statistic/foreigninvestment/.

BIBLIOGRAPHY

Abramowitz, Morton, Yoichi Funabashi, and Jisi Wang. *China-Japan-U.S. Relations: Meeting New Challenges*. Tokyo: Japan Center for International Exchange, 2002.

Akiyama, Masahiro. "Use of Seas and Management of Ocean Space: Analysis of the Policymaking Process for Creating the Basic Ocean Law." *Ocean Policy Studies* 5 (2007): 1–29.

Amako Satoshi. *Chūgoku, ajia, nihon—taikokuka suru "kyoryū" ha kyōi ka* [*China, Asia, Japan—Is the Emerging Superpower a Threat?*] Tokyo: Chikuma shobō, 2006.

Amako Satoshi and Atsumi Sugako. "Taitō suru chūgoku wo dō yomuka" [How to Read a Rising China]. *Research and Problems* (National Chengchi University International Relations Research Center) 36, no. 5 (2007): 115–28.

Amako Satoshi, Fujiwara Kiichi, Yamamoto Yoshinobu, and Iokibe Makoto. *Nitchū kankei wo dō kōchiku suruka—ajia no kyōsei to kyōryoku wo mezashite* [*How to Construct Japan-China Relations—For Harmonious Coexistence and Cooperation in Asia*]. Tokyo: Iwanami shoten, 2004.

Anami Koreshige. "Ajia chōsakai kōenkai, chūgoku no taitō to nihon no taiō" [Asia Reseach Institute Lecture, China's Rise and Posture Toward Japan]. *Asia Times* 38, nos. 1–2 (2007): 4–25.

Aoki Ken. "Chūgoku no taitō to nichibei bōeki kōzō no henka" [The Rise of China and the Changing Structure of U.S.-Japan Trade]. *International Economy*, no. 57 (2006):109–48.

Asano Akira. "Chūgoku no taigai seisaku 'chūgoku no taitō,' chūgoku imeji, anzenhoshō" [China's Foreign Policy—"China's Rise," China's Image, Security]. *Foreign Affairs* 56, no. 2 (2008): 17–34.

Association for the Safety of Imported Food, Japan. *Shokuhin yunyū handobukku: shokuhin wo anzen ni yunyū surutami ni Compliance with the Law* [*The Handbook for Food Imports: How to Comply with the Law and Safely Import Food*]. Tokyo: Association for the Safety of Imported Food, 2010.

Bedeski, Robert E. *The Fragile Entente: The 1978 Japan-China Peace Treaty in a Global Context*. Boulder, Colo.: Westview Press, 1983.

Brown, David G. "Chinese Economic Leverage in Sino-Japanese Relations." *Asian Survey* 12, no. 9 (1972): 753–71.

Calder, Kent E. "China and Japan's Simmering Rivalry." *Foreign Affairs* 85, no. 2 (2006): 129–39.

Camphausen, Roy, Michael Mochizuki, and Tomoyuki Kojima. "Tokuhō kōen tōronkai—chūgoku no taitō to nichibei anzen hoshō he no eikyō" [Dispatch Lecture and Debates—China's Rise and Its Impact on the U.S.-Japan Security Treaty]. *Asia Times* 36, no. 10 (2005): 22–49.

Cathcart, Adam, and Patricia Nash. "War Criminals and the Road to Sino-Japanese Normalization: Zhou Enlai and the Shenyang Trials." *Twentieth Century China* 34, no. 2 (2008): 89–111.

Chambers, Michael P. "Rising China: The Search for Power and Plenty." In *Strategic Asia 2006–07: Trade Interdependence, and Security*, 65–103, edited by Ashley J. Tellis and Michael Wills. Seattle: National Bureau of Asian Research, 2006.

Chen Wen-hung. "Chūgoku no taitō to higashi ajia sangyō no bungyō kōzō no henka no keikō (higashi ajia keizai no tōgō renkei no shinten wo fumaeta miraizō)—(dai isshō higashi ajia no keizai tōgō)" [China's Rise and the Trend of Division of Industrial Labor in East Asia (First Chapter—East Asian Economic Integration)]. *NIRA Policy Research* 17, no. 5 (2004): 24–28.

Cheng, Li. *China's Changing Political Landscape: Prospects for Democracy*. Washington, D.C.: Brookings Institution Press, 2008.

Cheng, Joseph Y. S. "Sino-Japanese Relations, 1957–60." *Asian Affairs* 8, no. 1 (1977): 70–84.

——. "Sino-Japanese Relations in the Twenty-First Century." *Journal of Contemporary Asia* 2 (2003): 251–73.

Dadwal, Shebonti Ray. "The Sino-Japanese Rare Earths Row: Will China's Loss Be India's Gain?" *Strategic Analysis* 35, no. 2 (2011): 181–85.

Deans, Phil. "Contending Nationalisms and the Diaoyutai/Senkaku Dispute." *Security Dialogue* 31, no.1 (2000): 119–31.

Drifte, Reinhard. "From 'Sea of Confrontation' to 'Sea of Peace, Cooperation, and Friendship'? Japan Facing China in the East China Sea." *Journal of Current Chinese Affairs* 16, no. 3 (2008): 27–51.

——. "Japanese-Chinese Territorial Disputes in the East China Sea: Between Military Confrontation and Economic Cooperation." Asia Research Centre Working Paper. London: London School of Economics and Political Science, 2008.

——. "Territorial Conflicts in the East China Sea: From Missed Opportunities to Negotiations Stalemate (1)." *Japan Focus*, June 1, 2009.

Eto, Shinkichi. "Recent Developments in Sino-Japanese Relations." *Asian Survey* 20, no. 7 (1980): 726–43.

Fishman, Ted C. *China, Inc.: How the Rise of the Next Superpower Challenges America and the World.* New York: Scribner, 2006.

Fravel, Taylor M. "Power Shifts and Escalation: Explaining China's Use of Force in Territorial Disputes." *International Security* 32, no. 3 (2007–2008): 44–83.

Fu Sei. *Chūgoku kaigun to kindai nitchū kankei* [*The Chinese Navy and Modern Japan-China Relations*]. Tokyo: Kinseisha, 2011.

Funabashi Yoichi. "Kyōchō seisaku no mosaku no haikei wo yomu chūgoku ha mizukara ni 'kinkoju' wo kakeru koto ga dekiru ka (tokushū chūgoku, heiwateki taitō no jitsuzō)" [Reading the Background of the Search for Cooperation Policy—Can China Place a "kinkoju" on Itself? ("China, the Real Image of the Peaceful Rise", special edition)]. *Chūōkōron* 119, no. 8 (2004): 104–14.

Gifford, Rob. *China Road: A Journey into the Future of a Rising Power.* New York: Random House, 2007.

Gill, Bates, and Yanzhong Huang. "Sources and Limits of Chinese 'Soft Power.'" *Survival* 48, no. 2 (2006): 17–36.

Gries, Peter Hays. "Nationalism, Indignation, and China's Japan Policy." *SAIS Review* 25, no. 2 (2005): 105–14.

Hagström, Linus. *Japan's China Policy: A Relational Power Analysis.* Abingdon: Routledge, 2005.

——. "Quit Power: Japan's China Policy in Regard to the Pinnacle Islands." *Pacific Review* 18, no. 2 (2005): 159–88.

Hellman, Donald C. "Japan's Relations with Communist China." *Asian Survey* 4, no. 10 (1964): 1085–92.

Hills, Carla A., and Dennis C. Blair. *U.S.-China Relations—An Affirmative*

Agenda, a Responsible Course. Task Force Report no. 59. New York: Council on Foreign Relations Press, 2007.

Hiramatsu Shigeo. *Chūgoku ha nihon wo heigō suru* [China Will Annex Japan]. Tokyo: Kodansha International, 2006.

Hisano Katsukuni. *Chūgokujin to nihonjin: gurōbaru kankyō he no taiō* [*The Chinese and the Japanese: Adaptation to the Global Environment*]. Tokyo: Waseda, 2011.

Hiwatashi Yumi. "'Chūgoku no taitō' to dōmei riron (tokushū: seiji bunseki no furontia to gendai nihon no seiji hendō)" ["The Rise of China" and Alliance Theory (Feature: Frontiers of Political Analysis and Political Change in Contemporary Japan)]. *Social Science Research* 54, no. 2 (2003): 77–100.

Hosaka Masayoshi. *Shōwashi nanatsu no nazo* [*History of the Shōwa Period: Seven Puzzles*]. Tokyo: Kodansha, 2003.

——. *Shōwashi no taiga wo iku 1—yasukuni to iu nayami* [*In the Great Flow of Shōwa History, no. 1—The Yasukuni Problem*]. Tokyo: Chūōkōron shinsha, 2013.

Hsiao, Gene. T. "Prospects for a New Sino-Japanese Relationship." *China Quarterly* 60 (1974): 720–49.

——. "The Sino-Japanese Rapprochement: A Relationship of Ambivalence." *China Quarterly* 57 (1974): 101–23.

Hsiung, James C., ed. *China and Japan at Odds: Deciphering the Perpetual Conflict.* New York: Palgrave Macmillan, 2007.

——. "Sea Power, the Law of the Sea, and the Sino-Japanese East China Sea 'Resource War.'" *American Foreign Policy Interests* 27, no. 6 (2006): 513–29.

Hughes, Christopher R. "Japan in the Politics of Chinese Leadership Legitimacy: Recent Developments in Historical Perspective." *Japan Forum* 20, no. 2 (2008): 245–66.

Hughes, Christopher W. "The Slow Death of Japanese Techno-Nationalism? Emerging Comparative Lessons for China's Defense Production." *Journal of Strategic Studies* 34, no. 3 (2011): 451–79.

Ijiri, Hidenori. "Sino-Japanese Controversy Since the 1972 Diplomatic Normalization." *China Quarterly*, no. 124 (1990): 639–61.

Ikuo Chihara. "Chūgoku no gunji teki taitō to rendō suru futatsu no mondai" [China's Militaristic Rise and Two Problems with Working Together]. *Chūōkōron* 120, no. 12 (2005): 96–103.

Ikenberry, G. John, ed. *America Unrivaled: The Future of the Balance of Power.* Ithaca, N.Y.: Cornell University Press, 2002.

——. "The Rise of China and the Future of the West: Can the Liberal System Survive?" *Foreign Affairs* 87, no. 1 (2008): 23–37.

Iriye, Akira. *China and Japan in the Global Setting.* Cambridge, Mass.: Harvard University Press, 1992.

Ishikawa, Shigeru. "Sino-Japanese Economic Co-operation." *China Quarterly,* no. 109 (1987): 1–21.

Itō Motoshige and Ministry of Finance, Policy Research Institute. *Nitchū kankei no keizai bunseki—kūdōkaron, chūgoku kyōiron no gokai* [*An Economic Analysis of Japan-China Relations—The Falsehood of Hollowing Out and China as a Threat*]. Tokyo: Tōyō keizai shinpōsha, 2003.

Jansen, Marius B. *Japan and China: From War to Peace, 1894–1972.* Chicago: Rand McNally, 1975.

Japan Center for Economic Research. *Chūgoku no keizai kōzō kaikaku—jizoku kanō na seichō wo mezashite* [*Structural Reform of the Chinese Economy—For Sustainable Growth*]. Tokyo: *Nikkei shinbun,* 2006.

Japan-China Friendship Association. *Nitchū yūkō undō gojūnen* [*Fifty Years of Japan-China amity*]. Tokyo: Tōhō shoten, 2000.

Ji, Guoxing. "The Legality of the 'Impeccable Incident.'" *China Security* 5, no. 2 (2009): 16–21.

Jinbo, Ken, et al. "Japan's Security Strategy Toward China: Integration, Balancing, and Deterrence." Project Proposal. Tokyo: Tokyo Foundation, October 2011.

Johnstone, Christopher B. "Japan's China Policy: Implications for U.S.-Japan Relations." *Asian Survey* 38, no. 11 (1998): 1071–78.

Kadokura Takashi. *BRICs: shinkō suru taikoku to nihon* [*BRICs: Rising Superpowers and Japan*]. Tokyo: Heibonsha, 2006.

——. *Zusetsu BRICs keizai: taitō suru burajiru, rosia, indo, chūgoku no subete* [*BRICs Economies: The Rise of Brazil, Russia, India and China*]. Tokyo: Nikkei shinbunsha, 2005.

Kan Shiyū and Shu Kenei. *Chūgoku no keizai daironsō* [*China's Economic Controversy*]. Tokyo: Keisō shobō, 2008.

Katō Kōzō. "Doru taisei to ajia taiheiyō chiiki sōgo izon (tokushū: seiji bunseki no furontia to gendai nihon no seiji hendō)" [The Dollar System and Interdependence in the Asia Pacific Region (Feature: Frontiers of Political Analysis and Political Change in Contemporary Japan)]. *Social Science Research* 54, no. 2 (2003): 101–26.

Kim, Hong N. "The Fukuda Government and the Politics of the Sino-Japanese Peace Treaty." *Asian Survey* 19, no. 3 (1979): 297–313.

——. "Sino-Japanese Relations in the Post-Mao Era." *Asian Affairs* 7, no. 3 (1980): 161–81.

——. "The Tanaka Government and the Politics of the Sino-Japanese Civil Aviation Pact, 1972–74." *World Affairs* 137, no. 4 (1975): 286–302.

Kishi Toshihiko, Tanigaki Mariko, and Fukamachi Hideo. *Mosaku suru kindai nitchū kankei: taiwa to kyōzon no jidai* [*Exploring Modern Japan-China Relations: The Age of Dialogue and Competitive Coexistence*]. Tokyo: University of Tokyo Press, 2009.

Kleine-Ahlbrandt, Stephanie. "China's Dictatorship Diplomacy." *Foreign Affairs* 87, no. 1 (2008): 38–56.

Kō Bunyū. *Tsukeagaruna chūgokujin, urotaeruna nihonjin—21 seiki nitchū bunmei no shōtotsu* [*Don't Get Too Confident, China; Don't Panic, Japan—The Clash of Japan-China Civilizations in the 21st Century*]. Tokyo: Tokuma shoten, 2006.

Kojima Tomoyuki. *Chūgoku no seiji shakai—fukyō taikoku he no mosaku* [*China's Political World—Exploring Paths to a Rich and Powerful Nation*]. Tokyo: Ashi shobō, 2000.

——. *Fukyō taikoku no chūgoku—kō takumin kara ko kintō he* [*Rich and Powerful China—From Jiang Zemin to Hu Jintao*]. Tokyo: Ashi shobō, 2003.

——. "Sino-Japanese Relations: A Japanese Perspective." *Asia-Pacific Review* 3, no.1 (1996): 73–106.

Kokubun Ryōsei. *Chūgoku ha ima* [*China Is Now*]. Tokyo: Iwanami shinsho, 2011.

Kokubun Ryōsei, Soeya Yoshihide, Kawashima Shin, and Takahara Akio, eds. *Ni'chū kankeishi* [*Modern History of Japan-China Relations*]. Tokyo: Yuhikako, 2013.

Kondō Daisuke. *Nihon yo, chūgoku to dōmei seyo!* [*Japan, Form an Alliance with China!*]. Tokyo: Kobunsha, 2006.

Konomoto Shingo. *2015 nen no chūgoku—ko kintō seiken ha nani wo mezasunoka?* [*China in 2015—What Will the Hu Jintao Government Aim For?*]. Tokyo: Tōyō keizai shinpōsha, 2008.

Koo, Min Gyo. "The Senkaku/Diaoyu Dispute and Sino-Japanese Political-Economic Relations: Cold Politics and Hot Economics." *Pacific Review* 22, no. 2 (2009): 205–32.

Kuroda Atsuro. "Chūgoku sangyō no taitō to ajia, nihon" [The Rise of Chinese Industry and Asia, Japan]. *Gakushikai kaihō* 2003, no. 3 (2003): 22–42.

Kwan C. H. "Chūgoku no taitō to ajia keizai meian wo wakeru chūgoku to no hokansei to kyōgōsei (tokushū chūgoku: keizai taikoku he no michi)" [China's Rise and Separating the Good and Bad from China on Complementarity and Competition in Asia's Economy]. *Nippon hyōronsha*, June 2005, 18–21.

——. "Chūgoku no taitō to nihon" [China's Rise and Japan]. *Japan Economic Research Monthly Report*, no. 297 (2003): 2–13.

——. "Heiwa taitō wo mezasu chūgoku—gurōbaru keizai taikoku no senryaku to kadai" [China's Peaceful Rise—Topics and Strategy on Becoming a Global Economic Power]. *International Issues*, no. 540 (2005): 58–69.

——. "Sekai jōsei seminaa 'chūgoku no taitō to nihon,' sekai keizai jihō" [World Affairs Seminar—The Rise of China and Japan]. *World Economic Times*, no. 131 (2003): 1–24.

Lampton, David M. "The Faces of Chinese Power." *Foreign Affairs* 86, no. 1 (2007): 115–27.

Lee, Chae-jin. "The Politics of Sino-Japanese Trade Relations, 1963–68." *Pacific Affairs* 42, no. 2 (1969): 129–44.

Lee, Wei-chin. "Troubles Under the Water: Sino-Japanese Conflict of Sovereignty on the Continental Shelf in the East China Sea." *Ocean Development and International Law* 18, no. 5 (1987): 585–611.

Lee, Yong Wook. *The Japanese Challenge to the American Neoliberal World Order: Identity, Meaning, and Foreign Policy*. Stanford, Calif.: Stanford University Press, 2008.

Liao, Xuanli. "The Petroleum Factor in Sino-Japanese Relations: Beyond Energy Cooperation." *International Relations of the Asia Pacific* 7, no. 1 (2007): 23–46.

Lieberthal, Kenneth. "How Domestic Forces Shape the PRC's Grand Strategy & International Impact." In *Strategic Asia 2007–08: Domestic Political Change and Grand Strategy*, edited by Ashley J. Tellis and Michael Wills, 29–66. Seattle: National Bureau of Asian Research, 2007.

Lin Kenryō. *Nihon yo, konna chūgoku to tsukiaeruka? [Japan, Can We Deal with a China Like This?]*. Tokyo: Namiki shobō, 2006.

Lum, Thomas, and Dick K. Nanto. *China's Trade with United States and the World*. CRS Report for Congress. Washington, D.C.: Government Printing Office, 2007.

Makino Matsuyo. *Kaihatsu tojō taikoku chūgoku no chiiki kaihatsu—keizai seichō, chiiki kakusa, hinkon [The Regional Development of China—Economic Growth, Regional Disparities, and Poverty]*. Tokyo: University Education Press, 2001.

Manicom, James. "Sino-Japanese Cooperation in the East China Sea: Limitations and Prospects." *Contemporary Southeast Asia* 31, no. 3 (2008): 455–78.

Mann, James. *The China Fantasy.* New York: Viking, 2007.

Marukawa Tomoo. *Chūgoku nashi de seikatsu dekiruka: bōeki kara yomitoku nitchū kankei no shinjitsu* [*Can We Live Without China? The Truth About Japan-China Relations from the Perspective of Trade and Commerce*]. Tokyo: PHP Institute, 2009.

Mastro, Oriana Skylar. "Signaling and Military Provocation in Chinese National Security Strategy: A Closer Look at the Impeccable Incident." *Journal of Strategic Studies* 34, no. 2 (2011): 219–44.

Masuda Masayuki. "Chūgoku no taitō to nitchū anzen hoshō kankei nitchū bōei kōryū no rōdomappu" [China's Rise and Sino-Japanese Security Relations—Road Map for Sino-Japanese Defense Exchanges]. *East Asia*, no. 483 (2007): 76–85.

Matsudaira Nagayoshi. "Dare ga mitama wo yogoshita no ka—yasukuni hōshi jūyonen no munen" [Who Dishonored the Spirit of the Dead: Regrets from Fourteen Years of Yasukuni Service]. *Bungei shunjū*, December 5, 1992, 162–71.

McVadon, Eric A. "The Reckless and the Resolute: Confrontation in the South China Sea." *China Security* 5, no. 2 (2009): 1–15.

Medeiros, Evan, et al. *Pacific Currents: The Responses of U.S. Allies and Security Partners in East Asia to China's Rise.* Santa Monica, Calif.: RAND, 2008.

Mendl, Wolf. *Issues in Japan's China Policy.* New York: Palgrave Macmillan, 1978.

Mitcham, Chad J. *China's Economic Relations with the West and Japan, 1949–79.* London: Routledge, 2005.

Miyamoto Yūji. *Korekara, chūgoku to dō tsukiauka* [*How to Deal with China in the Future*]. Tokyo: Nikkei Publishing, 2010.

Mizutani Naoko. *Hannichi izen—chūgoku tainichi kōsakusha tachi no kaisō* [*Before "Anti-Japan"—Memoirs of Chinese Agents in Japan*]. Tokyo: Bungei shunjūsha, 2006.

Mong Cheung. "Political Survival and the Yasukuni Controversy in Sino-Japanese Relations." *Pacific Review* 23, no. 4 (2010): 527–48.

Mori Kazuko. *Gendai chūgoku no kōzō hendō: taikoku chūgoku he no shiza* [*Structural Change of Modern China: Perspective on Superpower China*]. Tokyo: University of Tokyo Press, 2000.

——. *Nitchū kankei—sengo kara shin jidai he* [*Japan-China Relations—From the Postwar Period to the New Age*]. Tokyo: Iwanami shoten, 2006.

Morino, Tomozō. "China-Japan Trade and Investment Relations." *Proceedings of the Academy of Political Science* 28, no. 2 (1991): 87–94.

Morrison, Wayne M. "China-U.S. Trade Issues." Washington, D.C.: Congressional Research Service Report, 2007.

Munakata Naoko. *Nitchū kankei no tenki—higashi ajia keizai tōgō he no chosen* [*A Turning Point in Japan-China Relations—The Challenge of East Asian Economic Integration*]. Tokyo: Tōyō keizai shinpōsha, 2001.

Nagasawa Michio. *Naze korehodo rekishi ninshiki ga chigaunoka—nitchū kankei no hikari to kage* [*Why Do Our Understandings of History Differ So Much?—The Light and Shadow of Japan-China Relations*]. Tokyo: Kojinsha, 2006.

Nakanishi Terumasa. *Teikoku to shite no chūgoku—haken no ronri to genjitsu* [*China as Empire—The Logic and Truth of Hegemony*]. Tokyo: Tōyō keizai shinpōsha, 2004.

Naughton, Barry. *The Chinese Economy: Transitions and Growth*. Cambridge, Mass.: MIT Press, 2007.

Odom, Jonathan G. "The True 'Lies' of the Impeccable Incident: What Really Happened, Who Disregarded International Law, and Why Every Nation (Outside of China)Should Be Concerned." *Michigan State Journal of International Law* 18, no. 3 (2010): 1–42.

Ogawa Eiji and Ministry of Finance, Policy Research Institute. *Chūgoku no taitō to higashi ajia no kinyū shijō* [*The Rise of China and the East Asian Financial Market*]. Tokyo: Nippon hyōronsha, 2006.

Okabe Tatsumi. *Chūgoku no taigai senryaku* [*China's Foreign Policy*]. Tokyo: University of Tokyo Press, 2002.

——. *Chūgoku wo meguru kokusai kankyō* [*The International Environment Around China*]. Tokyo: Iwanami shoten, 2001.

——. *Nitchū kankei no kako to shōrai—gokai wo koete* [*The Past and Future of Japan-China Relations—Overcoming Misunderstandings*]. Tokyo: Iwanami shoten, 2006.

Okamoto Nobuhiro. *Chūgoku keizai no bokkō to ajia no sangyō saihen* [*The Rise of the Chinese Economy and the Asian Industrial Reorganization*]. Tokyo: IDE-JETRO, 2007.

Ōkita, Saburō. "Japan, China, and the United States: Economic Relations and Prospects." *Foreign Affairs* 57, no. 5 (1979): 1090–1110.

Ōnishi Yasuo. *Chūgoku ASEAN keizai kankei no shin tenkai—sōgo tōshi to FTA no jidai he* [*New Developments in China-ASEAN Economic Relations—Toward an Age of Mutual Investment and FTAs*]. Tokyo: IDE-JETRO, 2006.

Ōtake Hideo. *Koizumi jun'ichirō popyurizumu no kenkyū—sono senryaku to shuhō* [*Research on Koizumi Jun'ichirō's Populism—Strategies and Methods*]. Tokyo: Toyō keizai shinpōsha, 2006.

Pan, Zhongqi. "Sino-Japanese Dispute over the Diaoyu/Senkaku Islands: The Pending Controversy from the Chinese Perspective." *Journal of Chinese Political Science* 12, no. 1 (2007): 71–92.

Pedrozo, Raul. "Close Encounters at Sea: The USNS Impeccable Incident." *Naval War College Review* 62, no. 3 (2009): 102–11.

Peng Er Lam. *Japan's Relations with China: Facing a Rising Power.* Abingdon: Sheffield Centre for Japanese Studies / Routledge Series, 2009.

Pollack, Jonathan D. "The Sino-Japanese Relationship and East Asian Security: Patterns and Implications." *China Quarterly,* no. 124 (1990): 714–29.

Rahman, Chris, and Martin Tsamenyi. "A Strategic Perspective on Security and Naval Issues in the South China Sea." *Ocean Development and International Law* 41, no. 4 (2010): 315–33.

Rose, Caroline. "Managing China: Risk and Risk Management in Japan's China Policy." *Japan Forum* 22, nos. 1–2 (2010): 149–68.

——. "Patriotism Is Not Taboo: Nationalism in China and Japan and Its Implications for Sino-Japanese Relations." *Japan Forum* 12, no. 2 (2000): 169–81.

Roy, Denny. "China's Reaction to American Predominance." *Survival* 45, no. 3 (2003): 57–58.

——. "The Sources and Limits of Sino-Japanese Tensions." *Survival* 47, no. 2 (2005): 191–214.

——. "Stirring Samurai, Disapproving Dragon: Japan's Growing Security Activity and Sino-Japan Relations." *Asian Affairs* 31, no. 2 (2004): 86–101.

Saitō Michihiko. *Nitchū kankeishi no shomondai* [*The Problems of the History of Japan-China Relations*]. Tokyo: Chūō University Press, 2009.

Samuels, Richard J. *3.11: Disaster and Change in Japan.* Ithaca, N.Y.: Cornell University Press, 2013.

Satō Toyoshi and Li Enmin. *Higashi ajia kyōdōtai no kanōsei—nitchū kankei no sankentō* [*The Potential of the East Asia Community—Reconsidering Japan-China Relations*]. Tokyo: Ochanomizu shobō, 2006.

Scissors, Derek. "Deng Undone." *Foreign Affairs* 88, no. 3 (2009): 24–39.

Sekiyama Ken. *Nitchū no keizai kankei ha kō kawatta—tai chūgoku en shakkan 30 nen no kiseki* [*How the Japan-China Economic Relations Have Changed—The 30-Year History of Yen Loans to China*]. Tokyo: Kōbunken, 2008.

Shambaugh, David. "China Engages Asia: Reshaping the Regional Order." *International Security* 29, no. 3 (2004–2005): 64–99.

Shimizu Miwa. *Jinmin chūgoku no shūen—kyōsantō wo nomikomu "shin-fujin" no taitō* [*The End of the People's China—The Rise of China's*

"New Wealthy Class" and Its Challenge to the CCP]. Tokyo: Kodansha, 2006.

Shimizu Yoshikazu. *Chūgoku ha naze "han-nichi" ni nattaka?* [*Why Did China Become "Anti-Japan"?*]. Tokyo: Bungei shunjū, 2003.

Shin Kaitō. *Nitchū kankei shinka he no atarashii kokoromi—"kankyō kyōryoku" wo kīwādo ni* [*New Efforts to Promote Japan-China Relations—"Environmental Cooperation" as the Keyword*]. Tokyo: Duan Press, 2004.

Shinoda Tomohito. *Koizumi Diplomacy: Japan's Kantei Approach to Foreign and Defense Affairs*. Seattle: University of Washington Press, 2007.

Shirk, Susan L. *China: Fragile Superpower: How China's Internal Politics Could Derail Its Peaceful Rise*. Oxford: Oxford University Press, 2007.

Shū Bokushi. *Chūgoku keizairon—kōdo seichō no mekanizumu to kadai* [*The Chinese Economy—The Mechanism and Challenges of Rapid Growth*]. Tokyo: Nihon keizai hyōronsha, 2007.

Smith, Paul J. "China-Japan Relations and the Future Geopolitics of East Asia." *Asian Affairs* 35, no. 2 (2009): 230–56.

Sone Shika. "Chūgoku keizai no taitō to 'chūgoku kyōi' ron" [The Rise of China's Economy and the "China Threat" Theory]. *Seikei ronsō* 71, nos. 3–4 (2003): 517–48.

Still, Ellen M. "The Sino-Japanese Treaty: Will It Ever Be Ratified?" *Asian Affairs* 3, no. 4 (1976): 247–53.

Sugiyama Katsumi. *Gunji teikoku chūgoku no saishū mokuteki—sono toki, nihon ha, amerika ha* [*The Final Objective of China's Military Empire—What Will Japan and America Do?*]. Tokyo: Shōdensha, 2005.

Sunohara Tsuyoshi. *Antō senkaku kokuyūka* [*Secret Feud: The National Purchase of the Senkakus*]. Tokyo: Shinchōsha, 2013.

Sutter, Robert G. "China and Japan: Trouble Ahead?" *Washington Quarterly* 25, no. 4 (2002): 37–49.

——. *China's Rise in Asia: Promises and Perils*. Blue Ridge Summit, Pa.: Rowman & Littlefield, 2005.

Suzuki Jūryō, Furukawa Mantarō, and Sakai Makoto, eds. *Nitchū yūkō undō 50-nen* [*50 Years of Japan-China Friendship Activities*]. Tokyo: Tōhō shoten, 2000.

Swaine, Michael D. *America's Challenge: Engaging a Rising China in the Twenty-First Century*. Washington, D.C.: Carnegie Endowment for International Peace, 2011.

Takagi Naoto. *Tenkanki no chūgoku tōhoku keizai—kakudai suru tai-nichi keizai kōryū* [*The Turning Point of the Economy of Northeast China—*

Expansion of Economic Exchanges with Japan]. Fukuoka: Kyushu University Press, 1997.

Takahara, Akio. *Issues and Future Prospects for Japan-China Relations*. Tokyo: Tokyo Foundation, April 2011.

——. "Japan's Political Response to the Rise of China." In *The Rise of China and a Changing East Asian Order*, edited by Jisi Wang and Ryosei Kokubun, 48–71. Tokyo: Japan Center for International Exchange, 2004.

Tokyo Foundation. *Japan's Security Strategy Toward China: Integration, Balancing, and Deterrence in the Era of Power Shift*. Tokyo: Tokyo Foundation, 2011.

Tow, William T. "Sino-Japanese Security Cooperation: Evolution and Prospects." *Pacific Affairs* 56, no. 1 (1983): 51–83.

Tretiak, Daniel. "The Sino-Japanese Treaty of 1978: The Senkaku Incident Prelude." *Asian Survey* 18, no. 12 (1978): 1235–49.

Tsuchiya, Masaya. "Recent Developments in Sino-Japanese Trade." *Law and Contemporary Problems* 38, no. 2 (1973): 240–48.

Tsugami Toshiya. "Chūgoku taitō—nihon ha nani wo nasubekika?" [The Rise of China—What Should Japan Do?]. *Economy, Trade, and Industry Journal* 36, no. 3 (2003): 42–45.

Uemura Kōji. "Dai-jūkyūkai ajia taiheiyō shō kinnen kōenkai chō kyodai kokka chūgoku no taitō to meisō ga imi suru mono" [The Nineteenth Asia Pacific Award Memorial Lecture: The Rise of China as a Superpower and the Meaning of Its Straying Off Course]. *Asia Times* 39, no. 3 (2008): 4–25.

Valencia, Mark J. "The East China Sea Dispute: Context, Claims, Issues, and Possible Solutions." *Asia Perspective* 31, no. 1 (2007): 127–67.

——. "The Impeccable Incident: Truth and Consequences." *China Security* 5, no. 2 (2009): 22–28.

Wakamiya Yoshibumi. *Sengo hoshu no ajiakan* [*The Postwar Conservative View of Asia*]. Tokyo: Asahi shinbunsha, 1995. [English translation: Wakamiya, Yoshibumi. *The Postwar Conservative View of Asia: How the Political Right Has Delayed Japan's Coming to Terms with Its History of Aggression in Asia*. Tokyo: LTCB International Library Foundation, 1998.]

Walt, Stephen. *The Origins of Alliances*. Ithaca, N.Y.: Cornell University Press, 1987.

Wan Ming. *Nitchū shinjidai wo hiraku tenkanki nitchū kankeiron no saizensen: chūgoku toppu rīdā no shiten* [*The Front Line of Japan-China Relations in a Transitional Period That Opens a New Age for Japan-China Relations: The Perspective of Top Chinese Leaders*]. Tokyo: Sanwa shoseki, 2011.

——. "Sino-Japanese Relations Adrift in a Changing World." *Asia-Pacific Review* 18, no. 1 (2011): 73–83.

——. "Tensions in Recent Sino-Japanese Relations: The May 2002 Shenyang Incident." *Asian Survey* 43, no. 5 (2003): 826–44.

Wang, Jisi. "China's Search for Stability with America." *Foreign Affairs* 84, no. 5 (2005): 39–48.

Whiting, Allen S., and Xin Jianfei. "Sino-Japanese Relations: Pragmatism and Passion." *World Policy Journal* 8, no. 1 (1990–1991): 107–35.

Wu, Xinbo. "The Security Dimensions of Sino-Japanese Relations: Warily Watching One Another." *Asian Survey* 40, no. 2 (2000): 296–310.

Yahuda, Michael. "Sino-Japanese Relations: Partners and Rivals?" *Korean Journal of Defense Analysis* 21, no. 4 (2009): 365–79.

Yang, Bojiang. "Redefining Sino-Japanese Relations After Koizumi." *Washington Quarterly* 29, no. 4 (2006): 129–37.

Yang, Daqing, et al., eds. *Toward a History Beyond Borders: Contentious Issues in Sino-Japanese Relations*. Cambridge, Mass.: Harvard University Asia Center, 2012.

Yasukuni sengo hishi: A-kyusenpan wo goshi shita otoko [Yasukuni's Postwar Secret: The Man Who Enshrined the Class-A War Criminals]. Tokyo: Mainichi shinbunsha, 2007.

Yinan, He. "History, Chinese Nationalism, and the Emerging Sino-Japanese Conflict." *Journal of Contemporary China* 16, no. 50 (2007): 1–24.

——. "Ripe for Cooperation or Rivalry? Commerce, Realpolitik, and War Memory in Sino-Japanese Relations." *Asian Security* 4, no. 2 (2008): 162–97.

Yomiuri shinbun, China Coverage Team. *Bōchō chūgoku—shin nashonarizumu to yuganda seichō* [*Expanding China—New Nationalism and Distorted Growth*]. Tokyo: Chūōkōron shinsha, 2006.

Yomiuri shinbunsha, ed. *Gaikō wo kenka ni shita otoko: koizumi gaikō 2000 nichi no shinjitsu* [*The Man Who Fought for Foreign Policy: The Truth Behind 2000 Days of Koizumi Diplomacy*]. Tokyo: Shinchosha, 2006.

Yong, Deng. "Chinese Relations with Japan: Implications for Asia-Pacific Regionalism." *Pacific Affairs* 70, no. 3 (1997): 373–91.

Yoshida, Shigenobu. "Sino-Japanese Relations on the Move—On a Collision Course in the Asia-Pacific Region." *Australian Journal of Chinese Affairs*, no. 3 (1980): 81–89.

Yoshioka Keiko. *Aikoku keizai chūgoku no zenkyūka* [*The Patriotic Economy and China's Globalization*]. Tokyo: Asahi shinbunsha, 2008.

Zhang, Bijian. "China's Peaceful Rise to Great Power Status." *Foreign Affairs* 84, no. 5 (2005): 18–24.

Zhang Xiangshan and Suzuki Eiji. *Nitchū kankei no kanken to kenshō—kokkō seijōka 30 nen no ayumi* [*A Personal Memoir and Analysis of Japan-China Relations—30 Years of History Since Diplomatic Normalization*]. Tokyo: Sanwa shoseki, 2002.

Zhao Quansheng. *Nitchū kankei to nihon no seiji* [*Japan-China Relations and Japanese Politics*]. Tokyo: Iwanami shoten, 1999.

INDEX

Numbers in italics refer to pages on which figures appear.